ACCA

Paper F9

Financial management

Complete text

British library cataloguing-in-publication data

A catalogue record for this book is available from the British Library.

Published by:
Kaplan Publishing UK
Unit 2 The Business Centre
Molly Millars Lane
Wokingham
Berkshire
RG41 2QZ

ISBN 978 1 84710 524 0

© Kaplan Financial Limited, 2008

Printed in the UK by CPI William Clowes Beccles NR34 7TL

Acknowledgements

We are grateful to the Association of Chartered Certified Accountants and the Chartered Institute of Management Accountants for permission to reproduce past examination questions. The answers have been prepared by Kaplan Publishing.

Contents

KAPLAN PUBLISHING

chapter

Introduction

How to Use the Materials

These Kaplan Publishing learning materials have been carefully designed to make your learning experience as easy as possible and to give you the best chances of success in your examinations.

The product range contains a number of features to help you in the study process. They include:

(1) Detailed study guide and syllabus objectives

(2) Description of the examination

(3) Study skills and revision guidance

(4) Complete text or essential text

(5) Question practice

The sections on the study guide, the syllabus objectives, the examination and study skills should all be read before you commence your studies. They are designed to familiarise you with the nature and content of the examination and give you tips on how to best to approach your learning.

The **complete text or essential text** comprises the main learning materials and gives guidance as to the importance of topics and where other related resources can be found. Each chapter includes:

- The **learning objectives** contained in each chapter, which have been carefully mapped to the examining body's own syllabus learning objectives or outcomes. You should use these to check you have a clear understanding of all the topics on which you might be assessed in the examination.

- The **chapter diagram** provides a visual reference for the content in the chapter, giving an overview of the topics and how they link together.

- The **content** for each topic area commences with a brief explanation or definition to put the topic into context before covering the topic in detail. You should follow your studying of the content with a review of the illustration/s. These are worked examples which will help you to understand better how to apply the content for the topic.

- **Test your understanding** sections provide an opportunity to assess your understanding of the key topics by applying what you have learned to short questions. Answers can be found at the back of each chapter.

- **Summary diagrams** complete each chapter to show the important links between topics and the overall content of the paper. These diagrams should be used to check that you have covered and understood the core topics before moving on.

- **Question practice** is provided at the back of each text.

Icon Explanations

Definition - Key definitions that you will need to learn from the core content.

Key Point - Identifies topics that are key to success and are often examined.

Expandable Text - Expandable text provides you with additional information about a topic area and may help you gain a better understanding of the core content. Essential text users can access this additional content on-line (read it where you need further guidance or skip over when you are happy with the topic)

Illustration - Worked examples help you understand the core content better.

Test Your Understanding - Exercises for you to complete to ensure that you have understood the topics just learned.

Tricky topic - When reviewing these areas care should be taken and all illustrations and test your understanding exercises should be completed to ensure that the topic is understood.

On-line subscribers

Our on-line resources are designed to increase the flexibility of your learning materials and provide you with immediate feedback on how your studies are progressing. Ask your local customer services staff if you are not already a subscriber and wish to join.

If you are subscribed to our on-line resources you will find:

(1) On-line referenceware: reproduces your Complete or Essential Text on-line, giving you anytime, anywhere access.

(2) On-line testing: provides you with additional on-line objective testing so you can practice what you have learned further.

(3) On-line performance management: immediate access to youron-line testing results. Review your performance by key topics and chart your achievement through the course relative to your peer group.

Syllabus

Paper background

The aim of ACCA Paper F9, Financial management, is to develop the knowledge and skills expected of a financial manager, relating to issues affecting investment, financing, and dividend policy decisions.

Objectives of the syllabus

- Discuss the role and purpose of the financial management function.

- Assess and discuss the impact of the economic environment on financial management.

- Discuss and apply working capital management techniques.

- Carry out effective investment appraisal.

- Identify and evaluate alternative sources of business finance.

- Explain and calculate cost of capital and the factors which affect it.

- Discuss and apply principles of business and asset valuations.

- Explain and apply risk management techniques in business.

Core areas of the syllabus

- Financial management function.
- Financial management environment.
- Working capital management.
- Investment appraisal.
- Business finance.
- Cost of capital.
- Business valuations.
- Risk management.

Syllabus objectives

We have reproduced the ACCA's syllabus below, showing where the objectives are explored within this book. Within the chapters, we have broken down the extensive information found in the syllabus into easily digestible and relevant sections, called Content Objectives. These correspond to the objectives at the beginning of each chapter.

Syllabus learning objective and Chapter reference:

A FINANCIAL MANAGEMENT FUNCTION

1 The nature and purpose of financial management

(a) Explain the nature and purpose of financial management.[1] **Ch. 1**

(b) Explain the relationship between financial management and financial and management accounting.[1] **Ch. 1**

2 Financial objectives and the relationship with corporate strategy

(a) Discuss the relationship between financial objectives, corporate objectives and corporate strategy.[2] **Ch. 1**

(b) Identify and describe a variety of financial objectives, including:[2] **Ch.1**
   (i) shareholder wealth maximisation
   (ii) profit maximisation
   (iii) earnings per share growth.

3 Stakeholders and impact on corporate objectives

(a) Identify the range of stakeholders and their objectives. [2] **Ch. 2**

(b) Discuss the possible conflict between stakeholder objectives.[2]**Ch. 2**

(c) Discuss the role of management in meeting stakeholder objectives, including the use of agency theory.[2]**Ch. 2**

(d) Describe and apply ways of measuring achievement of corporate objectives including:[2] **Ch. 3**
   (i) ratio analysis using appropriate ratios such as return on capital employed, return on equity, earnings per share and dividend per share

   (ii) changes in dividends and share prices as part of total shareholder return.

(e) Explain ways to encourage the achievement of stakeholder objectives, including:[2] **Ch. 2**
   (i) managerial reward schemes such as share options and performance-related pay

   (ii) regulatory requirements such as corporate governance codes of best practice and stock exchange listing regulations

4 Financial and other objectives in not-for-profit organisations

(a) Discuss the impact of not-for-profit status on financial and other objectives.[2] **Ch. 4**

(b) Discuss the nature and importance of Value for Money as an objective in not-for-profit organisations.[2] **Ch. 4**

(c) Discuss ways of measuring the achievement of objectives in not-for-profit organisations.[2] **Ch. 4**

B FINANCIAL MANAGEMENT ENVIRONMENT

1 The economic environment for business

(a) Identify and explain the main macroeconomic policy targets.[1] **Ch. 14**

(b) Define and discuss the role of fiscal, monetary, interest rate and exchange rate policies in achieving macroeconomic policy targets.[1] **Ch. 14**

(c) Explain how government economic policy interacts with planning and decision-making in business.[2] **Ch. 14**

(d) Explain the need for and the interaction with planning and decision-making in business of:[1] **Ch. 14**

    (i) competition policy

    (ii) government assistance for business

    (iii) green policies

    (iv) corporate governance regulation.[2]

2 The nature and role of financial markets and institutions

(a) Identify the nature and role of money and capital markets, both national and international, in the UK financial system.[2] **Ch. 14**

(b) Explain the role of financial intermediaries.[1] **Ch. 14**

(c) Explain the functions of a stock market and a corporate bond market.[2] **Ch. 14**

(d) Explain the nature and features of different securities in relation to the risk/return trade-off.[2] **Ch. 14**

C WORKING CAPITAL MANAGEMENT

1 The nature, elements and importance of working capital

(a) Describe the nature of working capital and identify its elements.[1] **Ch. 5**

(b) Identify the objectives of working capital management in terms of liquidity and profitability, and discuss the conflict between them.[2] **Ch. 5**

(c) Discuss the central role of working capital management in financial management.[2] **Ch. 5**

2 Management of inventories, accounts receivable, accounts payable and cash

(a) Explain the cash operating cycle and the role of accounts payable and receivable.[2] **Ch. 5**

(b) Explain and apply relevant accounting ratios, including: [2] **Ch. 5**

   (i)   current ratio and quick ratio

   (ii)   inventory turnover ratio, average collection period and average payable period

   (iii) sales revenue/net working capital ratio.

(c) Discuss, apply and evaluate the use of relevant techniques in managing inventory, including the Economic Order Quantity model and Just-in-Time techniques.[2] **Ch. 6**

(d) Discuss, apply and evaluate the use of relevant techniques in managing accounts receivable, including: **Ch. 7**

   (i)   assessing creditworthiness[1]

   (ii)   managing accounts receivable[1]

   (iii) collecting amounts owing[1]

   (iv) offering early settlement discounts[2]

   (v)   using factoring and invoice discounting[2]

   (vi) managing foreign accounts receivable.[2]

(e) Discuss and apply the use of relevant techniques in managing accounts payable, including: **Ch. 7**

   (i)   using trade credit effectively[1]

   (ii)   evaluating the benefits of discounts for early settlement and bulk purchase[2]

   (iii) managing foreign accounts payable.[1]

(f) Explain the various reasons for holding cash, and discuss and apply the use of relevant techniques in managing cash, including:[2] **Ch. 8**

   (i)   preparing cash flow forecasts to determine future cash flows and cash balances

   (ii)   assessing the benefits of centralised treasury management and cash control

   (iii) cash management models, such as the Baumol model and the Miller-Orr model

   (iv) investing short-term

3 Determining working capital needs and funding strategies

(a) Calculate the level of working capital investment in current assets and discuss the key factors determining this level, including:[2] **Ch. 5**

    (i) the length of the working capital cycle and terms of trade

    (ii) an organisation's policy on the level of investment in current assets

    (iii) the industry in which the organisation operates.

(b) Describe and discuss the key factors in determining working capital funding strategies, including:[2] **Ch. 5**

    (i) the distinction between permanent and fluctuating current assets

    (ii) the relative cost and risk of short-term and long-term finance

    (iii) the matching principle

    (iv) the relative costs and benefits of aggressive, conservative and matching funding policies management attitudes to risk, previous funding decisions and organisation size.[1]

D INVESTMENT APPRAISAL

1 The nature of investment decisions and the appraisal process

(a) Distinguish between capital and revenue expenditure, and between fixed asset and working capital investment.[2] **Ch. 9**

(b) Explain the role of investment appraisal in the capital budgeting process.[2] **Ch. 9**

(c) Discuss the stages of the capital.[2] **Ch. 9**

2 Non-discounted cash flow techniques

(a) Identify and calculate relevant cash flows for investment projects.[2] **Ch. 9**

(b) Calculate payback period and discuss the usefulness of payback as an investment appraisal method.[2] **Ch. 9**

(c) Calculate return on capital employed (accounting rate of return) and discuss its usefulness as an investment appraisal method.[2] **Ch. 9**

3 Discounted cash flow (DCF) techniques

(a) Explain and apply concepts relating to interest and discounting, including:[2]

   (i) the relationship between interest rates and inflation, and between real and nominal interest rates **Ch. 11**

   (ii) the calculation of future values and the application of the annuity formula **Ch. 10**

   (iii) the calculation of present values, including the present value of an annuity and a perpetuity, and the use of discount and annuity tables **Ch. 10**

   (iv) the time value of money and the role of cost of capital in appraising investments **Ch. 10**

(b) Calculate net present value and discuss its usefulness as an investment appraisal method.[2] **Ch. 10**

(c) Calculate internal rate of return and discuss its usefulness as an investment appraisal method.[2] **Ch. 10**

(d) Discuss the superiority of DCF methods over non-DCF methods.[2] **Ch. 10**

(e) Discuss the relative merits of NPV and IRR.[2] **Ch. 10**

4 Allowing for inflation and taxation in DCF

(a) Apply and discuss the real-terms and nominal-terms approaches to investment appraisal.[2] **Ch. 11**

(b) Calculate the taxation effects of relevant cash flows, including the tax benefits of capital allowances and the tax liabilities of taxable profit.[2] **Ch. 11**

(c) Calculate and apply before- and after-tax discount rates. [2] **Ch. 11**

5 Adjusting for risk and uncertainty in investment appraisal

(a) Describe and discuss the difference between risk and uncertainty in relation to probabilities and increasing project life.[2] **Ch. 12**

(b) Apply sensitivity analysis to investment projects and discuss the usefulness of sensitivity analysis in assisting investment decisions.[2] **Ch. 12**

(c) Apply probability analysis to investment projects and discuss the usefulness of probability analysis in assisting investment decisions.[2] **Ch. 12**

(d) Apply and discuss other techniques of adjusting for risk and uncertainty in investment appraisal, including: **Ch. 12**

    (i) simulation[1]

    (ii) adjusted payback[1]

    (iii) risk-adjusted discount rates.[2]

6 Specific investment decisions (Lease or buy, asset replacement, capital rationing, etc)

(a) Evaluate leasing and borrowing to buy using the before- and after-tax costs of debt.[2] **Ch. 13**

(b) Evaluate asset replacement decisions using equivalent annual cost.[2] **Ch. 13**

(c) Evaluate investment decisions under single-period capital rationing, including:[2] **Ch. 13**

    (i) the calculation of profitability indexes for divisible investment projects

    (ii) the calculation of the NPV of combinations of non-divisible investment projects

    (iii) a discussion of the reasons for capital rationing.

E BUSINESS FINANCE

1 Sources of and raising short-term finance

(a) Identify and discuss the range of short-term sources of

(b) finance available to businesses, including:[2] **Ch. 15**

    (i) overdraft

    (ii) short-term loan

    (iii) trade credit

    (iv) lease finance.

2 Sources of, and raising, long-term finance

(a) Identify and discuss the range of long-term sources of finance available to businesses, including:[2] **Ch.15**

    (i) equity finance

    (ii) debt finance

    (iii) lease finance

    (iv) venture finance.

(b) Identify and discuss methods of raising equity finance,including:[2] **Ch.15**

    (i) rights issue

    (ii) placing

    (iii) public offer

    (iv) stock exchange listing.

3 Internal sources of finance and dividend policy

(a) Identify and discuss internal sources of finance,including:[2] **Ch.15**

    (i) retained earnings

    (ii) increasing working capital management efficiency.

(b) Discuss the relationship between the dividend decision

(c) and the financing decision[2] **Ch.15**

(d) Discuss practical influences on the dividend decision,including: **Ch.15**

    (i) legal constraints[1]

    (ii) liquidity[1]

    (iii) shareholder expectations[2]

    (iv) alternatives to cash dividends.[2]

4 Gearing and capital structure considerations

(a) Identify and discuss the problem of high levels of gearing.[2] **Ch.16**

(b) Assess the impact of sources of finance on financial position and financial risk using appropriate measures,including: **Ch.16**

    (i) ratio analysis using balance sheet gearing,operational and financial gearing, interest coverage ratio and other relevant ratios[2]

    (ii) cash flow forecasting[2]

    (iii) effect on shareholder wealth.[2]

5 Finance for small and medium-sized entities (SMEs)

(a) Describe the financing needs of small businesses. [2] **Ch.17**

(b) Describe the nature of the financing problem for small businesses in terms of the funding gap, the maturity gap and inadequate security.[2] **Ch.17**

(c) Explain measures that may be taken to ease the financing problems of SMEs, including the responses of government departments and financial institutions. [1] **Ch.17**

(d) Identify appropriate sources of finance for SMEs and evaluate the financial impact of different sources of finance on SMEs.[2]**Ch.17**

F COST OF CAPITAL

1 Sources of finance and their relative costs

(a) Describe the relative risk-return relationship and the relative costs of equity and debt.[2] **Ch.18**

(b) Describe the creditor hierarchy and its connection with the relative costs of sources of finance.[2] **Ch.18**

2 Estimating the cost of equity

(a) Apply the dividend growth model and discuss its weaknesses.[2] **Ch.18**

(b) Describe and explain the assumptions and components of the capital asset pricing model (CAPM).[2] **Ch.18**

(c) Apply the CAPM to valuing shares.[2] **Ch.18**

(d) Explain and discuss the advantages and disadvantages of the CAPM.[2] **Ch.18**

3 Estimating the cost of debt and other capital instruments

(a) Calculate the cost of capital of a range of capital instruments, including:[2] **Ch.18**

    (i) irredeemable debt

    (ii) redeemable debt

    (iii) convertible debt

    (iv) preference shares

    (v) bank debt.

4 Estimating the overall cost of capital

(a) Distinguish between average and marginal cost of capital.[2] **Ch.18**

(b) Calculate the weighted average cost of capital (WACC) using book value and market value weightings.[2] **Ch.18**

5 Capital structure theories and practical considerations

(a) Describe the traditional view of capital structure and its assumptions.[2] **Ch.19**

(b) Describe the views of Miller and Modigliani on capital structure, both without and with corporate taxation, and their assumptions.[2] **Ch.19**

(c) Identify a range of capital market imperfections and describe their impact on the views of Miller and Modigliani on capital structure.[2] **Ch.19**

(d) Explain the relevance of pecking order theory to the selection of sources of finance.[1] **Ch.19**

6 Impact of cost of capital on investments

(a) Explain the relationship between company value and cost of capital.[2] **Ch.19**

(b) Discuss the circumstances under which WACC can be used in investment appraisal.[2] **Ch.19**

(c) Discuss the advantages of the CAPM over WACC in determining a project-specific cost of capital.[2] **Ch.19**

(d) Apply the CAPM in calculating a project-specific discount rate.[2] **Ch.19**

G BUSINESS VALUATIONS

1 Nature and purpose of the valuation of business and financial assets

(a) Identify and discuss reasons for valuing businesses and financial assets.[2]**Ch.20**

(b) Identify information requirements for valuation and discuss the limitations of different types of information. [2] **Ch.20**

2 Models for the valuation of shares

(a) Dividend valuation model, including the dividend growth model.[2] **Ch.20**

(b) Market capitalisation.[2] **Ch.20**

(c) Asset-based valuation models, including:[2] **Ch.20**
   (i) net asset value (balance sheet basis)

   (ii) net asset value (net realisable value basis)

   (iii) net asset value (replacement cost basis).

(d) Income-based valuation models, including:[2] **Ch.20**
   (i) price/earnings ratio method

   (ii) earnings yield method

   (iii) discounted cash flow basis.

3 The valuation of debt and other financial assets

(a) Apply appropriate valuation methods to:[2] **Ch.20**
   (i) irredeemable debt

   (ii) redeemable debt

   (iii) convertible debt

   (iv) preference shares.

4 Efficient market hypothesis (EMH) and practical considerations in the valuation of shares

(a) Distinguish between and discuss weak form efficiency,semi-strong form efficiency and strong form efficiency.[2] **Ch.21**

(b) Discuss practical considerations in the valuation of shares, including:[2] **Ch.21**

   (i)   marketability and liquidity of shares

   (ii) availability and sources of information

   (iii) market imperfections and pricing anomalies.

(c) Describe the significance of investor speculation and the explanations of investor decisions offered by behavioural finance.[1] **Ch.21**

H RISK MANAGEMENT

1 The nature and types of risk and approaches to risk management

(a) Describe and discuss different types of foreign currency risk: [2] **Ch.22**

   (i)   translation risk

   (ii) transaction risk

   (iii) economic risk.

(b) Describe and discuss different types of interest rate risk:[1] **Ch.23**

   (i)   gap exposure

   (ii) basis risk

2 Causes of exchange rate differences and interest rate fluctuations

(a) Describe the causes of exchange rate fluctuations, including: **Ch.22**

   (i)   balance of payments[1]

   (ii) purchasing power parity theory[2]

   (iii) interest rate parity theory[2]

   (iv) four-way equivalence.[2]

(b) Forecast exchange rates using:[2] **Ch.22**

   (i)   purchasing power parity

   (ii) interest rate parity.

(c) Describe the causes of interest rate fluctuations, including: [2] **Ch.23**

    (i) structure of interest rates and yield curves

    (ii) expectations theory

    (iii) liquidity preference theory

    (iv) market segmentation.

3 Hedging techniques for foreign currency risk

(a) Discuss and apply traditional methods of foreign currency risk management, including: **Ch.23**

    (i) currency of invoice[1]

    (ii) netting and matching[2]

    (iii) leading and lagging[2]

    (iv) forward exchange contracts[2]

    (v) money market hedging[2]

    (vi) asset and liability management.[1]

(b) Compare and evaluate traditional methods of foreign currency risk management.[2] **Ch.22**

(c) Identify the main types of foreign currency derivates used to hedge foreign currency risk and explain how they are used in hedging.[1] **Ch.22**

4 Hedging techniques for interest rate risk

(a) Discuss and apply traditional methods of interest rate risk management, including: **Ch.23**

    (i) matching and smoothing[1]

    (ii) asset and liability management[1]

    (iii) forward rate agreements.[2]

(b) Identify the main types of interest rate derivates used to hedge interest rate risk and explain how they are used in hedging.[1] **Ch.23**

The superscript numbers in square brackets indicate the intellectual depth at which the subject area could be assessed within the examination. Level 1 (knowledge and comprehension) broadly equates with the Knowledge module, Level 2 (application and analysis) with the Skills module and Level 3 (synthesis and evaluation) to the Professional level. However, lower level skills can continue to be assessed as you progress through each module and level.

The examination

Examination format

The syllabus for Paper F9, Financial management, has the aim of developing in students the skills expected from a financial manager who is responsible for the finance function of a business. The paper also prepares candidates for more advanced and specialist study in Paper P4, Advanced financial management. The examination paper contains four questions, all of which are compulsory. Each question is worth 25 marks and has both computational and discursive elements. The balance between computational and discursive content will continue in line with the pilot paper. Candidates are provided with a formulae sheet and tables of discount factors and annuity factors.

Four 25-mark questions. Number of marks 100. Total time allowed: 3 hours and 1. 5 minutes reading time.

Paper-based examination tips

Spend the fifteen minutes of reading time **reading the paper** and planning your answers. During the reading time you may annotate the question paper but not write in the answer booklet. In particular you should use this time to ensure that you understand the requirements, highlighting key verbs, consider which parts of the syllabus are relevant and plan key calculations.

Divide the time you spend on questions in proportion to the marks on offer. One suggestion for this examination is to allocate 1 and 4/5 minutes to each mark available, so a 10-mark question should be completed in approximately 18 minutes.

Unless you know exactly how to answer the question, spend some time **planning** your answer. Stick to the question and **tailor your answer** to what you are asked. Pay particular attention to the verbs in the question.

Spend the last five minutes reading through your answers and making any additions or corrections.

If you **get completely stuck** with a question, leave space in your answer book and **return to it later**.

If you do not understand what a question is asking, state your assumptions. Even if you do not answer in precisely the way the examiner hoped, you should be given some credit, if your assumptions are reasonable.

You should do everything you can to make things easy for the marker. The marker will find it easier to identify the points you have made if your answers are legible.

Essay questions: Some questions may contain short essay-style requirements. Your essay should have a clear structure. It should contain a brief introduction, a main section and a conclusion. Be concise. It is better to write a little about a lot of different points than a great deal about one or two points.

Computations: It is essential to include all your workings in your answers. Many computational questions require the use of a standard format. Be sure you know these formats thoroughly before the exam and use the layouts that you see in the answers given in this book and in model answers.

Case studies: Most questions will be based on specific scenarios. To write a good case study, first identify the area in which there is a problem, outline the main principles/theories you are going to use to answer the question, and then apply the principles/theories to the case.

Reports, memos and other documents: some questions ask you to present your answer in the form of a report or a memo or other document. So use the correct format - there could be easy marks to gain here.

Study skills and revision guidance

This section aims to give guidance on how to study for your ACCA exams and to give ideas on how to improve your existing study techniques.

Preparing to study

Set your objectives

Before starting to study decide what you want to achieve – the type of pass you wish to obtain. This will decide the level of commitment and time you need to dedicate to your studies.

Devise a study plan

Determine which times of the week you will study.

Split these times into sessions of at least one hour for study of new material. Any shorter periods could be used for revision or practice.

Put the times you plan to study onto a study plan for the weeks from now until the exam and set yourself targets for each period of study – in your sessions make sure you cover the course, course assignments and revision.

If you are studying for more than one paper at a time, try to vary your subjects as this can help you to keep interested and see subjects as part of wider knowledge.

When working through your course, compare your progress with your plan and, if necessary, re-plan your work (perhaps including extra sessions) or, if you are ahead, do some extra revision/practice questions.

Effective studying

Active Reading

You are not expected to learn the text by rote, rather, you must understand what you are reading and be able to use it to pass the exam and develop good practice. A good technique to use is SQ3Rs – Survey, Question, Read, Recall, Review:

(1) **Survey** the chapter – look at the headings and read the introduction, summary and objectives, so as to get an overview of what the chapter deals with.

(2) **Question** – whilst undertaking the survey, ask yourself the questions that you hope the chapter will answer for you.

(3) **Read** through the chapter thoroughly, answering the questions and making sure you can meet the objectives. Attempt the exercises and activities in the text, and work through all the examples.

(4) **Recall** – at the end of each section and at the end of the chapter, try to recall the main ideas of the section/chapter without referring to the text. This is best done after a short break of a couple of minutes after the reading stage.

Review – check that your recall notes are correct. You may also find it helpful to re-read the chapter to try to see the topic(s) it deals with as a whole.

Note-taking

Taking notes is a useful way of learning, but do not simply copy out the text. The notes must:

- be in your own words
- be concise
- cover the key points
- be well-organised
- be modified as you study further chapters in this text or in related ones.

Three ways of taking notes:

Summarise the key points of a chapter.

Make linear notes – a list of headings, divided up with subheadings listing the key points. If you use linear notes, you can use different colours to highlight key points and keep topic areas together. Use plenty of space to make your notes easy to use.

Try a diagrammatic form – the most common of which is a mind-map. To make a mind-map, put the main heading in the centre of the paper and put a circle around it. Then draw short lines radiating from this to the main sub-headings, which again have circles around them. Then continue the process from the sub-headings to sub-sub-headings, advantages, disadvantages, etc.

Highlighting and underlining

You may find it useful to underline or highlight key points in your study text – but do be selective. You may also wish to make notes in the margins.

Revision

The best approach to revision is to revise the course as you work through it. Also try to leave four to six weeks before the exam for final revision. Make sure you cover the whole syllabus and pay special attention to those areas where your knowledge is weak. Here are some recommendations:

Read through the text and your notes again and condense your notes into key phrases. It may help to put key revision points onto index cards to look at when you have a few minutes to spare.

Review any assignments you have completed and look at where you lost marks -put more work into those areas where you were weak.

Practise exam standard questions under timed conditions. If you are short of time, list the points that you would cover in your answer and then read the model answer, but do try to complete at least a few questions under exam conditions.

Also **practise producing answer plans** and comparing them to the model answer.

If you are **stuck** on a topic find somebody (a tutor) to explain it to you.

Read good newspapers and professional journals, especially ACCA's Student Accountant – this can give you an advantage in the exam.

Ensure you know the structure of the exam – how many questions and of what type you will be expected to answer. During your revision attempt all the different styles of questions you may be asked.

Further reading

You can find further reading and technical articles under the student section of ACCA's website.

MATHEMATICAL TABLES

Formulae and tables

Economic order quantity

$$= \sqrt{\frac{2C_O D}{C_H}}$$

Miller – Orr Model

$$\text{Return point} = \text{Lower limit} + (\tfrac{1}{3} \times \text{spread})$$

$$\text{Spread} = 3 \left[\frac{\tfrac{3}{4} \times \text{transaction cost} \times \text{variance of cash flows}}{\text{interest rate}} \right]^{\frac{1}{3}}$$

The Capital Asset Pricing Model

$$E(r_i) = R_f = \beta_i \, (E(r_m) - R_f)$$

The asset beta formula

$$\beta_a = \left[\frac{V_e}{(V_e + V_d (1-T))} \beta_e \right] + \left[\frac{V_d (1-T)}{(V_e + V_d (1-T))} \beta_d \right]$$

The Growth Model

$$P_0 = \frac{D_0 (1+g)}{(r_e - g)}$$

Gordon's growth approximation

$$g = br_e$$

The weighted average cost of capital

$$\text{WACC} = \left[\frac{V_e}{V_e + V_d} \right] k_e + \left[\frac{V_d}{V_e + V_d} \right] k_d \, (1-T)$$

The Fisher formula

$$(1 + i) = (1 + r)(1 + h)$$

Purchasing power parity and interest rate parity

$$S_1 = S_0 \times \frac{(1 + h_c)}{(1 + h_b)} \qquad\qquad F_0 = S_0 \times \frac{(1 + i_c)}{(1 + i_b)}$$

Present value table

Present value of 1, i.e. $(1 + r)^{-n}$

Where   r = discount rate

         n = number of periods until payment

Periods	Discount rate (r)									
(n)	1%	2%	3%	4%	5%	6%	7%	8%	9%	10%
1	0.990	0.980	0.971	0.962	0.962	0.943	0.935	0.926	0.917	0.909
2	0.980	0.961	0.943	0.925	0.907	0.890	0.873	0.857	0.842	0.826
3	0.971	0.942	0.915	0.889	0.864	0.840	0.816	0.794	0.772	0.751
4	0.961	0.924	0.888	0.855	0.823	0.792	0.763	0.735	0.708	0.683
5	0.951	0.906	0.863	0.822	0.784	0.747	0.713	0.681	0.650	0.621
6	0.942	0.888	0.837	0.790	0.746	0.705	0.666	0.630	0.596	0.564
7	0.933	0.871	0.813	0.760	0.711	0.665	0.623	0.583	0.547	0.513
8	0.923	0.853	0.789	0.731	0.677	0.627	0.582	0.540	0.502	0.467
9	0.914	0.837	0.766	0.703	0.645	0.592	0.544	0.500	0.460	0.424
10	0.905	0.820	0.744	0.676	0.614	0.558	0.508	0.463	0.422	0.386
11	0.896	0.804	0.722	0.650	0.585	0.527	0.475	0.429	0.388	0.350
12	0.887	0.788	0.701	0.625	0.557	0.497	0.444	0.397	0.356	0.319
13	0.879	0.773	0.681	0.601	0.530	0.469	0.415	0.368	0.326	0.290
14	0.870	0.758	0.661	0.577	0.505	0.442	0.388	0.340	0.299	0.263
15	0.861	0.743	0.642	0.555	0.481	0.417	0.362	0.315	0.275	0.239

Periods	Discount rate (r)									
(n)	11%	12%	13%	14%	15%	16%	17%	18%	19%	20%
1	0.901	0.893	0.885	0.877	0.870	0.862	0.855	0.847	0.840	0.833
2	0.812	0.797	0.783	0.769	0.756	0.743	0.731	0.718	0.706	0.694
3	0.731	0.712	0.693	0.675	0.658	0.641	0.624	0.609	0.593	0.579
4	0.659	0.636	0.613	0.592	0.572	0.552	0.534	0.516	0.499	0.482
5	0.593	0.567	0.543	0.519	0.497	0.476	0.456	0.437	0.419	0.402
6	0.535	0.507	0.480	0.456	0.432	0.410	0.390	0.370	0.352	0.335
7	0.482	0.452	0.425	0.400	0.376	0.354	0.333	0.314	0.296	0.279
8	0.434	0.404	0.376	0.351	0.327	0.305	0.285	0.266	0.249	0.233
9	0.391	0.361	0.333	0.308	0.284	0.263	0.243	0.225	0.209	0.194
10	0.352	0.322	0.295	0.270	0.247	0.227	0.208	0.191	0.176	0.162
11	0.317	0.287	0.261	0.237	0.215	0.195	0.178	0.162	0.148	0.135
12	0.286	0.257	0.231	0.208	0.187	0.168	0.152	0.137	0.124	0.112
13	0.258	0.229	0.204	0.182	0.163	0.145	0.130	0.116	0.104	0.093
14	0.232	0.205	0.181	0.160	0.141	0.125	0.111	0.099	0.088	0.078
15	0.209	0.183	0.160	0.140	0.123	0.108	0.095	0.084	0.074	0.065

KAPLAN PUBLISHING

Annuity Table

Present value of an annuity of 1, i.e. $\dfrac{1-(1+r)^{-n}}{r}$

Where   r = discount rate

             n = number of periods until payment

Periods (n)	Discount rate (r)									
	1%	2%	3%	4%	5%	6%	7%	8%	9%	10%
1	0.990	0.980	0.971	0.962	0.952	0.943	0.935	0.926	0.917	0.909
2	1.970	1.942	1.913	1.886	1.859	1.833	1.808	1.783	1.759	1.736
3	2.941	2.884	2.829	2.775	2.723	2.673	2.624	2.577	2.531	2.487
4	3.902	3.808	3.717	3.630	3.546	3.465	3.387	3.312	3.240	3.170
5	4.853	4.713	4.580	4.452	4.329	4.212	4.100	3.993	3.890	3.791
6	5.795	5.601	5.417	5.242	5.076	4.917	4.767	4.623	4.486	4.355
7	6.728	6.472	6.230	6.002	5.786	5.582	5.389	5.206	5.033	4.868
8	7.652	7.325	7.020	6.733	6.463	6.210	5.971	5.747	5.535	5.335
9	8.566	8.162	7.786	7.435	7.108	6.802	6.515	6.247	5.995	5.759
10	9.471	8.983	8.530	8.111	7.722	7.360	7.024	6.710	6.418	6.145
11	10.368	9.787	9.253	8.760	8.306	7.887	7.499	7.139	6.805	8.495
12	11.255	10.575	9.954	9.385	8.863	8.384	7.943	7.536	7.161	6.814
13	12.134	11.348	10.635	9.986	9.394	8.853	8.358	7.904	7.487	7.103
14	13.004	12.106	11.296	10.563	9.899	9.295	8.745	8.244	7.786	7.367
15	13.865	12.849	11.938	11.118	10.380	9.712	9.108	8.559	8.061	7.606

Periods (n)	Discount rate (r)									
	11%	12%	13%	14%	15%	16%	17%	18%	19%	20%
1	0.901	0.893	0.885	0.877	0.870	0.862	0.855	0.847	0.840	0.833
2	1.713	1.690	1.668	1.647	1.626	1.605	1.585	1.566	1.547	1.528
3	2.444	2.402	2.361	2.322	2.283	2.246	2.210	2.174	2.140	2.106
4	3.102	3.037	2.974	2.914	2.855	2.798	2.743	2.690	2.639	2.589
5	3.696	3.605	3.517	3.433	3.352	3.274	3.199	3.127	3.058	2.991
6	4.231	4.111	3.998	3.889	3.784	3.685	3.589	3.498	3.410	3.326
7	4.712	4.564	4.423	4.288	4.160	4.039	3.922	3.812	3.706	3.605
8	5.146	4.968	4.799	4.639	4.487	4.344	4.207	4.078	3.954	3.837
9	5.537	5.328	5.132	4.946	4.772	4.607	4.451	4.303	4.163	4.031
10	5.889	5.650	5.426	5.216	5.019	4.833	4.659	4.494	4.339	4.192
11	6.207	5.938	5.687	5.453	5.234	5.029	4.836	4.656	4.486	4.327
12	6.492	6.194	5.918	5.660	5.421	5.197	4.968	4.793	4.611	4.439
13	6.750	6.424	6.122	5.842	5.583	5.342	5.118	4.910	4.715	4.533
14	6.982	6.628	6.302	6.002	5.724	5.468	5.229	5.008	4.802	4.611
15	7.191	6.811	6.462	6.142	5.847	5.575	5.324	5.092	4.876	4.675

The financial management function

Chapter learning objectives

Upon completion of this chapter you will be able to:

- explain the nature of financial management

- explain all the purposes of financial management (raising finance, allocation of financial resources, maintaining control over resources)

- define financial management, financial accounting and management accounting

- distinguish between financial management and financial and management accounting and explain the relationship between them

- define and distinguish between corporate strategy and corporate objectives

- define and distinguish between financial strategy and financial objectives

- describe the relationship between corporate strategy, corporate objectives and financial objectives

- explain the features of the financial objective of shareholder wealth maximisation

- distinguish between shareholder wealth maximisation and satisficing in a scenario

- explain the features of the financial objective of profit maximisation

- explain the features of the financial objective of earnings per share (EPS) growth.

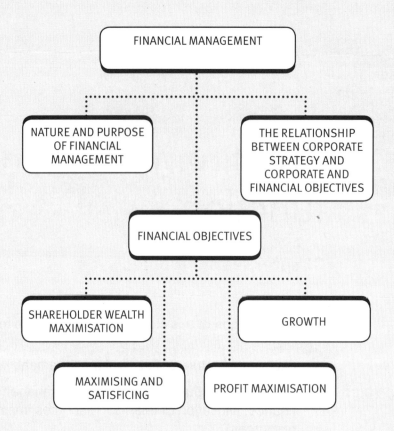

1 The nature and purpose of financial management

Key decisions for financial managers

Financial management is concerned with the efficient acquisition and deployment of both short- and long-term financial resources, to ensure the objectives of the enterprise are achieved.

Key areas of focus:

*   identifying and setting appropriate corporate financial objectives
*   achieving financial objectives, by taking decisions in three key areas:
    *   investment – should proposed investments (including potential acquisitions) be undertaken?
    *   finance – from what sources should funds be raised?
    *   dividends – how should cash funds be allocated to shareholders?

An understanding of these three key areas is fundamental for the examination.

*   Controlling resources to ensure efficient and effective use.

In all of the above areas the financial manager will need to take account of:

- the broader economic environment in which the business operates

- the potential risks associated with the decision and methods of managing that risk.

The F9 syllabus covers all these key aspects of financial management.

The balance sheet (statement of financial position) and financial management

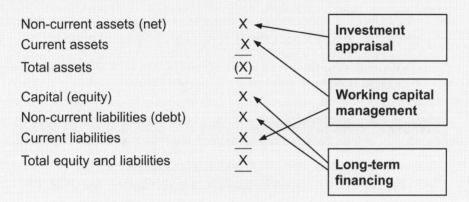

Non-current assets (net)	X
Current assets	X
Total assets	(X)
Capital (equity)	X
Non-current liabilities (debt)	X
Current liabilities	X
Total equity and liabilities	X

- Investment appraisal
- Working capital management
- Long-term financing

Expandable text

Financial management is concerned with all aspects of a business's financing decisions and these decisions will inevitably directly affect the balance sheet.

- Investment appraisal considers the long-term plans of the business and identifies the right projects to adopt to ensure financial objectives are met. The projects undertaken will nearly always involve the purchase of non-current assets at the start of the process.

- For a business to be successful, as well as identifying and implementing potentially successful projects, it must survive day to day. Working capital management is concerned with the management of liquidity – ensuring debts are collected, inventory levels are kept at the minimum level compatible with efficient production, cash balances are invested appropriately and payables are paid on a timely basis.

- All businesses need finance. A key financial management decision is the identification of the most appropriate sources, taking into account the requirements of the company, the likely demands of the investors and the amounts likely to be made available.

Financial management in context

Financial management should be distinguished from other important financial roles:

- management accounting – concerned with providing information for the more day to day functions of control and decision making
- financial accounting – concerned with providing information about the historical results of past plans and decisions.

Expandable text

Management accounting and financial management are both concerned with the use of resources to achieve a given target. Much of the information used and reported is common to both functions.

The main difference is in the time scales. **Financial management** is concerned with the **long-term raising of finance** and the **allocation and control of resources**; it involves targets, or objectives, that are generally long-term by nature, whilst management accounting usually operates within a 12-month time horizon.

Management accounting is concerned with providing information for the more day-to-day functions of control and decision making. This will involve budgeting, cost accounting, variance analysis, and evaluation of alternative uses of short-term resources.

Financial accounting is not directly involved in the day-to-day planning, control and decision making of an organisation. Rather, it is concerned with providing information about the historical results of past plans and decisions. Its purpose is to keep the owners (shareholders) and other interested parties informed of the overall financial position of the business, and it will not be concerned with the detailed information used internally by management accountants and financial managers.

Test your understanding 1

	Management accounting	Financial management	Financial accounting
• Review of overtime spending			
• Depreciation of non-current assets			
• Establishing dividend policy			
• Evaluating proposed expansion plans			
• Apportioning overheads to cost units			
• Identifying accruals and prepayments			

2 The relationship between corporate strategy and corporate and financial objectives

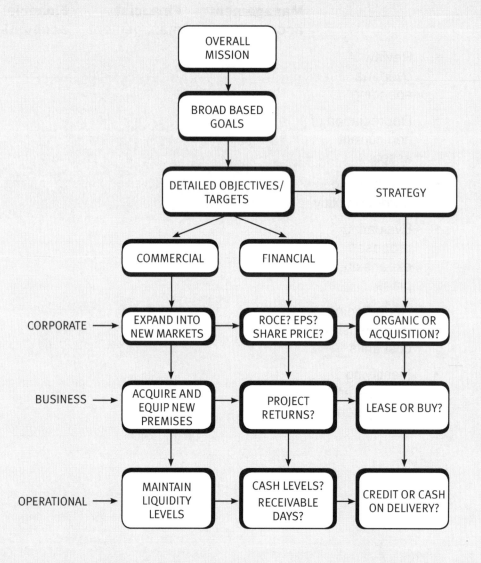

- The diagram above is key to understanding how financial management fits into overall business strategy.

- The distinction between 'commercial' and 'financial' objectives is to emphasise that not all objectives can be expressed in financial terms and that some objectives derive from commercial marketplace considerations.

Objectives/targets define **what** the organisation is trying to achieve. Strategy considers **how** to go about it.

Expandable text

Development of strategy follows on from the process of setting objectives. The starting point is the overriding purpose of the business. At first broad based, these general objectives are then broken down into more detailed aims:

- mission
- goals
- objectives and targets.

Once firm-wide commercial and financial objectives have been developed, these are cascaded down through the organisation:

- corporate objectives
- business objectives
- operational objectives.

Strategies are then developed at every level within the organisation to ensure that all departments and functions are working towards the same overall goals. The strategies are specifically designed to achieve the objectives set for that level of the organisation.

- Corporate strategy - concerns the decisions made by senior management about the overall purpose and scope of an organisation.
- Business strategy – how to compete successfully in particular markets.
- Operational strategy – how the component parts of an organisation deliver the corporate and business level strategies effectively.

Almost all strategies developed by the business will have financial implications and the financial manager has a key role to play in helping business strategies succeed.

Expandable text

Before strategy can be developed, commercial and financial objectives must be identified. These will be based on an assessment of the wishes and needs of organisational stakeholders (which will be further explored below). The business should recognise its overriding purpose or mission and develop broad based goals for the business to pursue to ensure it fulfils that purpose.

Each goal is then further broken down into detailed commercial and financial objectives, each of which should have appropriate identifiable, measurable targets so that progress towards them can be monitored.

These are then cascaded down throughout the organisation in a consistent manner so that all parts of the business are working to achieve the same overall goal. For example, the receivables days target of the credit control department should be linked to the cash needs of the investment projects, and the projects should be selected to achieve the overall corporate aim such as improving the share price. This in turn then satisfies the shareholders by increasing their wealth.

Once objectives and targets are set, the enterprise must then work to achieve them by developing and implementing appropriate strategies. Strategies will be developed at all levels of the business.

- Corporate strategy concerns the decisions made by senior management about matters such as the particular business the company is in, whether new markets should be entered or whether to withdraw from current markets. Such decisions can often have important financial implications. If, for example, a decision is taken to enter a new market, an existing company in that market could be bought, or a new company be started from scratch.

- Business strategy concerns the decisions to be made by the separate strategic business units within the group. Each unit will try to maximise its competitive position within its chosen market. This may involve for example choosing whether to compete on quality or cost.

- Operational strategy concerns how the different functional areas within a strategic business unit plan their operations to satisfy the corporate and business strategies being followed. We are, of course, most interested in the decisions facing the finance function. These day-to-day decisions include all aspects of working capital management.

KAPLAN PUBLISHING

Expandable text

The following list contains some commercial objectives/targets, some financial objectives/targets and some strategies, all at different levels of the business. Identify which is which.

- Implement a Just-In-Time (JIT) inventory system.
- Increase EPS by 5% on prior year.
- Acquire a rival in a share-for-share purchase.
- Buy four new cutting machines for $250,000 each.
- Achieve returns of 15% on new manufacturing investment.
- Improve liquidity ratio from 1.7 to 1.85.
- Reduce unsold inventory items by 12%.
- Update manufacturing capacity to incorporate new technology.
- Improve brand awareness within the UK.

	Commercial objectives / targets	Financial objectives / targets	Strategies
Corporate level			
Business level			
Operational level			

Solution

	Commercial objectives / targets	Financial objectives / targets	Strategies
Corporate level	Improve brand awareness within the UK.	Increase EPS by 5% on prior year.	Acquire rival chain in a share-for-share purchase.
Business level	Update manufacturing capacity to incorporate new technology.	Achieve returns of 15% on new manufacturing investment.	Buy four new cutting machines for $250,000 each.
Operational level	Reduce unsold inventory items by 12%.	Improve liquidity ratio from 1.7 to 1.85.	Implement a JIT inventory system.

3 Financial objectives

Shareholder wealth maximisation

If strategy is developed in response to the need to achieve objectives, it is obviously important to be clear about what those objectives are.

Most companies are owned by shareholders and originally set up to make money for those shareholders. The primary objective of most companies is thus to maximise shareholder wealth. (This could involve increasing the share price and/or dividend payout.)

Shareholder wealth maximisation is a fundamental principle of financial management. You should seek to understand the different aspects of the syllabus (e.g. finance, dividend policy, investment appraisal) within this unifying theme.

Many other objectives are also suggested for companies including: profit maximisation growthmarket sharesocial responsibilities.

- profit maximisation
- growth
- market share
- social responsibilities

KAPLAN PUBLISHING

Note: The objectives of other stakeholders are considered in more detail in chapter 2.

Maximising and satisficing

The objective of management has been deemed to be primarily one of maximising shareholder wealth. However in practice a distinction must be made between maximising and satisficing:

- maximising – seeking the best possible outcome
- satisficing – finding a merely adequate outcome.

Expandable text

Management could, on the one hand, constantly seek the maximum level of returns, even though this might involve exposure to risk and much higher management workloads. On the other hand, management might decide to hold returns at a satisfactory level, avoid risky ventures and reduce workloads.

Within a company, management might seek to maximise the return to some groups (e.g. shareholders) and satisfy the requirements of other groups (e.g. employees). The discussion about objectives is really about which group's returns management is trying to maximise.

The issue is clouded by the fact that the management may itself be unclear about the difference between maximising and satisficing. Thus management may believe that it is, say, maximising shareholder returns, when in fact it has reduced effort and accepted a merely satisfactory level of shareholder return.

Nevertheless, the objectives, if not the applications, of maximising as compared to satisficing should be clear.

Profit maximisation

An alternative objective of profit rather than shareholder wealth maximisation was mentioned above. There are a number of potential problems with taking this approach:

- short-termism
- risk
- not cash based.

The likelihood of this objective being adopted by management is greater where managerial performance targets (and financial rewards) are linked to profit measures such as ROCE.

Expandable text

In financial management we assume that the objective of the business is to maximise shareholder wealth. This is not necessarily the same as maximising profit or EPS.

Firms often find that share prices bear little relationship to reported profit figures (e.g. biotechnology companies and other 'new economy' ventures).

There are three main reasons behind this.

- Long-run versus short-run issues: In any business it is possible to boost short-term profits at the expense of long-term profits. For example discretionary spending on training, advertising, repairs and research and development (R&D) may be cut. This will improve reported profits in the short-term but damage the long-term prospects of the business. The stock exchange will normally see through such a tactic and share prices will fall.

- Quality (risk) of earnings: A business may increase its reported profits by taking a high level of risk. However the risk may endanger the returns available to shareholders. The stock exchange will then generally regard these earnings as being of a poor quality and the more risk-averse shareholders may sell. Once again the share price could fall.

- Cash: Accounting profits are just a paper figure. Dividends are paid with cash. Investors will therefore consider cash flow as well as profit.

Shareholder wealth is (in theory) determined by the present value of the future cash flows anticipated from the investment calculated by applying a discount rate that reflects the risks involved.

EPS growth

A widely used measure of corporate success is EPS, and it is therefore a commonly pursued objective.

However it is a measure of profitability, not wealth generation, and it is therefore open to the same criticisms as profit maximisation above.

Expandable text

EPS is widely used as a measure of return to equity.

The disadvantage of EPS is that it does not represent income of the shareholder. Rather, it represents that investor's share of the income generated by the company according to an accounting formula.

Whilst there is obviously a correlation between earnings and the wealth received by individual shareholders, they are not synonymous.

Chapter summary

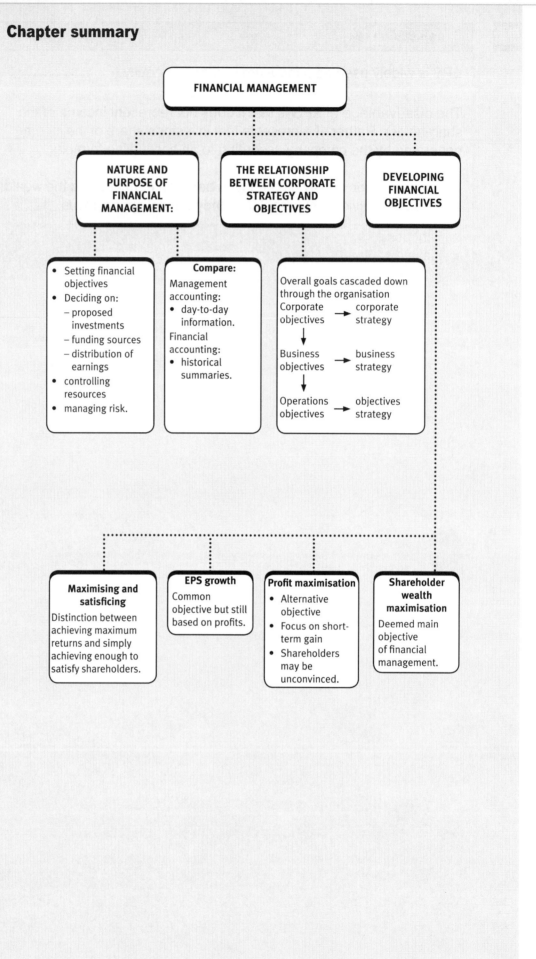

Test your understanding answers

Test your understanding 1

	Management accounting	Financial management	Financial accounting
Review of overtime spending	√		
Depreciation of non-current assets			√
Establishing dividend policy		√	
Evaluating proposed expansion plans			
Apportioning overheads to cost units	√		
Identifying accruals and prepayments			√

Management and the achievement of stakeholder objectives

Chapter learning objectives

Upon completion of this chapter you will be able to:

- list all the significant stakeholders in a company and identify the likely objectives of each

- identify and describe the main possible conflicts between the objectives of the significant stakeholders in a company

- identify the potential conflicts between stakeholder objectives in a scenario

- describe the role played by management in ensuring stakeholder objectives are met

- explain the risk of management not behaving in a goal congruent manner when pursuing stakeholder objectives

- describe the principle of agency theory

- describe the range of managerial remuneration packages designed to encourage managers to achieve stakeholder objectives

- select appropriate remuneration packages to encourage managers in a scenario to achieve stakeholder objectives

- explain the guidance within the corporate codes of governance that relates to encouraging managerial goal congruence

- explain the terms in the stock exchange listing regulations that encourage managerial goal congruence.

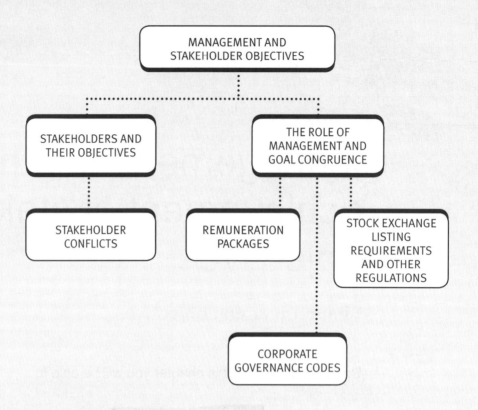

1 Stakeholder objectives

Corporate stakeholders

A stakeholder group is one with a vested interest in the company.

In the previous chapter we stated that the primary objective of a company is to maximise the wealth of shareholders. However many argue that a business must adopt the stakeholder view, which involves balancing the competing claims of a wide range of stakeholders, and taking account of broader economic and social responsibilities.

Typical stakeholders for an organisation would include:

- the community at large
- company employees
- company managers/directors
- equity investors (ordinary shareholders)
- customers
- suppliers
- finance providers
- the government.

Modern organisations vary in type, and talk of pursuing single objectives is perhaps a little simplistic. We see an assortment of small to large organisations ranging from those in the public sector through regulated utilities and not-for-profit organisations to purely private-sector operations. Each of these types of organisation is likely to have slightly different objectives. While many, particularly in the USA, would argue that the strategic objective of a private sector organisation is the long-term goal of maximising shareholder wealth, there is an alternative approach known as the **stakeholder view**.

This argues that in practice organisations have to balance the many competing claims of the community at large, employees, customers, shareholders and the environment. **Professor Charles Handy** is a prominent advocate of this view, arguing that maximisation of shareholder wealth, while important, cannot be the single overall objective of organisations, and account must be taken of broader economic and social responsibilities. Increasing globalisation, and the fact that some multinational companies have a turnover in excess of the incomes of small countries, puts these responsibilities sharply into focus. Typical stakeholders for an organisation might include the following.

- The community at large – this is a particularly important group for public sector enterprises and will have, in particular, environmental expectations from private sector or regulated organisations, such as organic foods, safe trains and cleaner petrol. For organisations there are problems of measurement – what are returns to the community at large? The goals of the community will be broad but will include such aspects as legal and social responsibilities, pollution control and employee welfare. Recently, environmental pressure groups have achieved considerable prominence and it is very clear that organisations cannot separate themselves from the societies and environments in which they operate.

- Company employees – obviously, many trade unionists would like to see their members as the residual beneficiaries of any surplus the company creates. Certainly, there is no measurement problem: returns = wages or salaries. However, maximising the returns to employees does assume that risk finance can be raised purely on the basis of satisficing, i.e. providing no more than an adequate return to shareholders.

- Company managers/directors – such senior employees are in an ideal position to follow their own aims at the expense of other stakeholders. Their goals will be both long-term (defending against takeovers, sales maximisation) and short-term (profit margins leading to increased bonuses).

- Equity investors (ordinary shareholders) – within any economic system, the equity investors provide the risk finance. In the UK, it is usually ordinary shareholders, or sometimes the government. There is a very strong argument for maximising the wealth of equity investors. In order to attract funds, the company has to compete with risk-free investment opportunities, e.g. government securities. The attraction is the accrual of any surplus to the equity investors. In effect, this is the risk premium which is essential for the allocation of resources to relatively risky investments in companies.

- Customers – satisfaction of customer needs will be achieved through the provision of value-for-money products and services. There remains, of course, the requirement for organisations to accurately identify precisely what those needs are.

- Suppliers – suppliers to the organisation will have short-term goals such as prompt payment terms alongside long-term requirements including contracts and regular business. The importance of the needs of suppliers will depend upon both their relative size and the number of suppliers.

- Finance providers – providers of finance (banks, loan creditors) will primarily be interested in the ability of the organisation to repay the finance including interest. As a result it will be the organisation's ability to generate cash both long- and short-term that will be the basis of interest to these providers.

- The government – the government will have political and financial interests in the organisation. Politically they will wish to increase exports and decrease imports whilst monitoring companies via the Competition Commission. Financially they require long-term profits to maximise taxation income. Equally importantly the government via its own agencies or via the legal system will seek to ensure that organisations observe health and safety, planning and minimum wage legislation. Also, on behalf of the community at large, government must consider modifying the behaviour of both individuals and organisations for environmental/health reasons, e.g. banning smoking in certain public places and restricting the advertising of tobacco companies.

The stakeholder view argues that it is simplistic to assume that organisations are motivated by a single goal and that the interests of all stakeholders must be taken into consideration. Critics of this view, however, would argue that while the interests of these other groups must obviously be balanced and managed, only shareholders have a relationship with organisations which is one of risk and return, and so practically the long-term financial objective of a private sector organisation is to maximise the wealth of equity investors. The debate will continue, but there seems to be an acceptance that organisations need to have a greater awareness of the societies in which they operate and this is reflected in the later debate on ethics.

Potential conflicts of objectives

With so many different groups having a vested interest in a company it is inevitable that at times those interests will conflict.

Conflict between and within groups of stakeholders and the need for management to balance the various interests is a key issue.

Test your understanding 1

Suggest the potential conflicts in objectives which could arise between the following groups of stakeholders in a company.

Stakeholders		Potential conflict
Employees	⇔ Shareholders	
Customers	⇔ Community at large	
Shareholders	⇔ Finance providers	
Customers	⇔ Shareholders/ managers	
Government	⇔ Shareholders	
Shareholders	⇔ Managers	

Expandable text

Mincorp is a mining company. Its mission is to 'maximise profits for shareholders whilst recognising its responsibilities to society'. It is considering a mining opportunity abroad in a remote country area where there is widespread poverty. The mining work will destroy local vegetation and may pollute the immediate water supply for some years to come. The company directors believe that permission for the mining work is likely to be granted by the government as there are few people or animals living in the area and the company will be providing much-needed jobs.

Identify the likely stakeholders in the company's decision. Consider their possible objectives and describe three likely conflicts in those objectives.

Solution

Stakeholder groups would include:

potential employees, local residents, wider community, environmental pressure groups, government, company directors/managers and prestige shareholders

Possible conflicts between their objectives would include:

Local residents/ pressure groups Managers/ shareholders
Local damage will have lasting impact on the environment. Local people/pressure groups may consider this unacceptable whilst shareholders may think that provided compensation is paid it is a reasonable consequence.

Company directors/ managers Employees/Pressure groups
Company directors may do only the minimum to comply with any health and safety legislation in order to save money. Potential employees may be desperate for work and un-informed and may therefore take risks with their own health. The wider community and pressure groups will focus on employee health as a priority.

Shareholders Government
Shareholders will want to see their own wealth increased by way of a return on their investment. The government may regard the wealth as belonging to the country and seek to prevent profits being taken out.

Note: Again any number of possible conflicts could be identified here. The scenario demonstrates the danger of focussing on improving share wealth to the exclusion of all other objectives.

2 The role of management and agency theory
Agency theory

Agency theory is often used to describe the relationships between the various interested parties in a firm and can help to explain the various duties and conflicts that occur:

 Agency relationships occur when one party, **the principal**, employs another party, **the agent**, to perform a task on their behalf. In particular, directors (agents) act on behalf of shareholders (principals).

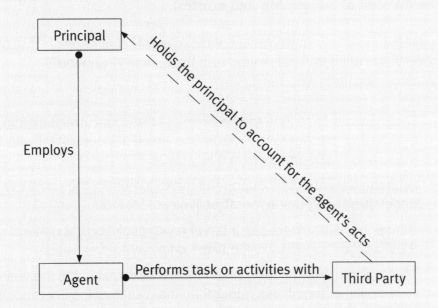

Expandable text

Agency theory can help to explain the actions of the various interest groups in the corporate governance debate.

For example, managers can be seen as the agents of shareholders, employees as the agents of managers, managers and shareholders as the agents of long- and short-term creditors, etc. In most of these principal-agent relationships, conflicts of interest will exist.

The problem lies in the fact that once the agent has been appointed he is able to act in his own selfish interests rather than pursuing the objectives of the principal.

Test your understanding 2

Fill in the gaps in the following table of agency relationships in a company.

Principal: Shareholders .... Loan creditors
Agent: .... Employees   ....
Agent's responsibility: ....

The divorce of ownership and control

By far the most important conflict of those mentioned above is that between the interests of shareholders who own the company and the directors/managers who run it.

- Finding ways to reduce the problems of the agency relationship and ensure that managers take decisions which are consistent with the objectives of shareholders is a key issue.

- Shareholders are reliant upon the management of the company to understand and pursue the objectives set for them.

- Although shareholders can intervene via resolutions at general meeting, the managers are usually left alone on a day-to-day basis.

- Management are uniquely placed to make decisions to maximise their own wealth or happiness rather than the wealth of the shareholders.

In the past 15 or so years, the following accusations of non-goal-congruent behaviour have been made against management:

- excessive remuneration levels
- empire building
- creative accounting
- off-balance-sheet financing
- inappropriate reaction to takeover bids
- unethical activities.

Expandable text

During the past 15 years or so, and particularly following the Maxwell scandal and others, attention has focused increasingly on the activities of directors. There has been an allegation that

directors have been making corporate decisions in their own interests rather than for the benefit of the company as a whole and the shareholders in particular.

KAPLAN PUBLISHING

Remuneration

The UK recession in the early 1990s and the economic slowdown in 2002-2003 led to many companies reporting sharply-reduced profits and laying off staff or cutting levels of employee pay. At the same time many directors were awarded large increases in pay, citing comparative pay levels in the US and in other companies as justification. During the 1990s the public failed to understand why 'fat cat' senior executives in newly-privatised utility companies should enjoy substantial pay rises after privatisation for doing essentially the same job as before. In 2003, criticisms were made of large pay awards to senior directors when the share price of their company and company profits had both fallen dramatically.

Empire building

The high level of corporate takeover activity in the 1980s led to many chief executives believing that building as large a group as possible was a valid aim in itself, an objective described as empire building. Executives gained prestige from successful bids and from being in charge of large conglomerates, but the returns to shareholders were often disappointing.

Creative accounting

The directors are responsible for selecting the accounting policies to be used by their company, subject to UK accounting standards and the opinion of the auditors. Despite the constraints upon them, the directors are still free to use creative accounting techniques to flatter their published accounts and perhaps artificially boost the share price. Examples of such techniques are: capitalising expenses on the balance sheet (e.g. development expenditure, advertising expenditure), not depreciating non-current assets, maximising the value of intangibles on the balance sheet (e.g. putting a value to brands), recognising revenue on long-term contracts at the earliest possible time (e.g. profits on leasing photocopiers), other forms of off-balance-sheet financing (see below).

The Accounting Standards Board's (ASB) continuing work programme aims to cut out creative accounting practices as much as is practically possible.

Off-balance-sheet finance refers to ways of financing assets where the method of funding is not recorded on the balance sheet.

One example is the use of leased, rather than purchased, assets. Before SSAP 21 a lessee's obligation to the lessor was omitted from the lessee's balance sheet and he could therefore report a lower gearing ratio and raise new funds at lower interest rates. SSAP 21 requires that assets acquired under finance leases must be capitalised on the lessee's balance sheet together with the corresponding obligation to the lessor. The ASB FRS 5 aims to restrict off-balance-sheet finance still further, for example by requiring quasi subsidiaries to be consolidated into the group accounts. The collapse of Enron in the US in late 2001 has put the spotlight on the various forms of off-balance-sheet finance used, and further scrutiny and regulation is inevitable.

Takeover bids

Boards of directors often spend considerable amounts of time and money attempting to defend their companies against takeover bids, even when it appears that the takeover would be in the best interests of the target company's shareholders. These directors are accused of trying to protect their own jobs, fearing that they will be retired if their company is taken over. Directors of public companies must now comply with the City Code on Takeovers and Mergers during a bid period.

Unethical activities

Unethical activities might not be prohibited by the Companies Acts or stock exchange regulations, but are believed by many to be undesirable to society as a whole. Examples are trading with countries ruled by dictatorships, testing products on animals, emitting pollution or carrying out espionage against competitors. The importance of **good business ethics** and **corporate social responsibility** (CSR) has been recognised in recent years and it is hoped that further progress is being made in the new millennium.

Although directors are supposed to be acting in the interests of the shareholders of their company, they stand accused in recent years of having made decisions on the basis of their own self-interest.

Expandable text

Managerial reward schemes

One way to help ensure that managers take decisions which are consistent with the objectives of shareholders is to introduce carefully designed remuneration packages. The schemes should:

- be clearly defined, impossible to manipulate and easy to monitor
- link rewards to changes in shareholder wealth
- match managers' time horizons to shareholders' time horizons
- encourage managers to adopt the same attitudes to risk as shareholders.

Common types of reward schemes include:

- remuneration linked to:
    - minimum profit levels
    - economic value added (EVA)
    - turnover growth
- executive share option schemes (ESOP).

Expandable text

Alternative reward systems

Types of remuneration schemes include:

A bonus based upon a minimum level of pre-tax profit

This scheme would be easy to set up and monitor.

Disadvantages are that the scheme may lead to managers taking decisions that would result in profits being earned in the short-term at the expense of long-term profitability. It could also lead to managers under-achieving, i.e. relaxing as soon as the minimum is achieved. The scheme might also tempt managers to use creative accounting to boost the profit figure.

A bonus linked to the EVA achieved by the company during the period. EVA could be defined in a number of different ways, but is essentially a measure of the increase in the value of shareholder wealth in the period. Schemes such as these are therefore designed to more closely align the interests of the employee and the shareholder.

Some organisations are going further than this and are using EVA as a way of structuring performance-linked variable remuneration where the EVA component may be a significant proportion of total remuneration.

A potential disadvantage is that calculating the bonus may be complex.

A bonus based on turnover growth

Growth of the business and higher production levels can lead to economies of scale which in turn can help the business compete more successfully on price.

However, turnover growth could be achieved at the expense of profitability, e.g. by reducing selling prices or by selecting high revenue product lines which may not necessarily be the most profitable. Maximising turnover is therefore unlikely to maximise shareholder wealth.

An ESOP

This scheme has the advantage that it will encourage managers to maximise the value of the shares of the company, i.e. the wealth of the shareholders. When an executive is awarded share options, the theory is that it is in their interests for the share price to rise, so they will do whatever possible to improve the share price. Their interests will be best served by working towards a goal that is also in the interests of the shareholders.

Such schemes are normally set up over a relatively long period thereby encouraging managers to make decisions to invest in positive return projects which should result in an increase in the price of the company shares. However, efficient managers may be penalised at times when share prices in general are falling.

There are several criticisms of ESOPs.

- When directors exercise their share options, they tend to sell the shares almost immediately to cash in on their profit. Unless they are awarded more share options, their interest in the share price therefore ends when the option exercise date has passed.

- If the share price falls when options have been awarded, and the options go 'underwater' and have no value, they cannot act as an incentive.

- If a company issues large quantities of share options, there could be some risk of excessive dilution of the equity interests of the existing shareholders. As a result, it has been suggested that companies should recognise the cost of share options to their shareholders, by making some form of charge for options in the income statement.

- Directors may distort reported profits (creative accounting) to protect the share price and the value of their share options.

Test your understanding 3

What are the benefits and potential problems with the reward schemes suggested?

Reward scheme	Benefits	Potential problems
Earnings linked to minimum profit levels		
Earnings linked to EVA		
Earnings linked to turnover growth		
ESOP		

Expandable text

Gretsch Inc, a listed company, has developed a highly successful new product and is thus growing rapidly. However, with this growth the firm is experiencing cash flow problems. Managers are currently awarded bonuses if there is growth in reported earnings per share

Comment on the current remuneration scheme.

Solution

Advantages

- Goal congruence – managers will work to achieve growth in EPS, which will make shareholders feel that their wealth is increasing.

- The figure is difficult (but not impossible!) to manipulate from one period to another as it will be audited.

Disadvantages

- There is little incentive for managers to control working capital and cash flow – a pressing problem. Growth may be at the expense of liquidity and ultimately compromise the firm's future survival.

- Managers may gain bonuses simply because of the products concerned rather than their own efforts. A target growth in EPS would be better.

- Long-term shareholder value and EPS are not well correlated.

- There is only one measure that focuses on final effects rather than operational causes.

Expandable text

Corporate governance codes

The director/shareholder conflict has also been addressed by the requirements of a number of corporate governance codes. The following key areas relate to this conflict.

- Non-executive directors (NEDs)
    - important presence on the board
    - must give obligation to spend sufficient time with the company
    - should be independent.

- Executive directors
    - separation of chairman and chief executive officer (CEO)
    - submit for re-election
    - clear disclosure of emoluments
    - outnumbered by the NEDs.

- Remuneration committees.

- Nomination committees.

- Annual general meeting (AGM).

After a number of high-profile firms collapsed, concerns over how the companies had been run led to a determination to ensure good corporate governance in future. A number of committees met and produced reports containing recommendations on how to improve corporate governance procedures. One of the areas addressed was the conflict between director and shareholder interests. Below is a selection of the current requirements:

NEDs

- At least half of the members of the board, excluding the chairman, should be independent NEDs. These are directors who do not take part in the running of the business. They attend board meetings, provide advice, listen to what is said and are generally meant to act as a control on the actions of the executive directors. Independence means they are free of any business or other relationship, which could materially interfere with the exercise of their independent judgement. Boards should disclose in the annual report which of the NEDs are considered to be independent.

- NEDs should get extra fees for chairing company committees but should not hold share options in their company. There was concern that allowing NEDs to hold share options in a company could encourage corporate excess or wrongdoing.

- One of the independent NEDs should be appointed a senior independent NED who would act as a champion for the interests of shareholders.

- Prospective NEDs should conduct due diligence before accepting the role. They should satisfy themselves that they have the knowledge, skills, experience and time to make a positive contribution to the company board.

- On appointment, the NEDs would also undertake that they have the time to meet their obligations. Company nomination committees would examine their performance, and make an assessment of whether they were devoting enough time to their duties.

Executive directors

- The chairman and the CEO roles should be separate, and a CEO should not become chairman of the same company.

- The chairman should be independent at the time of his appointment. Note that the effect of this, combined with the point about independent NEDs making up at least half of the board, will be to place independent NEDs in a majority on the board.

- All directors should submit themselves for re-election at least every three years.

- There should be clear disclosure of directors' total emoluments and those of the chairman and highest-paid UK director.

- Boards should set as their objective the reduction of directors' contract periods to one year or less.

Remuneration committees

- Executive directors' pay should be subject to the recommendations of a remuneration committee made up wholly of independent NEDs.

- Remuneration committees should objectively determine executive remuneration and individual packages for each executive director.

- The broad framework and cost of remuneration should be a matter for the board on the advice of the remuneration committee.

Nomination committees

- This committee will consist of NEDs with the aim of bringing an independent view to the selection and recruitment of both executive directors and NEDs.

- It will meet when required and effectively 'headhunt' directors. It will be a high-profile committee so as to demonstrate to stakeholders that a reasonable degree of objectivity exists in the selection process.

AGM

- Companies whose AGMs are well attended should consider providing a business presentation, with a question and answer session.

- Shareholders should be able to vote separately on each substantially separate issue; and the practice of 'bundling' unrelated proposals in a single resolution should cease.

Stock exchange listing requirements and other regulations

Although adherence to the principles of the corporate governance codes is voluntary, they are often referred to in the listing requirements of stock exchanges.

Illustration - Stock exchange listing requirements

The UK Combined Code is attached to the UK Listing Rules so that listed companies in the UK are under pressure to comply. Under an amendment to the UK Listing Rules, listed companies must:

- disclose how they have applied the principles and complied with the Code's provisions in their annual report and accounts

- state and explain any deviation from the recommended best practice.

Similarly some aspects of governance have moved into the statute books.

Illustration – Stock exchange listing requirements

The Directors' Remuneration Report Regulations 2002 in the UK amends the Companies Act 1985 and apply to quoted companies. The main provisions of the Regulations are as follows:

- a directors' remuneration report must be produced each year containing details of:
    - the remuneration for the year of each individual director
    - 'golden handshakes
    - ' payments into a pension scheme for a director
    - details of share option arrangements
- the report should be submitted to the shareholders for approval by vote at the AGM.

Chapter summary

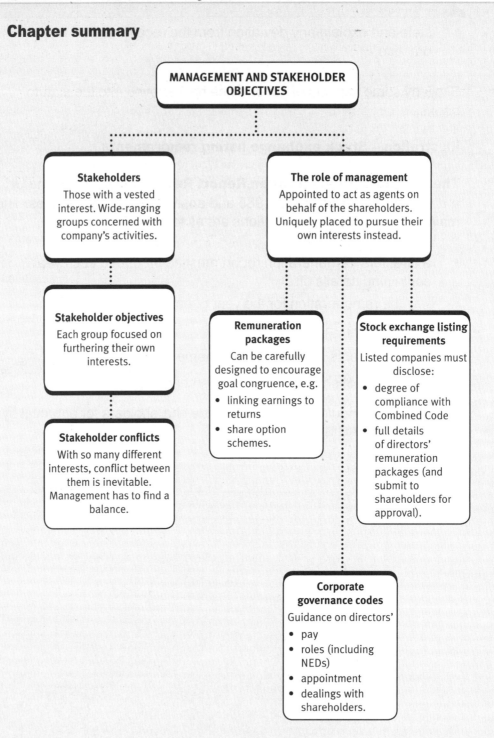

Test your understanding answers

Test your understanding 1

Stakeholders	Potential conflict
Employees ⇔ Shareholders	Employees may resist the introduction of automated processes which would improve efficiency but cost jobs. Shareholders may resist wage rises demanded by employees as uneconomical.
Customers ⇔ Community at large	Customers may demand lower prices and greater choice, but in order to provide them a company may need to squeeze vulnerable suppliers or import products at great environmental cost.
Shareholders ⇔ Finance providers	Shareholders may encourage management to pursue risky strategies in order to maximise potential returns, whereas finance providers prefer stable lower-risk policies that ensure liquidity for the payment of debt interest.
Customers ⇔ Shareholders/ managers	Customers may require higher service levels (such as 24 rather than 48 hour delivery) which are resisted by shareholders as too expensive or by management due to increased workload.
Government ⇔ Shareholders	Government will often insist upon levels of welfare (such as the minimum wage and health and safety practices) which would otherwise be avoided as an unnecessary expense.
Shareholders ⇔ Managers	Shareholders are concerned with the maximisation of their wealth. Managers may instead pursue strategies focused on growth as these may bring the greatest personal rewards.

> **Note:** You may have come up with different suggestions. The point is to recognise that there is a huge range of potential conflicts of interest and senior management will need to work to achieve a balance.

Test your understanding 2

Principal:	Shareholders	Management	Loan creditors
Agents:	Management	Employees	Management
Agent's responsibility:	To run the company in the best interests of the shareholders.	To work hard as instructed by management.	To manage the funds lent without taking excessive risks.

Test your understanding 3

Reward scheme	Benefits	Potential problems
Earnings linked to minimum profit levels	Easy to set up and monitor.	Managers may: • pursue short-term profits rather than real increases in shareholder wealth • 'relax' once minimum profits are achieved • use creative accounting to manipulate profitability figures.
Earnings linked to EVA	Closely aligns manager and shareholder interests.	Complex to calculate.
Earnings linked to turnover growth	Growth can lead to economies of scale.	Turnover increase not likely to lead to improved shareholder wealth.
ESOP	Directly aligns manager and shareholder interests.	• Only works until options exercised. • Does not work if shares fall in value. • Can dilute existing shareholders' holdings. • May incentivise creative accounting.

Measuring achievement of corporate objectives

Chapter learning objectives

Upon completion of this chapter you will be able to:

- calculate return on capital employed (ROCE) with data provided
- explain the meaning and usefulness of a calculated ROCE figure
- calculate earnings per share (EPS) and price earnings (PE) ratio with data provided
- explain the meaning and usefulness of an EPS figure and a PE ratio
- calculate return on equity (ROE) with data provided
- explain the meaning and usefulness of a calculated ROE figure
- calculate dividend per share (DPS) with data provided
- explain the meaning and usefulness of a DPS figure
- calculate dividend yield with data provided
- explain the meaning and usefulness of a dividend yield figure
- calculate total shareholder return (TSR) (dividend yield plus capital growth) with data provided
- explain the meaning and usefulness of a TSR (dividend yield plus capital growth) figure
- select appropriate ratios to measure changes in shareholder wealth within a scenario and discuss the relevance of the findings.

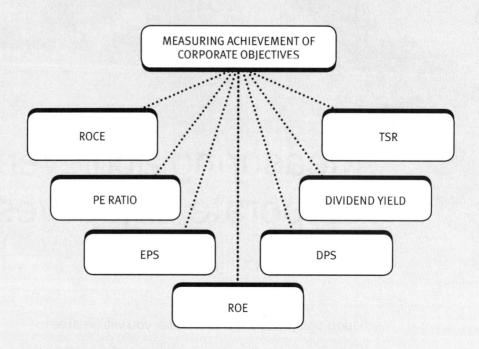

1 Measuring achievement of corporate objectives

For a company, the primary objective has been identified as the maximisation of shareholder wealth. However in the short-term the management may set profitability targets (either as interim goals or because they better represent the concerns of the managers). This section looks at the calculation of a range of measures designed to assess both profitability and increase in wealth. Some of the ratios have been met before in F5 but are covered here in full for completeness.

Taken in isolation, the calculations are relatively meaningless when assessing performance. Comparatives such as prior-year information, targets, industry averages and other forms of benchmarking are required if the measures are to be interpreted and the underlying causes investigated.

KAPLAN PUBLISHING

All the ratios calculated in the chapter are based upon the following information:

Balance sheets(Statements of finanacial position) as at 31 May

	20X6	20X5
	$000	$000
Non-current assets	1,800	1,400
Current assets		
Inventory	1,200	200
Receivables	400	800
Cash	100	100
Total Assets	3,500	2,500
Equity and Liabilities		
Ordinary share capital (50c shares)	1,200	500
Share premium	600	0
Reserves	200	100
	2,000	600
Non-current liabilities		
10% Loan notes	1,000	600
Current liabilities		
Loans and other borrowing	200	500
Other payables	300	800
	3,500	2,500

Income statements

	20X6	20X5
	$000	$000
Revenue	2,000	1,000
Cost of sales	(1,300)	(700)
Gross profit	700	300
Distribution costs	(260)	(90)
Administration expenses	(100)	(60)
Operating profit	340	150
Interest	(100)	(60)
Profit before taxation	240	90
Taxation	(50)	(20)
Profit after taxation	190	70
Ordinary dividends	(90)	(50)
Retained profit for the year	100	20
Profit and loss b/fwd	100	80
Profit and loss c/fwd	200	100
Share price ($)	1.30	1.26
Industry information:		
Industry PE ratio	22	20
Industry average growth in EPS (%)	12	8

2 ROCE

Considered to be a key ratio, ROCE gives a measure of how efficiently a business is using the funds available. It measures how much is earned per $1 invested.

$$\text{ROCE} = \frac{\text{Profit before interest and tax}}{\text{Capital Employed}} = \frac{\text{PBIT}}{\text{CE}}$$

PBIT = Operating profit
CE = Non-current assets + Current assets - Current liabilities
= Share capital + Reserves + Long-term loans

Disadvantage of ROCE:

- uses profit which is not directly linked to the objective of maximising shareholder wealth.

Illustration 1 – ROCE

		20X6	20X5
ROCE			
$\frac{\text{PBIT}}{\text{CE}} \times 100$		340	150
		3,000	1,200
		11.33%	12.50%

The company's ROCE has decreased in 20X6, i.e. for every $100 of capital invested the company earned $11.33 in 20X6 compared with $12.50 in 20X5.

---

3 EPS

This is the basic measure of a company's performance from an ordinary shareholder's point of view. It is the amount of profit, in cents, attributable to each ordinary share.

The principles of calculating EPS are simple:

$$EPS = \frac{\text{Profit after interest, after tax and after preference dividends}}{\text{Number of ordinary shares in issue}}$$

EPS can be analysed by studying the growth rate over time – trend analysis.

Disadvantage of EPS.

• EPS does not represent actual income of the shareholder and it uses earnings which are not directly linked to the objective of maximising shareholder wealth.

Illustration 2 – EPS

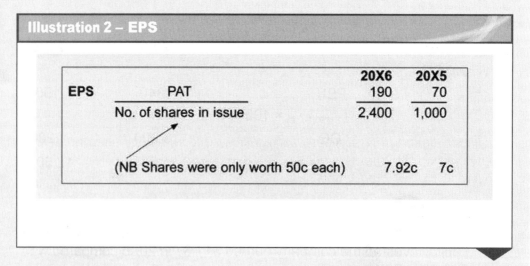

		20X6	20X5
EPS	$\dfrac{\text{PAT}}{\text{No. of shares in issue}}$	190 2,400	70 1,000
	(NB Shares were only worth 50c each)	7.92c	7c

Solution

The EPS is an improvement on the prior year. It has grown by:

$$\frac{92}{700} = 0.13 \qquad\qquad = 13\%$$

This is slightly higher than the industry average (12%).

Expandable text

Although the ratio is simple in principle, in practice there may be a number of complications as both the definitions of **earnings** and **shares in issue** require careful analysis. Accounting treatment may cause the ratios to be distorted, if for example the earnings figure includes the effects of extraordinary items.

When calculating the EPS you cannot compare EPS of one company with EPS of another, as the answer would be meaningless. You should first calculate the growth rate of the EPS and then compare it with the growth of similar companies.

EPS does not represent the income of the shareholder. Rather, it represents the investor's share of profit after tax generated by the company according to an accounting formula. Whilst there is obviously a correlation between earnings applicable to individual shareholders and their wealth, they are not equal.

*Price
earnings
Ratio*

*How much you are paying for
each dollar of earnings.
The lower it is the better it is.*

4 PE ratio

A PE ratio gives a basic measure of company performance. It expresses the amount the shareholders are prepared to pay for the share as a multiple of current earnings.

$$PE = \frac{\text{Share price}}{\text{EPS}}$$

A high PE ratio indicates that investors perceive the firm's earnings to be of high quality – usually a mixture of high growth and/or lower risk expectations.

Expandable text

This is the basic measure of a company's performance from the market's point of view. Investors estimate a share's value as the amount they are willing to pay for each unit of earnings. It expresses the current share price as a multiple of the most recent EPS.

If a PE ratio is high, investors expect profits to rise. This does not necessarily mean that all companies on high PE ratios are expected to perform to a high standard, merely that they are expected to do significantly better than in the past. They may have greater growth potential because they are coming from a low base.

Illustration 3 – PE Ratio

PE Ratio		20X6	20X5
	Share price	130	126
	EPS	7.92	7
		16.4 times	18 times

Investors are willing to buy shares in the company at 16.4 times last year's earnings compared with the previous year's position when they were willing to pay 18 times the earnings.

This fall may be because the company is not expected to grow as much as in the previous year. The industry average PE increased year-on-year from 20 to 22, which may suggest that this company is expected to generate slower growth or carries more risk than the industry average.

5 ROE

ROE measures how much profit a company generates for its ordinary shareholders with the money they have invested in the company.

It is useful for comparing the profitability of a company with other firms in the same industry.

It is calculated as

$$ROE = \frac{\text{Profit after tax and preference dividends}}{\text{Ordinary share capital + reserves}} \times 100\%$$

Where there are no preference shares this is simplified to give:

$$ROE = \frac{PAT}{\text{Shareholders' funds}} \times 100\%$$

ROE is similar to ROCE except:

- PAT is used instead of operating profit
- Shareholders' funds are used instead of CE (debt + equity).

Disadvantages of ROE:

- it uses profits which are an unreliable measure and not directly linked to shareholder wealth
- it is sensitive to gearing levels – ROE will increase as gearing ratio increases.

Expandable text

The value of ROE, is that it can help cut through the references to 'achieving record earnings' in many companies' annual reports. Achieving higher earnings each year is straightforward because a successful company generates profits every year. If management simply invested those earnings in a savings account paying 5% pa, they would be able to report 'record earnings' because of the interest they earned. But the shareholders would not be as well off as if the money had been returned to them for re-investment in another business opportunity.

So investors cannot take rising earnings per share each year as a sign of success. However the ROE figure takes into account the retained earnings from previous years, and so tells investors how effectively their capital is being reinvested. It is therefore a far better measure of management's abilities than the annual EPS.

However, apart from the obvious criticism that ROE still relies on the profit figure calculated, it is also sensitive to gearing levels. Assuming that the proceeds of debt finance can be re-invested at a return greater than the borrowing rate, then the greater the levels of debt in the capital structure, the higher the ROE will be.

Illustration 4 – ROE

ROE

	20X6	20X5
PAT	190	70
Shareholders' funds	2000	600
	9.5%	11.7%

The ROE is falling. What is more, it is falling at a time when the industry average has risen from 12% to 15%. This suggests that the company is failing to make the most of the shareholders' investment. This analysis accords with the findings of the ROCE and the PE ratio.

6 DPS

The DPS helps individual (ordinary) shareholders see how much of the overall dividend payout they are entitled to.

$$DPS = \frac{\text{Total ordinary dividend}}{\text{Total number of shares issued}}$$

Usually given in the company's financial statements.

Illustration 5 – DPS

		20X6	20X5
Dividend per share			
	Dividends for the period	90	50
	Total number of shares issued	2,400	1,000
		3.75c	50c

The DPS is falling. This would usually be regarded as bad news by investors, although here it is probably related to the share issue in 20X6. If it was a rights issue, e.g. the shareholders will now each own a greater number of shares.

Expandable text

Since the shareholders are the owners of the business, they are entitled to their share of the profits. This is most simply achieved by paying the amount out as a dividend. It is usually expressed as an amount per share. This is because the total amount a shareholder gets has to reflect their share of the company. If they are only a small shareholder and do not own many shares, they should only get a small share of the profit.

There is a tendency amongst investors to regard the level of dividend payout as a form of information about the company's performance. A falling DPS is regarded as a sign of problems. As a result many companies try to maintain a stable and slowly rising DPS, by resisting making high payouts during particularly good years.

7 Dividend yield

This provides a direct measure of the wealth received by the (ordinary) shareholder. It is the annual dividend per share expressed as an annual rate of return on the share price.

$$\text{Dividend yield} = \frac{\text{DPS}}{\text{Market price per share}}$$

It can be used to compare the return with that from a fixed-rate investment.

Disadvantage of dividend yield:

- it fails to take account of any anticipated capital growth so does not represent the total return to the investor.

Illustration 6 – Dividend yield

		20X6	20X5
Dividend yield			
DPS		3.75	5
Market price per share		130	126
		2.9%	4.0%

This return may compare unfavourably with interest rates but is not a full measure of company performance as the investor will also benefit from any increase in share price. As stated before, the low DPS may well be, in part, because of the recent share issue and this will also clearly impact the dividend yield.

Expandable text

The dividend yield is regarded as being significant in the context of reaching decisions about whether to buy or sell shares. Investors are concerned with the amount of cash, in present value terms, which they will receive from their investment in shares. This cash is the result of:

- dividends received
- proceeds when the shares are ultimately sold.

No ratio provides full information about future cash flows but dividend yield is regarded as being a useful pointer.

Dividend yield is, however, incomplete in that it ignores the capital gain on the share which most shareholders would expect. A better measure would be TSR.

8 TSR   *Total Shareholders Return*

This measures the returns to the investor by taking account of:

- dividend income
- capital growth.

$$TSR = \frac{DPS + \text{change in share price}}{\text{Share price at start of period}}$$

TSR makes comparing returns between investments simple, irrespective of the size of the underlying investment.

Illustration 7 – TSR

If we assume that the share price was $1.20 at 31 May 20X4, then the TSR for the two years can be calculated:

	20X6	20X5
$TSR = \dfrac{DPS + \text{Change in share price}}{\text{Share price at start of period}}$	$\dfrac{3.75 + (130 - 126)}{126}$	$\dfrac{5 + (126 - 120)}{120}$
	6.15%	9.17%

Expandable text

Probably the best measure of returns to equity, TSR takes account of the dividend income paid to shareholders and the capital growth of the share.

The TSR from an investment can easily be compared between companies or benchmarked against industry or market returns without having to worry about differences in size of the business.

The actual return received by the investor will depend on the shareholder's marginal rate of income tax and the capital gains tax suffered on any realised capital gain. Whether the shareholders prefer high dividend income or high capital gains will therefore depend very much on their tax position.

Being able to select relevant ratios in a given scenario, calculate and interpret them is a key skill that you need to develop for the examination.

Test your understanding 1

Summarised balance sheet(Statement of financial posotion) at 31 December 20X6

		$000	$000
Non-current assets			
Cost *less* depreciation			2,200
Current assets			
	Inventory	400	
	Receivables	500	
	Cash	100	
			1,000
Total assets			3,200

Equity and liabilities

Share capital

	Ordinary shares ($1 each)	1,000
	Preference shares (10%) ($1 each)	200
	Reserves	800
		2000

Non-current liabilities

	Loan notes (10% Secured)	600

Current liabilities

	Payables	400	
	Corporation tax	100	
	Dividends	100	
			600

Total equity and liabilities	3,200

Summarised income statement for the year ended 31 December 20X6

	$000	$000
Turnover		3,000
PBIT		400
Interest		(60)
Profit before tax		
		340
Corporation tax		(180)
PAT		160

Dividends

Ordinary – proposed and paid	125
Preference	20
	─────
	(145)
	─────
Transferred to revenue reserves	15
Current quoted price of $1 ordinary shares	$1.40
Price of $1 ordinary shares at 31/12/X5	$1.22

Using the information above, calculate the following ratios and comment on your findings:

(a) **ROCE – prior year 11%**

(b) **EPS – prior year 13.5c, industry average growth 3.5%**

(c) **PE ratio – industry average 7**

(d) **ROE – prior year 7%, industry average 7.5%**

(e) **DPS – prior year 12.5c**

(f) **Dividend yield**

(g) **TSR – prior year 20%, industry average 19%.**

Chapter summary

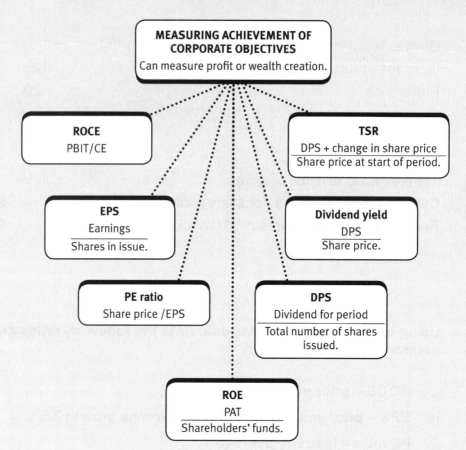

Test your understanding answers

Test your understanding 1

(a) **ROCE**

	20X6

$$\frac{PBIT}{CE} \times 100 \qquad \frac{400}{2,600}$$

15.4%

This short-term measure has improved suggesting the company is improving the efficient use of its funds.

(b) **EPS**

	20X6

$$\frac{\text{Profit available to ordinary shareholders}}{\text{Number of ordinary shares in issue}} \qquad \frac{160 - 20}{1,000}$$

14c

$$\text{Growth of EPS} = \frac{0.5}{3.5} = 3.7\%$$

The EPS is growing at a rate marginally above the industry average, which suggests an acceptable level of profitability is being achieved.

(c) **PE ratio**

	20X6
Share price	140
————————	———
EPS	14
	10 times

The PE ratio is higher than the industry average. This may be because the company is perceived to have good growth prospects. It is likely to be seen as having good investment potential since investors are prepared to pay ten times over the current earnings for the shares.

The current growth in EPS is fairly low but the company may be expected to make great improvements in the coming years.

(d) **ROE**

	20X6
PAT and pref. dividend	160 - 20
———————————————	———————
Shareholders' funds	1,800
	7.8%

The ROE is higher than last year. So in addition to the rising EPS it appears that the company is re-investing the funds it earns effectively. It also appears to be doing better than the industry as a whole. It would be useful to know what the industry average figure was in the previous year in order to determine the trend in its performance.

This finding is in line with the high PE ratio – if the firm is re-investing the funds it earns effectively it will be perceived as likely to develop good growth opportunities.

(e) **DPS**

	20X6
Dividends paid and proposed	125
Total number of shares issued	1,000
	12.5c

The DPS is unchanged despite an increase in EPS. This would make sense, as management are often reluctant to increase dividends too quickly, in case poor trading conditions in future years would then require a dividend cut. Dividend cuts are not well liked by investors.

Since the high PE ratio suggests good growth prospects, management may delay a dividend increase until these come to fruition.

(f) **Dividend yield**

	20X6
DPS	12.5
Market price per share	140
	8.9%

Prior year dividend yield can be calculated as prior year DPS divided by previous share price:

$$\frac{12.5}{122} = 10.2\%$$

It is inevitable that the dividend yield is falling, since the dividend has not been increased whilst the share price has grown. This shows the weakness of dividend yield as a measure – the shareholders are also benefiting from the increased share price but dividend yield does not take account of it.

(g) **TSR**

	20X6
DPS + Change in share price	12.5 + (140 - 122)
———————————————	————
Share price at start of period	122
	25%

The overall TSR is above industry average and increasing (prior year = 20%). This can be explained by the increase in share price which supplements the dividends received. This increase is a sign of increased investor expectations of future income.

Overall, this appears to be an efficient growing company with promising prospects recognised by shareholders. Managers are prudently delaying increasing dividend payments too early, to avoid later drops fuelling investor dissatisfaction and a resulting fall in share price.

4

Financial and other objectives in not-for-profit organisations

Chapter learning objectives

Upon completion of this chapter you will be able to:

- explain the impact of not-for-profit status on an organisation's non-financial objectives

- explain the impact of not-for-profit status on an organisation's financial objectives

- explain the concept of value for money (VFM)

- explain the importance of VFM as an objective in not-for-profit organisations (NFPs or NPOs)

- describe the 3 Es (economy, efficiency and effectiveness) and how they are used in NFPs to measure achievement of objectives

- suggest appropriate measures of achievement for use in a scenario based on an NFP.

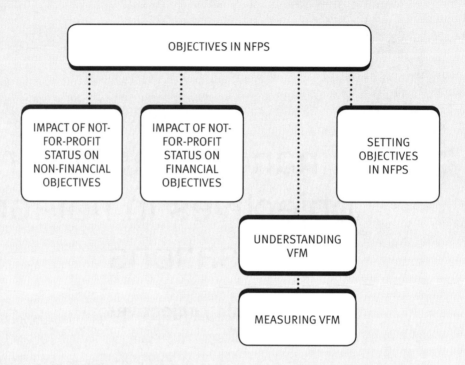

1 Objective setting in NFPs

NFPs (or NPOs) have been discussed before in F1. In F9 we are more concerned with the setting and measurement of objectives of such organisations.

The primary objective of NFPs is not to make money but to benefit prescribed groups of people.

Test your understanding 1

List types of organisation that might be considered not-for-profit and consider what groups they are set up to benefit.

Planning influences

A number of factors influence the way in which management objectives are determined in NFPs, which distinguish them from commercial businesses:

- wide range of stakeholders

- high level of interest from stakeholder groups

- significant degree of involvement from funding bodies and sponsors

- little or no financial input from the ultimate recipients of the service

- funding often provided as a series of advances rather than as a lump sum

- projects typically have a longer-term planning horizon
- may be subject to government influence/government macroeconomic policy.

Expandable text

List the influences a school headmaster may face when setting objectives.

Solution

- Wide range of stakeholders – pupils, parents, school governors, teachers, government.

- High level of interest from stakeholder groups – especially parents and governors.

- Funding is primarily from government who will have their own objectives such as performance in league tables, pass rates, etc.

- Little or no financial input from the ultimate recipients of the service – pupils.

- Projects typically have a longer-term planning horizon, e.g. new buildings.

- Education is a high-profile area of government policy.

Non-financial objectives

As with any organisation, NFPs will use a mixture of financial and non-financial objectives.

However, with NFPs the non-financial objectives are often more important and more complex because of the following.

- Most key objectives are very difficult to quantify, especially in financial terms, e.g. quality of care given to patients in a hospital.

- Multiple and conflicting objectives are more common in NFPs, e.g. quality of patient care versus number of patients treated.

These are discussed in more detail below.

For a company listed on the stock market we can take the maximisation of shareholder wealth as a working objective and know that the achievement of this objective can be monitored with reference to share price and dividend payments.

For an NFP the situation is more complex. There are two questions to be answered:

- in whose interests is it run?
- what are the objectives of the interested parties?

Many such organisations are run in the interests of society as a whole and therefore we should seek to attain the position where the gap between the benefits they provide to society and the costs of their operation is the widest (in positive terms).

The cost is relatively easily measured in accounting terms. However, many of the benefits are intangible. For example, the benefits of such bodies as the National Health Service (NHS) or local education authorities (LEAs) are almost impossible to quantify.

Because of the problem of quantifying the non-monetary objectives of such organisations most public bodies operate under objectives determined by the government (and hence ultimately by the electorate).

It is worth noting that some of the issues facing NFPs also have relevance in the commercial but public service-orientated industries such as utilities providers and the Post Office (many of which were originally owned by government). Although they have commercial status, there remains a prevailing concern about how well they serve the interests of society, which is not a test applied to the purely commercial sector.

Financial objectives

Since the services provided are limited primarily by the funds available, key objectives for NFPs will be to:

- raise as large a sum as possible
- spend funds as effectively as possible.

Targets may then be set for different aspects of each accounting period's finances such as:

- total to be raised in grants and voluntary income
- maximum percentage of this total that fund-raising expenses represents
- amounts to be spent on specified projects or in particular areas
- maximum permitted administration costs
- meeting budgets
- breaking even in the long run.

The actual figures achieved can then be compared with these targets and control action taken if necessary.

2 VFM as an objective

VFM can be defined as 'achieving the desired level and quality of service at the most economical cost'.

The concept of VFM is of particular importance in NFPs (particularly those in the public sector) because they:

- often use public funds raised through taxation or donation
- do not produce financial results such as profit figures
- have no clear priority of objectives
- face an increasing demand for accountability.

Expandable text

Because a significant number of NFPs are funded from the public purse, the lack of clear financial performance measures has been seen as a particular problem. It is argued that the public are entitled to reassurance that their money (in the form of taxes for public sector organisations or donations for charities) is being properly spent.

In addition, the complex mix of objectives with no absolute priority has also led to concern that the money may be being directed towards the wrong ends.

These issues, along with a growth in the perceived need for greater accountability among public officials, led to the development of the concept of evaluating VFM in public sector organisations. The principles developed are now widely applied in NFPs.

3 Measuring objectives in NFPs

Expandable text

Systems analysis

A more detailed analysis of what is meant by VFM can be achieved by viewing the organisation as a system set up to achieve its objectives by means of processing inputs into outputs.

The organisation as a system

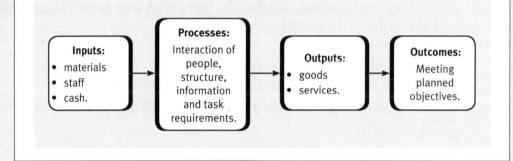

The three Es

Assessing whether the organisation provides value for money involves looking at the functioning of all aspects of the system. Performance measures have been developed to permit evaluation of each part separately.

VFM

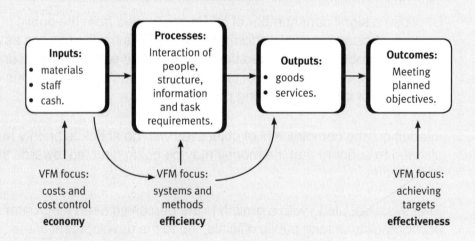

Economy: Minimising the costs of inputs required to achieve a defined level of output.

Efficiency: Ratio of outputs to inputs – achieving a high level of output in relation to the resources put in (input driven) or providing a particular level of service at reasonable input cost (output-driven).

Effectiveness: Whether outputs are achieved that match the predetermined objectives.

Use of the 3Es as a performance measure and a way to assess VFM is a key issue for examination questions that relate to NFPs and public sector organisations.

Expandable text

Known as the 3 Es these measures are fundamental to an understanding of VFM. An organisation achieving economy, efficiency and effectiveness in each part of the system is considered to be providing good VFM.

Public sector organisations are subject to regular VFM (or best value) reviews and the results have important impacts on future plans and funding decisions.

Economy

Acquiring resources of appropriate quality and quantity at the lowest cost. Note that whilst obtaining low prices is an important consideration it is not the only one. Achieving true economy will include ensuring the purchases are fit for purpose and meet any predetermined standards.

Efficiency

Maximising the useful output from a given level of resources, or minimising the inputs required to produce the required level of output.

Some public services fall within the first definition as they try to provide as much of a service as possible with strictly limited resources and few opportunities to generate further income sources. This is defined as 'input-driven' efficiency. This would include services such as library provision.

However in many areas, there is a statutory obligation to provide a particular standard of service, for example prison services, which cannot be significantly reduced or withdrawn. In this case the obligation is to provide the service at a reasonable cost and is known as 'output-driven' efficiency.

In both areas, the key consideration is whether the resources used were put to good use and the methods and processes carried out represent best practice.

Effectiveness

Ensuring that the output from any given activity is achieving the desired result.

For example the cheapest site on which to build and run a sports centre may be a disused brownfield site on the edge of town. However, if the council's objectives included reduction in car use and accessible opportunities for health improvement, then the output of the building process – the sports centre, even if built economically and efficiently, would not be considered effective as it failed to meet the stated objectives.

Expandable text

A subsidised college canteen service is to be evaluated by the local council to assess amongst other things, whether it is financially sound and offers value for money. Suggest appropriate measures of achievement that could be set for the service.

Solution

Financial measures:

- proportion of overall funds spent on administration costs
- ability to stay within budget/break even
- revenue targets met.

Economy targets:

- costs of purchasing provisions of suitable nutritional quality
- costs of negotiating for and purchasing equipment
- negotiation of bulk discounts
- pay rates for staff of appropriate levels of qualification.

Efficiency targets:

- numbers of portions produced
- cost per meal sold
- levels of wastage of unprepared and of cooked food
- staff utilisation
- equipment life.

Effectiveness targets:

- numbers using the canteen
- customer satisfaction ratings
- nutritional value of meals served.

Chapter summary

Objectives in not-for-profit organisations

e.g. charities, public services, local government, trade unions, sports associations, professional institutes.

Impact of not-for-profit status on non-financial objectives

- Wide-ranging high-interest stakeholders
- Involvement of sponsors
- No 'price' for end user
- Funding in tranches.

Impact of not-for-profit status on financial objectives

Limited funds so targets set on:
- total to be raised
- amount spent on fund-raising
- amount to be spent on specified projects
- adminisration spending
- staying within budget
- breaking even.

Setting objectives in NFPs

Set financial targets and targets in each of the 3 Es for all parts of the system.

Understanding VFM

Achieving the desired level and quality of service at the most economical cost.

Measuring VFM

Economy
Efficiency
Effectiveness.

Test your understanding answers

Test your understanding 1

Not-for-profit organisations and the groups they are set up to benefit would include:

- charities – those with unmet needs in a specific area

- public services including schools and hospitals – the general public in the location

- local government – the local citizens

- trade unions – members of the union

- sports associations – members of the association and others involved in the sport

- professional institutes – members of the institute and others in the profession.

Working capital management

Chapter learning objectives

Upon completion of this chapter you will be able to:

- define working capital and identify its elements

- explain the objectives of working capital management in terms of liquidity and profitability, and discuss the conflict between them

- explain the importance of working capital management to good financial management

- describe the principle and components of the cash operating cycle including the impact on it of accounts payable and receivable

- calculate the length of the cash operating cycle from supplied data

- calculate the current ratio and explain its relevance

- calculate the quick ratio and explain its relevance

- calculate the inventory turnover ratio and the inventory holding period and explain their relevance

- calculate the average collection period for receivables and explain its relevance

- calculate the average payable period for payables and explain its relevance

- calculate the length of a company's cash operating cycle by selecting relevant data from the company's accounts and discuss the implications for the company

- calculate the sales revenue/net working capital ratio and explain its relevance

- calculate the level of working capital investment in current assets from supplied data

- discuss the effect of a business' terms of trade on the length of the working capital cycle

- explain the policies a company may adopt on the level of investment in current assets

- discuss the effect of the industry in which the organisation operates on the length of the working capital cycle

- calculate the level of working capital investment in current assets by selecting relevant data from the company's accounts and discuss the implications for the company.

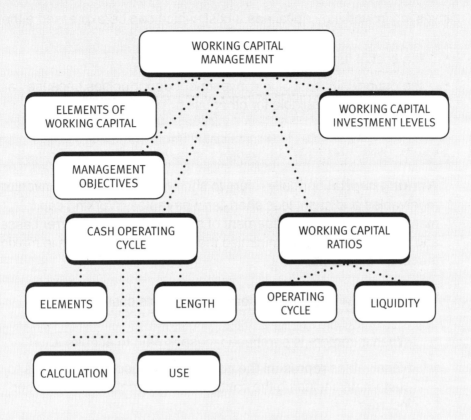

1 The elements of working capital

Working capital is the capital available for conducting the day-to-day operations of an organisation; normally the excess of current assets over current liabilities.

Working capital management is the management of all aspects of both current assets and current liabilities, to minimise the risk of insolvency while maximising the return on assets.

$= CA - CL$

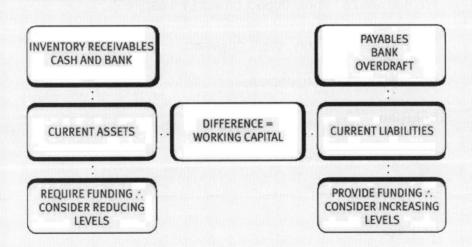

Investing in working capital has a cost, which can be expressed either as:

- the cost of funding it, or

- the opportunity cost of lost investment opportunities because cash is tied up and unavailable for other uses.

Expandable text

Working capital normally refers to short-term net assets – inventory, receivables and cash, less short-term payables. Working capital management is the management of all aspects of both current assets and current liabilities, to minimise the risk of insolvency while maximising the return on assets.

Working capital is an investment which affects cash flows.

- When inventory is purchased, cash is paid to acquire it.

- Receivables represent the cost of selling goods or services to customers, including the costs of the materials and the labour incurred.

- The cash tied up in working capital is reduced to the extent that inventory is financed by trade payables. If suppliers give a firm time to pay, the firm's cash flows are improved and working capital is reduced.

Expandable text

A company buys a large quantity of goods on credit and immediately sells them all on credit at a profit. Which of the following would increase? What would be the net impact on working capital?

Receivables, inventory, cash, payables.

Net impact: increase, decrease.

Solution

Buying goods on credit:

Dr   Purchase

Cr   Payables

Selling goods on credit:

Dr   Receivables

Cr   Sales

Therefore both payables and receivables would increase.

- All items were sold so inventory levels will have returned to pre-purchase levels.
- The receivables figure is higher than the payables figure since it includes a profit margin.
- Therefore overall current assets will rise by more than current liabilities and there will be a net increase in working capital.

2 The objectives of working capital management

Current assets are a major balance sheet item and especially significant to smaller firms.

Mismanagement of working capital is a common cause of business failure, e.g.:

- inability to meet bills as they fall due
- overtrading during periods of growth
- overstocking.

The main management objective, therefore, will be to get the balance of current assets and current liabilities right.

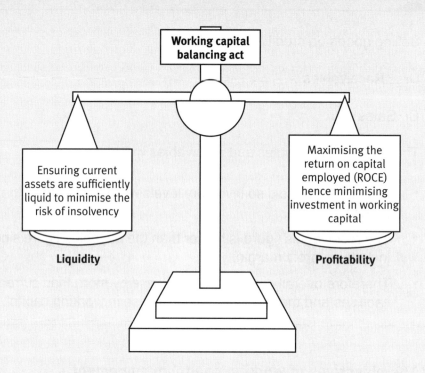

This can also be seen as the trade-off between cash flow versus profits.

Cash flow is the lifeblood of the thriving business. Effective and efficient management of the working capital investment is essential to maintaining control of business cash flow. Management must have full awareness of the profitability versus liquidity trade-off.

The need for adequate cash flow information is vital to enable management to fulfil this responsibility.

The trade-off between liquidity and profitability and its role in determining a business' overall investment in working capital is fundamental to your understanding of working capital management for the examination.

Expandable text

The decision regarding the level of overall investment in working capital is a cost/benefit trade-off – **liquidity versus profitability**, or **cash flow versus profits**.

Liquidity in the context of working capital management means having enough cash or ready access to cash to meet all payment obligations when these fall due. The main sources of liquidity are usually:

- cash in the bank

- short-term investments that can be cashed in easily and quickly

- cash inflows from normal trading operations (cash sales and payments by receivables for credit sales)

- an overdraft facility or other ready source of extra borrowing.

A firm choosing to have a lower level of working capital than rivals is said to have an 'aggressive' approach, whereas a firm with a higher level of working capital has a 'defensive' approach.

Cash flow is the lifeblood of the thriving business. Effective and efficient management of the working capital investment is essential to maintaining control of business cash flow. Management must have full awareness of the profitability versus liquidity trade-off.

For example, healthy trading growth typically produces:

- increased profitability
- the need to increase investment in non-current assets and working capital.

Here there is a trade-off under which trading growth and increased profitability squeeze cash. Ultimately, if not properly managed, increased trading can carry with it the spectre of overtrading and inability to pay the business creditors.

It is worth while stressing the difference between cash flow and profits. Cash flow is as important as profit. Unprofitable companies can survive if they have liquidity. Profitable companies can fail if they run out of cash to pay their liabilities (wages, amounts due to suppliers, overdraft interest, etc.).

Some examples of transactions that have this 'trade-off' effect on cash flows and on profits are as follows:

(a) Purchase of non-current assets for cash. The cash will be paid in full to the supplier when the asset is delivered; however profits will be charged gradually over the life of the asset in the form of depreciation.

(b) Sale of goods on credit. Profits will be credited in full once the sale has been confirmed; however the cash may not be received for some considerable period afterwards.

(c) With some payments such as tax there may be a significant timing difference between the impact on reported profit and the cash flow.

Clearly, cash balances and cash flows need to be monitored just as closely as trading profits. The need for adequate cash flow information is vital to enable management to fulfil this responsibility.

Expandable text

Fill in the blanks in the table to identify the advantages of having more or less working capital.

Advantages of keeping it high ⬆		Advantages of keeping it low ⬇
	INVENTORY	
	+	
	RECEIVABLES	
	+	
	CASH	
	=	
	CURRENT ASSETS	
	−	
	TRADE PAYABLES	
	=	
	WORKING CAPITAL	

Advantages of keeping it high		Advantages of keeping it low
Few stockouts		Less cash tied up in inventory
Bulk purchase discounts Reduced ordering costs	**INVENTORY**	Lower storage costs Flexibility
	+	
Customers like credit – ∴ profitable as attracts more sales	**RECEIVABLES**	Less cash tied up Less chance of irrecoverable debts Reduced costs of credit control
	+	
Able to pay bills on time Take advantage of unexpected opportunities Avoid high borrowing costs	**CASH**	Can invest surplus to earn high returns Less vulnerable to takeover
	=	
	CURRENT ASSETS	
	–	
Preserves own cash – cheap source of finance	**TRADE PAYABLES**	Lose prompt payment discounts Loss of credit status Less favourable supplier treatment
	=	
	WORKING CAPITAL	

3 The cash operating cycle

The elements of the operating cycle

The cash operating cycle is the length of time between the company's outlay on raw materials, wages and other expenditures and the inflow of cash from the sale of goods.

The faster a firm can 'push' items around the cycle the lower its investment in working capital will be.

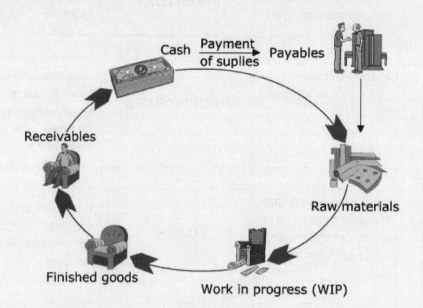

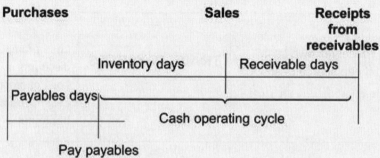

The cash operating cycle reflects a firm's investment in working capital as it moves through the production process towards sales. The investment in working capital gradually increases, first being only in raw materials, but then in labour and overheads as production progresses. This investment must be maintained throughout the production process, the holding period for finished goods and up to the final collection of cash from trade receivables.

(**Note:** The net investment can be reduced by taking trade credit from suppliers.)

Calculation of the cash operating cycle

For a manufacturing business, the cash operating cycle is calculated as:

Raw materials holding period	X
Less: payables' payment period	(x)
WIP holding period	X
Finished goods holding period	X
Receivables' collection period	X
	——
	X
	——

For a wholesale or retail business, there will be no raw materials or WIP holding periods, and the cycle simplifies to:

Inventory holding period	X
Less: payables' payment period	(x)
Receivables' collection period	X
	——
	X
	——

The cycle may be measured in days, weeks or months.

Expandable text

Illustration – Calculation of the cash operating cycle

A company generally pays its suppliers six weeks after receiving an invoice, whilst receivables usually pay within four weeks of invoicing. Raw materials inventory is held for a week before processing begins. Processing itself takes three weeks. Finished goods stay in inventory for an average of two weeks.

How long is the company's cash operating cycle?

Solution

Cash operating cycle = 1 – 6 + 3 + 2 + 4 = 4 weeks

Test your understanding 1

A company has provided the following information:

Receivables collection period	56 days
Raw material inventory holding period	21 days
Production period (WIP)	14 days
Suppliers' payment period	42 days
Finished goods holding period	28 days

Calculate the length of the operating cycle

P - 106

Use of the cash operating cycle

The cash operating cycle is a critical measure of the overall cash requirements for working capital.

The amount of cash required to fund the operating cycle will increase as either:

- the cycle gets longer
- the level of activity/sales increases.

KAPLAN PUBLISHING

This can be summed up as follows:

Activity/sales	Length of cycle	Funds needed increase proportionate to:
Stays constant =	Increases ↑	Days in cycle
Increase ↑	Stays constant =	Sales

Expandable text

Where level of activity (sales) is constant and the number of days of the operating cycle increase the amount of funds required for working capital will increase in approximate proportion to the number of days.

Where the cycle remains constant but activity (sales) increase the funds required for working capital will increase in approximate proportion to sales.

By monitoring the operating cycle the manager gains a macro view of the relative efficiency of the working capital utilisation. Further it may be a key target to reduce the operating cycle to improve the efficiency of the business.

Factors affecting the length of the operating cycle

Length of the cycle depends on:

- liquidity versus profitability decisions
- management efficiency
- industry norms, e.g. retail versus construction.

The optimum level of working capital is the amount that results in no idle cash or unused inventory, but that does not put a strain on liquid resources.

Expandable text

The length of the cycle depends on how the balancing act between liquidity and profitability is resolved, the efficiency of management and the nature of the industry.

The optimum level is the amount that results in no idle cash or unused inventory, but that does not put a strain on liquid resources. Trying to shorten the cash cycle may have detrimental effects elsewhere, with the organisation lacking the cash to meet its commitments and losing sales since customers will generally prefer to buy from suppliers who are prepared to extend trade credit, and who have items available when required.

Additionally, any assessment of the acceptability or otherwise of the length of the cycle must take into account the nature of the business involved.

A supermarket chain will tend to have a very low or negative cycle – they have very few, if any, credit customers, they have a high inventory turnover and they can negotiate quite long credit periods with their suppliers.

A construction company will have a long cycle – their projects tend to be long-term, often extending over more than a year, and whilst progress payments may be made by the customer (if there is one), the bulk of the cash will be received towards the end of the project.

4 Working capital ratios – operating cycle

The periods used to determine the cash operating cycle are calculated by using a series of working capital ratios.

The ratios for the individual components (inventory, receivables and payables) are normally expressed as the number of days/weeks/months of the relevant income statement figure they represent.

Illustration 1 – Working capital ratios – operating cycle

X plc has the following figures from its most recent accounts:

	$m
Receivables	4
Trade payables	2
Average raw material inventory	1
Average WIP inventory	1.3
Average finished goods inventory	2
Sales (80% on credit)	30
Materials usage	20
Materials purchases (all on credit)	18
Production cost	23
Cost of sales	25

Required:

Calculate the relevant working capital ratios. Round your answers to the nearest day.

Raw material inventory holding period

The length of time raw materials are held between purchase and being used in production.

Calculated as:

$$= \frac{\text{Average inventory held}}{\text{Material usage}} \times 365$$

$$= \frac{(\text{Opening inventory} + \text{closing inventory}) \div 2}{\text{Material usage}} \times 365$$

NB. Where usage cannot be calculated, purchases gives a good approximation.

Expandable text

Solution 1 to illustration 1

$$\frac{\$1m}{\$20m} \times 365 = 18 \text{ days}$$

WIP holding period

The length of time goods spend in production.

Calculated as:

$$= \frac{\text{Average WIP}}{\text{Production cost}} \times 365$$

NB. Where production cost cannot be calculated, cost of goods sold gives a good approximation.

Expandable text

Solution 2 to illustration 1

$$\frac{\$1.3m}{\$23m} \times 365 = 21 \text{ days}$$

Finished goods inventory period

The length of time finished goods are held between completion or purchase and sale.

Calculated as:

$$= \frac{\text{Average finished goods in inventory}}{\text{Cost of goods sold}} \times 365$$

Expandable text

Solution 3 to illustration 1

$$\frac{\$2m}{\$25m} \times 365 \qquad = 29 \text{ days}$$

Interpreting inventory period ratios

Usually low ratios are seen as a sign of good management.

In general, the shorter the inventory-holding period the better working capital management is considered to be. It is very expensive to hold inventory and thus minimum inventory holding usually points to good practice.

Compare with:

- prior years
- industry average/leaders

for a more precise analysis.

For each ratio, the corresponding turnover ratio can be calculated as:

$$\text{Inventory turnover (no of times)} = \frac{\text{Cost}}{\text{Average inventory held}}$$

Generally this is less useful in the examination.

Expandable text

Solution 4 to illustration 1

Using finished goods information above:

$$\text{Inventory turnover} = \frac{\$25m}{\$2m} = 12.5 \text{ times}$$

Thus finished goods inventory turns round/is turned into sales 12.5 times in the year.

Expandable text

Companies have to strike a balance between being able to satisfy customers' requirements out of stock and the cost of having too much capital tied up in inventory. However, not all industries can operate a Just-In-Time (JIT) policy and unless the nature of the business is known, it is not possible to say whether either 92 days or 30 days is satisfactory or unsatisfactory. A jeweller will have a high inventory-holding period, but a fishmonger selling fresh fish has a very low one.

Trade receivables days

The length of time credit is extended to customers.

Calculated as:

$$= \frac{\text{Average receivables}}{\text{Credit sales}} \times 365$$

Generally shorter credit periods are seen as financially sensible but the length will also depend upon the nature of the business.

Expandable text

Solution 5 to illustration 1

$$\frac{\$4m}{\$30m} \times 80\% \qquad \times 365 \qquad = 61 \text{ days}$$

Expandable text

Businesses which sell goods on credit terms specify a credit period. Failure to send out invoices on time or to follow up late payers will have an adverse effect on the cash flow of the business. The receivables collection period measures the average period of credit allowed to customers.

In general, the shorter the collection period the better because receivables are effectively 'borrowing' from the company. Remember, however, that the level of receivables reflects not only the ability of the credit controllers but also the sales and marketing strategy adopted, and the nature of the business. Any change in the level of receivables must therefore be assessed in the light of the level of sales.

Trade payables days

The average period of credit extended by suppliers.

Calculated as:

$$= \frac{\text{Average payables}}{\text{Credit purchases}} \times 365$$

Expandable text

Solution 6 to illustration 1

$$\frac{\$2m}{\$18m} \times 365 = 41 \text{days}$$

Generally, increasing payables days suggests advantage is being taken of available credit but there are risks:

- losing supplier goodwill
- losing prompt payment discounts
- suppliers increasing the price to compensate.

The operating cycle

The ratios can then be brought together to produce the cash operating cycle.

	Days
Raw material inventory days	18
Trade payables days	(41)
WIP period	21
Finished goods inventory days	29
Receivables days	61
Length of cash operating cycle	88

The cash operating cycle tells us it takes X plc 88 days between paying out for material inventories and eventually receiving cash back from customers.

As always this must then be compared with prior periods or industry average for meaningful analysis.

Additional points for calculating ratios

The ratios may be needed to provide analysis of a company's performance or simply to calculate the length of the operating cycle.

There are a few simple points to remember which will be of great use in the examination:

- Where the period is required in days, the multiple in the ratios is 365, for months the multiple is 12, or 52 for weeks.

- If you are required to compare ratios between two balance sheets, it is acceptable to base each holding period on balance sheet figures, rather than an average, in order to see whether the ratio has increased or decreased.

- For each ratio calculated above, the corresponding turnover ratio can be calculated by inverting the ratio given and removing the multiple.

- When using the ratios to appraise performance, it is essential to compare the figure with others in the industry or identify the trend over a number of periods.

- Ratios have their limitations and care must be taken because:
    - the balance sheet values at a particular time may not be typical
    - balances used for a seasonal business may not represent average levels, e.g. a fireworks manufacturer
    - ratios can be subject to window dressing/manipulation
    - ratios concern the past (historic) not the future
    - figures may be distorted by inflation and/or rapid growth.

Working capital turnover

When assessing company performance, return on capital employed (ROCE) is often broken down as follows:

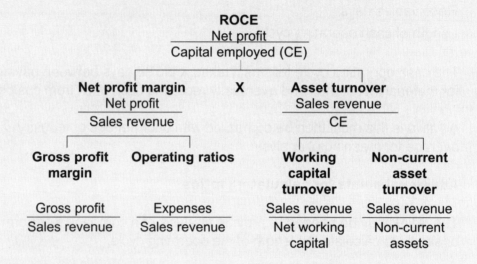

Therefore the one final ratio that relates to working capital is the working capital turnover ratio and is calculated as:

$$\frac{\text{Sales revenue}}{\text{Net working capital}}$$

This measures how efficiently management is utilising its investment in working capital to generate sales.

It must be interpreted in the light of the other ratios used.

5 Working capital ratios – liquidity

Two key measures, the current ratio and the quick ratio, are used to assess short-term liquidity. Generally a higher ratio indicates better liquidity.

Current ratio

 Measures how much of the total current assets are financed by current liabilities.

$$\text{Current ratio} = \frac{\text{Current assets}}{\text{Current liabilities}}$$

A measure of 2:1 means that current liabilities can be paid twice over out of existing current assets.

Quick (acid test) ratio

 The quick or acid test ratio:

- measures how well current liabilities are covered by liquid assets
- is particularly useful where inventory holding periods are long.

$$\text{Quick ratio (acid test)} = \frac{\text{Current assets - Inventory}}{\text{Current liabilities}}$$

A measure of 1:1 means that the company is able to meet existing liabilities if they all fall due at once.

Expandable text

These liquidity ratios are a guide to the risk of cash flow problems and insolvency. If a company suddenly finds that it is unable to renew its short-term liabilities (for instance if the bank suspends its overdraft facilities) there will be a danger of insolvency unless the company is able to turn enough of its current assets into cash quickly.

In general, high current and quick ratios are considered 'good' in that they mean that an organisation has the resources to meet its commitments as they fall due. However, it may indicate that working capital is not being used efficiently, for example that there is too much idle cash that should be invested to earn a return.

Conventional wisdom has it that an ideal current ratio is 2 and an ideal quick ratio is 1. It is very tempting to draw definite conclusions from limited information or to say that the current ratio should be 2, or that the quick ratio should be 1.

However, this is not very meaningful without taking into account the type of ratio expected in a similar business or within a business sector. Any assessment of working capital ratios must take into account the nature of the business involved.

For example a supermarket business operating a JIT system will have little inventory and since most of sales are for cash they will have few receivables. In addition the ability to negotiate long credit periods with suppliers can result in a large payables figure. This can result in net current liabilities and a current ratio below 1 – but does not mean the business has a liquidity problem.

KAPLAN PUBLISHING

Some companies use an overdraft as part of their long-term finance, in which case the current and quick ratios may appear worryingly low. In such questions you could suggest that the firm reschedule the overdraft as a loan. Not only would this be cheaper but it would also improve liquidity ratios.

Test your understanding 2

You have been given the following information for a company:

Summarised balance sheets(Statement of financial position) at 30 June

	20X7		20X6	
	$000	$000	$000	$000
Non-current assets (carrying value)		130		139
Current assets:				
Inventory	42		37	
Receivables	29		23	
Bank	3		5	
		74		65
Total assets		204		204
Equity and liabilities				
Ordinary share capital (50 cent shares)		35		35
Share premium account		17		17
Revaluation reserve		10		-
Profit and loss account		31		22
		93		74
Non-current liabilities				
5% secured loan notes		40		40
8% Preference shares ($1 shares)		25		25
Current liabilities				
Trade payables	36		55	
Taxation	10		10	
		46		65
Total equity and liabilities		204		204

Summarised income statement for the year ended 30 June

	20X7		20X6	
	$000	$000	$000	$000
Sales		209		196
Opening inventory	37		29	
Purchases	162		159	
	199		188	
Closing inventory	42		37	
		157		151
Gross profit		52		45
Finance costs	2		2	
Depreciation	9		9	
Sundry expenses	14		11	
		25		22
Net profit		27		23
Taxation		10		10
Net profit after taxation		17		13
Dividends:				
Ordinary shares	6		5	
Preference shares	2		2	
		8		7
Retained profit		9		6

From an examination point of view, calculating the ratios is only the start – interpretation is the key to a good answer. Try to build a cumulative picture, e.g. the current ratio looks good until we find out from calculating the inventory holding period that there are high levels of illiquid inventory.

Do not be afraid to point out further information that may be required to provide a better interpretation of your calculations, e.g. the company credit policy, industry benchmarks, etc.

Expandable text

Working capital investment levels

The level of working capital required is affected by the following factors:

(1) The nature of the business, e.g. manufacturing companies need more inventory than service companies.

(2) Uncertainty in supplier deliveries. Uncertainty would mean that extra inventory needs to be carried in order to cover fluctuations.

(3) The overall level of activity of the business. As output increases, receivables, inventory, etc. all tend to increase.

(4) The company's credit policy. The tighter the company's policy the lower the level of receivables.

(5) The length of the operating cycle. The longer it takes to convert material into finished goods into cash the greater the investment in working capital

(6) The credit policy of suppliers. The less credit the company is allowed to take, the lower the level of payables and the higher the net investment in working capital.

The working capital ratios shown above can be used to predict the future levels of investment required.

X plc has the following expectations for the forthcoming period.

	$m
Sales	10
Materials	(6)
Other costs	(2)
Profit	2

The following working capital ratios are expected to apply.

Inventory days	30 days
Receivables days	60 days
Payables days	40 days

Required:

Compute the working capital requirement.

Solution

We need to use the ratios to calculate balance sheet values in order to construct the projected working capital position.

				$m
Inventory	=	30 ÷ 365	× $6m	= 0.49
Receivables	=	60 ÷ 365	× $10m	1.64
Trade payables	=	40 ÷ 365	× $6m	= (0.66)
Working capital required				1.47

Expandable text

Illustration - Working capital investment levels

A company's annual sales are $8 million with a mark-up on cost of 60%. It normally settles payables two months after purchases are made, holding one month's worth of demand in inventory. It allows receivables 1½ months' credit and its cash balance currently stands at $1,250,000. What are its current and quick ratios?

Solution

Step 1 Calculate annual cost of sales, using the cost structure.

	%	$m
Sales	160	8
Cost of sales (COS)	100	5
Gross profit	60	3

Step 2 Calculate payables, receivables and inventory.

			20X6	20X5

$$\text{Payables} = \frac{2}{12} \times \text{annual COS} = \frac{2}{12} \times \$5m = \$0.833m$$

$$\text{Receivables} = \frac{1.5}{12} \times \text{annual sales} = \frac{1.5}{12} \times \$8m = \$1m$$

$$\text{Inventory} = \frac{1}{12} \times \text{annual COS} \quad \frac{1}{12} \times \$5m = \$0.417m$$

Step 3 Calculate the ratios.

$$\text{Current ratio} = \frac{\text{Inventory + receivables + cash}}{\text{Payables}} = \frac{0.417 + 1 + 1.25}{0.833} = 3.2$$

$$\text{Quick ratio} = \frac{\text{Receivables + cash}}{\text{Payables}} = \frac{1 + 1.25}{0.833} = 2.7$$

Expandable text

The following data relate to Mugwump Co, a manufacturing company.

Sales revenue for year:	$1,500,000
Costs as percentage of sales:	30%

Direct materials	
Direct labour	25%
Variable overheads	10%
Fixed overheads	15%
Selling and distribution	5%

Average statistics relating to working capital are as follows:

- receivables take 2½ months to pay
- raw materials are in inventory for three months
- WIP represents two months' half-produced goods
- finished goods represent one month's production
- credit is taken

– Materials	2 months
– Direct labour	1 week
– Variable overheads	1 month
– Fixed overheads	1 month
– Selling and distribution	½ month

WIP and finished goods are valued at the cost of material, labour and variable expenses.

Compute the working capital requirement of Mugwump Co assuming that the labour force is paid for 50 working weeks in each year.

Solution

1. Costs incurred

	$
Direct materials 30% of $1,500,000	450,000
Direct labour 25% of $1,500,000	375,000
Variable overheads 10% of $1,500,000	150,000
Fixed overheads 15% of $1,500,000	225,000
Selling and distribution 5% of $1,500,000	75,000

2. Average value of current assets

	$	$
Finished goods 1/12 × $975,000		81,250
Raw materials 3/12 × $450,000		112,500
WIP:		
(2 months @ half produced –		
1 month equivalent cost)		
Materials		
1/12 × $450,000	37,500	
Labour 1/12 × $375,000	31,250	
Variable overheads 1/12 × $150,000	12,500	
		81,250
Receivables 2 ½ /12 × $1,500,000		312,500
		587,500

3. Average value of current liabilities

	$	$
Materials 2/12 × $450,000	75,000	
Labour 1/50 × $375,000	7,500	
Variable overheads 1/12 × $150,000	12,500	
Fixed overheads 1/12 × $225,000	18,750	
Selling and distribution 1/24 × $75,000	3,125	
		(116,875)

4. Working capital required	470,625

Chapter summary

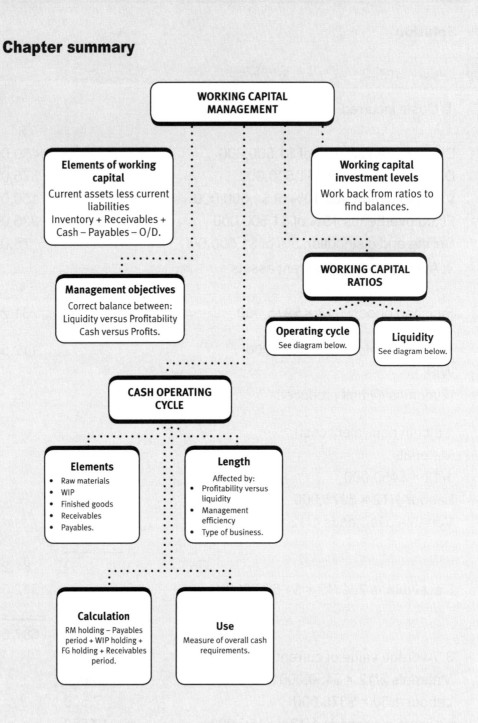

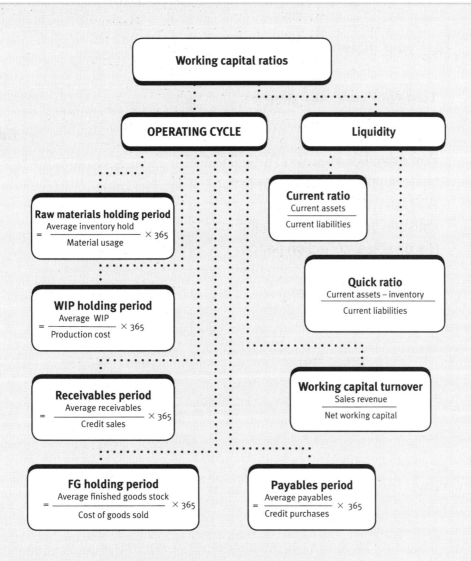

Test your understanding answers

Test your understanding 1

	Days
Raw materials inventory holding period	21
Less: suppliers' payment period	(42)
WIP holding period	14
Finished goods holding period	28
Receivables' collection period	56
	————
Operating cycle (days)	77
	————

Test your understanding 2

The current ratio:

20X7			**20X6**	
$\dfrac{74}{46}$	= 1.6		$\dfrac{65}{65}$	= 1.0

The quick (or acid test) ratio:

20X7			**20X6**	
$\dfrac{32}{46}$	= 0.7		$\dfrac{28}{65}$	= 0.4

Both of these ratios show an improvement. The extent of the change between the two years seems surprising and would require further investigation. It would also be useful to know how these ratios compare with those of a similar business, since typical liquidity ratios for supermarkets, say, are quite different from those for heavy engineering firms.

In 20X7 current liabilities were well covered by current assets. Liabilities payable in the near future are 70% covered by cash and receivables (a liquid asset, close to cash).

To better understand the liquidity ratios we can then look at each individual component of working capital:

The inventory holding period:

20X7	**20X6**
$\dfrac{(\tfrac{1}{2}\,(37 + 42) \times 365\ \text{days})}{157} = 92\ \text{days}$	$\dfrac{(\tfrac{1}{2}\,(29 + 37) \times 365\ \text{days})}{151} = 80\ \text{days}$

The inventory holding period has lengthened. In general, the shorter the stock holding period the better. It is very expensive to hold stock and thus minimum stock holding usually points to good management.

The current ratio calculation now seems less optimistic, considering the holding period for inventory of 92 days. Inventory that takes nearly four months to sell is not very liquid! It would be better to focus attention on the acid test ratio.

Receivables days:

	20X7	20X6
Average daily sales	$209,000	$196,000
	$\dfrac{209{,}000}{365} = \$573$	$\dfrac{196{,}000}{365} = \$537$
Closing trade receivables	$29,000	$23,000
Receivables days	$29,000	$23,000
	$\dfrac{29{,}000}{573} = 51 \text{ days}$	$\dfrac{23{,}000}{537} = 43 \text{ days}$

Or more quickly:

20X7	20X6
$\dfrac{29{,}000}{209{,}000} \times 365 \text{ days} = 50.6 \text{ days}$	$\dfrac{23{,}000}{196{,}000} \times 365 = 42.8 \text{ days}$

Compared with 20X6, the receivables collection period has worsened in 20X7. It would be important to establish the company policy on credit allowed. If the average credit allowed to customers was, say, 30 days, then something is clearly wrong. Further investigation might reveal delays in sending out invoices or failure to 'screen' new customers.

This situation suggests yet a further review of the liquidity ratios. The acid test ratio ignores inventory but still assumes receivables are liquid. If debt collection is a problem then receivables too are illiquid and the company could struggle to pay its current liabilities were they all to fall due in a short space of time.

Payables days:

	20X7	20X6
Average daily purchases	$162,000	$159,000
	$\dfrac{162{,}000}{365} = \$444$	$\dfrac{159{,}000}{365} = \$436$
Closing trade receivables	$36,000	$55,000
Payables' payment period	81 days	126 days

Or more quickly:

20X6

$$\frac{36,000}{162,000} \times 365 \text{ days} = 81.1 \text{ days}$$

20X6

$$\frac{55,000}{159,000} \times 365 = 126.3 \text{ days}$$

The payables' payment period has reduced substantially from last year. It is, however, in absolute terms still a high figure. Often, suppliers request payment within 30 days. The company is taking nearly three months. Trade creditors are thus financing much of the working capital requirements of the business, which is beneficial to the company.

A high level of creditor days may be good in that it means that all available credit is being taken, but there are three potential disadvantages of taking extended credit:

- Future supplies may be endangered.
- Availability of cash discounts is lost.
- Suppliers may quote a higher price for the goods knowing the company takes extended credit.

Additionally when viewed alongside the previous ratios calculated, this might suggest a cash flow problem causing suppliers to be left unpaid.

Length of the operating cycle:

	20X7 days	20X6 days
Inventory holding period	92	80
+		
Receivables' collection period	51	43
–		
Payables' payment period	(81)	(126)
=		
Cash operating cycle	62 days	(3 days)

Our example shows that, in 20X7, there is approximately a 62-day gap between paying cash to suppliers for goods, and receiving the cash back from customers. However, in 20X6, there was the somewhat unusual situation where cash was received from the customers, on average, more than 3 days before the payment to suppliers was needed.

Working capital management – inventory control

Chapter learning objectives

Upon completion of this chapter you will be able to:

- explain the objective of inventory management

- define and explain lead time and buffer inventory

- explain and apply the basic economic order quantity (EOQ) formula to data provided

- calculate the EOQ taking account of quantity discounts and calculate the financial implications of discounts for bulk purchases

- define and calculate the re-order level where demand and lead time are known

- describe and evaluate the main inventory management systems including Just-In-Time (JIT) techniques

- suggest appropriate inventory management techniques for use in a scenario.

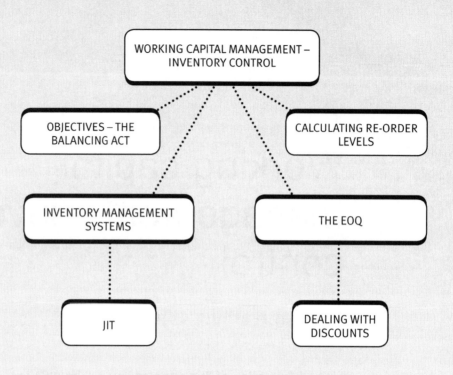

1 The objectives of inventory management

Inventory is a major investment for many companies. Manufacturing companies can easily be carrying inventory equivalent to between 50% and 100% of the revenue of the business. It is therefore essential to reduce the levels of inventory held to the necessary minimum.

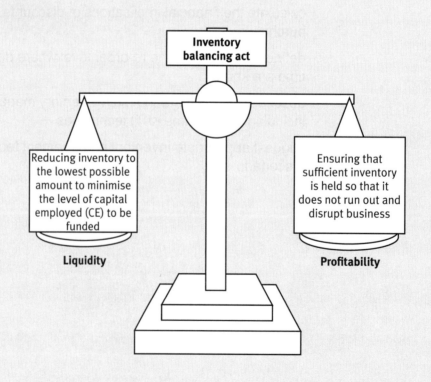

Costs of high inventory levels

Keeping inventory levels high is expensive owing to:

- purchase costs
- holding costs:
  - storage
  - stores administration
  - risk of theft/damage/obsolescence.

Expandable text

Carrying inventory involves a major working capital investment and therefore levels need to be very tightly controlled. The cost is not just that of purchasing the goods, but also storing, insuring, and managing them once they are in inventory.

Purchase costs: once goods are purchased, capital is tied up in them and until sold on (in their current state or converted into a finished product), the capital earns no return. This lost return is an opportunity cost of holding the inventory.

Stores administration: in addition, the goods must be stored. The company must incur the expense of renting out warehouse space, or if using space they own, there is an opportunity cost associated with the alternative uses the space could be put to. There may also be additional requirements such as controlled temperature or light which require extra funds.

Other risks: once stored, the goods will need to be insured. Specialist equipment may be needed to transport the inventory to where it is to be used. Staff will be required to manage the warehouse and protect against theft and if inventory levels are high, significant investment may be required in sophisticated inventory control systems.

The longer inventory is held, the greater the risk that it will deteriorate or become out of date. This is true of perishable goods, fashion items and high-technology products, for example.

Costs of low inventory levels

If inventory levels are kept too low, the business faces alternative problems:

- stockouts:
    - lost contribution
    - production stoppages
    - emergency orders
- high re-order/setup costs
- lost quantity discounts.

Expandable text

Stockout: if a business runs out of a particular product used in manufacturing it may cause interruptions to the production process – causing idle time, stockpiling of work-in-progress (WIP) or possibly missed orders. Alternatively, running out of goods held for onward sale can result in dissatisfied customers and perhaps future lost orders if custom is switched to alternative suppliers. If a stockout looms, the business may attempt to avoid it by acquiring the goods needed at short notice. This may involve using a more expensive or poorer quality supplier.

Re-order/setup costs: each time inventory runs out, new supplies must be acquired. If the goods are bought in, the costs that arise are associated with administration – completion of a purchase requisition, authorisation of the order, placing the order with the supplier, taking and checking the delivery and final settlement of the invoice. If the goods are to be manufactured, the costs of setting up the machinery will be incurred each time a new batch is produced.

Lost quantity discounts: purchasing items in bulk will often attract a discount from the supplier. If only small amounts are bought at one time in order to keep inventory levels low, the quantity discounts will not be available.

The challenge

The objective of good inventory management is therefore to determine:

- the optimum re-order level – how many items are left in inventory when the next order is placed, and

- the optimum re-order quantity – how many items should be ordered when the order is placed

for all material inventory items.

In practice, this means striking a balance between holding costs on the one hand and stockout and re-order costs on the other.

Other key terms associated with inventory management include:

- lead time – the lag between when an order is placed and the item is delivered

- buffer inventory – the basic level of inventory kept for emergencies. A buffer is required because both demand and lead time will fluctuate and predictions can only be based on best estimates.

Ensure you can distinguish between the various terms used: re-order level, re-order quantity, lead time and buffer inventory. The balancing act between liquidity and profitability, which might also be considered to be a trade-off between holding costs and stockout/re-order costs, is key to any discussion on inventory management.

Expandable text

A catering company is reviewing its inventory management processes. Identify the likely costs and benefits of holding high levels of food inventory.

Solution

Costs	Benefits
Freezers – purchase and running costs.	Cope with unexpected demand.
Refrigeration expenses.	Will not run out and miss contribution from lost sales.

Storage space.	Can take advantage of bulk discounts.
Risk of theft.	Fewer trips to cash and carry.
Potential for deterioration.	Less time spent placing and paying for orders.
May attract vermin.	
Cash tied up in purchase cost.	

2 EOQ

For businesses that do not use JIT (discussed in more detail below), there is an optimum order quantity for inventory items, known as the EOQ.

The challenge

The aim of the EOQ model is to minimise the total cost of holding and ordering inventory.

The relevant costs are:

- variable costs of holding the inventory – C_H – holding cost per unit pa

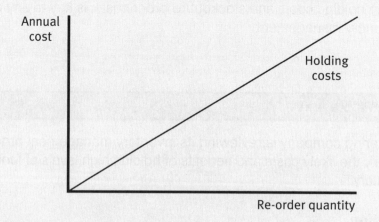

- fixed costs of placing the order – C_O – fixed costs (order setup costs) per order.

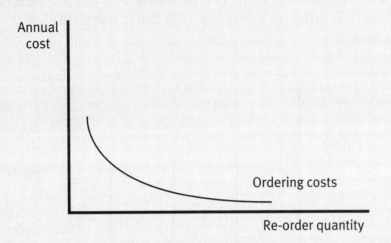

 When the re-order quantity chosen minimises the total cost of holding and ordering, it is known as the EOQ.

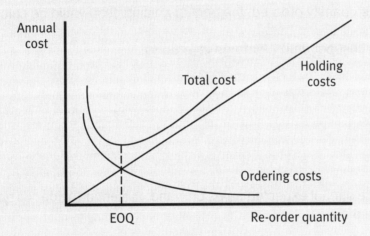

Assumptions

The following assumptions are made:

- demand and lead time are constant and known
- purchase price is constant
- no buffer inventory held (not needed).

These assumptions are critical and should be discussed when considering the validity of the model and its conclusions, e.g. in practice, demand and/or lead time may vary.

When new batches or items of inventory are purchased or made at periodic intervals, the inventory levels are assumed to exhibit the following pattern over time.

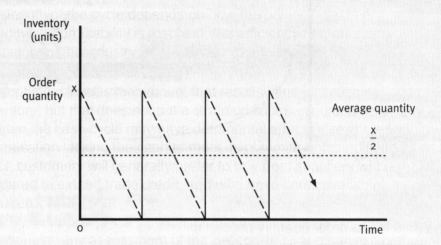

If x is the quantity ordered, the annual holding cost would be calculated as:

Holding cost per unit × Average inventory:

$$C_H \times \frac{x}{2}$$

If D is the annual expected sales demand, the annual order cost is calculated as:

Order cost per order × no. of orders pa.

$$C_O \times \frac{D}{x}$$

Expandable text

Illustration – Assumptions

A company requires 1,000 units of material X per month. The cost per order is $30 regardless of the size of the order. The holding costs are $2.88 per unit pa.

Required:

Investigate the total cost of buying the material in quantities of 400, 500, 600 or 700 units at one time. What is the cheapest option?

Expandable text

Solution

	Order quantity			
	400 units	**500 units**	**600 units**	**700 units**
Average inventory	200	250	300	350
No. of orders pa	30	24	20	17.14
	$	$	$	$
Holding cost – average units × $2.88	576	720	864	1,008

	Order quantity			
	400 units	500 units	600 units	700 units
Ordering cost – no. of orders × $30	900	720	600	514.2
Total cost	1,476	1,440	1,464	1,522.2

Therefore the best option is to order 500 units each time.

Note that this is the point at which total cost is minimised and the holding costs and order costs are equal.

The calculation

The EOQ can be more quickly found using a formula (given in the examination):

$$EOQ = \sqrt{\frac{2C_OD}{C_H}}$$

where:

C_O = cost per order

D = annual demand

C_H = cost of holding one unit for one year.

Expandable text

Illustration – The calculation

A company requires 1,000 units of material X per month. The cost per order is $30 regardless of the size of the order. The holding costs are $2.88 per unit pa.

Required:

Calculate the EOQ using the formula.

Expandable text

Solution:

$$EOQ = \sqrt{\frac{2C_OD}{C_H}}$$

$C_O = 30$

D = 1,000 × 12 = 12,000

$C_H = 2.88$

$$EOQ = \sqrt{\frac{2 \times 30 \times 12,000}{2.88}} = 500$$

Test your understanding 1

Monthly demand for a product is 10,000 units. The purchase price is $10/unit and the company's cost of finance is 15% pa. Warehouse storage costs per unit pa are $2/unit. The supplier charges $200 per order for delivery.

Calculate the EOQ.

Dealing with quantity discounts

Discounts may be offered for ordering in large quantities. If the EOQ is smaller than the order size needed for a discount, should the order size be increased above the EOQ?

Procedure:

Step 1 Calculate EOQ, ignoring discounts.

Step 2 If this is below the level for discounts, calculate total annual inventory costs. If this would qualify for a discount, then recalculate C_H (if neccessary) and the EOQ. Then calculate the total annual inventory costs.

Step 3 Recalculate total annual inventory costs using the order size required to just obtain each discount.

Step 4 Compare the cost of Steps 2 and 3 with the saving from the discount, and select the minimum cost alternative.

Step 5 Repeat for all discount levels.

Expandable text

Illustration – Dealing with quantity discounts

W Co is a retailer of barrels. The company has an annual demand of 30,000 barrels. The barrels cost $12 each. Fresh supplies can be obtained immediately, with ordering and transport costs amounting to $200 per order. The annual cost of holding one barrel in stock is estimated to be $1.20.

A 2% discount is available on orders of at least 5,000 barrels and a 2.5% discount is available if the order quantity is 7,500 barrels or above.

Required:

Calculate the EOQ ignoring the discount and determine if it would change once the discount is taken into account.

Expandable text

Solution

Step 1 Calculate EOQ, ignoring discounts.

$$EOQ = \sqrt{\frac{2C_O D}{C_H}}$$

$C_O = 200$

$D = 30,000$

$C_H = 1.20$

$$EOQ = \sqrt{\frac{2 \times 200 \times 30,000}{1.2}} = 3,162$$

Step 2 As this is below the level for discounts, calculate total annual inventory costs.

Total annual costs for the company will comprise holding costs plus re-ordering costs.

= (Average inventory × C_H) + (Number of re-orders pa × C_O)

= $\dfrac{3{,}162}{2} \times \$1.20 \div \dfrac{30{,}000}{3{,}1062} \times \$200$

= \$1,897.20 + \$1,897.53

= \$3,794.73

= \$3,795

Step 3 Recalculate total annual inventory costs using the order size required to just obtain the discount.

At order quantity 5,000, total costs are as follows.

5,000 × \$1.20/2 + 30,000 × \$200/5000 = \$4,200

	\$
Extra costs of ordering in batches of 5,000 (4,200 – 3,795)	(405)
Less: Saving on discount 2% × \$12 × 30,000	7,200
Step 4 Net cost saving	6,795

Hence batches of 5,000 are worthwhile.

Step 3 (again) _quantity_

At order quality 7,500, total costs are as follows:

7,500 × \$1.20 ÷ 2 + 30,000 × \$200 ÷ 7,500 = \$5,300

Extra costs of ordering in batches of 7,500 (5,300 - 4,200)	(1,100)
Less: Saving on extra discount (2.5 - 2%) × 30,000 × 12	1,800
	700

Step 4 Net cost saving

So a further cost saving can be made on orders of 7,500 units.

Note: If Step 1 produces an EOQ at which a discount would have been available, and the holding cost would be reduced by taking the discount, i.e. where C_H is based on the purchase price × the cost of finance, the EOQ must be recalculated using the new C_H before the above steps are followed.

Test your understanding 2

D Co uses component V22 in its construction process. The company has a demand of 45,000 components pa. They cost $4.50 each. There is no lead time between order and delivery, and ordering costs amount to $100 per order. The annual cost of holding one component in inventory is estimated to be $0.65.

A 0.5% discount is available on orders of at least 3,000 components and a 0.75% discount is available if the order quantity is 6,000 components or above.

Calculate the optimal order quantity.

3 Calculating the re-order level (ROL)
Known demand and lead time

Having decided how much inventory to re-order, the next problem is when to re-order. The firm needs to identify a level of inventory which can be reached before an order needs to be placed.

The **ROL** is the quantity of inventory on hand when an order is placed.

When demand and lead time are known with certainty the ROL may be calculated exactly, i.e. ROL = demand in the lead time.

Expandable text

Illustration – Known demand and lead time

Using the data for W Co, assume that the company adopts the EOQ as its order quantity and that it now takes two weeks for an order to be delivered. How frequently will the company place an order? How much inventory will it have on hand when the order is placed?

Solution

- Annual demand is 30,000. The original EOQ is 3,162. The company will therefore place an order once every

  3,162 ÷ 30,000 × 365 days = 38 days

- The company must be sure that there is sufficient inventory on hand when it places an order to last the two weeks' lead time. It must therefore place an order when there is two weeks' worth of demand in inventory:

  i.e. ROL 2 ÷ 52 × 30,000 = 1,154 units

Test your understanding 3

Using the data relating to D Co, and ignoring discounts, assume that the company adopts the EOQ as its order quantity and that it now takes three weeks for an order to be delivered.

(a) **How frequently will the company place an order?**

(b) **How much inventory will it have on hand when the order is placed?**

ROL with variable demand or variable lead time

When lead time and demand are known with certainty, ROL = demand during lead time. Where there is uncertainty, an optimum level of buffer inventory must be found.

This depends on:

- variability of demand
- cost of holding inventory
- cost of stockouts.

You will not be required to perform this calculation in the examination.

Expandable text

If there were certainty, then the last unit of inventory would be sold as the next delivery is made. In the real world, this ideal cannot be achieved. Demand will vary from period to period, and ROL must allow some buffer (or safety) inventory, the size of which is a function of maintaining the buffer (which increases as the levels increase), running out of inventory (which decreases as the buffer increases) and the probability of the varying demand levels.

---

4 Inventory management systems

A number of systems have been developed to simplify the inventory management process:

- bin systems
- periodic review
- JIT.

Bin systems

A simple visual reminder system for re-ordering is to use a bin system.

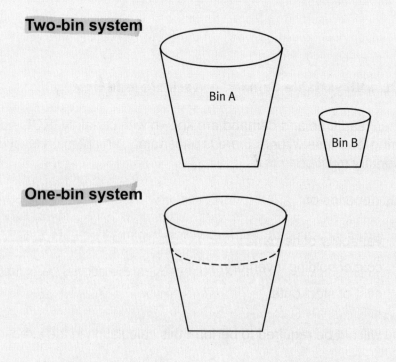

These methods rely on accurate estimates of:

- lead time
- demand in lead time.

Action must therefore be taken if inventory levels:

- fall below a preset minimum
- exceed a preset maximum.

 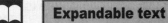

Expandable text

Two-bin system

This system utilises two bins, e.g. A and B. Inventory is taken from A until A is empty. An order for a fixed quantity is placed and, in the meantime, inventory is used from B. The standard inventory for B is the expected demand in the lead time (the time between the order being placed and the inventory arriving), plus some 'buffer' inventory.

When the new order arrives, B is filled up to its standard level and the rest is placed in A. Inventory is then drawn as required from A, and the process is repeated.

One-bin system

The same sort of approach is adopted by some firms for a single bin with a red line within the bin indicating the ROL.

Control levels

In bin systems, where order quantities are constant, it is important to identify alterations to the estimates on which that quantity was based. The inventory controller should be notified when the inventory level exceeds a maximum or falls below a minimum.

Maximum inventory level would represent the normal peak holding, i.e. buffer inventory plus the re-order quantity. If the maximum is exceeded, a review of estimated demand in the lead time is needed.

Minimum inventory level usually corresponds with buffer inventory. If inventory falls below that level, emergency action to replenish may be required.

The levels would also be modified according to the relative importance/cost of a particular inventory item.

Periodic review system (constant order cycle system)

Inventory levels are reviewed at fixed intervals, e.g. every four weeks. The inventory in hand is then made up to a predetermined level, which takes account of:

- likely demand before the next review

- likely demand during the lead time.

Thus a four-weekly review in a system where the lead time was two weeks would demand that inventory be made up to the likely maximum demand for the next six weeks.

Test your understanding 4

A company has estimated that for the coming season weekly demand for components will be 80 units. Suppliers take three weeks on average to deliver goods once they have been ordered and a buffer inventory of 35 units is held.

If the inventory levels are reviewed every six weeks, how many units will be ordered at a review where the count shows 250 units in inventory?

Expandable text

Bin systems versus periodic review

Advantage of bin systems	Advantage of periodic review system
Inventory can be kept at a lower level because of the ability to order whenever inventory falls to a low level, rather than having to wait for the next re-order date.	Order office load is more evenly spread and easier to plan. For this reason the system is popular with suppliers.

Slow-moving inventory

Management need to review inventory usage to identify slow-moving inventory. An aged inventory analysis should be produced and reviewed regularly so that action can be taken. Actions could include:

- elimination of obsolete items

- slow-moving inventory items only ordered when actually needed

- review of demand level estimates on which re-order decisions are based.

Expandable text

Certain items may have a high individual value, but be subject to infrequent demand.

In most organisations, about 20% of items held make up 80% of total usage (the 80/20 rule). Slow-moving items may be ordered only when required, unless a minimum order quantity is imposed by the supplier.

A regular report of slow-moving items is useful in that management is made aware of changes in demand and of possible obsolescence. Arrangements may then be made to reduce or eliminate inventory levels or, on confirmation of obsolescence, for disposal.

JIT systems

JIT is a series of manufacturing and supply chain techniques that aim to minimise inventory levels and improve customer service by manufacturing not only at the exact time customers require, but also in the exact quantities they need and at competitive prices.

In JIT systems the balancing act is dispensed with. Inventory is reduced to an absolute minimum or eliminated altogether.

Aims of JIT are:

- a smooth flow of work through the manufacturing plant

- a flexible production process which is responsive to the customer's requirements

- reduction in capital tied up in inventory.

This involves the elimination of all activities performed that do not add value = waste.

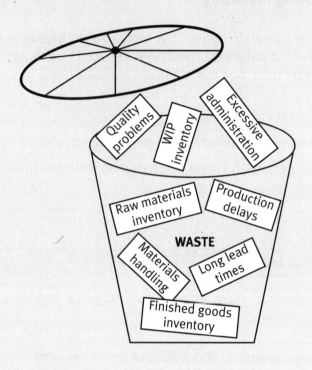

Achieved by:

- reducing batch sizes
- delivering raw material inventory to point of use
- designing shop floor for seamless movement of WIP
- emphasising total quality
- reducing finished goods level by making to order.

Implications for the supplier relationship include:

- dependent on quality and reliability
- long-term trusting relationships
- physical proximity.

Expandable text

JIT extends much further than a concentration on inventory levels. It centres around the elimination of waste. Waste is defined as any activity performed within a manufacturing company which does not add value to the product. Examples of waste are:

- raw material inventory

- WIP inventory

- finished goods inventory

- materials handling

- quality problems (rejects and reworks, etc.)

- queues and delays on the shop floor

- long raw material lead times

- long customer lead times

- unnecessary clerical and accounting procedures.

JIT attempts to eliminate waste at every stage of the manufacturing process, notably by the elimination of:

- WIP, by reducing batch sizes (often to one)

- raw materials inventory, by the suppliers delivering direct to the shop floor JIT for use

- scrap and rework, by an emphasis on total quality control of the design, of the process, and of the materials

- finished goods inventory, by reducing lead times so that all products are made to order

- material handling costs, by re-design of the shop floor so that goods move directly between adjacent work centres.

The combination of these concepts in JIT results in:

- a smooth flow of work through the manufacturing plant

- a flexible production process which is responsive to the customer's requirements

- reduction in capital tied up in inventory.

A JIT manufacturer looks for a single supplier who can provide **high quality**, **frequent** and **reliable** deliveries, rather than the lowest price. In return, the supplier can expect more business under **long-term purchase orders**, thus providing **greater certainty** in forecasting activity levels.

Long-term contracts and single sourcing strengthen buyer-supplier relationships and tend to result in a higher quality product. Inventory problems are shifted back onto suppliers, with deliveries being made as required.

The spread of JIT in the production process inevitably affects those in delivery and transportation. Smaller, more frequent loads are required at shorter notice. The haulier is regarded as almost a partner to the manufacturer, but tighter schedules are required of hauliers, with penalties for non-delivery.

Reduction in inventory levels reduces the time taken to count inventory and the clerical cost. However with JIT, although inventory holding costs are close to zero, inventory ordering costs are high.

Expandable text

Select the appropriate choices in the following table:

Inventory management system	Order date	Order quantity
Periodic review	Known/Unknown	Known/Unknown
Two-bin	Known/Unknown	Known/Unknown

Solution

Inventory management system	Order date	Order quantity
Periodic review	Known	Unknown
Two-bin	Unknown	Known

You need to be able to outline the key features of each stock control system and the impact they may have on ordering and holding costs and/or order dates and quantities. Ensure you can discuss the implications of JIT for production processes and supplier relationships as well as inventory levels.

Test your understanding 5

A company expects annual demand for product X to be 255,380 units. Product X is purchased for $11 per unit from a supplier, MKR Co. TNG places an order for 50,000 units of product X at regular intervals throughout the year. Because the demand for product X is to some degree uncertain, TNG maintains a safety (buffer) inventory of product X which is sufficient to meet demand for 28 working days. The cost of placing an order is $25 and the storage cost for product X is 10 cents per unit per year.

The company uses a working year consisting of 365 days.

P-138

(a) **Calculate the annual cost of the current ordering policy.**

(b) **Calculate the annual saving if the EOQ model is used to determine an optimal ordering policy.**

(c) **Critically discuss the limitations of the EOQ model as a way of managing inventory.**

(d) **Discuss the advantages and disadvantages of using JIT inventory management methods.**

Chapter summary

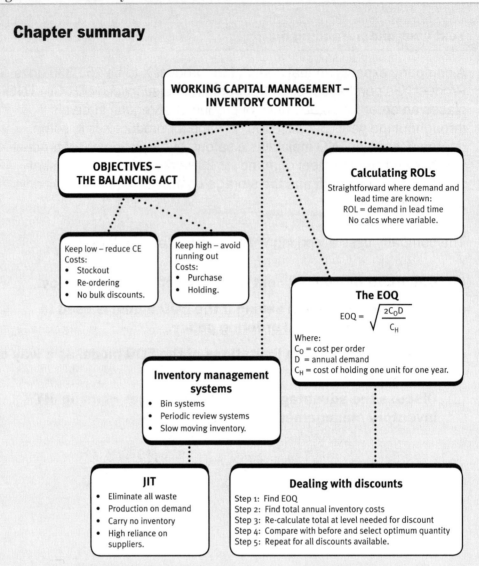

WORKING CAPITAL MANAGEMENT –
INVENTORY CONTROL

**OBJECTIVES –
THE BALANCING ACT**

Keep low – reduce CE
Costs:
• Stockout
• Re-ordering
• No bulk discounts.

Keep high – avoid
running out
Costs:
• Purchase
• Holding.

Calculating ROLs
Straightforward where demand and
lead time are known:
ROL = demand in lead time
No calcs where variable.

The EOQ

$$EOQ = \sqrt{\frac{2C_O D}{C_H}}$$

Where:
C_O = cost per order
D = annual demand
C_H = cost of holding one unit for one year.

**Inventory management
systems**
• Bin systems
• Periodic review systems
• Slow moving inventory.

JIT
• Eliminate all waste
• Production on demand
• Carry no inventory
• High reliance on
  suppliers.

Dealing with discounts
Step 1: Find EOQ
Step 2: Find total annual inventory costs
Step 3: Re-calculate total at level needed for discount
Step 4: Compare with before and select optimum quantity
Step 5: Repeat for all discounts available.

Test your understanding answers

Test your understanding 1

$$EOQ = \sqrt{\frac{2C_o D}{C_H}}$$

$C_O = 200$

$D = 10{,}000 \times 12 = 120{,}000$

$C_H = (10 \times 0.15) + 2 = 3.5$

$$EOQ = \sqrt{\frac{2 \times 200 \times 120{,}000}{3.5}} = 3{,}703$$

Test your understanding 2

Step 1

$$EOQ = \sqrt{\frac{2C_OD}{C_H}}$$

$C_O = 100$

$D = 45,000$

$C_H = 0.65$

$$EOQ = \sqrt{\frac{2 \times 100 \times 45,000}{0.65}} = 3,721 \text{, which would qualify for a 0.5\% discount}$$

Step 2

Total annual costs for the company will comprise holding costs plus re-ordering costs.

= (Average inventory × C_H) + (Number of re-orders pa × C_O)

$$= \frac{3,721}{2} \times \$0.65 + \frac{45,000}{3,721} \times \$100$$

$$= \left(\frac{3,721}{2} \times \$0.65\right) + \left(\frac{45,000}{3,721} \times \$100\right)$$

Step 3

At order quantity 6,000, total costs are as follows.

6,000 × \$0.65/2 + 45,000 × \$100 ÷ 6,000 = \$2,700

	\$
Extra costs of ordering in batches of 6,000 (2,700 − 2,419)	(281)
Less: Saving on extra discount	

$(0.75\% - 0.5\%) \times \$4.5 \times 45{,}000$	506.25
Step 4	
Net cost saving	225.25

So a saving can be made on orders of 6,000 units.

Test your understanding 3

(a) Annual demand is 45,000. The original EOQ is 3,721.

The company will therefore place an order once every

3,721 ÷ 45,000 × 365 days = 30 days

(b) The company must be sure that there is sufficient inventory on hand when it places an order to last the three weeks' lead time. It must therefore place an order when there is three weeks' worth of demand in inventory:

3/52 × 45,000 = 2,596 units

Test your understanding 4

Demand per week is 80 units. The next review will be in six weeks by which time 80 × 6 = 480 units will have been used.

An order would then be placed and during the lead time – three weeks – another 80 × 3 = 240 units will be used.

The business therefore needs to have 480 + 240 = 720 units in inventory to ensure a stockout is avoided. Since buffer inventory of 35 units is required, the total number needed is 755 units.

Since the current inventory level is 250 units, an order must be placed for 755 – 250 = 505 units.

Test your understanding 5

The company has a current order size of 50,000 units.

Average number of orders per year = demand order size = 255,380 ÷ 50,000 = 5.11 orders.

Annual ordering cost = 5.11 × 25 = $127.75.

Buffer inventory held = 255,380 × 28 ÷ 365 = 19,591 units.

Average inventory held = 19,591 + (50,000 ÷ 2) = 44,591 units.

Annual holding cost = 44,591 × 0.1 = $4,459.10.

Annual cost of current ordering policy = 4,459.10 + 127.75 = $4,587.

We need to calculate the EOQ:

$$EOQ = \sqrt{\frac{2C_o D}{C_H}}$$

$C_O = 25$

$D = 255,380$

$C_H = 0.10$

$$EOQ = \sqrt{\frac{2 \times 25 \times 255,380}{0.10}} = 11,300 \text{ units}$$

Average number of orders pa = 255,380 ÷ 11,300 = 22.6 orders.

Annual ordering cost = 22.6 × 25 = $565.00.

Average inventory held = 19,591 + (11,300 ÷ 2) = 25,241 units.

Annual holding cost = 25,241 × 0.1 = $2,524.10.

Annual cost of EOQ ordering policy = 2,524.10 + 565.00 = $3,089.

Saving compared to current policy = 4,587 − 3,089 = $1,498.

The EOQ model is based on a cost function for holding inventory which has two terms: holding costs and ordering costs.

With the EOQ, the total cost of having inventory is minimised when holding cost is equal to ordering cost. The EOQ model assumes certain knowledge of the variables on which it depends and for this reason is called a deterministic model.

Demand for inventory, holding cost per unit pa and order cost are assumed to be certain and constant for the period under consideration. In practice, demand is likely to be variable or irregular and costs will not remain constant. The EOQ model also ignores the cost of running out of inventory (stockouts). This has caused some to suggest that the EOQ model has little to recommend it as a practical model for inventory management.

The model was developed on the basis of zero lead time and no buffer inventory, but these are not difficulties that prevent the practical application of the EOQ model. As our earlier analysis has shown, the EOQ model can be used in circumstances where buffer inventory exists and provided that lead time is known with certainty it can be ignored.

The EOQ model also serves a useful purpose in directing attention towards the costs that arise from holding inventory. If these costs can be reduced, working capital tied up in inventory can be reduced and overall profitability can be increased.

JIT inventory management methods seek to eliminate any waste that arises in the manufacturing process as a result of using inventory. JIT purchasing methods apply the JIT principle to deliveries of material from suppliers. With JIT production methods, inventory levels of raw materials, WIPand finished goods are reduced to a minimum or eliminated altogether by improved work-flow planning and closer relationships with suppliers.

Advantages

JIT inventory management methods seek to eliminate waste at all stages of the manufacturing process by minimising or eliminating inventory, defects, breakdowns and production delays. This is achieved by improved work flow planning, an emphasis on quality control and firm contracts between buyer and supplier.

One advantage of JIT inventory management methods is a stronger relationship between buyer and supplier. This offers security to the supplier, who benefits from regular orders, continuing future business and more certain production planning. The buyer benefits from lower inventory holding costs, lower investment in inventory and WIP, and the transfer of inventory management problems to the supplier. The buyer may also benefit from bulk purchase discounts or lower purchase costs.

The emphasis on quality control in the production process reduces scrap, reworking and setup costs, while improved production design can reduce or even eliminate unnecessary material movements. The result is a smooth flow of material and work through the production system, with no queues or idle time.

Disadvantages

A JIT inventory management system may not run as smoothly in practice as theory may predict, since there may be little room for manoeuvre in the event of unforeseen delays. There is little room for error, e.g. on delivery times.

The buyer is also dependent on the supplier for maintaining the quality of delivered materials and components. If delivered quality is not up to the required standard, expensive downtime or a production standstill may arise, although the buyer can protect against this eventuality by including guarantees and penalties in the supplier's contract. If the supplier increases prices, the buyer may find that it is not easy to find an alternative supplier who is able, at short notice, to meet his needs.

Working capital management – accounts receivable and payable

Chapter learning objectives

Upon completion of this chapter you will be able to:

- explain how to establish and implement a credit policy for accounts receivable

- explain the administration involved in collecting amounts owing from accounts receivable

- explain the pros and cons of offering early settlement discounts to accounts receivable

- calculate the financial implications of offering discounts for early settlement

- define and explain the features of factoring

- discuss the advantages and disadvantages of factoring

- define and explain the features of invoice discounting

- suggest and evaluate suitable techniques for managing accounts receivable within a scenario question

- explain the factors involved in the effective management of trade credit

- calculate the effective cost of an early settlement discount offered on an account payable

- explain the specific factors to be considered when managing foreign accounts receivable

- explain the specific factors to be considered when managing foreign accounts payable.

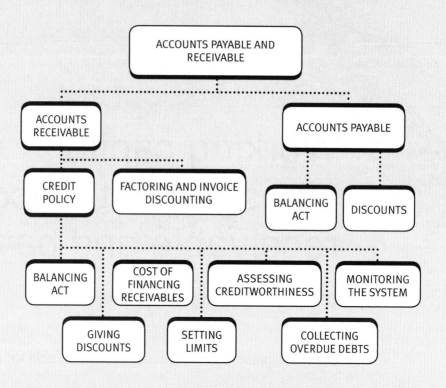

1 Accounts receivable – establishing a credit policy

The balancing act

Management must establish a credit policy. The optimum level of trade credit extended represents a balance between two factors:

- profit improvement from sales obtained by allowing credit
- the cost of credit allowed.

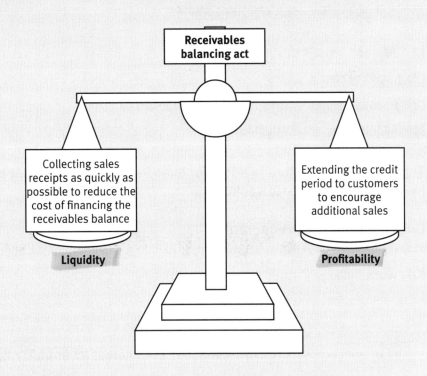

 Remember this trade-off is a key factor in determining the company's working capital investment

Influenced by:

- demand for products
- competitors' terms
- risk of irrecoverable debts
- financing costs
- costs of credit control.

Expandable text

A firm must establish a policy for credit terms given to its customers. Ideally the firm would want to obtain cash with each order delivered, but that is impossible unless substantial settlement (or cash) discounts are offered as an inducement. It must be recognised that credit terms are part of the firm's marketing policy. If the trade or industry has adopted a common practice, then it is probably wise to keep in step with it.

A lenient credit policy may well attract additional customers, but at a disproportionate increase in cost.

A credit policy has four key aspects:

(1) Assess creditworthiness.

(2) Control credit limits.

(3) Invoice promptly and collect overdue debts.

(4) Monitor the credit system.

This is a useful structure to adopt for examination questions that ask about the management of receivables.

Costs of financing receivables

Key working:

> Finance cost = Receivable balance × Interest (overdraft) rate
>
> $$\text{Receivable balance} = \text{Sales} \times \frac{\text{Receivable days}}{365}$$

Illustration 1 – Costs of financing receivables

Paisley Co has sales of $20 million for the previous year, receivables at the year end were $4 million, and the cost of financing receivables is covered by an overdraft at the interest rate of 12% pa.

Required:

(a) calculate the receivables days for Paisley

(b) calculate the annual cost of financing receivables.

Expandable text

Solution

(a) Receivables days = $4m ÷ $20m × 365 = 73 days

(b) Cost of financing receivables = $4m × 12% = $480,000.

Expandable text

Watch Co has sales of $32 million for the previous year, receivables at the year end were $7.5 million, and the cost of financing receivables is covered by an overdraft at the interest rate of 8% pa.

(a) **Calculate the receivables days for Watch.**

(b) **Calculate the cost of financing receivables.**

Solution

(a) Receivables days = $7.5m ÷ $32m × 365 = 86 days

(b) Cost of financing receivables = $7.5m × 8% = $600,000.

Assessing creditworthiness

A firm should assess the creditworthiness of:

- all new customers immediately
- existing customers periodically.

Information may come from:

- bank references
- trade references
- competitors
- published information
- credit reference agencies
- company sales records
- credit scoring.

Expandable text

To minimise the risk of irrecoverable debts occurring, a company should investigate the creditworthiness of all new customers (credit risk), and should review that of existing customers from time to time, especially if they request that their credit limit should be raised. Information about a customer's credit rating can be obtained from a variety of sources.

These include:

- Bank references – A customer's permission must be sought. These tend to be fairly standardised in the UK, and so are not perhaps as helpful as they could be.

- Trade references – Suppliers already giving credit to the customer can give useful information about how good the customer is at paying bills on time. There is a danger that the customer will only nominate those suppliers that are being paid on time.

- Competitors – in some industries such as insurance, competitors share information on customers, including creditworthiness.

- Published information – The customer's own annual accounts and reports will give some idea of the general financial position of the company and its liquidity.

- Credit reference agencies – Agencies such as Dunn & Bradstreet publish general financial details of many companies, together with a credit rating. They will also produce a special report on a company if requested. The information is provided for a fee.

- Company's own sales records – For an existing customer, the sales ledgers will show how prompt a payer the company is, although they cannot show the ability of the customer to pay.

- Credit scoring – Indicators such as family circumstances, home ownership, occupation and age can be used to predict likely creditworthiness. This is useful when extending credit to the public where little other information is available. A variety of software packages is available which can assist with credit scoring.

Credit limits

Credit limits should be set to reflect both the:

- amount of credit available
- length of time allowed before payment is due.

The ledger account should be monitored to take account of orders in the pipeline as well as invoiced sales, before further credit is given.

Invoicing and collecting overdue debts

A credit period only begins once an invoice is received so prompt invoicing is essential. If debts go overdue, the risk of default increases, therefore a system of follow-up procedures is required:

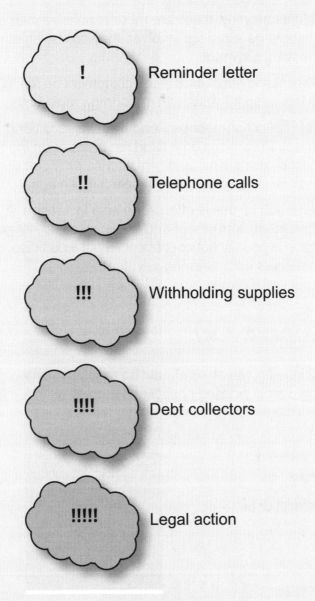

! Reminder letter

!! Telephone calls

!!! Withholding supplies

!!!! Debt collectors

!!!!! Legal action

 Expandable text

The longer a debt is allowed to run, the higher the probability of eventual default. A system of follow-up procedures is required, bearing in mind the risk of offending a valued customer to such an extent that their business is lost.

Techniques for 'chasing' overdue debts include the following:

- Reminder letters: these are often regarded as being a relatively poor way of obtaining payment, as many customers simply ignore them. Sending reminders by fax or email is usually more productive than using the post.

- Telephone calls: these are more expensive than reminder letters but where large sums are involved they can be an efficient way of speeding payment.

- Withholding supplies: putting customers on the 'stop list' for further orders or spare parts can encourage rapid settlement of debts.

- Debt collection agencies and trade associations: these offer debt collection services on a fixed fee basis or on 'no collection no charge' terms. The quality of service provided varies considerably and care should be taken in selecting an agent.

- Legal action: this is often seen as a last resort. A solicitor's letter often prompts payment and many cases do not go to court. Court action is usually not cost effective but it can discourage other customers from delaying payment.

Monitoring the system

The position of receivables should be regularly reviewed as part of managing overall working capital and corrective action taken when needed. Methods include:

- age analysis

- ratios

- statistical data.

Expandable text

Management will require regular information to take corrective action and to measure the impact of giving credit on working capital investment. Typical management reports on the credit system will include the following points.

Age analysis of outstanding debts.

- Ratios, compared with the previous period or target, to indicate trends in credit levels and the incidence of overdue and irrecoverable debts.

- Statistical data to identify causes of default and the incidence of irrecoverable debts among different classes of customer and types of trade.

2 Accounts receivable – early settlement discounts

Cash discounts are given to encourage early payment by customers. The cost of the discount is balanced against the savings the company receives from having less capital tied up due to a lower receivables balance and a shorter average collection period. Discounts may also reduce the number of irrecoverable debts.

Test your understanding 1

Consider the advantages and disadvantages of offering early settlement discounts to customers.

Illustration 2 – Accounts receivable – early settlement discounts

Paisley Co has sales of $20 million for the previous year, receivables at the year end of $4 million and the cost of financing receivables is covered by an overdraft at the interest rate of 12% pa. It is now considering offering a cash discount of 2% for payment of debts within 10 days. Should it be introduced if 40% of customers will take up the discount?

Expandable text

Solution

Discount as a percentage of amount paid = 2 ÷ 98 = 2.04%

Receivables days are 73 per illlustration1, so:

Saving is 63 days (dropping from 73 days to 10) and there are 365 ÷ 3 = 5.794 periods in a year

Annualised cost of discount % is

$(1 + 0.0204)^{5.794} - 1 = 0.1241 = 12.41\%$.

The overdraft rate is 12%.

It would be marginally cheaper to borrow the money from the bank rather than offer the discount.

The calculation of the annual cost can therefore be expressed as a formula:

$$\text{Annual cost of discount} = \left[1 + \frac{\text{discount}}{\text{amount left to pay}}\right]^{\text{no.of periods}} - 1$$

where no. of periods = $\dfrac{365 \,/\, 52 \,/\, 12}{\text{no. of days / weeks / months}}$ earlier the money is received.

Notice that the annual cost calculation is always based on the amount left to pay, i.e. the amount net of discount.

If the cost of offering the discount exceeds the rate of overdraft interest then the discount should not be offered.

Expandable text

A company is offering a cash discount of 2.5% to receivables if they agree to pay debts within one month. The usual credit period taken is three months.

What is the effective annualised cost of offering the discount and should it be offered, if the bank would loan the company at 18% pa?

Solution

Discount as a percentage of amount paid = 2.5/97.5 = 2.56%

Saving is 2 months and there are 12/2 = periods in a year.

Annualised cost of discount % is

$(1+0.0256)^6 - 1 = 0.1638 = 16.38\%$.

The loan rate is 18%.

It would therefore be worthwhile offering the discount.

3 Accounts receivable – factoring and invoice discounting

Factoring and invoice discounting are both ways of speeding up the receipt of funds from accounts receivable.

Factoring

Factoring is the outsourcing of the credit control department to a third party.

The debts of the company are effectively sold to a factor (normally owned by a bank). The factor takes on the responsibility of collecting the debt for a fee. The company can choose some or all of the following three services offered by the factor:

(1) debt collection and administration – recourse or non-recourse

(2) financing

(3) credit insurance.

These are of particular value to:

*   smaller firms
*   fast growing firms.

Make sure you can discuss the various services offered and remember that non-recourse factoring is more expensive as the factor bears the costs of any irrecoverable debts.

Expandable text

Debt collection and administration – the factor takes over the whole of the company's sales ledger, issuing invoices and collecting debts.

Financing provision – in addition to the above, the factor will advance up to 80% of the value of a debt to the company; the remainder (minus finance costs) being paid when the debts are collected. The factor becomes a source of finance. Finance costs are usually 1.5% to 3% above bank base rate and charged on a daily basis.

Credit insurance – the factor agrees to insure the irrecoverable debts of the client. The factor would then determine to whom the company was able to offer credit.

Some companies realise that, although it is necessary to extend trade credit to customers for competitive reasons, they need payment earlier than agreed in order to assist their own cash flow. Factors exist to help such companies.

Factoring is most suitable for:

- small and medium-sized firms which often cannot afford sophisticated credit and sales accounting systems, and

- firms that are expanding rapidly. These often have a substantial and growing investment in inventory and receivables, which can be turned into cash by factoring the debts. Factoring debts can be a more flexible source of financing working capital than an overdraft or bank loan.

Factoring is primarily designed to allow companies to accelerate cash flow, providing finance against outstanding trade receivables. This improves cash flow and liquidity.

Factoring can be arranged on either a 'without recourse' basis or a 'with recourse' basis.

- When factoring is without recourse or 'non-recourse', the factor provides protection for the client against irrecoverable debts. The factor has no 'comeback' or recourse to the client if a customer defaults. When a customer of the client fails to pay a debt, the factor bears the loss and the client receives the money from the debt.

- When the service is with recourse ('recourse factoring'), the client must bear the loss from any irrecoverable debt, and so has to reimburse the factor for any money it has already received for the debt.

Credit protection is provided only when the service is non-recourse and this is obviously more costly.

Typical factoring arrangements

Administration and debt collection

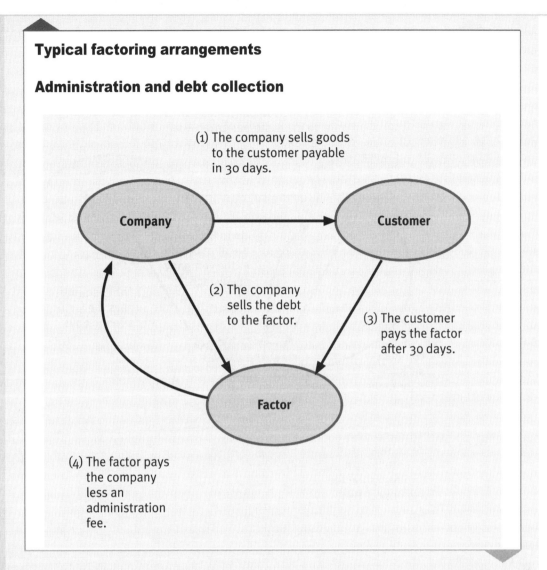

(1) The company sells goods to the customer payable in 30 days.

(2) The company sells the debt to the factor.

(3) The customer pays the factor after 30 days.

(4) The factor pays the company less an administration fee.

Including financing

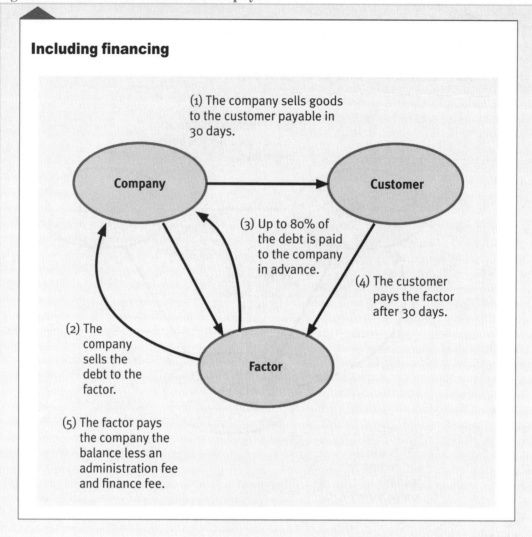

(1) The company sells goods to the customer payable in 30 days.

(3) Up to 80% of the debt is paid to the company in advance.

(4) The customer pays the factor after 30 days.

(2) The company sells the debt to the factor.

(5) The factor pays the company the balance less an administration fee and finance fee.

Advantages	Disadvantages
(1) Saving in administration costs.	(1) Likely to be more costly than an efficiently run internal credit control department.
(2) Reduction in the need for management control.	(2) Factoring has a bad reputation associated with failing companies; using a factor may suggest your company has money worries.
(3) Particularly useful for small and fast growing businesses where the credit control department may not be able to keep pace with volume growth.	(3) Customers may not wish to deal with a factor.
	(4) Once you start factoring it is difficult to revert easily to an internal credit control system.
	(5) The company may give up the opportunity to decide to whom credit may be given (non-recourse factoring).

Expandable text

The benefits of factoring are as follows.

- A business improves its cash flow, because the factor provides finance for up to 80% or more of debts within 24 hours of the invoices being issued. A bank providing an overdraft facility secured against a company's unpaid invoices will normally only lend up to 50% of the invoice value. (Factors will provide 80% or so because they set credit limits and are responsible for collecting the debts.)

- A factor saves the company the administration costs of keeping the sales ledger up to date and the costs of debt collection.

- A business can use the factor's credit control system to assess the creditworthiness of both new and existing customers.

- Non-recourse factoring is a convenient way of obtaining insurance against irrecoverable debts.

Problems with factoring.

- Although factors provide valuable services, companies are sometimes wary about using them. A possible problem with factoring is that the intervention of the factor between the factor's client and the debtor company could endanger trading relationships and damage goodwill. Customers might prefer to deal with the business, not a factor.

- When a non-recourse factoring service is used, the client loses control over decisions about granting credit to its customers.

- For this reason, some clients prefer to retain the risk of irrecoverable debts, and opt for a 'with recourse' factoring service. With this type of service, the client and not the factor decides whether extreme action (legal action) should be taken against a non-payer.

- On top of this, when suppliers and customers of the client find out that the client is using a factor to collect debts, it may arouse fears that the company is beset by cash flow problems, raising fears about its viability. If so, its suppliers may impose more stringent payment terms, thus negating the benefits provided by the factor.

- Using a factor can create problems with customers who may resent being chased for payment by a third party, and may question the supplier's financial stability.

Illustration 3 – Typical factoring arrangements

Edden is a medium-sized company producing a range of engineering products, which it sells to wholesale distributors. Recently, its sales have begun to rise rapidly due to economic recovery. However, it is concerned about its liquidity position and is looking at ways of improving cash flow.

Its sales are $16 million pa, and average receivables are $3.3 million (representing about 75 days of sales).

One way of speeding up collection from receivables is to use a factor. The factor will operate on a service-only basis, administering and collecting payment from Edden's customers. This is expected to generate administrative savings of $100,000 each year.

The factor has undertaken to pay outstanding debts after 45 days, regardless of whether the customers have actually paid or not. The factor will make a service charge of 1.75% of Edden's turnover. Edden can borrow at an interest rate of 8% pa.

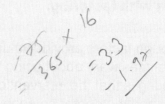

Required : Determine the relative costs and benefits of using the factor.

Expandable text

Solution

Reduction in receivables days = 75 - 45 = 30 day

Reduction in receivables	= 30 ÷ 365 × $16m	= $1,315,068
Saving in finance cost	= (8% × $1,315,068)	= $105,205
		say $105,000
Administrative savings		= $100,000
Service charge	= (1.75% × $16m)	= $280,000

Summary

	$
Service charge	(280,000)
Finance cost saved by reducing receivables	105,000
Administration costs saved	100,000
Net annual cost of the service	(75,000)

Edden will have to balance this cost against the security offered by improved cash flows and greater liquidity.

Test your understanding 2

As in Edden, a company has sales of $16 million pa, and average receivables are $3.3 million (representing about 75 days of sales). It is now considering a factoring arrangement with a different factor where 80% of the book value of invoices is paid immediately, with finance costs charged on the advance at 10% pa.

Suppose that this factor will charge 1% of sales as their fee for managing the sales ledger, that there will be administrative savings of $100,000 as before, but that outstanding balances will be paid after 75 days (i.e. there is no change in the typical payment pattern by customers this time).

> **Determine the relative costs and benefits of using this factor.**

Invoice discounting

Invoice discounting is a method of raising finance against the security of receivables without using the sales ledger administration services of a factor.

While specialist invoice discounting firms exist, this is a service also provided by a factoring company. Selected invoices are used as security against which the company may borrow funds. This is a temporary source of finance, repayable when the debt is cleared. The key advantage of invoice discounting is that it is a confidential service, and the customer need not know about it.

In some ways it is similar to the financing part of the factoring service without control of credit passing to the factor.

Ensure you can explain the difference between factoring and invoice discounting, and the situations where one may be more appropriate than the other.

Expandable text

Typical arrangement

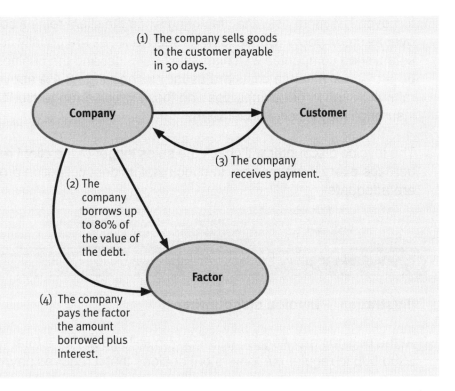

Invoice discounting is a method of raising finance against the security of receivables without using the sales ledger administration services of a factor. With invoice discounting, the business retains control over its sales ledger, and confidentiality in its dealings with customers. Firms of factors will also provide invoice discounting to clients.

The method works as follows:

- The business sends out invoices, statements and reminders in the normal way, and collects the debts. With 'confidential invoice discounting', its customers are unaware that the business is using invoice discounting.

- The invoice discounter provides cash to the business for a proportion of the value of the invoice, as soon as it receives a copy of the invoice and agrees to discount it. The discounter will advance cash up to 80% of face value.

- When the business eventually collects the payment from its customer, the money must be paid into a bank account controlled by the invoice discounter. The invoice discounter then pays the business the remainder of the invoice, less interest and administration charges.

Invoice discounting can help a business that is trying to improve its cash flows, but does not want a factor to administer its sales ledger and collect its debts. It is therefore equivalent to the financing service provided by a factor.

Administration charges for this service are around 0.5-1% of a client's turnover. It is more risky than factoring since the client retains control over its credit policy. Consequently, such facilities are usually confined to established companies with high sales revenue, and the business must be profitable. Finance costs are usually in the range 3-4% above base rate, although larger companies and those which arrange credit insurance may receive better terms.

The invoice discounter will check the sales ledger of the client regularly, perhaps every three months, to check that its debt collection procedures are adequate.

Expandable text

Illustration – Invoice discounting

At the beginning of August, Basildon plc sells goods for a total value of $300,000 to regular customers but decides that it requires payment earlier than the agreed 30-day credit period for these invoices.

A discounter agrees to finance 80% of their face value, i.e. $240,000, at an interest cost of 9% pa.

The invoices were due for payment in early September, but were subsequently settled in mid-September, exactly 45 days after the initial transactions. The invoice discounter's service charge is 1% of invoice value. A special account is set up with a bank, into which all payments are made.

The sequence of cash flows is:

August — Basildon receives cash advance of $240,000.

Mid-September — Customers pay $300,000.

Invoice discounter receives the full $300,000 paid into the special bank account.

Basildon receives the balance payable, less charges, i.e.

Service fee = 1% × $300,000 =	$3,000
Finance cost = 9% × $240,000 × 45/365 =	$2,663
Total charges	$5,663

Basildon receives:

Balance of payment from customer	$60,000
Less charges	$5,663
	$54,337

Summary $300,000 invoiced

Total receipts by Basildon: $240,000 + $54,337	$294,337
Invoice discounter's fee and interest charges	$5,663

Expandable text

A company has sales of $20 million for the previous year, receivables at the year end of $4 million and the overdraft which covers the financing of receivables is charged at a rate of 12% pa.

A factor has offered a debt collection service which should shorten the receivables collection period on average to 50 days. It charges 1.5% of turnover but should reduce administration costs to the company by $150,000.

(a) **Calculate the cost of the factoring facility.**

(b) **In addition, the factor has offered a finance provision of 80% of the debt immediately. They charge 14% but this is expected to save an additional $50,000. What is the overall cost of this service?**

Solution

(a) Finance cost = 50 days/365 days × $20m × 12%	=$328,767
Factor charge = $20m × 1.5% =	$300,000
Less: Admin savings =	($150,000)
Total cost	$478,767

Note: this compares with the current cost of financing via the overdraft:

$4m @ 12% = $480,000.

So factoring appears marginally cheaper.

(b) Finance cost:

Factor finance =

80% × 50 days/365 days × $20m × 14%	= $306,849
Overdraft finance =	
20% × 50 days/365 days × $20m × 12% =	$65,753
Factor charge = $20m × 1.5%	= $300,000
Less: Admin savings	= $(200,000)
Total cost	$472,602

4 Accounts payable – managing trade credit

Trade credit is the simplest and most important source of short-term finance for many companies.

 Again it is a balancing act between liquidity and profitability.

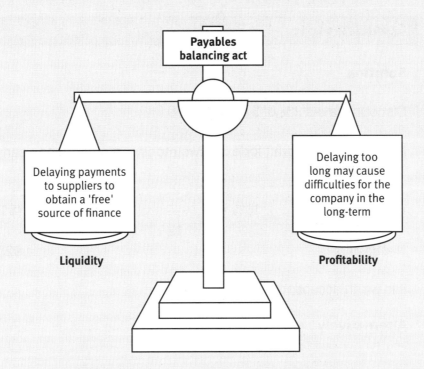

By delaying payment to suppliers companies face possible problems:

*   supplier may refuse to supply in future

*   supplier may only supply on a cash basis

*   there may be loss of reputation

*   supplier may increase price in future.

Trade credit is normally seen as a 'free' source of finance. Whilst this is normally true, it may be that the supplier offers a discount for early payment. In this case delaying payment is no longer free, since the cost will be the lost discount.

In the examination, you need to be able to calculate the cost of this discount foregone.

Expandable text

Illustration – Accounts payable – managing trade credit

One supplier has offered a discount to Box Co of 2% on an invoice for $7,500, if payment is made within one month, rather than the three months normally taken to pay. If Box's overdraft rate is 10% pa, is it financially worthwhile for them to accept the discount and pay early?

Expandable text

Solution

Discount saves 2% of $7,500 =$150

Financed by overdraft for extra two months in order to pay early:

$$\text{Cost} = 10\% \times \frac{2}{12} \times \$7,500 = (\$125)$$

Net saving = $25

It is worth accepting the discount.

Alternatively :

$$\text{Discount as a percentage of amount paid} = \frac{150}{7,350} = 2.04\%$$

$$\text{Saving is 2 months and there are } \frac{12}{2} = \text{6 periods in a year}$$

Annualised cost of not taking the discount (and therefore borrowing from the supplier) is:

$$(1+0.0204)^6 -1 = 0.1288 = 12.88\%$$

The overdraft rate is 10%.

It would be cheaper to borrow the money from the bank to pay early and accept the discount.

Test your understanding 3

Work out the equivalent annual cost of the following credit terms: 1.75% discount for payment within three weeks; alternatively, full payment must be made within eight weeks of the invoice date. Assume there are 50 weeks in a year.

Hint: Consider a $100 invoice.

Expandable text

Under **trade credit** a firm is able to obtain goods (or services) from a supplier without immediate payment, the supplier accepting that the firm will pay at a later date.

Trade credit periods vary from industry to industry and each industry will have what is a generally accepted norm which would be from seven days upwards. The usual terms of credit range from four weeks to the period between the date of purchase and the end of the month following the month of purchase.

However, considerable scope for flexibility exists and longer credit periods are sometimes offered, particularly where the type of business activity requires a long period to convert materials into saleable products, e.g. farming.

A proportion of the firm's suppliers will normally offer **settlement discounts** which should be taken up where possible by ensuring that special clearing treatment is given where settlement discount is allowed. However, if the firm is short of funds, it might wish to make maximum use of the credit period allowed by suppliers regardless of the settlement discounts offered.

It is a mistake to reduce working capital by holding on to creditors' money for a longer period than is allowed as, in the long-term, this will affect the supplier's willingness to supply goods and raw materials, and cause further embarrassment to the firm.

Favourable credit terms are one of several factors which influence the choice of a supplier. Furthermore, the act of accepting settlement discounts has an opportunity cost, i.e. the cost of finance obtained from another source to replace that not obtained from creditors.

Whilst trade credit may be seen as a source of **free credit** , there will be **costs** associated with extending credit taken beyond the norm – lost discounts, loss of supplier goodwill, more stringent terms for future sales.

In order to compare the cost of different sources of finance, all costs are usually converted to a rate pa basis. The cost of extended trade credit is usually measured by loss of discount, but the calculation of its cost is complicated by such variables as the number of alternative sources of supply, and the general economic conditions.

Certain assumptions have to be made concerning (a) the maximum delay in payment which can be achieved before the supply of goods is withdrawn by the supplier, and (b) the availability of alternative sources of supply.

Expandable text

Marton Co produces a range of specialised components, supplying a wide range of customers, all on credit terms. 20% of revenue is sold to one firm. Having used generous credit policies to encourage past growth, Marton Co now has to finance a substantial overdraft and is concerned about its liquidity.

Marton Co borrows from its bank at 13% pa interest. No further sales growth in volume or value terms is planned for the next year.

In order to speed up collection from customers, Marton Co is considering two alternative policies:

Option one

Factoring on a non-recourse basis, the factor administering and collecting payment from Marton Co's customers. This is expected to generate administrative savings of $200,000 pa and to lower the average receivable collection period by 15 days. The factor will make a service charge of 1% of Marton Co's revenue and also provide credit insurance facilities for an annual premium of $80,000.

Option two

Offering discounts to customers who settle their accounts early. The amount of the discount will depend on speed of payment as follows.

Payment within 10 days of despatch of invoices 3%

Payment within 20 days of despatch of invoices 1.5%

It is estimated that customers representing 20% and 30% of Marton Co's sales respectively will take up these offers, the remainder continuing to take their present credit period.

Extracts from Marton Co's most recent accounts are given below:

	($000)	($000)
Sales (all on credit)		20,000
Cost of sales		(17,000)
Operating profit		3,000

Current assets:

inventory	2,500
receivables	4,500
cash	Nil

Calculate the relative costs and benefits in terms of annual profit before tax of each of the two proposed methods of reducing receivables, and recommend the most financially advantageous policy. Comment on your results .

Solution

The relative costs and benefits of each option are calculated as follows:

Option 1 – Factoring

Reduction in receivables days	=15 days	
Reduction in receivables	= 15 ÷ 365 × $20m =	$821,916
Effect on profit before tax:		
Finance cost saving	= (13% × $821,916) =	$106,849
Administrative savings	=	$200,000
Service charge	= (1% × $20m) =	($200,000)
Insurance premium	=	($80,000)
Net profit benefit	=	$26,849

Option 2 – The discount

With year-end receivables at $4.5 million, the receivables collection period was: $4.5m ÷ $20m × 365 = 82 days.

The scheme of discounts would change this as follows:

10 days for 20% of customers

20 days for 30% of customers

82 days for 50% of customers

Average receivables days become:

(20% × 10) + (30% × 20) + (50% × 82) = 49 days

Hence, average receivables would reduce from the present $4.5 million to:

49 × $20m ÷ 365 = $2,684,932

Finance cost saving = 13% × ($4.5m – $2.685m) = $235,950

The cost of the discount:

(3% × 20% × $20m) + (1.5% × 30% × $20rn) = ($210,000)

The net benefit to profit before tax : $25,950

The figures imply that factoring is marginally the more attractive, but this result relies on the predicted proportions of customers actually taking up the discount and paying on time. It also neglects the possibility that some customers will insist on taking the discount without bringing forward their payments. Marton Co would have to consider a suitable response to this problem.

Conversely, the assessment of the value of using the factor depends on the factor lowering Marton Co's receivables days. If the factor retains these benefits for itself, rather than passing them on to Marton Co, this will raise the cost of the factoring option. The two parties should clearly specify their mutual requirements from the factoring arrangement on a contractual basis.

Expandable text

Accounts receivable and payable – managing foreign trades

Overseas accounts receivable and payable bring additional risks that need to be managed:export credit riskforeign transaction exposure.check creditworthiness of all customers negotiate secure payment terms ensure proper documents are presented for payment insist that payment is in a convertible currency.

Export credit risk

Export credit risk is the risk of failure or delay in collecting payments due from foreign customers.

May be caused by:

- insolvent customers
- bank failure
- unconvertible currencies
- political risk.

Solutions include:

- using banks as intermediaries
- irrevocable letter of credit (ILC)
- acquiring guarantees
- taking out export cover
- good business management!!:

Foreign exchange risk

Many trade transactions involve foreign currencies:

- buying from abroad in a foreign currency
- denominating sales to export customers in a foreign currency.

Since many of the transactions are arranged on credit, the foreign currency needed/owed will not be exchanged until some time after the contract date.

There is a risk that the value of the currency will change between the date of the contract and the date of settlement. This risk is known as foreign exchange transaction exposure.

Dealing with this risk is the subject of chapter 22.

In a question that deals with overseas receivables and payables remember to consider export credit risk and foreign transaction exposure as well as the normal points on the management of receivables and payables.

Expandable text

Whilst all of the basic management principles and techniques discussed so far apply equally to overseas receivables and payables, there are additional risks that will need to be managed, including:

- export credit risk and foreign exchange transaction exposure.

Export credit risk is the risk of failure or delay in collecting payments due from foreign customers. Possible causes of loss from such risk, which apply to all export trade of whatever size, include the following.

- Illiquidity or insolvency of the customer. This also occurs in domestic trading. When an export customer cannot pay however, suppliers have extra problems in protecting their positions in a foreign legal and banking system.
- Bankruptcy or failure of a bank in the remittance chain.
- A poorly-specified remittance channel.
- Inconvertibility of the customer's currency, and lack of access to the currency in which payment is due. This can be caused by deliberate exchange controls or by an unplanned lack of foreign exchange in the customer's central bank.
- Political risks. Their causes can be internal (change of regime, civil war) or external (war, blockade) to the country concerned.

Exporters can protect themselves against these risks by the following means.

- Use banks in both countries to act as the collecting channel for the remittance and to control the shipping documents so that they are only released against payment or acceptance of negotiable instruments (bills of exchange or promissory notes).
- Commit the customer's bank through an ILC.
- Require the ILC to be confirmed (effectively guaranteed) by a first class bank in the exporter's country. This makes the ILC a confirmed ILC (CILC).
- Obtain support from third parties, e.g.:
  - get a guarantee of payment from a local bank
  - get a letter from the local finance ministry or central bank confirming availability of foreign currency.
- Take out export credit cover.

- Use an intermediary such as a confirming, export finance, factoring or forfeiting house to handle the problems on their behalf; or possibly by giving no credit or selling only through agents who accept the credit risk (del credere agents) and are themselves financially strong.

None of these devices will enable the exporter to escape from certain hard facts of life.

- The need to avoid giving credit to uncreditworthy customers. Weak customers cannot obtain an ILC from their own bank, nor would they be cleared for credit by a credit insurer or intermediary.

- The need to negotiate secure payment terms, procedures and mechanisms which customers do not find congenial. An ILC and especially a CILC are costly to customers, and restrict their flexibility: if they are short of cash at the end of the month, they must still pay out if their bank is committed.

- Exporters can only collect under a letter of credit if they present exactly the required documents. They will not be able to do this if they have sent the goods by air and the credit requires shipping documents; or if they need to produce the customer's inspection certificates and the customer's engineer is mysteriously unavailable to inspect or sign.

- The need to insist that payment is in a convertible currency and in a form which the customer's authorities will permit to become effective as a remittance to where the exporters need to have the funds, usually in their own country. Often this means making the sale subject to clearance under exchange controls or import licensing regulations.

Introductory points about foreign exchange:

Many companies trade in foreign currencies, either buying from abroad in a foreign currency or denominating sales to export customers in a foreign currency.

If so they might need to:

- buy foreign currency to pay a supplier, or

- convert foreign currency receipts into domestic currency.

Like domestic trade, foreign trade is arranged on credit terms. Companies usually know in advance what foreign currency they will need to pay out and what currencies they will be receiving. Foreign exchange risk arises in these situations:

- If a company has to obtain foreign currency at a future date to make a payment there is a risk that the cost of buying the currency will rise (from what it would cost now) if the exchange rate moves and the currency strengthens in value.

- If a company will want to convert currency earnings into a domestic currency at a future date, there is a risk that the value of the currency will fall (from its current value) if the exchange rate moves and the currency falls in value.

Exposures to these risks of adverse changes in an exchange rate are known as 'foreign exchange transaction exposures'. These exposures can be 'hedged' (reduced or offset). The methods available to hedge the risks are covered in chapter 22.

KAPLAN PUBLISHING

Chapter summary

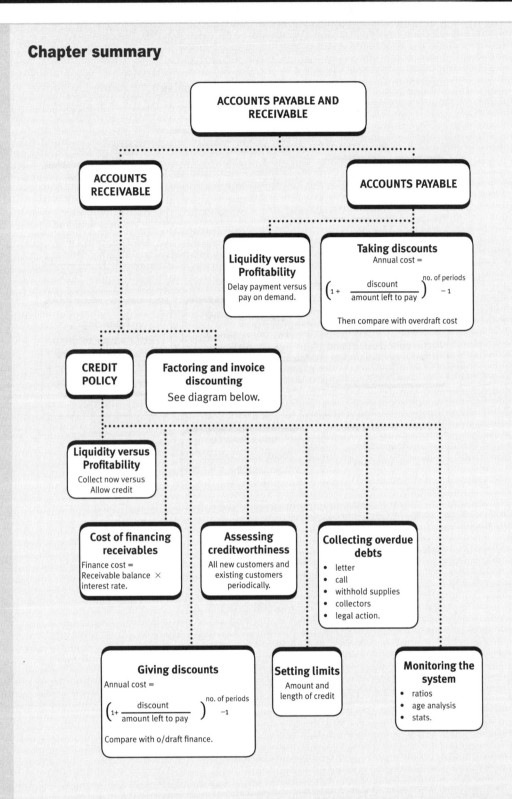

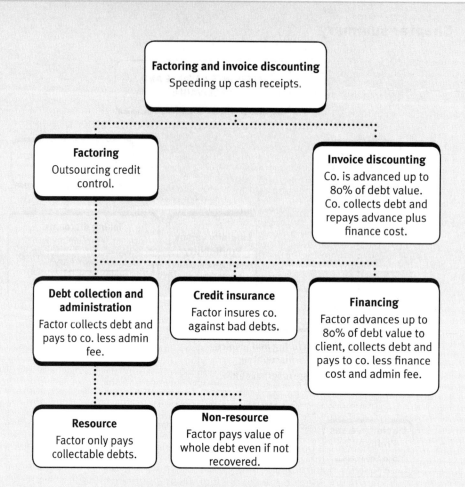

Test your understanding answers

Test your understanding 1

Advantages	Disadvantages
Early payment reduces the receivables balance and hence the finance costs.	Difficulty in setting the appropriate terms.
Potential to reduce the irrecoverable debts arising.	Uncertainty as to when cash receipts will be received, complicating cash budgeting.
Offers a choice to customers of payment terms.	Unlikely to reduce irrecoverable debts in practice.
	Customers pay over normal terms but still take the cash discount.

Test your understanding 2

	Costs of factoring	Savings
	$	$
Sales ledger administration 1% × $16m	160,000	
Administration cost savings		100,000
Cost of factor finance 10% × 80% × $3.3m	264,000	
Overdraft finance costs 8% × 80% × $3.3m saved		211,200
Total	424,000	311,200
Net cost of factoring	112,800	

As before the firm will have to balance this cost against the security offered by improved cash flows and greater liquidity.

Test your understanding 3

Step 1

Work out the discount available and the amount due if the discount were taken.

Discount available on a $100 invoice = 1.75% × $100 = $1.75.

Amount due after discount = $100 × $1.75 = $98.25

Step 2

The effective interest cost of not taking the discount is:

1.75 ÷ 98.25 = 0.0178

for an 8 – 3 = five-week period.

Step 3

Calculate the equivalent annual rate. There are ten five-week periods in a year.

The equivalent interest annual rate is $(1 + 0.018)^{10} - 1 = 0.195$ or 19.5%.

Working capital management – cash and funding strategies

Chapter learning objectives

Upon completion of this chapter you will be able to:

- explain the main reasons for a business to hold cash

- define and explain the use of cash budgets and cash flow forecasts

- prepare a cash flow forecast to determine future cash flows and cash balances

- discuss the advantages and disadvantages of centralised treasury management and cash control

- explain the points addressed by the Baumol cash management model

- calculate the optimum cash management strategy using the Baumol cash management model

- explain the logic of the Miller-Orr cash management model

- calculate the optimum cash management strategy using the Miller-Orr cash management model

- explain the ways in which a firm can invest cash short-term

- explain the ways in which a firm can borrow cash short-term

- calculate the level of working capital investment in current assets from supplied data

- explain the main strategies available for the funding of working capital

- explain the distinction between permanent and fluctuating current assets

- explain the relative costs and risks of short-term and long-term finance

- explain the logic behind matching short- and long-term assets and funding

- explain the relative costs and benefits of aggressive, conservative and matching funding policies

- explain the impact that factors such as management attitudes to risk, previous funding decisions and organisation size might have on the strategy chosen to fund working capital.

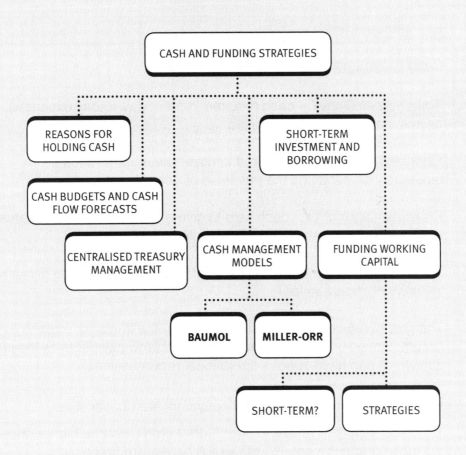

1 Reasons for holding cash

Although cash needs to be invested to earn returns, businesses need to keep a certain amount readily available. The reasons include:

- transactions motive
- finance motive
- precautionary motive
- investment motive.

Failure to carry sufficient cash levels can lead to:

- loss of settlement discounts
- loss of supplier goodwill
- poor industrial relations
- potential liquidation.

Expandable text

Cash is required for a number of reasons:

Transactions motive – cash required to meet day-to-day expenses, e.g. payroll, payment of suppliers, etc.

Finance motive – cash required to cover major items such as the repayment of loans and the purchase of non-current assets.

Precautionary motive – cash held to give a cushion against unplanned expenditure (the cash equivalent of buffer inventory).

Speculative motive – cash kept available to take advantage of market investment opportunities.

The cost of running out of cash depends on the firm's particular circumstances but may include not being able to pay debts as they fall due which can have serious operational repercussions:

- settlement discounts for early payment are unavailable

- trade suppliers refuse to offer further credit, charge higher prices or downgrade the priority with which orders are processed

- if wages are not paid on time, industrial action may well result, damaging production in the short-term and relationships and motivation in the medium-term

> • the court may be petitioned to wind up the company if it consistently fails to pay bills as they fall due.

Once again therefore the firm faces a balancing act:

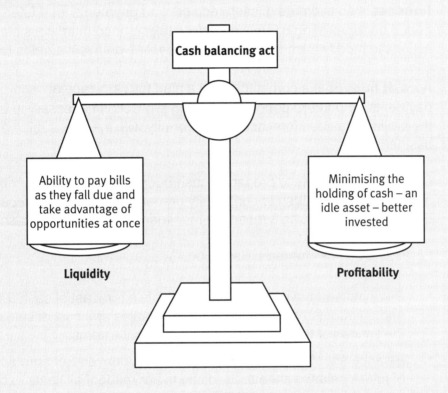

Remember to consider the four motives for holding cash and the liquidity/profitability trade-off in a question that asks for a discussion of cash management.

2 Cash budgets and cash flow forecasts

A **cash forecast** is an estimate of cash receipts and payments for a future period under existing conditions.

A **cash budget** is a commitment to a plan for cash receipts and payments for a future period after taking any action necessary to bring the forecast into line with the overall business plan.

Forecasts can be prepared from any of the following:

• planned receipts and payments

• balance sheet predictions

• working capital ratios.

Make sure you are aware of the difference between a cash budget and a cash forecast. The requirement to produce a forecast using working capital ratios has been a popular examination topic.

Expandable text

It is important to distinguish between a budget and a forecast. A **cash forecast** is an estimate of cash receipts and payments for a future period under existing conditions before taking account of possible actions to modify cash flows, raise new capital, or invest surplus funds.

A **cash budget** is a commitment to a plan for cash receipts and payments for a future period after taking any action necessary to bring the preliminary cash forecast into conformity with the overall plan of the business.

Companies are likely to prepare a cash budget as part of the annual master budget, but then to continually prepare revised cash forecasts throughout the year, as a means of monitoring and managing cash flows.

Forecasts can be prepared based on:

- Receipts and payments forecast. This is a forecast of cash receipts and payments based on predictions of sales and cost of sales and the timings of the cash flows relating to these items.

- Balance sheet forecast. This is a forecast derived from predictions of future balance sheets. Predictions are madeof all items except cash, which is then derived as a balancing figure.

- Working capital ratios. Future cash and funding requirements can be determined from the working capital ratios seen in Chapter 5. This has been a popular examination topic.

Receipts and payments budgets are much more detailed than balance sheet forecasts. They are normally used for short-termcash forecasting, whereas balance sheet forecasts are generally longer-term (say, longer than three to six months).

Cash budgets are used to:

- assess and integrate operating budgets

- plan for cash shortages and surpluses

- compare with actual spending.

Preparing a cash flow forecast from receipts and payments

Every type of cash inflow and receipt, along with their timings, must be forecast. Note that cash receipts and payments differ from sales and cost of sales in the income statement because:

- not all cash items affect the income statement
- some income statement items are not cash flows
- actual timing of cash flows may not correspond with the accounting period in which they are recorded.

Expandable text

Cash receipts and payments are not the same as sales and the costs of sales found in the firm's income statement because:

- not all cash receipts or payments affect the income statement, e.g. the issue of new shares or the purchase of a non-current asset
- some income statement items are derived from accounting conventions and are not cash flows, e.g. depreciation or the profit/loss on the sale of a non-current asset

> - the timing of cash receipts and payments does not coincide with the income statement accounting period, e.g. a sale is recognised in the income statement when the invoice is raised, yet the cash payment from the receivable may not be received until the following period or later.

The following approach should be adopted for examination questions.

Step 1 – Prepare a proforma

Month:	1	2	3	4
	$	$	$	$
Receipts (few lines)				
Sub total				
Payments (Many lines)				
Sub total				
Net cash flow				
Balance brought down				
Balance carried down				

Step 2 – Fill in the simple figures

Some payments need only a small amount of work to identify the correct figure and timing and can be entered straight into the proforma. These would usually include:

- wages and salaries
- fixed overhead expenses
- dividend payments
- purchase of non-current assets.

Step 3 – Work out the more complex figures

The information on sales and purchases can be more time consuming to deal with, e.g.:

- timings for both sales and purchases must be found from credit periods

- variable overheads may require information about production levels

- purchase figures may require calculations based on production schedules and inventory balances.

Expandable text

Illustration – Cash flow forecast from receipts and payments

A manufacturing company makes product WSX, for which the variable overhead cost is $2 per unit. Fixed costs are budgeted at $450,000 for the year, of which $130,000 are depreciation charges. The remaining fixed costs are incurred at a constant rate every month, with the exception of factory rental costs, which are $80,000 each year, payable 50% in December and 50% in June.

With the exception of rental costs, 10% of overhead expenses are paid for in the month in which they occur and the remaining 90% are paid in the following month.

The budgeted production quantities of product WSX are:

	Units
September	40,000
October	60,000
November	50,000
December	30,000

Required:

Prepare a month-by-month cash flow forecast for overhead payments in the period October–December.

Solution

Workings: fixed overheads

	$
Annual fixed overheads	450,000
Deduct depreciation	130,000
	———
Cash expenses	320,000
Deduct annual factory rental	80,000
	———

Regular cash expenses for the year	240,000
Regular cash expenses each month	20,000

These expenses will be paid for as follows: $2,000 in the month incurred and $18,000 in the following month. So total cash spending on these regular fixed cost items will be $20,000 in every month. An additional $40,000 is paid in June and December, for rent.

Workings: variable overheads

	Units	Variable overhead costs	Payment in		
			October	November	December
		$	$	$	$
September	40,000	80,000	72,000	–	–
October	60,000	120,000	12,000	108,000	–
November	50,000	100,000	–	10,000	90,000
December	30,000	60,000	–	–	6,000
Total payments			84,000	118,000	96,000

An overhead cash payments forecast can now be prepared.

	October	November	December
	$	$	$
Variable overheads	84,000	118,000	96,000
Fixed overheads	20,000	20,000	60,000
Total payments	104,000	138,000	156,000

Expandable text

Illustration – Cash flow forecast from receipts and payments

A business has estimated that 10% of its sales will be cash sales, and the remainder credit sales. It is also estimated that 50% of receivables will pay in the month following sale, 30% two months after sale, 15% three months after sale and irrecoverable debts will be 5% of credit sales.

Total sales figures are as follows:

Month	$
October	80,000
November	60,000
December	40,000
January	50,000
February	60,000
March	90,000

Required:

Prepare a month-by-month forecast of cash receipts from sales for the months January-March.

Solution

Receivables take up to three months to pay, so in the first month of the budget period, January, the business should expect some cash receipts for credit sales three months earlier, in October.

It might be useful to prepare a table for workings, as follows:

Sales month	Total sales	Cash receipts January	Cash receipts February	Cash receipts March
	$	$	$	$
October	80,000	10,800	–	–
November	60,000	16,200	8,100	–
December	40,000	18,000	10,800	5,400
January	50,000	5,000	22,500	13,500
February	60,000	–	6,000	27,000
March	90,000	–	–	9,000
Total receipts		50,000	47,400	54,900

For example, October sales were $80,000 and 90% of these ($72,000) were credit sales. Of these 15% are expected to pay three months later in January, so the cash receipts in January from October sales are expected to be $10,800 (15% of $72,000).

Similarly, November sales were $60,000 in total and of these $54,000 were credit sales. Of the credit sales, 30% will pay two months later in January and 15% three months later in February.

January sales are expected to total $50,000, of which $5,000 will be cash sales and $45,000 credit sales. Of the credit sales, there should be receipts from 50% ($22,500) in February and 30% ($13,500) in March.

Make sure that you can see how all the figures in this workings table have been calculated.

IIn this table receipts from cash sales and receipts from receivables are combined into a single figure for receipts from sales for the month. The receipts from cash sales and receipts from credit sales could be calculated separately if required.

Test your understanding 1

The forecast sales for an organisation are as follows:

	January $	February $	March $	April $
Sales	6,000	8,000	4,000	5,000

All sales are on credit and receivables tend to pay in the following pattern:

	%
In month of sale	10
In month after sale	40
Two months after sale	45

The organisation expects the rate of irrecoverable debts to be 5%.

Calculate the forecast cash receipts from receivables in April.

Test your understanding 2

A manufacturing business makes and sells widgets. Each widget requires two units of raw materials, which cost $3 each. Production and sales quantities of widgets each month are as follows:

Month	Sales and production units
December (actual)	50,000
January (budget)	55,000
February (budget)	60,000
March (budget)	65,000

In the past, the business has maintained its inventories of raw materials at 100,000 units. However, it plans to increase raw material inventories to 110,000 units at the end of January and 120,000 units at the end of February. The business takes one month's credit from its suppliers.

Calculate the forecast payments to suppliers each month, for raw material purchases.

Test your understanding 3

In the near future a company will purchase a manufacturing business for $315,000, this price to include goodwill ($150,000), equipment and fittings ($120,000), and inventory of raw materials and finished goods ($45,000).

A delivery van will be purchased for $15,000 as soon as the business purchase is completed. The delivery van will be paid for in the second month of operations.

The following forecasts have been made for the business following purchase:

I   Sales (before discounts) of the business's single product, at a mark-up of 60% on production cost will be:

Month	1	2	3	4	5	6
($000)	96	96	92	96	100	104

25% of sales will be for cash; the remainder will be on credit, for settlement in the month following that of sale. A discount of 10% will be given to selected credit customers, who represent 25% of gross sales.

II   Production cost will be $5 per unit. The production cost will be made up of:

Raw materials	$2.50
Direct labour	$1.50
Fixed overhead	$1.00

III   Production will be arranged so that closing inventory at the end of any month is sufficient to meet sales requirements in the following month. A value of $30,000 is placed on the inventory of finished goods, which was acquired on purchase of the business. This valuation is based on the forecast of production cost per unit given in (ii) above.

IV   The single raw material will be purchased so that inventory at the end of a month is sufficient to meet half of the following month's production requirements. Raw material inventory acquired on purchase of the business ($15,000) is valued at the cost per unit that is forecast as given in (ii) above. Raw materials will be purchased on one month's credit.

V   Costs of direct labour will be met as they are incurred in production.

VI   The fixed production overhead rate of $1.00 per unit is based upon a forecast of the first year's production of 150,000 units. This rate includes depreciation of equipment and fittings on a straight-line basis over the next five years. Fixed production overhead is paid in the month incurred.

VII Selling and administration overheads are all fixed, and will be
$208,000 in the first year. These overheads include depreciation of
the delivery van at 30% pa on a reducing balance basis. All fixed
overheads will be incurred on a regular basis, and paid in the month
incurred, with the exception of rent and rates. $25,000 is payable for
the year ahead in month one for rent and rates.

A **Prepare a monthly cash budget. You should include the
business purchase and the first four months of operations
following purchase.**

B **Calculate the inventory, receivables, and payables balances
at the end of the four-month period. Comment briefly upon
the liquidity situation.**

Expandable text

**Preparing a cash flow forecast from a balance sheet(Statement of
financial position)**

Used to predict the cash balance at the end of a given period, this
method will typically require forecasts of:

- changes to non-current assets (acquisitions and disposals)
- future inventory levels
- future receivables levels
- future payables levels
- changes to share capital and other long-term funding (e.g. bank
  loans)

- changes to retained profits.

Expandable text

Illustration – Cash flow forecast from a balance sheet(Statement of financial position)

Zed Co has the following balance sheet(Statement of financial position) at 30 June 20X3:

	$	$
Non-current assets:		
Plant and machinery		192,000
Current assets:		
Inventory	16,000	
Receivables	80,000	
Bank	2,000	
		98,000
Total assets		290,000
Equity and liabilities:		
Issued share capital		216,000
Retained profits		34,000
		250,000
Current liabilities		
Trade payables	10,000	
Dividend payable	30,000	
		40,000
Total equity and liabilities		290,000

(a) The company expects to acquire further plant and machinery costing $8,000 during the year to 30 June 20X4.

(b) The levels of inventories and receivables are expected to increase by 5% and 10% respectively by 30 June 20X4, due to business growth.

(c) Trade payables and dividend liabilities are expected to be the same at 30 June 20X4.

(d) No share issue is planned, and retained profits for the year to 30 June 20X4 are expected to be $42,000.

(e) Plant and machinery is depreciated on a reducing balance basis, at the rate of 20% pa, for all assets held at the balance sheet date.

Produce a balance sheet forecast as at 30 June 20X4, and predict what the cash balance or bank overdraft will be at that date.

Expandable text

Solution

Zed Co – Balance sheet(Statement of financial position) at 30 June 20X4

	$	$	$
Non-current assets:			
Plant and machinery[(192,000 + 8,000) × 80%]			160,000
Current assets:			
Inventory (16,000 × 105%)		16,800	
Receivables (80,000 × 110%)		88,000	
Bank (balancing figure)		67,200	
			172,000
Total assets			332,000
Equity and liabilities			
Issued share capital			216,000
Retained profits (34,000 + 42,000)			76,000
			292,000
Current liabilities:			
Trade payables		10,000	
Dividend payable		30,000	
			40,000
Total equity and liabilities			332,000

The forecast is that the bank balance will increase by $65,200 (i.e. $67,200 – $2,000). This can be reconciled as follows:

	$	$
Retained profit		42,000
Add: Depreciation (20% of ($192,000 + $8,000))		40,000
		82,000
Less: Non-current asset acquired		(8,000)
		74,000
Increase in inventory	800	
Increase in receivables	8,000	
		(8,800)
Increase in cash balance		65,200

Expandable text

Gee Co has the following balance sheet(Statement of financial position) at 30th June 20X5:

	$	$
Non-current assets:		
Plant and machinery		180,000
Current assets		
Inventory	12,000	
Receivables	70,000	
Bank	1,500	
		83,500
Total assets		263,500
Equity and liabilities		
Issued share capital		204,000
Retained profits		21,000
		225,000
Current liabilities:		
Trade payables	12,500	
Dividend payable	26,000	
		38,500
Total equity and liabilities		263,500

(a) The company expects to acquire further plant and machinery costing $5,000 during the year to 30 June 20X6.

(b) The levels of inventories and receivables are expected to increase by 3% and 7% respectively by 30 June 20X6, due to business growth.

(c) Trade payables and dividend liabilities are expected to be the same at 30 June 20X5.

(d) $20,000 is planned to be raised through a share issue, and retained profits for the year to 30 June 20X6 are expected to be $15,000.

(e) Plant and machinery is depreciated on a reducing balance basis, at the rate of 20% pa, for all assets held at the balance sheet date.

Produce a balance sheet(Statement of financial position) forecast as at 30 June 20X6, and predict what the cash balance or bank overdraft will be at that date.

Solution

Gee Co – Balance sheet(Statement of financial position) at 30 June 20X6

	$	$	$
Non-current assets:			
Plant and machinery[(180,000 + 5,000) × 80%]			148,000
Current assets:			
Inventory (12,000 × 103%)		12,360	
Receivables (70,000 × 107%)		74,900	
Bank (balancing figure)		63,240	
			150,500
Total assets			298,500
Equity and liabilities			
Issued share capital			224,000
Retained profits (21,000 + 15,000)			36,000
			260,000
Current liabilities:			
Trade payables		12,500	
Dividend payable		26,000	
			38,500
Total equity and liabilities			298,500

The forecast is that the bank balance will increase by $61,740(i.e. $63,240 – $1,500). This can be reconciled as follows:

	$	$
Retained profit		15,000
Add: Depreciation (20% of ($180,000 + $5,000))		37,000
		52,000
Plus: Cash raised through share issue		20,000
Less: Non-current asset acquired		(5,000)
		67,000
Increase in inventory	360	
Increase in receivables	4,900	
		(5,260)
Increase in cash balance		61,740

Expandable text

X Co has the following expectations for the forthcoming period.

	$m
Sales	10
Materials	(6)
Other non-production costs	(2)
Profit	2

The following working capital ratios are expected to apply.

Inventory days	30 days
Receivables days	60 days
Payables days	40 days

Required:

Compute the working capital requirement.

Solution

We need to use the ratios to calculate balance sheet values in order to construct the projected working capital position.

			$m
Inventory	=	30/365 × $6m =	0.49
Receivables	=	60/365 × $10m =	1.64
Trade payables	=	40/365 × $6m =	(0.66)
Working capital required			1.47

Expandable text

Preparing a cash flow forecast from working capital ratios

Working capital ratios can also be used to forecast future cash requirements.

The first stage is to use the ratios to work out the working capital requirement, as we have already seen in chapter 5.

This technique is used to help forecast overall cash flow. The proforma below is used.

	$
Operating profit	X
Add: Depreciation	X
Cash flow from operations	X
Add: Cash from sale of non-current assets	X
Long-term finance raised	X
Less: Purchase of non-current assets	(X)
Redemption of long-term funds	(X)
Interest paid	(X)
Tax paid	(X)
Dividend paid	(X)
Increase in working capital	(X)
Net cash flow	X

KAPLAN PUBLISHING

Note that the proforma given is not strictly in accordance with FRS 1. FRS 1 governs the production of cash flow statements in a company's financial statements but here we are calculating projected future cash flows rather that the historical cash flow for which the FRS was introduced.

Expandable text

Illustration – Cash flow forecast from working capital ratios

X Co had the following results for last year.

Income statement	$m
Sales	200
Cost of sales (including $20m depreciation)	120
Operating profit	80
Interest	5
Profit before tax	75
Tax	22
Profit after tax	53
Dividend proposed	10
Retained earnings	43

Balance sheet (extract)	$m	$m
Non-current assets		400
Current assets:		
Inventory	25	
Receivables	33	
Cash	40	
	98	
Current liabilities:		
Trade payables	20	
Dividend payable	10	
Tax payable	22	
	52	
Long term loan @ 10%		50

X Co expects the following for the forthcoming year.

Sales will increase by	10%
Plant and machinery will be purchased costing	$12m
Inventory days	80 days
Receivables days	75 days
Trade payables days	50 days
Depreciation will be	$15m

Required:

Prepare a cash flow projection for the forthcoming period.

Solution

Here we will assume that the gross profit percentage will remain unaltered in cash terms.

	$m
Last year	
Sales	200
Cost of sales less depreciation	100
Operating cash flow	100
Gross profit percentage	50%
	$m
This year	
Sales 110% × $200m	220
Cost of sales 50% × $220m	110
Operating cash flow	110

Next we calculate the working capital requirements (to the nearest $m).

		$m
Inventory	80 ÷ 365 × $110m =	24
Receivables	75 ÷ 365 × $220m =	45
Trade payables	50 ÷ 365 × $110m =	15

Now we assemble the information in the proforma given earlier.

Note		$m
1	Operating cash flow	110
2	Interest	(5)
3	Tax	(22)
3	Dividend	(10)
4	Purchase of plant and machinery	(12)
5	Reduction in inventory ($24m ÷ $25m)	1
5	Increase in receivables ($45m × $33m)	(12)
5	Reduction in trade payables ($15m × $20m)	(5)
	Net cash flow	45

Notes

(1) We have already calculated operating cash flow so do not need to adjust for depreciation of $15m.

(2) It is assumed that this is the same as last period, as the loans have not changed.

(3) The tax and dividend payables in last year's balance sheet will be paid in the forthcoming period

(4) This was given in the question.

(5) Increases in current assets are an outflow, reductions are an inflow. The reverse is the case for trade payables.

Expandable text

X Inc has the following results from last period.

Income statement

	$m
Turnover	500
Cost of sales	300
Operating profit	200
Interest	40
Profit before tax	160
Tax	70
Profit after tax	90
Dividends	50
Retained profit	40

Balance sheet(Statement of financial position)

	$m	$m
Non-current assets		750
Current assets:		
Inventory	60	
Receivables	120	
Cash	40	
		220
		970
10% loan notes		400
Current liabilities:		
Trade payables		50
Tax		70
Dividends		30

X Inc expects the following to apply next period.

Turnover increase to	$650m
Operating profit %	30%
Redemption of all the debentures at end of period for a discount of	$50m
Sales of non-current assets	$150m
Depreciation and loss on sale of non-current assets	$50m
Inventories at end of period	$100m
Receivables at end of period	$170m
Trade payables at end of period	$60m

Produce a statement to compute the cash flow over the forthcoming period.

Solution

	$m
Operating profit 30% × $650m	195
Add: Depreciation and loss on asset sales	50
	⎯⎯
Operating cash flow	245
Add: Proceeds from sale of non-current assets	150
	⎯⎯
	395
Less: Interest paid (from opening balance sheet)	(40)
Tax paid (from opening balance sheet)	(70)
Dividends paid (from opening balance sheet)	(30)
Redemption of debentures (400m – 50m)	(350)
	⎯⎯
	(95)
Increase in inventories (100m – 60m)	(40)
Increase in receivables (170m – 120m)	(50)
Increase in trade payables (60m – 50m)	10
	⎯⎯
Net cash flow	(175)
	⎯⎯

3 Centralised treasury management

The role of treasury management

Treasury management is concerned with liquidity and covers the following activities:

- banking and exchange
- cash and currency management
- investment in short-term assets
- risk and insurance
- raising finance.

Originally the activities were carried out within the general finance function, but today are often separated into a treasury department, particularly in large international companies. Reasons for the change include:

- increase in size and global coverage of the companies
- increasingly international markets
- increase in sophistication of business practices.

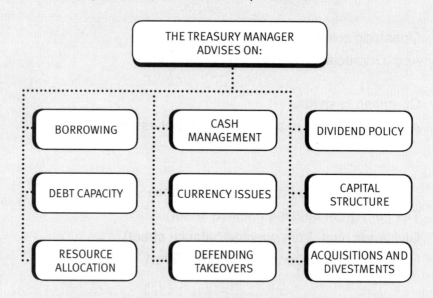

The case for centralising treasury management

A company must choose between having its treasury management:

- centralised
- decentralised

If they are centralised, each operating company holds only the minimum cash balance required for day-to-day operations, remitting the surplus to the centre for overall management.

If they are decentralised, each operating company must appoint an officer responsible for that company's own treasury operations.

Test your understanding 4

Consider the advantages and disadvantages of centralised treasury functions.

Ensure you can discuss the key arguments.

Centralised treasury management often results in a highly-skilled team, cheaper borrowing, lower bank charges and more effective hedging of currency risk, but some motivational and local knowledge benefits may be lost.

Expandable text

All treasury management activities are concerned with managing the liquidity of a business, the importance of which to the survival and growth of a business cannot be over-emphasised.

Why have a treasury department?

The functions carried out by the treasurer have always existed, but have been absorbed historically within other finance functions. A number of reasons may be identified for the modern development of separate treasury departments:

- size and internationalisation of companies: these factors add to both the scale and the complexity of the treasury functions

- size and internationalisation of currency, debt and security markets: these make the operations of raising finance, handling transactions in multiple currencies and investing, much more complex. They also present opportunities for greater gains

- sophistication of business practice: this process has been aided by modern communications, and as a result the treasurer is expected to take advantage of opportunities for making profits or minimising costs which did not exist a few years ago.

For these reasons, most large international corporations have moved towards setting up a separate treasury department.

Treasury departments tend to rely heavily on new technology for information.

Treasury responsibilities

The treasurer will generally report to the finance director (financial manager), with a specific emphasis on borrowing and cash and currency management. The treasurer will have a direct input into the finance director's management of debt capacity, debt and equity structure, resource allocation, equity strategy and currency strategy.

The treasurer will be involved in investment appraisal, and the finance director will often consult the treasurer in matters relating to the review of acquisitions and divestments, dividend policy and defence from takeover.

Treasury departments are not large, since they are not involved in the detailed recording of transactions.

Centralisation of treasury activities

Should treasury activities in a large international group be centralised or decentralised?

Advantages of centralisation are as follows.

- There is no need for treasury skills to be duplicated throughout the organisation. One highly-trained central department can assemble a highly-skilled team, offering skills that could not be available if every company had their own treasury.

- Necessary borrowings can be arranged in bulk, at keener interest rates than for smaller amounts. Similarly bulk deposits of surplus funds will attract higher rates of interest than smaller amounts.

- The group's foreign currency risk can be managed much more effectively from a centralised treasury, since only the treasury department can appreciate the total exposure situation. A total hedging policy is more efficiently carried out by head office, rather than each company doing its own hedging.

- Bank charges should be lower, since the carrying of both balances and overdrafts in the same currency should be eliminated.

Advantages of decentralisation are as follows.

- Greater autonomy leads to greater motivation. Individual companies will manage their cash balances more attentively if they are responsible for them, rather than simply remitting them up to head office.

- Local operating units should have a better feel for local conditions than head office and can respond more quickly to local developments.

4 Cash management models

Cash management models are aimed at minimising the total costs associated with movements between:

- a current account (very liquid but not earning interest) and
- short-term investments (less liquid but earning interest).

The models are devised to answer the questions:

- at what point should funds be moved?
- how much should be moved in one go?

The Baumol cash management model

Baumol noted that cash balances are very similar to inventory levels, and developed a model based on the economic order quantity (EOQ).

Assumptions:

- cash use is steady and predictable
- cash inflows are known and regular
- day-to-day cash needs are funded from current account
- buffer cash is held in short-term investments.

The formula calculates the amount of funds to inject into the current account or to transfer into short-term investments at one time:

$$Q = \sqrt{(2C_O D / C_H)}$$

where:

C_O = transaction costs (brokerage, commission, etc.)

D = demand for cash over the period

C_H = cost of holding cash.

The model suggests that when interest rates are high, the cash balance held in non-interest-bearing current accounts should be low. However its weakness is the unrealistic nature of the assumptions on which it is based.

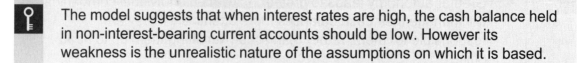

Expandable text

Illustration – The Baumol cash management model

A company generates $10,000 per month excess cash, which it intends to invest in short-term securities. The interest rate it can expect to earn on its investment is 5% pa. The transaction costs associated with each separate investment of funds is constant at $50.

Required:

(a) What is the optimum amount of cash to be invested in each transaction?

(b) How many transactions will arise each year?

(c) What is the cost of making those transactions pa?

(d) What is the opportunity cost of holding cash pa?

Expandable text

Solution

Q (cash investment) =

$$\sqrt{\left(\frac{2 \times 50 \times 10,000 \times 12}{0.05}\right)} = \$15,492$$

b. Number of transactions pa =

$$\frac{120{,}000}{15{,}492} = 7.75$$

c. Annual transaction cost = $7.75 \times \$50$ = $387

d. Annual opportunity cost = (holding cost)

$$5\% \times \frac{15{,}492}{2} = \$387$$

Expandable text

C_O = transaction costs are the costs of making a trade in securities or moving funds in and out of interest-bearing deposit accounts.

D = the demand for cash over the period relates to cash needs for day-to-day transactions.

C_H = the cost of holding cash will be the opportunity cost relating to either the return it could have earned in marketable securities or deposit accounts or the cost of borrowing in order to acquire cash.

Test your understanding 5

A company faces a constant demand for cash totalling $200,000 pa. It replenishes its current account (which pays no interest) by selling constant amounts of gilts which are held as an investment earning 6% pa. The cost per sale of gilts is a fixed $15 per sale.

What is the optimum amount of gilts to be sold each time an injection of cash is needed in the current account, how many transfers will be needed and what will the overall transaction cost be?

The Miller-Orr cash management model

The **Miller-Orr** model controls irregular movements of cash by the setting of upper and lower control limits on cash balances.

The **Miller-Orr** model is used for setting the target cash balance.

It has the advantage of incorporating uncertainty in the cash inflows and outflows.

The diagram below shows how the model works over time.

- The model sets higher and lower control limits, H and L, respectively, and a target cash balance, Z.

- When the cash balance reaches H, then (H-Z) dollars are transferred from cash to marketable securities, i.e. the firm buys (H-Z) dollars of securities.

- Similarly when the cash balance hits L, then (Z-L) dollars are transferred from marketable securities to cash.

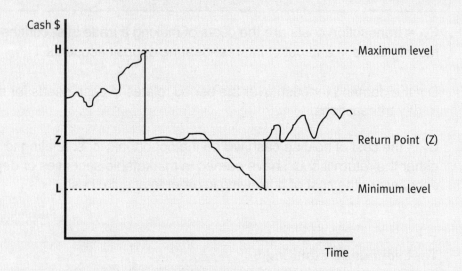

The lower limit, L is set by management depending upon how much risk of a cash shortfall the firm is willing to accept, and this, in turn, depends both on access to borrowings and on the consequences of a cash shortfall.

The formulae (given in the examination) for the **Miller-Orr** model are:

Return point = Lower limit + (1/3 × spread)

Spread = 3 [(3/4 × Transaction cost × Variance of cash flows) ÷ Interest rate] $^{1/3}$

Note: variance and interest rates should be expressed in daily terms.

Expandable text

Illustration – The Miller-Orr cash management model

The minimum cash balance of $20,000 is required at **Miller-Orr Co**, and transferring money to or from the bank costs $50 per transaction. Inspection of daily cash flows over the past year suggests that the standard deviation is $3,000 per day, and hence the variance (standard deviation squared) is $9 million. The interest rate is 0.03% per day.

Calculate:

(i)   the spread between the upper and lower limits

(ii) the upper limit

(iii) the return point.

Expandable text

Solution

(i)   Spread = 3 $(3/4 \times 50 \times 9{,}000{,}000/0.0003)^{1/3}$ = $31,200

(ii) Upper limit = 20,000 + 31,200 = $51,200

(iii) Return point = 20,000 + 31,200/3 = $30,400

Test your understanding 6

A company sets its minimum cash balance at $5,000 and has estimated the following:

- transaction cost = $15 per sale or purchase of gilts

- standard deviation of cash flows = $1,200 per day (i.e. variance = $1.44 million per day)

- interest rate = 7.3% pa = 0.02% per day.

(i)   **What is the spread between the upper and lower limits?**

(ii) **What is the upper limit?**

(iii) **What is the return point?**

Expandable text

The **Miller-Orr** model controls irregular movements of cash by the use of upper and lower limits on cash balances.

The lower limit has to be specified by the firm and the upper limit is calculated by the model. The cash balance of the firm is allowed to vary freely between the two limits but if the cash balance on any day goes outside these limits, action must be taken.

If the cash balance reaches the lower limit it must be replenished in some way, e.g. by the sale of marketable securities or withdrawal from a deposit account. The size of this withdrawal is the amount required to take the balance back to the return point. It is the distance between the return point (usually set in **Miller-Orr** as the lower limit plus one third of the distance up to the upper limit) and the lower limit.

If the cash balance reaches the upper limit, an amount must be invested in marketable securities or placed in a deposit account, sufficient to reduce the balance back to the return point. Again, this is calculated by the model as the distance between the upper limit and the return point.

The minimum cost upper limit is calculated by reference to brokeragecosts, holding costs and the variance of cash flows. The model has some fairly restrictive assumptions, e.g. normally distributed cash flows but, in tests, **Miller and Orr** found it to be fairly robust and claim significant potential cost savings for companies.

---

5 Short-term investment and borrowing solutions

The cash management models discussed above assumed that funds could be readily obtained when required either by liquidating short-term investments or by taking out short-term borrowing.

A company must choose from a range of options to select the most appropriate source of investment/funding.

Short-term cash investments

Short-term cash investments are used for temporary cash surpluses. To select an investment, a company has to weigh up three potentially conflicting objectives and the factors surrounding them.

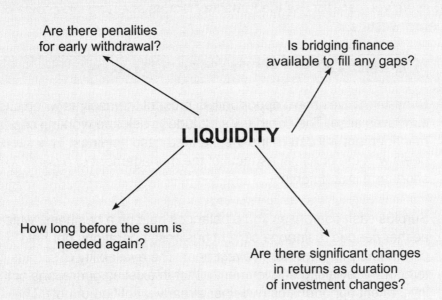

Are there penalities
for early withdrawal?

Is bridging finance
available to fill any gaps?

LIQUIDITY

How long before the sum is
needed again?

Are there significant changes
in returns as duration
of investment changes?

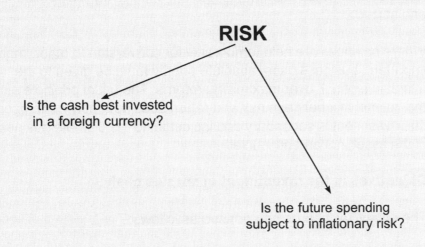

RISK

Is the cash best invested
in a foreigh currency?

Is the future spending
subject to inflationary risk?

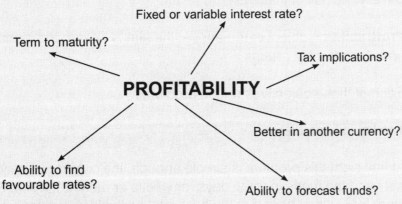

Fixed or variable interest rate?

Term to maturity?

Tax implications?

PROFITABILITY

Better in another currency?

Ability to find
favourable rates?

Ability to forecast funds?

Ensure you can discuss the three key factors affecting the choice of
short-term investment.

Ensure you can discuss the three key factors affecting the choice of short-term investment.

Expandable text

Short-term investment opportunities present themselves when cash surpluses arise. The company's attitude to risk and working capital management will determine the planned cash holdings. This section deals with the practical aspects of the management of a portfolio of short-term investments.

Surplus cash comprises liquid balances held by a business, which are neither needed to finance current business operations nor held permanently for short-term investment. The availability of surplus cash is temporary, awaiting employment either in existing operations or in new investment opportunities (whether already identified or not). The 'temporary' period can be of any duration, from one day to the indefinite future date at which the new investment opportunity may be identified and seized.

Where balances are held temporarily for conversion to other, more important, business uses, absolute priority must be given to the avoidance of risk over maximising returns. The usual principle of finding the optimal mix between risk and return does not apply here, because the investment is secondary and incidental to the ultimate business use of the asset, not an end in itself.

Objectives in the investment of surplus cash

The objectives can be categorised as follows:

Liquidity: the cash must be available for use when needed.

Safety: no risk of loss must be taken.

Profitability: subject to the above, the aim is to earn the highest possible after-tax returns.

Each of these objectives raises problems.

The liquidity problem

At first sight this problem is simple enough. If a company knows that it will need the funds in three days (or weeks or months), it simply invests them for just that period at the best rate available with safety. The solution is to match the maturity of the investment with the period for which the funds are surplus. However there are a number of factors to consider:

- The exact duration of the surplus period is not always known. It will be known if the cash is needed to meet a loan instalment, a large tax payment or a dividend. It will not be known if the need is unidentified, or depends on the build-up of inventory, the progress of construction work, or the hammering out of an acquisition deal.

- Expected future trends in interest rates (see below) affect the maturity of investments.

- Bridging finance may be available to bridge the gap between the time when the cash is needed and the subsequent date on which the investment matures.

- An investment may not need to be held to maturity, if either an earlier withdrawal is permitted by the terms of the instrument without excessive penalty, or there is a secondary market and its disposal in that market causes no excessive loss.

- A good example of such an investment is a certificate of deposit (CD), where the investor 'lends' the bank a stated amount for a stated period, usually between one and six months. As evidence of the debt and its promise to pay interest, the bank gives the investor a CD. There is an active market for CDs issued by the commercial banks and turning a CD into cash is easy and cheap.

The safety problem

Safety means there is no risk of loss. Superficially this again looks simple. The concept certainly includes the absence of credit risk. For example, the firm should not deposit with a bank which might conceivably fail within the maturity period and thus not repay the amount deposited.

However, safety is not necessarily to be defined as certainty of getting the original investment repaid at 100% of its original home currency value. If the purpose for which the surplus cash is held is not itself fixed in the local currency, then other criteria of safety may apply.

Examples

If the cash is being held to meet a future commitment, the ultimate amount of the commitment may be subject to inflationary rises (e.g. payment to building contractors for a new factory). In this case a safer investment instrument may be an index-linked gilt-edged bond with a maturity date close to the expected date of the payment.

If the cash is being held to meet a future payment in a foreign currency, the only riskless investment would be one denominated in that currency.

The profitability problem

The profitability objective looks deceptively simple at first: go for the highest rate of return subject to the overriding criteria of safety and liquidity. However, here there are even more complications.

Factor being considered Rule of thumb course of action

Fixed or variable rates	Invest long (fixed interest investments with late maturity dates – subject to the liquidity rule) if there are good reasons to expect interest rates to fall.
Term to maturity	Invest short (fixed interest investments with early maturity dates) or at variable rates if there are good grounds for expecting rates to go up.
Tax effects	Aim to optimise net cash flows after tax. Tax payments are a cash outflow. There are many tax-efficient investments for surplus cash, e.g. use of tax havens, or government securities which may be exempt from capital gains tax (CGT).
Use of other currencies	Investing in currencies other than the company's operating currency in which it has the bulk of its assets and in which it reports to its owners is clearly incompatible with the overriding requirement of safety, except in two possible sets of circumstances:

- the investment is earmarked for a payment due in another currency (as seen earlier) or

- both principal and interest are sold forward or otherwise hedged against the operating currency (hedging is covered in greater detail later in Chapter 23).

Difficulty in forecasting available funds	Segregate receipts and payments into the following categories: • The steadier and more forecastable flows, such as cash takings in retail trades. There may be predictable peaks, say at the end of the week and in the pre-Christmas period. • The less predictable but not individually large items. • Controllable items such as payments to normal suppliers. • Items such as collections from major customers, which are individually so large that it pays to spend some management time on them. This segregation can even be taken to the point where separate bank accounts are used for the different categories.
Difficulty in finding the most favourable rates	Know the available instruments and their current relative benefits. Shop around for the 'best buy' among investees who offer the most appropriate instrument.

Short-term borrowing

Short-term cash requirements can also be funded by borrowing from the bank. There are two main sources of bank lending:

- bank overdraft
- bank loans.

Bank overdrafts are mainly provided by the clearing banks and are an important source of company finance.

Advantages	Disadvantages
• Flexibility	• Repayable on demand
• Only pay for what is used, so cheaper	• May require security
	• Variable finance costs

Bank loans are a contractual agreement for a specific sum, loaned for a fixed period, at an agreed rate of interest. They are less flexible and more expensive than overdrafts but provide greater security.

Expandable text

Finance costs on bank loans and overdrafts are normally variable, i.e. they alter in line with base rates. Fixed rate loans are available, but are less popular with firms (and providers of finance).

Bank overdrafts

A common source of short-term financing for many businesses is a bank overdraft. These are mainly provided by the clearing banks and represent permission by the bank to write cheques even though the firm has insufficient funds deposited in the account to meet the cheques.

An overdraft limit will be placed on this facility, but provided the limit is not exceeded, the firm is free to make as much or as little use of the overdraft as it desires. The bank charges interest on amounts outstanding at any one time, and the bank may also require repayment of an overdraft at any time.

The advantages of overdrafts are the following.

- Flexibility – they can be used as required.

- Cheapness – interest is only payable on the finance actually used, usually at 2-5% above base rate (and all loan interest is a tax deductible expense).

The disadvantages of overdrafts are as follows.

- Overdrafts are legally repayable on demand. Normally, however, the bank will give customers assurances that they can rely on the facility for a certain time period, say six months.

- Security is usually required by way of fixed or floating charges on assets or sometimes, in private companies and partnerships, by personal guarantees from owners.

- Interest costs vary with bank base rates. This makes it harder to forecast and exposes the business to future increases in interest rates.

Overall, bank overdrafts are one of the most important sources of short-term finance for industry.

Bank loans

A bank loan represents a formal agreement between the bank and the borrower, that the bank will lend a specific sum for a specific period (one to seven years being the most common). Interest must be paid on the whole of this sum for the duration of the loan.

This source is, therefore, liable to be more expensive than the overdraft and is less flexible but, on the other hand, there is no danger that the source will be withdrawn before the expiry of the loan period. Interest rates and requirements for security will be similar to overdraft lending.

Comparison of bank loans and overdrafts

Consider a company that requires a maximum of $600 over the next four months. However, it is only halfway through month four that it actually requires the full amount.

The difference can be shown as follows:

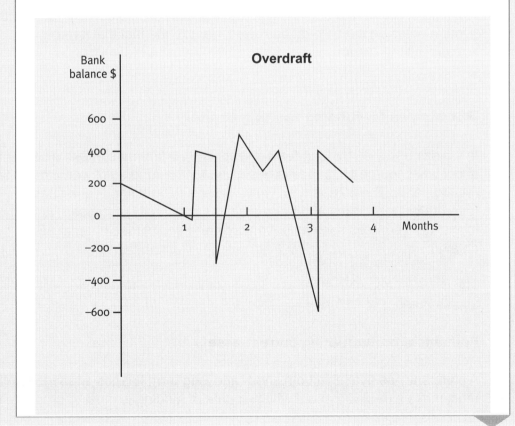

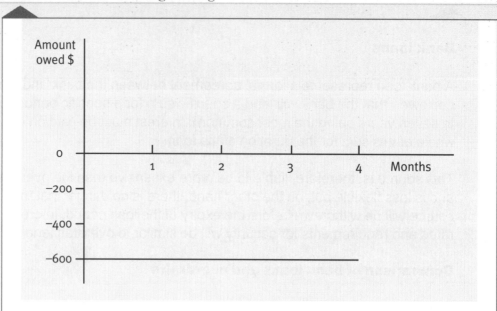

If an overdraft is used, the company will pay interest on the maximum amount part way through month 4. For the remainder of the period it will pay interest on an overdraft of substantially less than that, or it will pay no interest at all as it has a positive bank balance. If it borrows $600 by way of a bank loan at the beginning of the four months, it must pay interest for four months on the amount borrowed, despite the fact that it rarely requires the full sum.

6 Strategies for funding working capital

In the same way as for long-term investments, a firm must make a decision about what source of finance is best used for the funding of working capital requirements. The company will have access to both short-term finance (overdrafts, bank loans and trade credit as previously discussed) and longer-term sources such as debentures and equity (see chapter 15 for details).

The decision about whether to choose short- or long-term options depends upon a number of factors.

Permanent or fluctuating current assets

A company has available both short- and long-term finance. Management must make a decision about which source of funding is most appropriate to its needs.

Traditionally current assets were seen as short-term and fluctuating and best financed out of short-term credit which could be paid off when not required. Long-term finance was used for non-current assets, since it involves committing for a number of years and is not easily reversed.

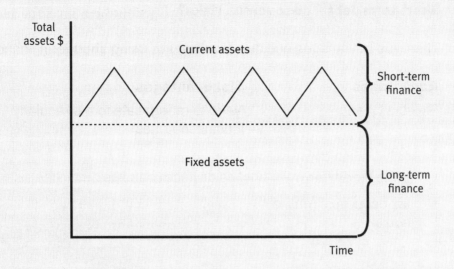

However this approach ignores the fact that in most businesses a proportion of the current assets are fixed over time, i.e. 'permanent'. For example:

- buffer inventory
- receivables during the credit period
- minimum cash balances.

If growth is included in the analysis, a more realistic picture emerges:

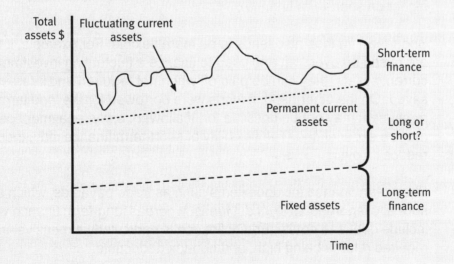

The choice of how to finance the permanent current assets is a matter for managerial judgement, but includes an analysis of the cost and risks of short-term finance.

Short-term debt – cost versus risks?

There are advantages and disadvantages to using short-term finance:

Advantages	Disadvantages
Flexible Cheap:	Need to renegotiate terms regularly Fluctuating rates

- loan rates lower
- trade credit free
- tax deductible (unlike equity)

Expandable text

The cost of short-term finance

Short-term finance is usually cheaper than long-term finance. This is largely due to the risks taken by creditors. For example, if a bank were considering two loan applications, one for one year and the other for 20 years, all other things being equal it would demand a higher interest rate on the 20-year loan. This is because it feels more exposed to risk on long-term loans, as more could go wrong with the borrower over a period of twenty years than a period of one year (although it should be noted that occasionally this situation is reversed, with rates of return being higher on short-term finance).

Short-term finance also tends to be more flexible. For example, if funds are raised on overdraft and used to finance a fluctuating investment in current assets, they can be paid off when not required and interest saved. On the other hand, if funds were borrowed for the long term, early repayment may not be possible, or, if allowed, early repayment penalties may be experienced. The flexibility of short-term finance may, therefore, reduce its overall cost.

Short-term finance includes items such as trade payables, which are normally regarded as low cost funds, whereas long-term finance will include debt and equity. Equity finance is particularly expensive, its required returns being high, and non-tax deductible.

The risks of short-term finance

Short-term financing has already been established as generally 'the cheaper option'. However, the price paid for reduced cost is increased risk for the borrower.

There may be:

Renewal problems – short-term finance may need to be continually renegotiated as various facilities expire and renewal may not always be guaranteed.

Unstable interest rates – if the company constantly has to renew its funding arrangements, it will be at the mercy of fluctuations in short-term interest rates.

feels more exposed to risk on long-term loans, as more could go wrong with the borrower over a period of 20 years than a period of one year (although it should be noted that occasionally this situation is reversed, with rates of return being higher on short-term finance).

Short-term finance also tends to be more flexible. For example, if funds are raised on overdraft and used to finance a fluctuating investment in current assets, they can be paid off when not required and interest saved. On the other hand, if funds were borrowed for the long-term, early repayment may not be possible, or, if allowed, early repayment penalties may be experienced. The flexibility of short-term finance may, therefore, reduce its overall cost.

Short-term finance includes items such as trade payables, which are normally regarded as low-cost funds, whereas long-term finance will include debt and equity. Equity finance is particularly expensive, its required returns being high, and non-tax deductible.

The risks of short-term finance

Short-term financing has already been established as generally 'the cheaper option'. However, the price paid for reduced cost is increased risk for the borrower.

There may be:

Renewal problems – short-term finance may need to be continually renegotiated as various facilities expire and renewal may not always be guaranteed.

Unstable interest rates – if the company constantly has to renew its funding arrangements, it will be at the mercy of fluctuations in short-term interest rates.

Aggressive, conservative and matching funding policies

There is no ideal funding package, but three approaches may be identified.

- Aggressive – finance most current assets, including 'permanent' ones, with short-term finance. Risky but profitable.

- Conservative – long-term finance is used for most current assets. Stable but expensive.

- Matching – the duration of the finance is matched to the duration of the investment.

Expandable text

Illustration – Aggressive, conservative matching funding policies

The following three companies have current asset financing structures that may be considered as aggressive, average and defensive (conservative):

Balance sheet	Aggressive	Average	Defensive
	$000	$000	$000
Non-current assets	50	50	50
Current assets	50	50	50
	100	100	100
Equity (50,000 $1 shares)	50	50	50
Long-term debt (average cost 10% pa)	–	25	40
Current liabilities (average cost 3% pa)	50	25	10
	100	100	100
Current ratio	1:1	2:1	5:1
Income statement	$	$	$
EBIT	15,000	15,000	15,000
Less: Interest	1,500	3,250	4,300
Earnings before tax	13,500	11,750	10,700

Corporation tax @ (say) 40%	5,400	4,700	4,280
Earnings available to equity	8,100	7,050	6,420
Earning per share (EPS)	16.2c	14.1c	12.84c

The aggressive company is so termed as it is prepared to take the risk of financing more of its business investment with short-term credit. The defensive company, at the other 'extreme', takes on board a high proportion of longer-term debt with, consequently, less short-term credit risk.

It can be seen that the aggressive company returns a higher profit but at the cost of greater risk. It is interesting to note that this higher risk is revealed in its relatively poor current ratio.

Essentially the final choice of working capital funding is down to the management of the individual companies, bearing in mind:

- the willingness of creditors to lend

- the risks of their commercial sector

- the attitude of management to risk and previous funding patterns.

Expandable text

Smaller companies may, by necessity, finance almost all their needs from short-term finance, since long-term debt and equity may be difficult to raise without marketable shares and a good track record.

If the commercial sector in which the company operates has volatile earnings, management may consider it best to take a conservative approach to funding to avoid particular problems in problem years.

The attitude to risk of the decision maker will ultimately determine the decision taken (see chapter 12 for more analysis of attitude to risk), and this in turn may be influenced by the attitudes and decisions of those who have gone before.

Chapter summary

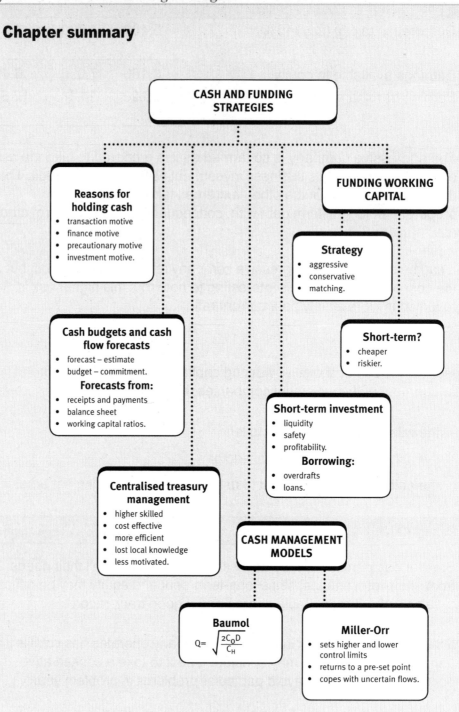

Test your understanding answers

Test your understanding 1

Cash from:		$
April sales:	10% × $5,000	500
March sales:	40% × $4,000	1,600
February sales:	45% × $8,000	3,600
		————
		5,700

Test your understanding 2

When inventories of raw materials are increased, the quantities purchased will exceed the quantities consumed in the period.

Figures for December are shown because December purchases will be paid for in January, which is in the budget period.

Quantity of raw material purchased in units:

	Units of widgets produced	Material (@ 2 units per widget)			
		December	January	February	March
	Units	Units	Units	Units	Units
December	50,000	100,000			
January	55,000		110,000		
February	60,000			120,000	
March	65,000				130,000
Increase in inventories		–	10,000	10,000	–
Total purchase quantities		100,000	120,000	130,000	130,000
At $3 per unit		300,000	360,000	390,000	390,000

Having established the purchases each month, we can go on to budget the amount of cash payments to suppliers each month. Here, the business will take one month's credit.

	January	February	March
	$	$	$
Payment to suppliers	300,000	360,000	390,000

At the end of March, there will be payables of $390,000 for raw materials purchased, which will be paid in April.

Test your understanding 3

A Monthly cash budget

	Month 1	Month 2	Month 3	Month 4
	$	$	$	$
Cash inflows:				
Cash sales	24,000	24,000	23,000	24,000
Credit sales		72,000	72,000	69,000
Less: Discounts		(2,400)	(2,400)	(2,300)
Total inflow	24,000	93,600	92,600	90,700
Cash outflows:				
Purchases **(W1)**	–	44,375	29,375	30,625
Labour **(W1)**	27,000	17,250	18,000	18,750
Production overhead **(W2)**	10,500	10,500	10,500	10,500
Selling and administration overhead **(W3)**	39,875	14,875	14,875	14,875
Purchase of business	315,000	–	–	–
Purchase of van	–	15,000	–	–
Total outflow	392,375	102,000	72,750	74,750
Net cash flow for month	(368,375)	(8,400)	19,850	15,950
Opening balance	0	(368,375)	(376,775)	(356,925)
Closing balance	(368,375)	(376,775)	(356,925)	(340,975)

Workings (W1)

	Month 1	Month 2	Month 3	Month 4	Month 5	Month 6
Sales ($)	96,000	96,000	92,000	96,000	100,000	104,000
Sales units	12,000	12,000	11,500	12,000	12,500	13,000
+ Closing inventory	12,000	11,500	12,000	12,500	13,000	
– Opening inventory	6,000	12,000	11,500	12,000	12,500	13,000
	────	────	────	────	────	────
Production (units)	18,000	11,500	12,000	12,500	13,000	
	────	────	────	────	────	
Raw material usage (Production × $2.50)	45,000	28,750	30,000	31,250	32,500	
+ Closing inventory	14,375	15,000	15,625	16,250		
– Opening inventory	15,000	14,375	15,000	15,625		
	────	────	────	────		
Purchases (one month delay)	44,375	29,375	30,625	31,875		
	────	────	────	────		
Labour cost (production × $1.50)	27,000	17,250	18,000	18,750		

(W2) – Production overheads

	$
Annual overheads (150,000 × $1)	150,000
Depreciation (120,000/5)	(24,000)
	────
	126,000
	────
Monthly cash outflow (126,000/12)	10,500

(W3) – Selling and administration overheads

	$
Annual overheads	208,000
Depreciation (15,000 × 0.3)	(4,500)
	203,500
Less: Rent and rates in month 1	25,000
Monthly cash outflow – months 2, 3, 4 (178500/12)	178,500
Month 1: 25,000 + 14,875	14,875
	39,875

B. Closing balances:

Inventory:	$
Finished goods (12,500 × $5)	62,500
Raw materials	16,250
	78,750

Receivables:	
Month 4 credit sales (96,000 × 0.75)	72,000
Less: Discount (10% × 0.25 × 96,000)	(2,400)
	69,600
Payables	31,875

Apart from the purchase of the business, which will require separate long-term finance, the cash flow forecast suggests that there will be sufficient cash inflows to meet the cash outflows on an ongoing basis. The current assets and receivables provide sufficient funds to cover the payables.

Test your understanding 4

Advantages	Disadvantages
Avoids duplication of skills.	Lack of autonomy for local areas – demotivating.
Can borrow/invest in bulk – better rates given.	Lack of local involvement – local knowledge lost.
Better exchange rate management – see total exposure.	Lack of local involvement – local management not concerned about treasury issues.
Potential to net off and therefore reduce amount to be borrowed and hence charged.	

Test your understanding 5

The optimum amount of gilts sold, Q, for each cash injection into the current account will be:

$$Q = \sqrt{(2 \times 200{,}000 \times 15 \div 0.06)} = \$10{,}000$$

The total number of transactions will be

$$200{,}000 \div 10.000 = 20$$

and the total transaction cost will be 20 × $15 = $300.

Test your understanding 6

The spread is calculated as:

$$3 \times [(3/4 \times 15 \times 1.44m) \div 0.0002]^{1/3}$$

$$= 3 \times \$4{,}327$$

$$= \$12{,}981$$

Therefore:

- lower limit (set by the company) = $5,000
- upper limit = 5,000 + 12,981 = $17,981
- return point = 5,000 + (1/3 × 12,981) = $9,327.

Capital budgeting and basic investment appraisal techniques

Chapter learning objectives

Upon completion of this chapter you will be able to:

- define and distinguish between capital and revenue expenditure

- distinguish between expenditure on non-current assets and working capital

- describe the capital budgeting process

- explain the role of investment appraisal in the capital budgeting process

- explain the relationship between the capital budgeting process and the development of corporate strategy

- define a relevant cash flow (and distinguish it from an accounting profit)

- identify and calculate relevant cash flows in a scenario

- calculate the payback period and use it to appraise an investment

- discuss the usefulness of payback as an investment appraisal method

- calculate return on capital employed (ROCE) (accounting rate of return) and use it to appraise an investment

- discuss the usefulness of ROCE as an investment appraisal method.

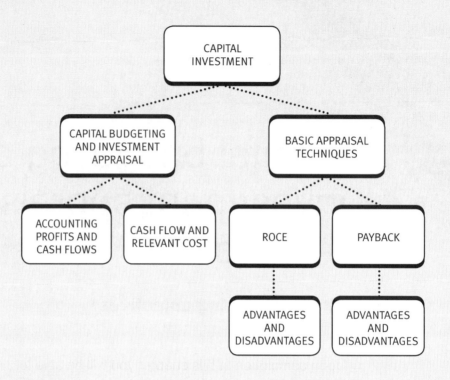

1 Capital investment

When a business spends money on new non-current assets it is known as capital investment or capital expenditure. Spending may be for:

- maintenance
- profitability
- expansion
- indirect purposes.

Spending is normally irregular and for large amounts. It is expected to generate long-term benefits.

Expandable text

Maintenance – spending to replace worn-out or obsolete assets, or to improve safety and security of existing non-current assets.

Profitability – spending to achieve cost savings, quality improvements, improvements to productivity, etc.

Expansion – spending to grow the business, make new products, open new outlets, invest in research and development (R&D), etc.

KAPLAN PUBLISHING

Indirect purposes – spending which is necessary for the smooth running of the business but not directly related to operations, e.g. renovating office buildings.

Compare:

- Revenue expenditure – regular spending on the day-to-day running of the business where the benefit is expected to last for only one specific accounting period.

- Working capital investment – investment in short-term net assets.

You must be able to distinguish between capital and revenue expenditure and expenditure on working capital.

Expandable text

Short-term net assets are primarily made up of inventory, receivables and cash less short-term payables.

Expandable text

An enterprise spends money on the following:

- annual rental payment for the warehouse

- a new fork-lift truck to replace one damaged in an accident

- increased inventory to fulfil a newly-won contract

- an automatic moulding machine to streamline a production process.

Identify the type of expenditure that each of the above represents.

Solution

- Annual rental payments for the warehouse are revenue expenditure. The benefit is only for that accounting period.

- The new fork-lift truck is a capital purchase. It is maintenance spending as it replaces one already owned but damaged.

- The increased inventory spending is an investment in working capital.

- The automatic moulding machine is also a capital expense. However since it was bought to streamline a production process, the purpose is profitability.

2 Capital budgeting and investment appraisal

A capital budget:

- is a programme of capital expenditure covering several years
- includes authorised future projects and projects currently under consideration.

The capital budgeting process consists of a number of stages:

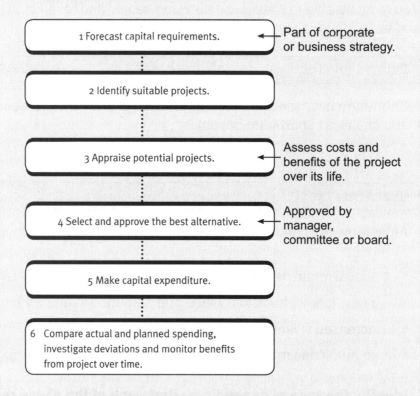

1 Forecast capital requirements. ← Part of corporate or business strategy.

2 Identify suitable projects.

3 Appraise potential projects. ← Assess costs and benefits of the project over its life.

4 Select and approve the best alternative. ← Approved by manager, committee or board.

5 Make capital expenditure.

6 Compare actual and planned spending, investigate deviations and monitor benefits from project over time.

The process of appraising the potential projects (stage 3 above) is known as **investment appraisal**. This appraisal has the following features:

- assessment of the level of expected returns earned for the level of expenditure made
- estimates of future costs and benefits over the project's life.

Expandable text

When a proposed capital project is evaluated, the costs and benefits of the project should be evaluated over its foreseeable life. This is usually the expected useful life of the non-current asset to be purchased, which will be several years. This means that estimates of future costs and benefits call for long-term forecasting.

A 'typical' capital project involves an immediate purchase of a non-current asset. The asset is then used for a number of years, during which it is used to increase sales revenue or to achieve savings in operating costs. There will also be running costs for the asset. At the end of the asset's commercially useful life, it might have a 'residual value'. For example, it might be sold for scrap or in a second-hand market. (Items such as motor vehicles and printing machines often have a significant residual value.)

A problem with long-term forecasting of revenues, savings and costs is that forecasts can be inaccurate. However, although it is extremely difficult to produce reliable forecasts, every effort should be made to make them as reliable as possible.

- A business should try to avoid spending money on non-current assets on the basis of wildly optimistic and unrealistic forecasts.

- The assumptions on which the forecasts are based should be stated clearly. If the assumptions are clear, the forecasts can be assessed for reasonableness by the individuals who are asked to authorise the spending.

Expandable text

What financial issues will management need to satisfy themselves about in each of the following capital investment projects?

- The purchase of a new heating system to replace a worn-out one.

- The opening of an additional branch of a retail outlet.

- The purchase of an updated cutting machine to reduce scrap levels.

Solution

New heating system – that there are no cheaper or more effective systems available. Management will need to compare the various systems available to decide on the best one.

New retail outlet – that the costs incurred in opening the outlet will be recovered and a satisfactory return made.

Updated cutting machine – that the costs incurred in obtaining the machine will be less than the savings made by reducing scrap levels.

Note that although all three projects require appraisal, the heating system is compared with other options. A return is required from the retail outlet and the cutting machine must save more than it costs. Therefore to appraise a project it is important to first be clear about the objectives of the investment.

Two basic appraisal techniques are covered in this chapter:

- ROCE
- payback.

More sophisticated methods of investment appraisal are dealt with in chapter 10.

Examination questions may ask you to compare and contrast the use of these two basic techniques.

3 ROCE

This is also known as accounting rate of return (ARR).

PBIT

$$ROCE = \frac{\text{Average annual profits before interest and tax}}{\text{Initial capital costs}} \times 100\%$$

Decision rule:

- If the expected ROCE for the investment is greater than the target or hurdle rate then the project should be accepted.

This is the method that should be used unless you are told otherwise. Other versions of this calculation, which you may come across in practice, include using:

- average carrying values of the assets over their life
- first year's profits
- total profits over the whole of the project's life.

Expandable text

Illustration – ROCE

A project involves the immediate purchase of an item of plant costing $110,000. It would generate annual cash flows of $24,400 for five years, starting in Year 1. The plant purchased would have a scrap value of $10,000 in five years, when the project terminates. Depreciation is on a straight-line basis.

Calculate the ROCE.

Expandable text

Solution

Annual cash flows are taken to be profit before depreciation.

Average annual depreciation $=$ ($110,000 – $10,000) ÷ 5

$=$ $20,000

Average annual profit $=$ $24,400 – $20,000

$=$ $4,400

ROCE

$$= \frac{\text{Average annual profit}}{\text{Initial capital cost}} \times 100\%$$

$$= \frac{\$4,400 \times 100\%}{\$110,000} = 4\%$$

Expandable text

Illustration – ROCE

Using average carrying values of investment

Using the figures above, produce revised calculations based on the average carrying value of the investment.

Expandable text

Solution

Average annual profits (as before)	= $4,400
Average book value of assets	= Initial capital cost + Final scrap value ÷ 2
	= $110,000 + $10,000 2 ÷ 2
	= $60,000
ROCE	= $4,400 ÷ $60,000 × 100
	= 7.33%

Test your understanding 1

A project requires an initital investment of $800,000 and then earns net cash inflows as follows:

Year	1	2	3	4	5	6	7
Cash inflows ($000)	100	200	400	400	300	200	150

In addition, at the end of the seven-year project the assets initially purchased will be sold for $100,000. *Scrap value*

Determine the project's ROCE using:

(a) **initial capital invested**

(b) **average capital invested.**

$$\frac{800000 - 100000}{7}$$

$$Dep = 100000$$

The initial capital cost could comprise any or all of the following:

- cost of new assets bought
- net book value (NBV) of existing assets to be used in the project
- investment in working capital
- capitalised R&D expenditure (**NB** ensure this is amortised against profit).

4 Advantages and disadvantages of ROCE

Advantages include:

- simplicity
- links with other accounting measures. ✓

Disadvantages include:

- no account is taken of project life
- no account is taken of timing of cash flows
- it varies depending on accounting policies
- it may ignore working capital
- it does not measure absolute gain
- there is no definitive investment signal.

In the examination it is important that you can discuss the features of ROCE as an investment appraisal technique, in addition to being able to calculate it.

Expandable text

Advantages

Simplicity – being based on widely-reported measures of return (profits) and asset (balance sheet values), it is easily understood and easily calculated.

Links with other accounting measures – annual ROCE, calculated to assess a business or sector of a business (and therefore the investment decisions made by that business), is a widely used measure. It is expressed in percentage terms with which managers and accountants are familiar.

Disadvantages

It fails to take account of either the project life or the timing of cash flows within that life. This therefore ignores the time value of money.

It will vary with specific accounting policies, and the extent to which project costs are capitalised. Profit measurement is thus 'subjective', and ROCE figures for identical projects would vary from business to business.

It might ignore working capital requirements.

Like all rate of return measures, it is not a measurement of absolute gain in wealth for the business owners.

There is no definite investment signal. The decision to invest or not remains subjective in view of the lack of an objectively set target ROCE.

5 Accounting profits and cash flows

In capital investment appraisal it is more appropriate to evaluate future cash flows than accounting profits, because:

- profits cannot be spent
- profits are subjective
- cash is required to pay dividends.

Expandable text

Cash flows are a better measure of the suitability of a capital investment because:

- cash is what ultimately counts – profits are only a guide to cash availability: they cannot actually be spent

- profit measurement is subjective – the time period in which income and expenses are recorded, and so on, are a matter of judgement

- cash is used to pay dividends – dividends are the ultimate method of transferring wealth to equity shareholders.

In practice, the cash flow effects of a project are likely to be similar to the project's effects on profits. Major differences in cash and profit flows will be linked to the following:

- changes in working capital
- asset purchase and depreciation
- deferred taxation
- capitalisation of research and development expenditure.

6 Cash flows and relevant costs

Only relevant cash flows should be considered. These are:

- future
- incremental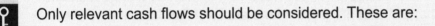
- cash-based.

Ignore:

- sunk costs
- committed costs
- non-cash items
- allocated costs.

Expandable text

The only cash flows that should be taken into consideration in capital investment appraisal are:

- cash flows that will happen in the future, and
- cash flows that will arise only if the capital project goes ahead.

These cash flows are direct revenues from the project and relevant costs. Relevant costs are future costs that will be incurred or saved as a direct consequence of undertaking the investment.

- Costs that have already been incurred are not relevant to a current decision. For example, suppose a company makes a non-returnable deposit as a down payment for an item of equipment, and then reconsiders whether it wants the equipment after all. The money that has already been spent cannot be recovered and so is not relevant to the current decision about obtaining the equipment.

- Costs that will be incurred anyway, whether or not a capital project goes ahead, cannot be relevant to a decision about investing in the project. Fixed cost expenditures are an example of 'committed costs'. For the purpose of investment appraisal, a project should not be charged with an amount for a share of fixed costs that will be incurred in any event.

- Non-cash items of cost can never be relevant to investment appraisal. In particular, the depreciation charges on a fixed asset are not relevant costs for analysis because depreciation is not a cash expenditure.

- Accounting treatment of costs is often irrelevant (e.g. depreciation, stock valuation, methods of allocating overheads) because it has no bearing on cash flows, except to the extent that it may affect taxation payable. Overheads attributed to projects should, in the examination, be taken as absorbed figures unless specified otherwise. It should be assumed there is no change to actual overhead paid, and thus no relevant cash flow.

Test your understanding 2

A company is evaluating a proposed expenditure on an item of equipment that would cost $160,000. A technical feasibility study has been carried out by consultants, at a cost of $15,000, into benefits from investing in the equipment. It has been estimated that the equipment would have a life of four years, and annual profits would be $8,000, after deducting annual depreciation of $40,000 and an annual charge of $25,000 for a share of the existing fixed cost of the company.

What are the relevant cash flows for this?

Expandable text

A manufacturing company is considering the production of a new type of widget. Each widget will take two hours to make. Fixed overheads are apportioned on the basis of $1 per labour hour. If the new widgets are produced, the company will have to employ an additional supervisor at a salary of $15,000 pa. The company will produce 10,000 widgets pa.

What are the relevant cash flows?

Solution

Only the $15,000 salary is relevant. The fixed overheads are not incremental to the decision and should be ignored.

7 Payback method of appraisal

The **payback** period is the time a project will take to pay back the money spent on it. It is based on expected cash flows and provides a measure of liquidity.

Decision rule:

- only select projects which pay back within the specified time period
- choose between options on the basis of the fastest payback
- provides a measure of liquidity.

(a) **Constant annual cash flows**

$$\text{Payback period} = \frac{\text{initial investment}}{\text{annual cash flow}}$$

Illustration 1 – Payback method of appraisal

An expenditure of $2 million is expected to generate net cash inflows of $500,000 each year for the next seven years.

What is the payback period for the project?

Expandable text

Solution

$$\text{Payback period} = \frac{\$2,000,000}{\$500,000} = 4 \text{ years}$$

Expandable text

The payback method provides a rough measure of the liquidity of a project, in other words how much annual cash flow it earns. It is not a measure of the profitability of a project over its life. In the example above, the fact that the project pays back within four years ignores the total amount of cash flows it will provide over seven years. A project costing $2 million and earning net cash inflows of $500,000 for just five years would have exactly the same payback period, even though it would not be as profitable.

A payback period may not be for an exact number of years.

Test your understanding 3

A project will involve spending $1.8 million now. Annual cash flows from the project would be $350,000.

What is the expected payback period?

Expandable text

Payback in years and months is calculated by multiplying the decimal fraction of a year by 12 months. In this example, 0.1429 years = 1.7 months (0.1429 × 12 months), which is rounded to 2 months.

(b) Uneven annual cash flows

In practice, cash flows from a project are unlikely to be constant. Where cash flows are uneven, payback is calculated by working out the cumulative cash flow over the life of the project.

KAPLAN PUBLISHING

Expandable text

Illustration – Payback method of appraisal

A project is expected to have the following cash flows:

Year	Cash flow
	$000
0	(2,000)
1	500
2	500
3	400
4	600
5	300
6	200

What is the expected payback period?

Solution

Year	Cash flow	Cumulative cash flow
	$000	$000
0	(2,000)	(2,000)
1	500	(1,500)
2	500	(1,000)
3	400	(600)
4	600	0
5	300	300
6	200	500

In the table above a column is added for cumulative cash flows for the project to date. Figures in brackets are negative cash flows.

Each year's cumulative figure is simply the cumulative figure at the start of the year plus the figure for the current year. The cumulative figure each year is therefore the expected position as at the end of that year.

As discussed above payback is not always an exact number of years.

Expandable text

Illustration - Payback method of appraisal

A project is expected to have the following cash flows:

Year	Cash flow
	$000
0	(1,900)
1	300
2	500
3	600
4	800
5	500

What is the expected payback period?

Solution

Year	Cash flow	Cumulative cash flow
	$000	$000
0	(1,900)	(1,900)
1	300	(1,600)
2	500	(1,100)
3	600	(500)
4	800	300
5	500	800

Payback is between the end of Year 3 and the end of Year 4 – that is during Year 4. Assuming a constant rate of cash flow throughout the year, payback would be after 3.625 years or 3 years 8 months.

Note that if cashflows were deemed to arise at the end of the year then the payback period would be 4 years.

KAPLAN PUBLISHING

Expandable text

If we assume a constant rate of cash flow throughout the year, we could estimate that payback will be three years plus ($500/800) of Year 4. This is because the cumulative cash flow is minus $500 at the start of the year and the Year 4 cash flow would be $800.

$500/800 = 0.625

Therefore payback is after 3.625 years.

Payback in years and months is calculated by multiplying the decimal fraction of a year by 12 months. In this example, 0.625 years = 7.5 months (0.625 × 12 months), which is rounded to 8 months.

Test your understanding 4

Calculate the payback period in years and months for the following project:

Year	Cash flow
	$000
0	(3,100)
1	1,000
2	900
3	800
4	500
5	500

8 Advantages and disadvantages of payback

Advantages include:

- it is simple
- it is useful in certain situations:
  - rapidly changing technology
  - improving investment conditions

- it favours quick return:
  - helps company growth
  - minimises risk
  - maximises liquidity
- it uses cash flows, not accounting profit.

Disadvantages include:

- it ignores returns after the payback period
- it ignores timings
- it is subjective – no definitive investment signal
- it ignores project profitability.

In the examination it is important that you can discuss the features of payback as an investment appraisal technique as well as being able to do the calculation.

Expandable text

Advantages

Simplicity – as a concept, it is easily understood and is easily calculated.

Rapidly changing technology – If new plant is likely to be scrapped in a short period because of obsolescence, a quick payback is essential.

Improving investment conditions – When investment conditions are expected to improve in the near future, attention is directed to those projects which will release funds soonest, to take advantage of the improving climate.

Payback favours projects with a quick return – It is often argued that these are to be preferred for three reasons:

(1) Rapid project payback leads to rapid company growth, but in fact such a policy will lead to many profitable investment opportunities being overlooked because their payback period does not happen to be particularly swift.

(2) Rapid payback minimises risk (the logic being that the shorter the payback period, the less there is that can go wrong). Not all risks are related to time, but payback is able to provide a useful means of assessing time risks (and only time risks). It is likely that earlier cash flows can be estimated with greater certainty.

(3) Rapid payback maximises liquidity – but liquidity problems are best dealt with separately, through cash forecasting.

Cash flows – Unlike the other traditional methods it uses cash flows, rather than profits, and so is less likely to produce an unduly optimistic figure distorted by assorted accounting conventions which might permit certain costs to be carried forward and not affect profit initially.

Disadvantages

Project returns may be ignored – cash flows arising after the payback period are totally ignored. payback ignores profitability and concentrates on cash flows and liquidity.

Timing ignored – cash flows are effectively categorised as pre-payback or post-payback, but no more accurate measure is made. In particular, the time value of money is ignored.

Lack of objectivity – there is no objective measure as to what length of time should be set as the minimum payback period. Investment decisions are therefore subjective.

Project profitability is ignored – payback takes no account of the effects on business profits and periodic performance of the project, as evidenced in the financial statements. This is critical if the business is to be reasonably viewed by users of the accounts.

Chapter summary

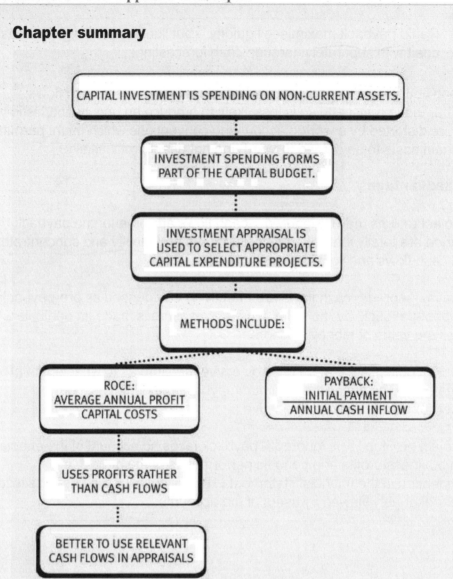

Test your understanding answers

Test your understanding 1

This uses profits rather than cash flows.

Average annual inflows = $1,750,000 ÷ 7		= $250,000
Average annual depreciation = ($800,000 − $100,000) ÷ 7		= $100,000

(A net $700,000 is being written off as depreciation over 7 years.)

Average annual profit = $250,000 − $100,000 = $150,000

The average capital invested is (800,000 + 100,000) ÷ 2 = $450,000

a. $$\text{ROCE} = \frac{\text{Average annual profit}}{\text{Initial investment}} \times 100 = \frac{\$150,000}{\$800,000} \times 100 = 33.33\%$$

b. $$\text{ROCE} = \frac{\text{Average annual profit}}{\text{Average investment}} \times 100 = \frac{\$150,000}{\$450,000} \times 100 = 18.75\%$$

Test your understanding 2

The $15,000 already spent on the feasibility study is not relevant, because it has already been spent. (It is a 'sunk cost'.) Depreciation and apportioned fixed overheads are not relevant. Depreciation is not a cash flow and apportioned fixed overheads represent costs that will be incurred anyway.

	$
Estimated profit	8,000
Add back depreciation	40,000
Add back apportioned fixed costs	25,000
Annual cash flows	73,000

The project's cash flows to be evaluated are:

Years	$
Now (Year 0) Purchase equipment	(160,000)
1-4 Cash flow from profits	73,000 each year

Test your understanding 3

$$Payback = \frac{\$1,800,000}{\$350,000} = 5.1429 \text{ years}$$

- 5.1 years
- 5 years 2 months

assuming cash flows occur evenly throughout the year.

Test your understanding 4

The payback period would be calculated as follows.

Year	Cash flow	Cumulative cash flow
	$000	$000
0	(3,100)	(3,100)
1	1,000	(2,100)
2	900	(1,200)
3	800	(400)
4	500	100
5	500	600

Payback is between the end of Year 3 and the end of Year 4, in other words during Year 4.

If we assume a constant rate of cash flow through the year, we could estimate that payback will be three years, plus ($400/500) of Year 4, which is 3.8 years.

0.8 years = 10 months (0.8 × 12)

We could therefore estimate that payback would be after 3 years 10 months.

Investment appraisal – discounted cash flow techniques

Chapter learning objectives

Upon completion of this chapter you will be able to:

- explain the concept of the time value of money

- calculate the future value of a sum by compounding

- calculate the present value (PV) of a single sum using formula

- calculate the PV of a single sum using discount tables

- calculate the PV of an annuity using formula

- calculate the PV of an annuity using annuity tables

- calculate the PV of a perpetuity using formula

- calculate the PV of advanced annuities and perpetuities

- calculate the PV of delayed annuities and perpetuities

- explain the basic principle behind the concept of a cost of capital

- calculate the net present value (NPV) of an investment and use it to appraise the proposal

- discuss the usefulness of NPV as an investment appraisal method and its superiority over non-discounted cash flows (DCF) methods

- calculate the internal rate of return (IRR) of an investment and use it to appraise the proposal

- discuss the usefulness of IRR as an investment appraisal method and its superiority over non-DCF methods

- discuss the relative merits of NPV and IRR.

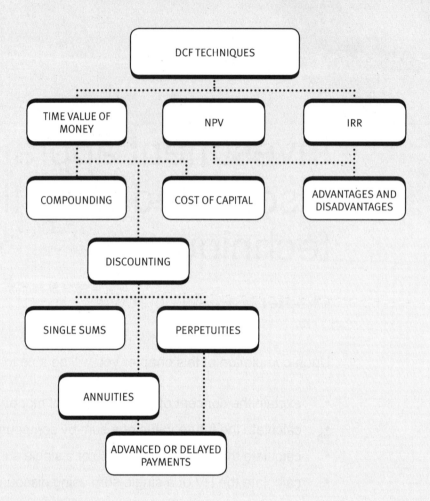

1 The time value of money

Money received today is worth more than the same sum received in the future, i.e. it has a **time value.**

This occurs for three reasons:

- potential for earning interest/cost of finance
- impact of inflation
- effect of risk.

This is a key concept in investment appraisal.

DCF techniques take account of this time value of money when appraising investments.

Expandable text

Potential for earning interest

If a capital investment is to be justified, it needs to earn at least a minimum amount of profit, so that the return compensates the investor for both the amount invested and also for the length of time before the profits are made. For example, if a company could invest $80,000 now to earn revenue of $82,000 in one week's time, a profit of $2,000 in seven days would be a very good return. However, if it takes four years to earn the money, the return would be very low.

Therefore money has a time value. It can be invested to earn interest or profits, so it is better to have $1 now than in one year's time. This is because $1 now can be invested for the next year to earn a return, whereas $1 in one year's time cannot. Another way of looking at the time value of money is to say that $1 in six years' time is worth less than $1 now.

Impact of inflation

In most countries, in most years prices rise as a result of inflation. Therefore funds received today will buy more than the same amount a year later, as prices will have risen in the meantime. The funds are subject to a loss of purchasing power over time.

Risk

The earlier cash flows are due to be received, the more certain they are – there is less chance that events will prevent payment. Earlier cash flows are therefore considered to be more valuable.

2 Compounding

A sum invested today will earn interest. Compounding calculates the future or terminal value of a given sum invested today for a number of years.

To compound a sum, the figure is increased by the amount of interest it would earn over the period.

Illustration 1 – Compounding

An investment of $100 is to be made today. What is the value of the investment after two years if the interest rate is 10%?

Expandable text

Solution

		$
Value after one year	100 × 1.1 =	110
Value after two years	110 × 1.1 =	121

The $100 will be worth $121 in two years at an interest rate of 10%.

The formula for calculating the future value of a sum is:

$$F = P(1 + r)^n$$

where F = Future value after n periods

P = Present or Initial value

r = Rate of interest per period

n = Number of periods

The terminal value is the value, in n years' time, of a sum invested now, at an interest rate of r%.

Expandable text

You have $5,000 to invest now for six years at an interest rate of 5% pa. What will be the value of the investment after six years?

Solution

$F = \$5{,}000 \, (1 + 0.05)^6$

$= \$5{,}000 \times 1.3401$

$= \$6{,}700$

3 Discounting

In a potential investment project, cash flows will arise at many different points in time. To make a useful comparison of the different flows, they must all be converted to a common point in time, usually the present day, i.e. the cash flows are discounted.

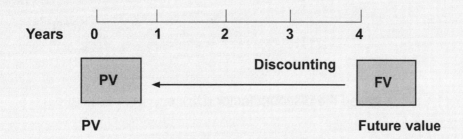

Assumptions used in discounting

Unless the examiner tells you otherwise, the following assumptions are made about cash flows when discounting:

- all cash flows occur at the start or end of a year
- initial investments occur at once (T_0)
- other cash flows start in one year's time (T_1).

Expandable text

- All cash flows occur at the start or end of a year.

Although in practice many cash flows accrue throughout the year, for discounting purposes they are all treated as occurring at the start or end of a year. Note also that if today (T_0) is 01/01/20X0, the dates 31/12/20X1 and 01/01/20X2, although technically separate days, can be treated for discounting as occurring at the same point in time, i.e. at T_1.

- Initial investments occur at once (T_0), other cash flows start in one year's time (T_1).

In project appraisal, the investment needs to be made before the cash flows can accrue. Therefore, unless the examiner specifies otherwise, it is assumed that investments occur in advance. The first cash flows associated with running the project are therefore assumed to occur one year after the project begins, i.e. at T_1.

Discounting a single sum

The PV is the cash equivalent now of money receivable/payable at some future date.

The PV of a future sum can be calculated using the formula:

$$P = \frac{F}{(1+r)^n} = F \times (1+r)^{-n}$$

$(1 + r)^{-n}$ is called the discount factor (DF), e.g. if r = 10% and n = 5.

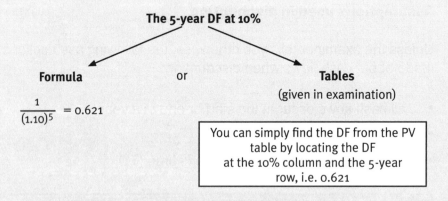

The 5-year DF at 10%

Formula　　　　or　　　　**Tables**
　　　　　　　　　　　　　　　(given in examination)

$$\frac{1}{(1.10)^5} = 0.621$$

You can simply find the DF from the PV table by locating the DF at the 10% column and the 5-year row, i.e. 0.621

Illustration 2 – Discounting a single sum

What is the PV of $115,000 receivable in nine years' time if r = 6%? Show your answer using both the formula and the DF tables.

Solution

$$P = \frac{F}{(1+r)^n} = \frac{115{,}000}{(1+0.06)^9} = \$68{,}068 \text{ (using formula)}$$

P = $115,000 × 0.592 = $68,080 (using tables)

The difference between the two answers is caused by rounding.

Expandable text

What amount should be invested now to receive \$10,000 in four years' time if r = 8% pa.

Solution

The amount to be invested is the PV of the future sum.

$P = \$10{,}000/(1.08)^4 = \$7{,}350$

P = $10,000 × 0.735 = $7,350 (using tables).

Test your understanding 1

The cash flows for a project have been estimated as follows:

Year	$
0	(25,000)
1	6,000
2	10,000
3	8,000
4	7,000

The cost of capital is 6%.

Convert these cash flows to a PV.

Add up the total of the PVs for each of the years.

Discounting annuities

An annuity is a constant annual cash flow for a number of years. The PV can be found using an annuity formula or annuity tables.

Illustration 3 – Discounting annuities

A payment of $1,000 is to be made every year for 6 years, the first payment occurring in one year's time. The interest rate is 10%. What is the PV of the annuity?

Solution

The PV of an annuity could be found by adding the PVs of each payment separately.

Time	Payment	DF @ 10%(from tables)	PV
	$		$
T1	1,000	0.909	909
T2	1,000	0.826	826
T3	1,000	0.751	751
T4	1,000	0.683	683
T5	1,000	0.621	621
T6	1,000	0.564	564
		_____	_____
		4.354	4,354
		_____	_____

However, you can see from the table that the sum of all the DF is 4.354.

Therefore the PV can be found more quickly:

$1,000 × 4.354 = $4,354.

The **annuity factor** (AF) is the name given to the sum of the individual DF.

The PV of an annuity is found using the formula:

PV = Annuity × AF

For a six-year annuity at 10%:

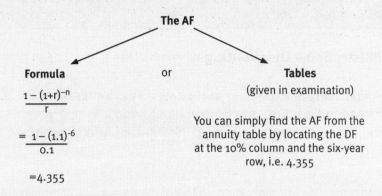

The AF

Formula　　　　or　　　　　**Tables**
(given in examination)

$$\frac{1-(1+r)^{-n}}{r}$$

You can simply find the AF from the
annuity table by locating the DF
at the 10% column and the six-year
row, i.e. 4.355

$$= \frac{1-(1.1)^{-6}}{0.1}$$

$$= 4.355$$

Test your understanding 2

A payment of \$3,600 is to be made every year for seven years, the first payment occurring in one year's time. The interest rate is 8%. What is the PV of the annuity.

Discounting perpetuities

A perpetuity is an annual cash flow that occurs forever.

It is often described by examiners as a cash flow continuing 'for the foreseeable future'.

The PV of a perpetuity is found using the formula:

$$PV = \frac{cashflow}{r}$$

or

$$PV = cashflow \times \frac{1}{r}$$

$\dfrac{1}{r}$ is known as the perpetuity factor.

Expandable text

Illustration – Discounting perpetuities

A company is expecting to receive rental income of $24,300 for the foreseeable future, the first receipt to occur in one year's time. What is the PV of the rental income if the interest rate is expected to be 4%?

Expandable text

Solution

$$PV = 24{,}300 \times \frac{1}{0.04} = \$607{,}500$$

Test your understanding 3

What is the PV of a payment of $5,736 to be made annually for the foreseeable future, starting in one year's time, if the interest rate is 12%?

Advanced annuities and perpetuities

Some regular cash flows may start at T_0 rather than T_1.

Calculate the PV by ignoring the payment at T_0 when considering the number of cash flows and then adding one to the annuity or perpetuity factor.

Expandable text

Illustration – Advanced annuities and perpetuities

A 5-year $600 annuity is starting today. Interest rates are 10%. Find the PV of the annuity.

Solution

This is essentially a standard 4-year annuity with an additional payment at T_0. The PV could be calculated as follows:

	T_0	T_1	T_2	T_3	T_4
CF	600	600	600	600	600
PV	600 +		$600 \times$ 4-year 10% AF		

PV = 600 + 600 × 3.17 = 600 + 1902 = $2,502

The same answer can be found more quickly by adding 1 to the AF:

PV = 600 × (1 + 3.17) = 600 × 4.17 = $2,502.

Expandable text

Illustration – Advanced annuities and perpetuities

A perpetuity of $2,000 is due to commence immediately. The interest rate is 9%. What is the PV?

Expandable text

Solution

This is essentially a standard perpetuity with an additional payment at T_0. The PV could be calculated as follows:

T_0		T_1	T_2	T_3	T_4 ....
2,000		$2,000 \to \infty$			

$$PV \left(2000\right) + \left(2000 \quad \times 9\% \text{ perpetuity formula}\right)$$

Again, the same answer can be found more quickly by adding 1 to the perpetuity factor.

$$2000 \times \left(1 + \frac{1}{0.09}\right) = 2000 \times 12.11 = \$24{,}222$$

Test your understanding 4

Find the PV of the following cash flows:

(1) A fifteen year annuity of $300 starting at once. Interest rates are 6%.

(2) A perpetuity of $33,000 commencing immediately. Interest rates are 22%.

Delayed annuities and perpetuities

Some regular cash flows may start later than T_1.

These are dealt with by:

(1) applying the appropriate factor to the cash flow as normal

(2) discounting your answer back to T_0.

Illustration – Delayed annuities and perpetuities

What is the PV of $200 incurred each year for four years, starting in three year's time, if the discount rate is 5%?

Solution

Method: A four-year annuity starting at T_3
(1-4)

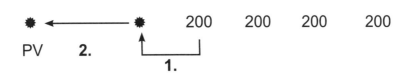

Step 1.   Discount the annuity as usual

200 × 4yr 5% AF = 200 × 3.456 = 709.2

Note that this gives the value of the annuity at T_2

Step 2.   Discount the answer back to T_0

709.2 × 2yr 5% DF = 709.2 × 0.907 = $643

Annuity or perpetuity factors will discount the cash flows back to give the value one year before the first cash flow arose. For standard annuities and perpetuities this gives the present (T_0) value since the first cash flow started at T_1.

However for delayed cash flows, applying the factor will find the value of the cash flows one year before they began, which in this example is T_2. To find the PV, an additional calculation is required – the value must be discounted back to T_0.

Care must be taken to discount back the appropriate number of years. The figure here was discounted back two years because the first step gave the value at T_2. It can help to draw a timeline as above and mark on the effect of the first step (as shown with a 1. here) to help you remember.

Test your understanding 5

The financial director of A Co has prepared the following schedule to enable her to appraise a new project. Interest rates are 10%. She wants to calculate the PV of the cash flows using two different assumptions regarding the project duration.

The assumptions are as follows:

A   That the real annual cash flow will be $250,000 from Year 4 for the foreseeable future.

B   That the real annual cash flow will be $250,000 from Year 4 to Year 18.

Year	T_0	T_1	T_2	T	Assumption (a) T_4onwards	Assumption (b) T_4-T_{18}
	$000	$000	$000	$000	$000	$000
Net cash flow	(2,000)	(440)	363	399	250	250

Find the sum of the PVs (known as the NPV) from the project under both assumptions.

4 A cost of capital

In the above discussions we referred to the rate of interest. There are a number of alternative terms used to refer to the rate a firm should use to take account of the time value of money:

- cost of capital
- discount rate
- required return.

Whatever term is used, the rate of interest used for discounting reflects the cost of the finance that will be tied up in the investment.

5 The NPV

To appraise the overall impact of a project using DCF techniques involves discounting all the relevant cash flows associated with the project back to their PV.

If we treat outflows of the project as negative and inflows as positive, the NPV of the project is the sum of the PVs of all flows that arise as a result of doing the project.

The NPV represents the surplus funds (after funding the investment) earned on the project, therefore:

- if the NPV is positive – the project is financially viable
- if the NPV is zero – the project breaks even
- if the NPV is negative – the project is not financially viable
- if the company has two or more mutually exclusive projects under consideration it should choose the one with the highest NPV
- the NPV gives the impact of the project on shareholder wealth.

Expandable text

What does the NPV actually mean?

Suppose, in an investment problem, we calculate the NPV of certain cash flows at 12% to be – $97, and at 10% to be zero, and yet at 8% the NPV of the same cash flows is + $108. Another way of expressing this is as follows.

- If the funds were borrowed at 12% the investor would be $97 out of pocket – i.e. the investment earns a yield below the cost of capital.

- If funds were borrowed at 10% the investor would break even – i.e. the investment yields a return equal to the cost of capital.

- If funds were borrowed at 8% the investor would be $108 in pocket – i.e. the investment earns a return in excess of the cost of capital.

In other words, a positive NPV is an indication of the surplus funds available to the investor now as a result of accepting the project.

Illustration 4 – The NPV

An organisation is considering a capital investment in new equipment. The estimated cash flows are as follows.

Year	Cash flow
	$
0	(240,000)
1	80,000
2	120,000
3	70,000
4	40,000
5	20,000

The company's cost of capital is 9%.

Calculate the NPV of the project to assess whether it should be undertaken.

Expandable text

Solution

Year	Cash flow	DF at 9%	PV
	$		$
0	(240,000)	1.000	(240,000)
1	80,000	0.917	73,360
2	120,000	0.842	101,040
3	70,000	0.772	54,040
4	40,000	0.708	28,320
5	20,000	0.650	13,000
NPV			+ 29,760

The PV of cash inflows exceeds the PV of cash outflows by $29,760, which means that the project will earn a DCF return in excess of 9%, i.e. it will earn a surplus of $29,760 after paying the cost of financing. It should therefore be undertaken.

Expandable text

A firm is considering investing in a new delivery vehicle which will make savings over the current out-sourced service.

The cost of the vehicle is $35,000 and it will have a five-year life.

The cash savings it will make over the period are as follows:

Year	$
1	8,000
2	9,000
3	12,000
4	9,500
5	9,000

The firm currently has a required return of 13% and this is considered to be its cost of capital. However there is some concern about this figure, and the investment is to be appraised using 13% and then again at 11% and 8%.

DFS

Year	13%	13%	13%
1	0.855	0.901	0.926
2	0.783	0.812	0.857
3	0.693	0.731	0.794
4	0.613	0.659	0.735
5	0.543	0.593	0.681

Calculate the NPV of the investment at each of the three discount rates given, and for each assumption, recommend whether or not the Investment should go ahead.

Solution

Discount rate 13%

Discount rate 13%

Year	Outflow	Inflow	DF @ 13%	NPV
	$	$		$
0	(35,000)		1.000	(35,000)
1		8,000	0.885	7,080
2		9,000	0.783	7,047
3		12,000	0.693	8,316
4		9,500	0.613	5,824
5		9,000	0.543	4,887

NPV (1,846)

Discount rate 11%

Year	Outflow	Inflow	DF @ 8%	NPV
	$	$		$
0	(35,000)		1.000	(35,000)
1		8,000	0.901	7,208
2		9,000	0.812	7,308
3		12,000	0.731	8,772
4		9,500	0.659	6,261
5		9,000	0.593	5,337

NPV (114)

		Discount rate 8%		
Year	**Outflow**	**Inflow**	**DF @ 8%**	**NPV**
	$	$		$
0	(35,000)		1.000	(35,000)
1		8,000	0.926	7,408
2		9,000	0.857	7,713
3		12,000	0.794	9,528
4		9,500	0.735	6,983
5		9,000	0.681	6,129
				NPV 2,761

Recommendation

At a cost of capital of 13%, the NPV is negative, i.e. the investment would reduce funds by $1,846, and so it should be rejected.

At a cost of capital of 11%, the NPV is also negative, but funds would be reduced by just $114. It should be rejected, but only just. In fact, at a discount rate of 10.87% the project exactly breaks even. This breakeven rate is known as the IRR and it is covered shortly.

At a cost of capital of 8%, the NPV is positive, i.e. the investment would increase funds by $2,761, and so should be accepted.

6 Advantages and disadvantages of using NPV

Advantages

Theoretically the NPV method of investment appraisal is superior to all others. This is because it:

- considers the time value of money
- is an absolute measure of return
- is based on cash flows not profits
- considers the whole life of the project
- should lead to maximisation of shareholder wealth.

Disadvantages

- It is difficult to explain to managers
- It requires knowledge of the cost of capital
- It is relatively complex.

Expandable text

When appraising projects or investments, NPV is considered to be superior (in theory) to most other methods. This is because it:

- considers the time value of money – discounting cash flows to PV takes account of the impact of interest, inflation and risk over time. (See later sessions for more on inflation and risk.) These significant issues are ignored by the basic methods of payback and annual rate of return (ARR)

- is an absolute measure of return – the NPV of an investment represents the actual surplus raised by the project. This allows a business to plan more effectively

- is based on cash flows not profits – the subjectivity of profits makes them less reliable than cash flows and therefore less appropriate for decision making. Neither ARR nor payback is an absolute measure

- considers the whole life of the project – methods such as payback only consider the earlier cash flows associated with the project. NPV takes account of all relevant flows associated with the project. Discounting the flows takes account of the fact that later flows are less reliable which ARR ignores

- should lead to maximisation of shareholder wealth. If the cost of capital reflects the investors' (i.e. shareholders') required return, then the NPV reflects the theoretical increase in their wealth (see session 18 later). For a company, this is considered to be the primary objective of the business.

However, there are some potential drawbacks:

- It is difficult to explain to managers. To understand the meaning of the NPV calculated requires an understanding of discounting. The method is not as intuitive as techniques such as payback.

- It requires knowledge of the cost of capital. As we will see later (session 18), the calculation of the cost of capital is, in practice, more complex than identifying interest rates. It involves gathering data and making a number of calculations based on that data and some estimates. The process may be deemed too protracted for the appraisal to be carried out.

- It is relatively complex. For the reasons explained above, NPV may be rejected in favour of simpler techniques.

7 IRR

The IRR is another project appraisal method using DCF techniques.

The IRR represents the discount rate at which the NPV of an investment is zero. As such it represents a breakeven cost of capital.

Decision rule:

- projects should be accepted if their IRR is greater than the cost of capital.

Expandable text

Using the NPV method, PVs are calculated by discounting cash flows at a given cost of capital, and the difference between the PV of costs and the PV of benefits is the NPV. In contrast, the IRR method of DCF analysis is to calculate the exact DCF rate of return that the project is expected to achieve.

If an investment has a positive NPV, it means it is earning more than the cost of capital. If the NPV is negative, it is earning less than the cost of capital. This means that if the NPV is zero, it will be earning exactly the cost of capital.

Conversely, the percentage return on the investment must be the rate of discount or cost of capital at which the NPV equals zero. This rate of return is called the IRR, or the DCF yield and if it is higher than the target rate of return then the project is financially worth undertaking.

The IRR may be calculated by a linear interpolation, i.e. by assuming a linear relationship between the NPV and the discount rate. Plotting a graph would give an approximate IRR, but the same point can also be found using a formula. It involves finding two NPVs at two different rates of interest and interpolating between them (that is, assuming the points are joined by a straight line). This gives an estimate of the IRR. (The exact IRR requires a more complex technique, best carried out using an Excel spreadsheet).

This technique can be illustrated on the graph below, which plots the NPV of an investment against the discount rate and shows both the true and estimated IRRs.

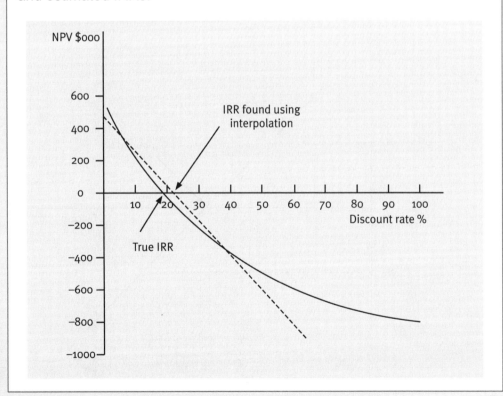

Calculating the IRR using linear interpolation

The steps in linear interpolation are:

(1) Calculate two NPVs for the project at two different costs of capital

(2) Use the following formula to find the IRR:

$$IRR = L + \frac{N_L}{N_L - N_H} \times (H - L)$$

where:

L = Lower rate of interest

H = Higher rate of interest

N_L = NPV at lower rate of interest

N_H = NPV at higher rate of interest.

The diagram below shows the IRR as estimated by the formula.

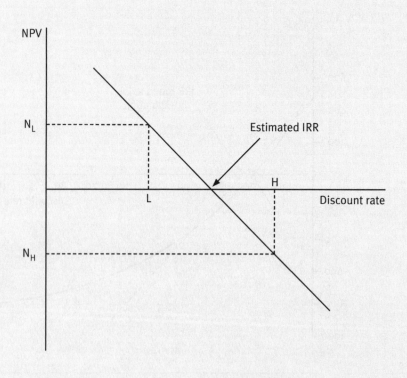

Expandable text

Step 1 Calculate two NPVs for the project at two different costs of capital. You can choose any costs of capital and get a fair result. However, it helps to find two costs of capital for which the NPV is close to 0, because the IRR will be a value close to them. Ideally, you should use one cost of capital where the NPV is positive and the other cost of capital where the NPV is negative, although this is not essential.

Step 2 Once the two NPVs have been calculated, they and their associated costs of capital can be used to calculate the IRR. In other words, we can estimate the IRR by finding the point where a line joining these points would cross the x-axis (the point where the NPV is zero) in a graph plotting the project NPV against various discount rates.

Illustration 5 – Calculating the IRR using linear interpolation

A potential project's predicted cash flows give a NPV of $50,000 at a discount rate of 10% and –$10,000 at a rate of 15%.

Calculate the IRR.

Expandable text

$$IRR = 10\% + \frac{50,000}{50,000-(-10,000)} \times (15\%-10\%) = 14.17\%$$

For the examination the choice of rates to estimate the IRR is less important than your ability to perform the calculation to estimate it.

Test your understanding 6

A business undertakes high-risk investments and requires a minimum expected rate of return of 17% pa on its investments. A proposed capital investment has the following expected cash flows:

Year	$
0	(50,000)
1	18,000
2	25,000
3	20,000
4	10,000

(1) **Calculate the NPV of the project if the cost of capital is 15%.**

(2) **Calculate the NPV of the project if the cost of capital is 20%.**

(3) **Use the NPVs you have calculated to estimate the IRR of the project.**

(4) **Recommend, on financial grounds alone, whether this project should go ahead.**

Calculating the IRR of a project with even cash flows

There is a simpler technique available, using annuity tables, if the project cash flows are annuities.

(1) Find the cumulative DF, Initial investment ÷ Annual inflow

(2) Find the life of the project, n.

(3) Look along the n year row of the cumulative DF until the closest value is found.

(4) The column in which this figure is found is the IRR.

Expandable text

Illustration – Calculating IRR of a project with even cash flows

Find the IRR of a project with an initial investment of $1.5 million and three years of inflows of $700,000 starting in one year.

Expandable text

Solution

NPV calculation:

Time		Cash flow $000	DF (c) %	PV $000
0	Investment	(1,500)	1	(1,500)
1-3	Inflow	700	(b)	(a)
				_____
NPV				Nil
				_____

- The aim is to find the discount rate (c) that produces an NPV of nil.
- Therefore the PV of inflows (a) must equal the PV of outflows, $1,500,000.
- If the PV of inflows (a) is to be $1,500,000 and the size of each inflow is $700,000, the DF required (b) must be 1,500,000 ÷ 700,000 = 2.143.
- The discount rate (c) for which this is the 3-year factor can be found by looking along the 3-year row of the cumulative DFS shown in the annuity table.
- The figure of 2.140 appears under the 19% column suggesting an IRR of 19% is the closest.

Calculating the IRR of a project where the cash flows are perpetuities

$$\text{IRR of a perpetuity} = \frac{\text{Annual inflow}}{\text{Initial investment}} \times 100$$

Expandable text

Illustration – Calculating IRR where cash flows are perpetuities

Find the IRR of an investment that costs $20,000 and generates $1,600 for an indefinitely long period.

Expandable text

Solution

$$IRR = \frac{\text{Annual inflow}}{\text{Initial investment}} \times 100 = \frac{\$1,600}{\$20,000} \times 100 = 8\%$$

Test your understanding 7

Find the IRR of an investment of $50,000 if the inflows are:

(a) $5,000 in perpetuity

(b) $8,060 for eight years.

8 Advantages and disadvantages of IRR

Advantages

The IRR has a number of benefits, e.g. it:

- considers the time value of money
- is a percentage and therefore easily understood
- uses cash flows not profits
- considers the whole life of the project
- means a firm selecting projects where the IRR exceeds the cost of capital should increase shareholders' wealth.

Disadvantages

- It is not a measure of absolute profitability.
- Interpolation only provides an estimate and an accurate estimate requires the use of a spreadsheet programme.
- It is fairly complicated to calculate.
- Non-conventional cash flows may give rise to multiple IRRs.

Advantages:

- IRR considers the time value of money. The current value earned from an investment project is therefore more accurately measured. As discussed above this is a significant improvement over the basic methods.

- IRR is a percentage and therefore easily understood. Although managers may not completely understand the detail of the IRR, the concept of a return earned is familiar and the IRR can be simply compared with the required return of the organisation.

- IRR uses cash flows not profits. These are less subjective as discussed above.

- IRR considers the whole life of the project rather than ignoring later flows (which would occur with payback for example).

- IRR a firm selecting projects where the IRR exceeds the cost of capital should increase shareholders' wealth. This holds true provided the project cash flows follow the standard pattern of an outflow followed by a series of inflows, as in the investment examples above.

However there are a number of difficulties with the IRR approach:

- It is not a measure of absolute profitability. A project of $1,000 invested now and paying back $1,100 in a year's time has an IRR of 10%. If a company's required return is 6%, then the project is viable according to the IRR rule but most businesses would consider the absolute return too small to be worth the investment.

- Interpolation only provides an estimate (and an accurate estimate requires the use of a spreadsheet programme). The cost of capital calculation itself is also only an estimate and if the margin between required return and the IRR is small, this lack of accuracy could actually mean the wrong decision is taken.

- For example if the cost of capital is found to be 8% (but is actually 8.7%) and the project IRR is calculated as 9.2% (but is actually 8.5%) the project would be wrongly accepted. Note that where such a small margin exists, the project's success would be considered to be sensitive to the discount rate (see session 12 on risk).

- Non-conventional cash flows may give rise to no IRR or multiple IRRs. For example a project with an outflow at T0 and T2 but income at T1 could, depending on the size of the cash flows, have a number of different profiles on a graph (see below). Even where the project does have one IRR, it can be seen from the graph that the decision rule would lead to the wrong result as the project does not earn a positive NPV at any cost of capital.

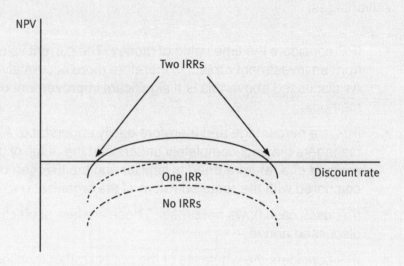

9 NPV versus IRR

Both NPV and IRR are investment appraisal techniques which discount cash flows and are superior to the basic techniques discussed in the previous session. However only NPV can be used to distinguish between two mutually-exclusive projects, as the diagram below demonstrates:

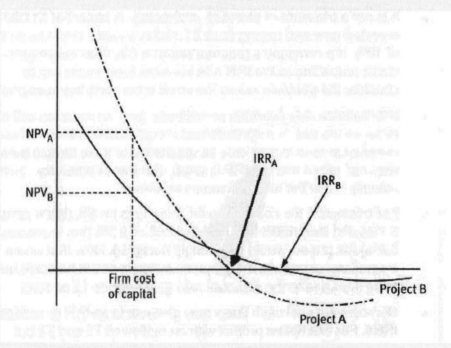

The profile of project A is such that it has a lower IRR and applying the IRR rule would prefer project B. However in absolute terms, A has the higher NPV at the company's cost of capital and should therefore be preferred.

NPV is therefore the better technique for choosing between projects.

The advantage of NPV is that it tells us the absolute increase in shareholder wealth as a result of accepting the project, at the current cost of capital. The IRR simply tells us how far the cost of capital could increase before the project would not be worth accepting.

Expandable text

Explain which of the factors impacting projects are taken into account when discounting and give two advantages that the use of DCF techniques has over the basic investment techniques covered in the previous session.

Solution

Discounting takes into account the impact over time of:

- interest
- inflation
- risk.

DCF techniques are superior because they:

- take account of the time value of money. They do this by building the impact of the factors above into the appraisal via the discount rate
- should ensure that projects accepted will increase the shareholders' wealth.

Chapter summary

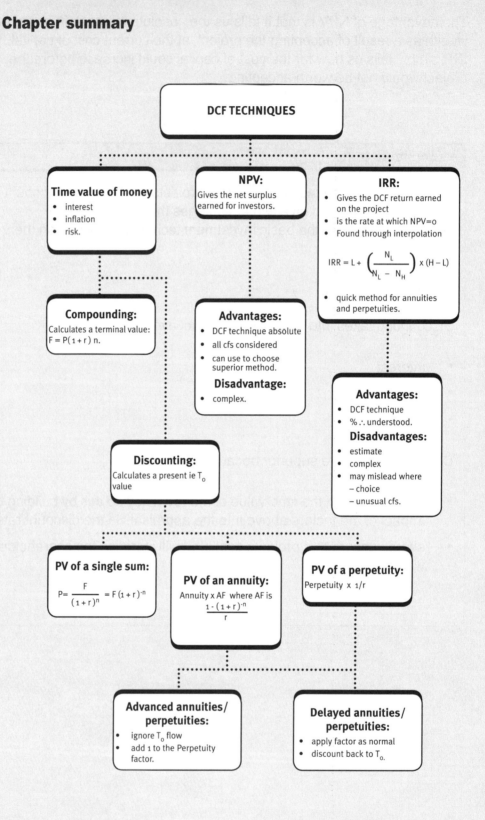

Test your understanding answers

Test your understanding 1

Year	Cash flow	DF	PV
	$	at 6%	$
0	(25,000)	1.000	(25,000)
1	6,000	0.943	5,658
2	10,000	0.890	8,900
3	8,000	0.840	6,720
4	7,000	0.792	5,544
			+ 1,822

As we will soon see, $1,822 is known as the **NPV** of the project.

Test your understanding 2

Using the formula:

$$\frac{1-(1+r)^{-n}}{r} = \frac{1-(1.08)^{-7}}{0.08} = 5.206$$

$3,600 × 5.206 = $18,741.60

Note that the AF could have been taken straight from the tables.

Test your understanding 3

$$PV = \frac{5,736 × 1}{0.12} = \$47,800$$

Test your understanding 4

(1) This is a standard 14-year annuity with one additional payment at T_0.

Step 1: Look up the 14-year AF ⇨

AF = 9.295

Step 2: Add 1 ⇨ 9.295 + 1 = 10.295

Step 3: Calculate the PV ⇨300 × 10.295 = $3,088.50

(2) This is simply a standard perpetuity with one additional payment at T_0.

Step 1: Calculate the perpetuity factor ⇨ 1/0.22 = 4.545

Step 2: Add 1 ⇨ 4.545 + 1 = 5.545

Step 3: Calculate the PV ⇨ 33,000 × 5.545 = $182,982

Test your understanding 5

Year	T_0	T_1	T_2	T_3	Assumption (a) T_4 onwards	Assumption (b) T_4 - T_{18}
	$000	$000	$000	$000	$000	$000
Net cash flow	(2,000)	(440)	363	399	250	250
Perpetuity factor (here discounts the cash flow to T_3)					$1 \div 0.1 = 10$	
AF (here discounts the cash flow to T_3)						15-yr 10% AF =7.606
DFs @ 10%	1.000	0.909	0.826	0.751	0.751	0.751
PV	(2,000)	(400)	300	300	1,878	1,428
NPV (a)					78	
NPV (b)						(372)

Test your understanding 6

Year	Cash flow	DF @ 15%	PV @ 15%	DF @ 20%	PV @ 20%
	$		$		$
0	(50,000)	1.000	(50,000)	1.000	(50,000)
1	18,000	0.870	15,660	0.833	14,994
2	25,000	0.756	18,900	0.694	17,350
3	20,000	0.658	13,160	0.579	11,580
4	10,000	0.572	5,720	0.482	4,820
NPV			+ 3,440		(1,256)

The IRR is above 15% but below 20%.

Using the interpolation method:

(1) The NPV is + 3,440 at 15%.

(2) The NPV is – 1,256 at 20%.

(3) The estimated IRR is therefore:

$$\text{IRR} = 15\% + \frac{3,440}{(440 - (-1,256))} \times (20 - 15)\%$$

$$= 15\% \quad + 3.7\%$$

$$= 18.7\%$$

(4) The project is expected to earn a DCF return in excess of the target rate of 17%, so on financial grounds (ignoring risk) it is a worthwhile investment.

Test your understanding 7

a. $\text{IRR} = \dfrac{\text{Annual inflow}}{\text{Initial investment}} \times 100 = \dfrac{\$5,000}{\$50,000} \times 100 = 10\%$

b. NPV calculation

Time		Cash flow $	DF(c) %	PV $
0	Investment	(50,000)	1	(50,000)
1-8	Inflow	8,060	(b)	(a)
			NPV	Nil

- The aim is to find the discount rate (c) that produces an NPV of nil.
- Therefore the PV of inflows (a) must equal the PV of outflows, $50,000.
- If the PV of inflows (a) is to be $50,000 and the size of each inflow is $8,060, the DF required must be 50,000 ÷ 8,060 = 6.20.
- The discount rate (c) for which this is the 8-year factor can be found by looking along the 8-year row of the cumulative DFS shown in the annuity table.
- The figure of $6.210 appears under the 6% column suggesting an IRR of 6% is the closest.

Investment appraisal – further aspects of discounted cash flows (DCF)

Chapter learning objectives

Upon completion of this chapter you will be able to:

- explain the impact of inflation on interest rates and define and distinguish between real and nominal (money) interest rates

- explain the difference between the real terms and nominal terms approaches to investment appraisal

- use the nominal (money) terms approach to appraise an investment

- use the real terms approach to appraise an investment

- explain the impact of tax on DCF appraisals

- calculate the tax cash flows associated with capital allowances and incorporate them into net present values (NPV) calculations

- calculate the tax cash flows associated with taxable profits and incorporate them into NPV calculations

- calculate and apply before- and after-tax discount rates

- explain the impact of working capital on an NPV calculation and incorporate working capital flows into NPV calculations.

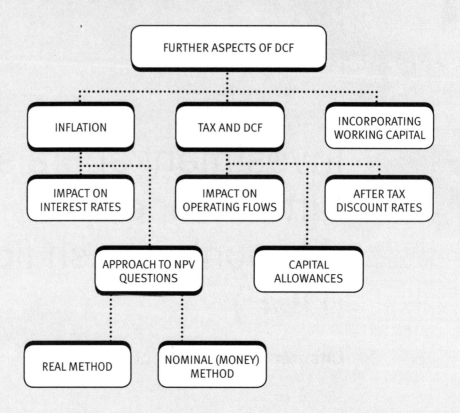

1 The relationship between inflation rates and interest rates

Inflation is a general increase in prices leading to a general decline in the real value of money.

In times of inflation, the fund providers will require a return made up of two elements:

- real return for the use of their funds (i.e. the return they would want if there were no inflation in the economy)

- additional return to compensate for inflation.

The overall required return is called the money or nominal rate of return.

Expandable text

Illustration – Relationship between inflation and interest rates

An investor is prepared to invest $100 for one year.

He requires a real return of 10% pa.

In addition, he requires compensation for loss of purchasing power resulting from inflation which is currently running at 5% pa.

What money rate of return will he require?

Expandable text

Solution

Just to compensate for inflation, his money needs to increase by 5%, to $100 × 1.05 = $105.

To give a real return on top of this, it must further increase by 10%, to $105 × 1.1 = $115.50.

Thus his money must increase overall by 1.05 × 1.1 = 1.155, i.e. by 15.5%.

So the investor's actual required return is 15.5%.

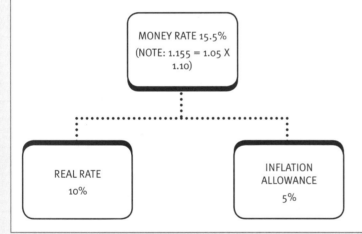

The real and money (nominal) returns are linked by the formula:

$(1 + i) = (1 + r)(1 + h)$

where

i = money rate

r = real rate

h = inflation

Expandable text

$1,000 is invested in an account that pays 10% interest pa. Inflation is currently 7% pa. Find the real return on the investment.

Solution

Real return = $1,000 × 1.1/1.07 = $1.028. A return of 2.8%.

Test your understanding 1

If the real rate of interest is 8% and the rate of inflation is 5%, what should the money rate of interest be?

2 Dealing with inflation in NPV calculations

In investment appraisal two types of inflation need consideration:

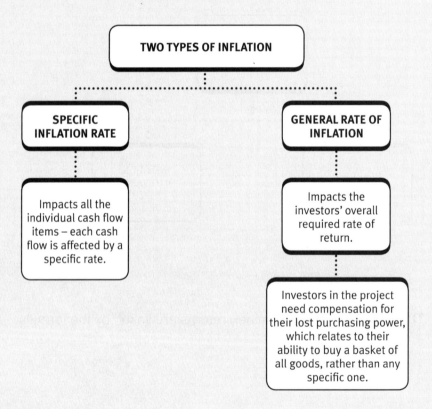

This inflation therefore impacts NPV calculation in two ways.

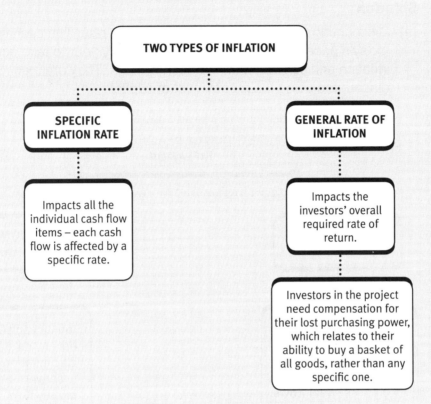

This inflationary impact can be dealt with in two different ways – both methods give the same NPV.

Illustration – Dealing with inflation in NPV calculations

Storm Co is evaluating Project X, which requires an initial investment of $50,000. Expected net cash flows are $20,000 pa for four years at today's prices. However these are expected to rise by 5.5% pa because of inflation. The firm's cost of capital is 15%. Find the NPV by:

(a) discounting money cash flows

(b) discounting real cash flows.

Solution

(a) Discounting money cash flow at the money rate: The cash flows at today's prices are inflated by 5.5% for every year to take account of inflation and convert them into money flows. They are then discounted using the money cost of capital.

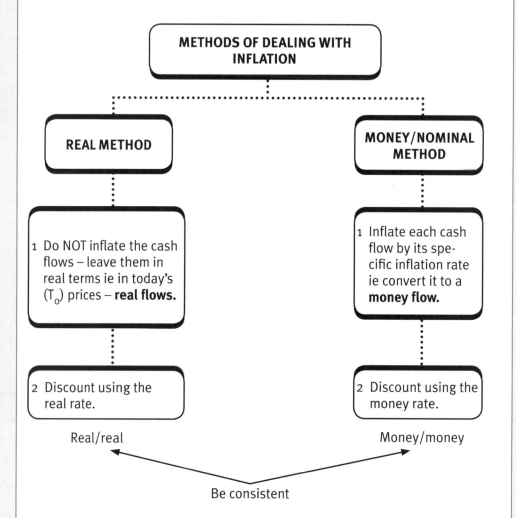

METHODS OF DEALING WITH INFLATION

REAL METHOD

1 Do NOT inflate the cash flows – leave them in real terms ie in today's (T_o) prices – **real flows.**

2 Discount using the real rate.

Real/real

MONEY/NOMINAL METHOD

1 Inflate each cash flow by its specific inflation rate ie convert it to a **money flow.**

2 Discount using the money rate.

Money/money

Be consistent

Note: The question simply refers to the 'firm's cost of capital'. You can assume this is the money rate – if you are given a real rate the examiner will always specify.

Time	Money cash flow	Discount rate	PV
	$	15%	$
0	(50,000)	1	(50,000)
1	21,100	0.870	18,357
2	22,261	0.756	16,829
3	23,485	0.658	15,453
4	24,776	0.572	14,172
		NPV =	14,811

(b) Discounting the real cash flows at the real rate.

Calculate the real rate by removing the general inflation from the money cost of capital:

$$(1+r) = \frac{(1+i)}{(1+h)}$$

$$(1+r) = \frac{(1+1.15)}{(1.055)}$$

$$(1+r) = 1.09$$

Therefore $r = 0.09$ i.e. 9.%

The real rate can now be applied to the real flows without any further adjustments.

Year	Real cash flow	Discount rate	PV
	$	9%	$
0	(50,000)	1	(50,000)
1-4	20,000	3.240	64,800
		NPV =	14,800

Note: Differences due to rounding.

Test your understanding 2

A project has the following cash flows before allowing for inflation, i.e. they are stated at their T_0 values.

Timing	Cash flow
	$
0	(750)
1	330
2	242
3	532

The company's money discount rate is 15.5%. The general rate of inflation is expected to remain constant at 5%.

Evaluate the project in terms of:

(a) **real cash flows and real discount rates**

(b) **money cash flows and money discount rates.**

The real method examples used above had all cash flows inflating at the general rate of inflation. In practice, inflation does not affect all costs to the same extent. In this case the money/money method should be used as it is much simpler.

In the examination, for a short life project, with cash flows inflating at different rates, it is best to set the NPV calculation out with the cash flows down the side and the time across the top.

Expandable text

Illustration – Dealing with inflation in NPV calculations

A company is considering a cost-saving project. This involves purchasing a machine costing $7,000, which will result in annual savings (in real terms) on wage costs of $1,000 and on material costs of $400.

The following forecasts are made of the rates of inflation each year for the next five years:

Wage costs	10%
Material costs	5%
General prices	6%

The cost of capital of the company, in money terms, is 15%.

Evaluate the project, assuming that the machine has a life of five years and no scrap value.

Expandable text

Solution

	T_0	T_1	T_2	T_3	T_4	T_5
	$	$	$	$	$	$
Investment	(7,000)					
Wages savings (inflating @ 10%)		1,100	1,210	1,331	1,464	1,610
Materials savings (inflating @ 5%)		420	441	463	486	510
Net cash flow	(7,000)	1,520	1,651	1,794	1,950	2,120
PV factor @ 15%	1.000	0.870	0.756	0.658	0.572	0.497
PV of cash flow	(7,000)	1,322	1,248	1,180	1,115	1,054

Therefore NPV = $(1,081) which suggests the project is not worthwhile.

Note: the general rate of inflation has not been used in, and is irrelevant to, this calculation.

Expandable text

The following is a useful summary of how to approach examination questions:

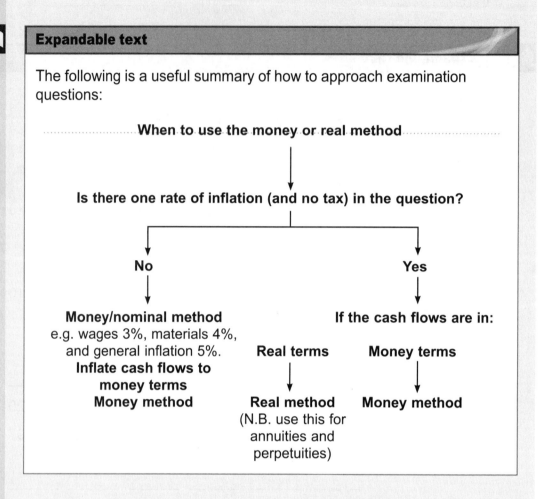

When to use the money or real method

Is there one rate of inflation (and no tax) in the question?

No

Money/nominal method
e.g. wages 3%, materials 4%, and general inflation 5%.
Inflate cash flows to money terms
Money method

Real terms

Real method
(N.B. use this for annuities and perpetuities)

Yes

If the cash flows are in:

Money terms

Money method

Expandable text

If there is one rate of inflation in the question both the real and money method will give the same answer. However it is easier to adjust one discount rate, rather than all the cash flows over a number of years. This is particularly true where the cash flows are annuities and the only method where they are perpetuities.

Although it is theoretically possible to use the real method in questions incorporating tax, it is extremely complex. It is therefore much safer (and easier) to use the money/nominal method in all questions where tax is taken into account.

Expandable text

A project under consideration has the following projected data. All cash flows are in current terms

	$000
Investment	1,700
Inflow at T_1	100
Inflow at T_2	200
Inflow at T_{3-10}	300

The rate of inflation (which will affect all cash flows equally) is 3% and the firm's required money return is 11.24%

Calculate the NPV of the project and determine whether the project is worth while.

Solution

Since the cash flows are in real terms, it is simpler to adjust the money rate to get a real rate and use the real method, particularly since the cash flows include an 8-year annuity, which it would be time consuming to inflate.

Real discount rate: 1.1124/1.03 = 1.08, therefore r = 8%.

NPV calculation

	T_0	T_1	T_2	T_{3-10}
	$000	$000	$000	$000
Net cash flows	(1,700)	100	200	300
8-year annuity factor (discounts to T_2)				5.747
DF	1.000	0.926	0.857	0.857
PV	(1,700)	93	171	1,478

NPV = $42.000

Expandable text

This exercise could have been done using the money method, but it is much longer and so not recommended here.

Money method : calculate the money cash flows for each year (by inflating up at 3%) and discount by the money discount rate (11.24%).

Years	0	1	2	3	4	5	6	7	8	9	10
Net cash flows	(1,700)	103	212	328	338	348	358	369	380	391	403
DF @ 11.24%	1	.899	.808	.726	.653	.587	.528	.474	.426	.383	.345
PV	(1,700)	93	171	238	221	204	189	175	162	150	139
NPV					42						

3 Dealing with tax in NPV calculations

Since most companies pay tax, the impact of corporation tax must be considered in any investment appraisal.

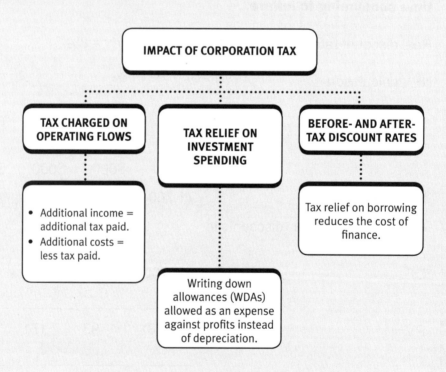

Tax on operating flows

Corporation tax charged on a company's profits is a relevant cash flow for NPV purposes. It is assumed, unless otherwise stated in the question, that:

- operating cash inflows will be taxed at the corporation tax rate

- operating cash outflows will be tax deductible and attract tax relief at the corporation tax rate

- tax is paid one year after the related operating cash flow is earned

- investment spending attracts capital or WDAs which get tax relief (see the section below)

- the company is earning net taxable profits overall (this avoids any issues of carrying losses forwards to reduce future taxation).

Use the following approach for examination questions :

YEAR	0	1	2	3

Add an extra year (if tax is delayed)

These five headings must be prepared for all taxation questions

(1) Net trading revenue — The inflows and outflows from trading (e.g. sales minus operating cash flows)

(2) Tax payable — The net trading revenue × tax rate (normally delayed by one year)

(3) Investment

(4) Residual/scrap value

(5) Tax relief on WDAs — Calculated as a separate cash flow in a working

(6) Working capital flows (no tax implications)

Expandable text

Taxation has the following effects on an investment appraisal problem:

- Project cash flows will give rise to taxation which itself has an impact on project appraisal. Normally we assume that tax paid on operating flows is due one year after the related cash flow. However, it is possible for alternative assumptions to be made and so you should read any examination question carefully to ascertain precisely what assumptions are made in the question.

- Organisations benefit from being able to claim capital allowances – a tax deductible alternative to depreciation. The effect of these is to reduce the amount of tax that organisations are required to pay. Again it is important to read any examination question carefully in order to identify what treatment is expected by the examiner. A common assumption is that WDAs at 25% pa are receivable.

Note that the **WDAs are not cash flows** and to calculate the tax impact we have to multiply each year's WDA by the corporation tax rate. The effect of a WDA is on the amount of tax payable, which is the relevant cash flow.

In dealing with these tax effects it is always assumed that:

- where a tax loss arises from the project, there are sufficient taxable profits elsewhere in the organisation to allow the loss to reduce any relevant (subsequent) tax payment (and it may therefore be treated as a cash inflow) and that the company has sufficient taxable profits to obtain full benefit from capital allowances.

In practice, the effects of taxation are complex, and are influenced by a number of factors including the following:

- the taxable profits and tax rate
- the company's accounting period and tax payment dates
- capital allowances
- losses available for set-off

but many of these issues are ignored or simplified for the purposes of NPV investment appraisal.

Capital allowances/WDAs

For tax purposes, a business may not deduct the cost of an asset from its profits as depreciation (in the way it does for financial accounting purposes).

Instead the cost must be deducted from taxable profits in the form of 'capital allowances' or WDAs. The basic rules are as follows:

- WDAs are calculated on a reducing balance basis (usually at a rate of 25%)
- the total WDAs given over the life of an asset equate to its fall in value over the period (i.e. the cost less any scrap proceeds)
- WDAs are claimed as early as possible

- WDAs are given for every year of ownership except the year of disposal
- in the year of sale or scrap a balancing allowance (BA) or charge arises (CA).

	$
Original cost of asset	X
Cumulative capital allowances claimed	(X)
Written down value of the asset	X
Disposal value of the asset	(X)
BA or BC	X

Expandable text

If a business buys a capital asset in one year and sells it several years later, the total tax relief it will receive is the tax on the cost of the asset less its eventual disposal value. For example, if a business buys equipment for $100,000 in Year 0 and disposes of it in Year 5 for $20,000, it will receive tax relief on the net cost of $80,000. If the rate of corporation tax is 30%, the reduction in tax payments over the five years would be 30% × $80,000 = $24,000.

Expandable text

BAs are given as a final deduction to ensure the full fall in value has been allowed. BCs occur where the total WDAs claimed exceed the fall in value of the asset. The excess claimed is treated as a taxable amount in the year of disposal.

Expandable text

Illustration – Capital allowances/WDA

An asset was purchased for $100,000. At the time of its disposal, the cumulative capital allowances claimed over the life of the asset were $68,000.

Calculate the BA or BC if the asset is disposed of for:

(a) $20,000

(b) $40,000

Expandable text

Solution

(a)	$
Original cost of asset	100,000
Cumulative capital allowances claimed	(68,000)
Written down value of the asset	32,000
Disposal value of the asset	(20,000)
BA (a deduction against profits)	12,000

(b)	$
Original cost of asset	100,000
Cumulative capital allowances claimed	(68,000)
Written down value of the asset	32,000
Disposal value of the asset	(40,000)
BC (taxable with profits)	(8,000)

Expandable text

An asset was purchased for $96,000. At the time of its disposal, the cumulative capital allowances claimed over the life of the asset were $73,000.

Calculate the BA or BC if the asset is disposed of for:

(a) **$27,000**

(b) **scrap with no sale proceeds.**

Solution

(a)

	$
Original cost of asset	96,000
Cumulative capital allowances claimed	(73,000)
Written down value of the asset	23,000
Disposal value of the asset	(27,000)
Balancing charge (taxable with profits	(4,000)

(b)

	$
Original cost of asset	96,000
Cumulative capital allowances claimed	(73,000)
Written down value of the asset	23,000
Disposal value of the asset	0
BA (a deduction against profits)	23,000

For tax purposes care must be taken to identify the exact time of asset purchase.

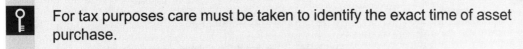

- Assets are assumed to be bought at T_0.

- This could be the very end of an accounting period (e.g. 31/21/X1) or the start of another (e.g.1/1/X2).

- There is no distinction between these dates for discounting, but there is for tax.

Asset bought at the start of an accounting period:

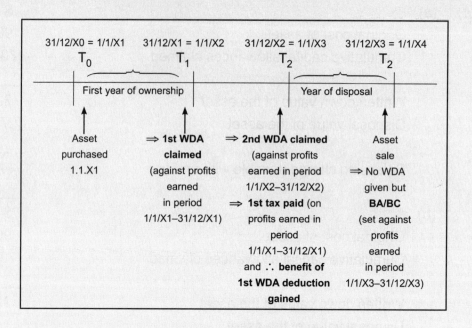

Asset bought at the end of an accounting period:

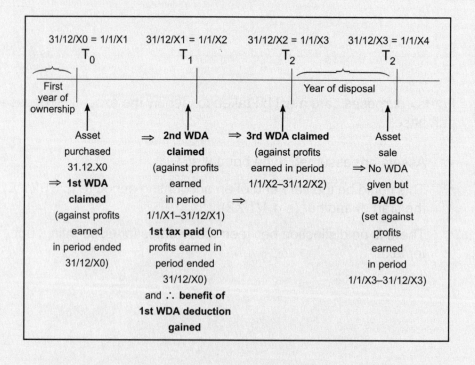

Expandable text

Although the total value of WDAs will not alter, the timing of the asset purchase affects how much of the total fall in value is claimed in each tax year. Because of the time value of money, the later the deductions are taken, and the corresponding tax relief claimed, the less worthwhile the WDAs will be.

- If an asset is bought at T_0 on 1/1/X2, the first year of ownership is the period 1/1/X2 – 31/12/X2, and the first WDA deduction will be set off against profits earned in that period. Since for NPV purposes cash flows are deemed to occur at year end, the WDA deduction will be claimed at T_1. Corresponding tax relief will therefore occur one year later at T_2.

- However, if the asset is bought, still at T_0, but at the end of an accounting period, e.g. on 31/12/X1, the first WDA will be allowed for set-off against profits earned in the accounting period 1/1/X1 – 31/12/X1 (i.e. a period earlier that in the past example) since this is now the first year of ownership, even though the asset was owned for only one day of the year. This means the WDA is claimed at T_0, at the same time as the purchase. The corresponding tax relief will therefore occur a year earlier than before at T_1.

Expandable text

Illustration – Capital allowances/WDA

An asset is bought on the first day of the year for $10,000 and will be used on a project for four years after which it will be disposed of on the final day of year 4. Tax is payable at 30%, one year in arrears, and capital allowances are available at 25% reducing balance.

Required:

(a) Calculate the WDA and hence the tax savings for each year if the proceeds on disposal of the asset are $2,500.

(b) If net trading income from the project is $4,000 pa and the cost of capital is 10% calculate the NPV of the project.

C   How would your answer change if the asset was bought on the last day of the previous accounting period?

Expandable text

Solution

(a)

Time		$	Tax saving @ 30%	Timing of tax relief
T_0	Initial investment	10,000		
T_1	WDA @ 25%	(2,500)	750	T_2
	Written down value	7,500		
T_2	WDA @ 25%	(1,875)	563	T_3
	Written down value	5,625		
T_3	WDA @ 25%	(1,406)	422	T_4
	Written down value	4,219		
T_4	Sale proceeds	(2,500)		
T_4	BA	1,719	516	T_5

Note:

- total WDAs = 2,500 + 1,875 + 1,406 + 1,719 = 7,500 = fall in value of the asset

- total tax relief = 750 + 563 + 422 + 516 = 2251 ≈ 7,500 × 30% (WDAs x tax rate)

(b)

Time	T$_0$	T$_1$	T$_2$	T$_3$	T$_4$	T$_5$
	$	$	$	$	$	$
Net trading inflows		4,000	4,000	4,000	4,000	
Tax payable (30%)			(1,200)	(1,200)	(1,200)	(1,200)
Initial investment	(10,000)					
Scrap proceeds					2,500	
Tax relief on WDAs			750	563	422	516
Net cash flows	(10,000)	4,000	3,550	3,363	5,722	(684)
DF @ 10%	1.000	0.909	0.826	0.751	0.683	0.621
PV	(10,000)	3,636	2,932	2,526	3,908	(425)
					NPV	2,577

(c) The asset is still bought at time T0 but falls into the previous accounting period for tax purposes. The overall value of WDAs claimed and therefore the total tax saving remains unchanged, but the timing and amount of the individual amounts will alter. Because of the time value of money, this will impact the final NPV.

Time			Tax saving @ 30%	Timing of relief
		$	$	
T_0	Initial investment	10,000		
T_0	WDA @ 25%	(2,500)	750	T_1
	Written down value	7,500		
T_1	WDA @ 25%	(1,875)	563	T_2
	Written down value	5,625		
T_2	WDA @ 25%	(1,406)	422	T_3
	Written down value	4,219		
T_3	WDA @ 25%	(1,055)	317	T_4
		3,164		
T_4	Sale proceeds	(2,500)		
T_4	BA	664	199	T_5

Note:

- total WDAs = 2,500 + 1,875 + 1,406 + 1,055 + 664 = 7,500 = fall in value of the asset

- total tax relief = 750 + 563 + 422 + 317 + 199 = 2251 ≈ 7,500 x 30% (WDAs x tax rate)

Time	T$_0$	T$_1$	T$_2$	T$_3$	T$_4$	T$_5$
	$	$	$	$	$	$
Net trading inflows		4,000	4,000	4,000	4,000	
Tax payable (30%)			(1,200)	(1,200)	(1,200)	(1,200)
Initial investment	(10,000)					
Scrap proceeds					2,500	
Tax relief on WDAs		750	563	422	317	199
Net cash flows	(10,000)	4,750	3,363	3,222	5,617	(1,001)
DF @ 10%	1.000	0.909	0.826	0.751	0.683	0.621
PV	4,318	2,778	2,420	3,836	(622)	
					NPV	$2,730

N.B. The NPV of the project is now higher as a result of acquiring the asset 1 day earlier.

Test your understanding 3

A company buys an asset on the last day of the accounting period for $26,000. It will be used on a project for three years after which it will be disposed of on the final day of year 3. Tax is payable at 30% one year in arrears, and capital allowances are available at 25% reducing balance.

(a) **Calculate the WDA and hence the tax savings for each year if the proceeds on disposal of the asset are $12,500.**

(b) **If net trading income from the project is $16,000 pa and the cost of capital is 8% calculate the NPV of the project.**

(c) **How would your answer change if the asset was bought on the first day of the accounting period?**

Expandable text

Before- and after-tax discount rates

Debt interest is tax deductible. This reduces the cost of loan finance to a company.

Expandable text

Illustration – Before and after tax discount rates

A company earns $100,000 pa and pays corporation tax at 30%. It has no long-term debt. Its position is as follows:

	$
Net income	100,000
Debt interest	–
Taxable income	100,000
Corporation tax	(30,000)
Earnings for shareholders	70,000

Compare the position if the company has a $100,000 bank loan on which the bank charges 10% interest.

	$
Net income	100,000
Debt interest	(10,000)
Taxable income	90,000
Corporation tax	(27,000)
Earnings for shareholder	63,000

The net impact of the loan is therefore:	$
Increased expense – debt interest	(10,000)
Saved tax cost (30,000 – 27,000)	3,000
Net interest cost	7,000

The after-tax cost of the loan is therefore 7,000/100,000 = 7%.

For a bank loan the after-tax cost of debt is therefore calculated as: $I(1 - T)$ where:

I = before tax (i.e. quoted) interest rate

T = corporation tax rate

Impact on NPV questions:

- Do not include interest payments on loans in the cash flows to be discounted.

- If the cost of capital is given you can assume that it incorporates the tax relief on debt interest.

- When calculating the cost of debt (see later sessions), the tax relief will need to be incorporated into the calculation.

Tax relief in debt interest will impact NPV calculations.

- The tax relief on interest payments will reduce the effective rate of interest which a firm pays on its borrowings, and hence the opportunity cost of capital.

- The discount rate given will be the 'after-tax' cost of capital and this rate should be used to discount the 'after-tax' project cash flows.

- This means that the actual interest payments on borrowing can be ignored, because they have already been provided for in calculating the cost of capital.

- The calculation of the cost of capital (see later) will include consideration of the before- and after-tax cost of debt.

4 Incorporating working capital

Investment in a new project often requires an additional investment in working capital, i.e. the difference between short-term assets and liabilities.

The treatment of working capital is as follows:

- initial investment is a cost at the start of the project

- if the investment is increased during the project, the increase is a relevant cash outflow

- at the end of the project all the working capital is 'released' and treated as a cash inflow.

Expandable text

Illustration – Incorporating working capital

A company expects sales for a new project to be $225,000 in the first year growing at 5% pa. The project is expected to last for 4 years. Working capital equal to 10% of annual sales is required and needs to be in place at the start of each year. Calculate the working capital flows for incorporation into the NPV calculation.

Expandable text

Solution

Step 1: Calculate the absolute amounts of working capital needed over the project:

	T_0	T_1	T_2	T_3	T_4
	$	$	$	$	$
Sales		225,000	236,250	248,063	260,466
Working capital required (10% sales)	22,500	23,625	24,806	26,047	

Step 2: Work out the **incremental** investment required each year (remember that the full investment is released at the end of the project):

	T₀	T₁	T₂	T₃	T₄
	$	$	$	$	$
Working		23,625 – 22,500	24,806 – 23,625	26,047 – 24,806	
Working capital investment	(22,500)	(1,125)	(1,181)	(1,241)	26,047

Test your understanding 4

A company anticipates sales for the latest venture to be $300,000 in the first year. Sales are then expected to increase at a rate of 8% pa over the three-year life of the project. Working capital equal to 10% of annual sales is required and needs to be in place at the start of each year.

Calculate the working capital flows.

5 Dealing with questions with both tax and inflation.

Combining tax and inflation in the same question does not make it any more difficult than keeping them separate.

Questions with both tax and inflation are best tackled using the money method.

- Inflate costs and revenues, where necessary, before determining their tax implications.
- Ensure that the cost and disposal values have been inflated (if necessary) before calculating WDAs.
- Always calculate working capital on these inflated figures, unless given.
- Use a post-tax money discount rate.

Proforma

YEAR	0	1	2	3

Add an extra year (if tax is delayed)

(1) Net trading revenue
The inflows and outflows from trading (e.g. sales minus operating cash flows)

Inflated where necessary

(2) Tax payable
The net trading revenue × tax rate (normally delayed by one year)

Calculated as normal on the money flows

(3) Investment

Shouldn't need inflating!

(4) Residual/scrap value

May need inflating but usually given in money terms

(5) Tax relief on WDAs

Calculated as normal

(6) Working capital flows

Calculate using money figures

Test your understanding 5

Ackbono Co is considering a potential project with the following forecasts:

	Now	T₁	T₂	T₃
Initial investment ($million)	(1,000)			
Disposal proceeds ($million)				200
Demand (millions of units)		5	10	6

The initial investment will be made on the first day of the new accounting period.

The selling price per unit is expected to be $100 and the variable cost $30 per unit. Both of these figures are given in today's terms.

Tax is paid at 30%, one year after the accounting period concerned.

WDA's are available at 25% reducing balance.

The company has a real required rate of return of 6.8%.

General inflation is predicted to be 3% pa but the selling price is expected to inflate at 4% and variable costs by 5% pa

Determine the NPV of the project.N.B. work in $ millions.

Chapter summary

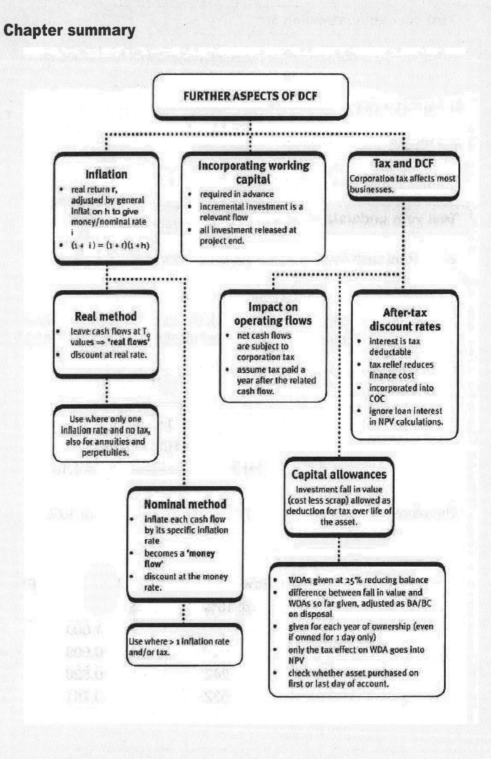

Test your understanding answers

Test your understanding 1

(1 + i) = (1 + r)(1 + h) = 1.08 × 1.05 = 1.134

m = 13.4%.

Test your understanding 2

(a) Real cash flows and real discount rates

Discount rate as per the question of 15.5% includes investor's/lender's inflation expectation of 5%. Hence 'real' discount rate, r, is given by:

$$1+r = \frac{1+i}{1+h}$$

$$1+r = \frac{1+0.155}{1 + 0.05} = 1.10$$

Therefore   r is   0.10   or 10%

Timing	Cash flow	PV factor	PV
$	@ 10%	$	
0	(750)	1.000	(750)
1	330	0.909	300
2	242	0.826	200
3	532	0.751	400
NVP			150

(b) Money cash flows and money discount rates

The discount rate as per the question of 15.5% is the money discount rate.

To convert real cash flows into money flows they will need to be increased by 5% each year from year 0, to allow for inflation.

Timing	Real/ cash flow (a) $	Inflation factor (b)	Money cash flow (a) × (b) $	DF @ 15.5%	PV $
0	(750)	1	(750)	1.000	(750)
1	330	$1 + 0.05$	346.5	0.866*	300
2	242	$(1 + 0.05)^2$	266.8	0.750	200
3	532	$(1 + 0.05)^3$	615.9	0.649	400
NPV					150

*$1/1.155 = 0.866$

$1/1.155^2 = 0.750$

$1/1.155^3 = 0.649$

Note that either approach yields identical conclusions (allowing for rounding).

Test your understanding 3

(a)

Time		$	$	Tax saving @ 30%	Timing of tax relief
T_0	Initial investment		26,000		
T_0	WDA @ 25%		(6,500)	1,950	T_1
	Written down value		19,500		
T_1	WDA @ 25%		(4,875)	1,463	T_2
	Written down value		14,625		
T_2	WDA @ 25%		(3,656)	1,097	T_3
	Written down value		10,969		
	Sale proceeds		(12,500)		
T_3	BC		(1,531)	(460)	T_4

(b)

Time	T₀	T₁	T₂	T₃	T₄
	$	$	$	$	$
Net trading inflows		16,000	16,000	16,000	
Tax payable (30%)			(4,800)	(4,800)	(4,800)
Initial investment	(26,000)				
Scrap proceeds				12,500	
Tax relief on WDAs		1,950	1,463	1,097	(460)
Net cash flows	(26,000)	17,950	12,663	24.797	5,260
DF @ 8%	1.000	0.926	0.857	0.794	0.735
PV	(26,000)	16,622	10,852	19,689	3,866
				NPV	$17,297

(c)

Time			$	$	Tax saving @30%	Timing of tax reief
T0	Initial investment		26,000			
T1	WDA @ 25%		(6,500)		1,950	T2
	Written down value		19,500			
T2	WDA @ 25%		(4,875)		1,463	T3
	Written down value		14,625			
	Sale proceeds		(12,500)			

Time	T0	T1	T2	T3	T4
Net trading inflows	$	$	$	$	$
Net trading inflows		16,000	16,000	16,000	
Tax payable (30%)			(4,800)	(4,800)	(4,800)
Initial investment	(26,000)				
Scrap proceeds				12,500	
Tax relief on WDAs			1,950	1,463	638
Net cash flows	(26,000)	16,000	13,150	25,163	4,162
DF @ 8%	1.000	0.926	0.857	0.794	0.735
PV	(26,000)	14,816	11,270	19,979	
NPV					$16,268

The NPV is lower as a result of the purchase being delayed.

Test your understanding 4

Step 1: Calculate the absolute amounts of working capital needed over the project:

	T_0	T_1	T_2	T_3
	$	$	$	$
Sales		300,000	324,000	349,920
Working capital required	30,000	32,400	34,992	

Step 2: Work out the incremental investment required each year, remembering to release all the working capital at the end of the project

	T_0	T_1	T_2	T_3
	$	$	$	$
Working		32,400-30,000	34,992-32,400	
Capital investment	(30,000)	(2,400)	(2,592)	34,992

Test your understanding 5

$ millions	T_0	T_1	T_2	T_3	T_4
Sales **(W1)**		520	1082	675	
Variable costs **(W1)**		(158)	(331)	(208)	
Net trading inflows		362	751	467	
Tax payable (30%)			(109)	(225)	(140)
Initial investment	(1,000)				
Scrap proceeds				200	
Tax relief on WDAs **(W2)**			75	56	109
Net cash flows	(1,000)	362	717	498	(31)
DF @ 10% **(W3)**	1	0.909	0.826	0.751	0.683
PV	(1,000)	329	592	374	(21)
				NPV	274

W1: revenue and costs

Revenue and costs need to be expressed in money terms.

e.g. revenue at T_2 = \$10m × 100 × $(1.04)2$ = \$1,081.6m.

W2: WDAs

Time		$m	Tax saving $m	Timing of tax relief
T_0	Initial investment	1000		
T_1	WDA @ 25%	(250)	75	T_2
	Written down value	750		
T_2	WDA @ 25%	(188)	56	T_3
	Written down value	562		
	Sale proceeds	(200)		
T_3	BA	362	109	T_4

W3: Discount rate

$(1+i) = (1+r) \times (1+h) = 1.068 \times 1.03 = 1.10$, giving m = 10%.

Investment appraisal under uncertainty

Chapter learning objectives

Upon completion of this chapter you will be able to:

- distinguish between risk and uncertainty in investment appraisal

- define sensitivity analysis and discuss its usefulness in assisting investment decisions

- apply sensitivity analysis to investment projects and explain the meaning of the findings

- define an expected value (EV) and discuss the usefulness of probability analysis in assisting investment decisions

- apply probability analysis to investment projects and explain the meaning of the findings

- discuss the use of simulation to take account of risk and uncertainty in investment appraisal

- discuss the use of discounted payback in investment appraisal

- use discounted payback to appraise an investment

- explain the principle of adjusting discount rates to take account of risk.

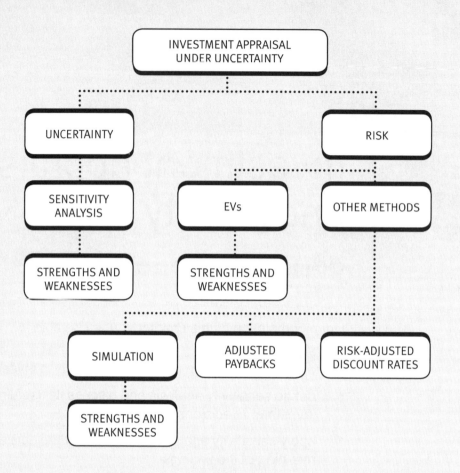

1 Risk and uncertainty

The difference between risk and uncertainty

Investment appraisal faces the following problems:

- all decisions are based on forecasts
- all forecasts are subject to uncertainty
- this uncertainty needs to be reflected in the financial evaluation.

 The decision maker must distinguish between:

- **risk** – quantifiable – possible outcomes have associated probabilities, thus allowing the use of mathematical techniques
- **uncertainty** – unquantifiable – outcomes cannot be mathematically modelled.

In investment appraisal the areas of concern are therefore the accuracy of the estimates concerning:

- project life

- predicted cash flows and associated probabilities

- discount rate used.

Incorporating risk and uncertainty

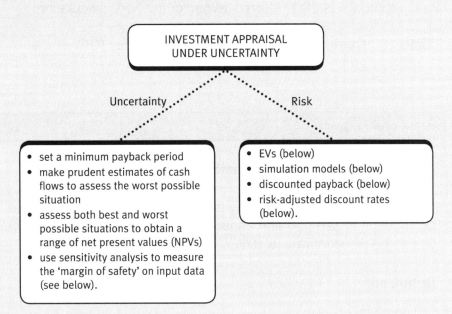

2 Sensitivity analysis

- Sensitivity analysis typically involves posing 'what if?' questions.

- For example, what if demand fell by 10% compared to our original forecasts? Would the project still be viable?

- Ideally we want to know how much demand could fall before the project should be rejected or, equivalently, the breakeven demand that gives an NPV of zero. We could then assess the likelihood of forecast demand being that low.

Calculating sensitivity

This maximum possible change is often expressed as a percentage:

$$\text{Sensitivity margin} = \frac{\text{NPV}}{\text{Present value (PV) of flow under consideration}} \times 100\%$$

This would be calculated for each input individually.

The lower the sensitivity margin, the more sensitive the decision to the particular parameter being considered, i.e. small changes in the estimate could change the project decision from accept to reject.

NB Because we will need the PV of each cash flow separately, the following tabular approach is the preferred layout for the NPV calculation:

Time	Cash flow	Discount factor (DF) at x%	PV

Expandable text

Illustration – Calculating sensitivity

An investment of $40,000 today is expected to give rise to annual contribution of $25,000 and annual fixed cost of $10,000 for the next four years; the discount rate is 10%.

Required:

(a) Calculate the NPV of this investment.

(b) Calculate the sensitivity of your calculation to the following:

    (i)   initial investment

    (ii) contribution

    (iii) fixed costs

    (iv) discount rate

    (v) life of the project.

(c) The annual contribution of $25,000 is based on selling one product, with a sales volume of 10,000 units, selling price of $12.50 and variable costs of $10. Calculate the sensitivity margin for:

(i)   the sales volume

(ii) the selling price.

Expandable text

Solution

(a)

Time	Narrative	Cash flow	DF	PV
		$	10%	$
0	Investment	(40,000)	1.000	(40,000)
1-4	Contribution	25,000	3.170	79,250
1-4	Fixed costs	(10,000)	3.170	(31,700)
			NPV =	7,550

Therefore the decision should be to accept the investment.

(b)

i. Sensitivity to initial investment = $\dfrac{7,550}{40,000}$ = 18.9%

i.e. an 18.9% increase in the cost of the initial investment would cause the NPV to fall to zero.

ii. Sensitivity to contribution = $\dfrac{7,550}{79,250}$ = 9.5%

i.e. a 9.5% decrease in the level of contribution would cause the NPV to fall to zero.

iii. Sensitivity to fixed cost = $\dfrac{7,550}{31,700}$ = 23.8%

iv. To calculate the sensitivity to the discount rate, it is necessary to find the rate at which the project NPV is zero, i.e. the internal rate of return (IRR) of the project.

Time	Cash flow	DF	PV
	$	×%?	$
0	(40,000)	1.000	(40,000)
1-4	15,000	2.667 **(W1)**	40,000
		NPV =	0

(W1) If the project NPV is set to zero, the PV of the net cash inflows would need to be $40,000. Hence the discount factor needed to make the NPV go down to 0 is 40,000÷15,000 = 2.667.

From tables, at four years, the closest annuity rate to 2.667 occurs at approximately 18%. This is therefore the breakeven discount rate, i.e. the IRR.

This quick method of finding the IRR will only work if all the inflows are in the form of annuities. Otherwise the usual linear interpolation route must be followed.

V.

Time	Cash flow	DF	PV
	$	10%	$
0	(40,000)	1.000	(40,000)
1 – n?	15,000	2.667	40,000
		NPV =	0

The DF needed to make the NPV go down to 0 is once again

$$\frac{40,000}{15,000} = 2.667$$

From tables, at 10%, the annuity rate of 2.667 occurs approximately midway between times 3 and 4. The project will therefore breakeven after approximately 3½ years.

This quick method of finding the breakeven life will only work if all the inflows are in the form of annuities. Otherwise a discounted payback must be calculated (see below).

(c)

(i) Sensitivity to sales volume:

The relevant cash flow is contribution, so the sensitivity margin will be the sensitivity to contribution as above (9.5%).

As sales volume affects both sales revenue and variable costs, being asked to find the sensitivity to sales volume is the same as sensitivity to contribution.

(ii) If selling price changes, the revenue will change, so the relevant cash flow will be revenue.

PV of revenue = $12.50 × 10,000 × 3.170 = $396,250

Sensitivity margin = $\frac{7,550}{396,250}$ × 100 = 1.9%

If price falls by more than 1.9%, the project will make a loss. It is most sensitive to price.

Test your understanding 1

Bacher Co is considering investing $500,000 in equipment to produce a new type of ball. Sales of the product are expected to continue for three years, at the end of which the equipment will have a scrap value of $80,000. Sales revenue of $600,000 pa will be generated at a variable cost of $350,000. Annual fixed costs will increase by $40,000.

(a) **Determine whether, on the basis of the estimates given, the project should be undertaken, assuming that all cash flows occur at annual intervals and that Bacher Co has a cost of capital of 15%.**

(b) **Find the percentage changes required in the following estimates for the investment decision to change:**

    (i)   **initial investment**

    (ii) **scrap value**

    (iii) **selling price**

    (iv) **unit variable cost**

    (v) **annual fixed cost**

    (vi) **sales volume**

    (vii) **cost of capital.**

Advantages and disadvantages of sensitivity analysis

Advantages

- simple
- provides more information to allow management to make subjective judgements
- identifies critical estimates.

Disadvantages:

- assumes variables change independently of each other
- does not assess the likelihood of a variable changing
- does not directly identify a correct decision.

Expandable text

Strengths of sensitivity analysis

- No complicated theory to understand.
- Information will be presented to management in a form which facilitates subjective judgement to decide the likelihood of the various possible outcomes considered.
- Identifies areas which are crucial to the success of the project. If the project is chosen, those areas can be carefully monitored.
- Indicates just how critical are some of the forecasts which are considered to be uncertain.

Weaknesses of sensitivity analysis

- It assumes that changes to variables can be made independently, e.g. material prices will change independently of other variables. This is unlikely. If material prices went up the firm would probably increase selling price at the same time and there would be little effect on NPV. A technique called simulation (see later) allows us to change more than one variable at a time.

- It only identifies how far a variable needs to change. It does not look at the probability of such a change. In the above analysis, sales volume appears to be the most crucial variable, but if the firm were facing volatile raw material markets a 65% change in raw material prices would be far more likely than a 29% change in sales volume.

- It is not an optimising technique. It provides information on the basis of which decisions can be made. It does not point directly to the correct decision.

3 EVs

When there are a number of possible outcomes for a decision and probabilities can be assigned to each, then an EV may be calculated.

 The EV is the weighted average of all the possible outcomes, with the weightings based on the probability estimates.

Calculating an EV

The formula for calculating an EV is:

$EV = \sum px$

where

p = the probability of an outcome

x = the value of an outcome.

The EV is not the most likely result. It may not even be a possible result, but instead it finds the long-run average outcome.

Illustration – Calculating an EV

- Cash flows from a new restaurant venture may depend on whether a competitor decides to open up in the same area.We have made the following estimates:

- The chance that the competitor opens up is 30%.

- NPV if competitor opens is $(10,000).

- NPV if competitor does not open is $20,000.

- What is the EV of the venture?

Solution

Competitor opens up	Probability	Project NPV	EV
		$	$
Yes	0.3	(10,000)	(3,000)
No	0.7	20,000	14,000
			11,000

The EV of the venture is $11,000. This is positive suggesting that the venture should be accepted.

The EV is the weighted average of the outcomes, with the weightings based on the probability estimates.

The EV does not necessarily represent what the outcome will be, nor does it represent the most likely result. What it really represents is the average pay-off per occasion if the project were repeated many times (i.e. a 'long-run' average).

There are two main problems with using EV to make decisions in this way:

- The project will only be carried out once. It could result in a sizeable loss and there may be no second chance to win our money back.

- The probabilities used are simply subjective estimates of our belief, on a scale from 0 to 1. There is probably little data on which to base these estimates.

Test your understanding 2

A firm has to choose between three mutually exclusive projects, the outcomes of which depend on the state of the economy. The following estimates have been made:

State of the economy	Recession	Stable	Growing
Probability	0.5	0.4	0.1
	NPV ($000)	NPV ($000)	NPV ($000)
Project A	100	200	1,400
Project B	0	500	600
Project C	180	190	200

Determine which project should be selected on the basis of expected market values.

Using EVs in larger NPV calculations

The EV technique can be used to simplify the available data in a larger investment appraisal question.

Illustration 1 – Using EVs in larger NPV calculations

Dralin Co is considering an investment of $460,000 in a non-current asset expected to generate substantial cash inflows over the next five years. Unfortunately the annual cash flows from this investment are uncertain, but the following probability distribution has been established:

Annual cash flow ($)	Probability
50,000	0.3
100,000	0.5
150,000	0.2

At the end of its five-year life, the asset is expected to sell for $40,000. The cost of capital is 5%.

Should the investment be undertaken?

Expandable text

Solution

Expected annual cash flows are:

Annual cash flow	Probability	PV
(x)	(p)	
50,000	0.3	15,000
100,000	0.5	50,000
150,000	0.2	30,000
		95,000

NPV calculation:

Time	Cash flow	DF 5%	PV
	$		$
0	(460,000)	1.000	(460,000)
1-5	95,000	4.329	411,255
5	40,000	0.784	31,360
		NPV =	(17,385)

As the ENPV is negative, the project should not be undertaken.

KAPLAN PUBLISHING

An alternative approach would be to calculate three separate NPVs and then combine them, giving the following figures:

	Annual cash flow	Probability	NPV
			$
	$		
	50,000	0.3	(212,190)
	100,000	0.5	4,260
	150,000	0.2	220,710

ENPV = 0.3 × (-212,190) + 0.5 × 4,260 + 0.2 × (220,710) = (17,385)

Even though the ENPV is negative these figures show that there is a 70% chance of the project giving a positive NPV. Some investors may consider the project acceptable on this basis.

Expandable text

A company is considering whether to invest in equipment for providing a new service to its clients. The equipment will cost $100,000 and will have a disposal value of $20,000 after four years. Estimates of sales and incremental fixed cost cash expenditures are as follows.

Annual sales	Probability
$	
600,000	0.4
700,000	0.4
800,000	0.2

The company expects to achieve a contribution/sales ratio of 40% on all the services it provides. Incremental fixed costs will be $215,000 per annum. The project has a four-year life.

The company's cost of capital is 9%.

Calculate the three possible NPVs and the expected NPV. Comment on your results.

Solution

Annual sales of $600,000

Timing	Narrative	CF	DF	PV
		$000		$000
0	Buy asset	(100)	1	(100)
4	Sell asset	20	0.708	14.16
1-4	Annual inflow (W)	25	3.240	81.00
NPV				**(4.84)**

(W) Annual inflow = (600,000 × 40%) - 215,000 = $25,000 p.a.

Annual sales of $700,000

Timing	Narrative	CF	DF	PV
		$000		$000
0	Buy asset	(100)	1	(100)
4	Sell asset	20	0.708	14.16
1-4	Annual inflow (W)	65	3.240	210.6
NPV				**124.76**

(W) Annual inflow = (700,000 × 40%) - 215,000 = $65,000 p.a.

Annual sales of $800,000

Timing	Narrative	CF	DF	PV
		$000		$000
0	Buy asset	(100)	1	(100)
4	Sell asset	20	0.708	14.16
1-4	Annual inflow (W)	105	3.240	340.2
NPV				**254.36**

(W) Annual inflow = (800,000 × 40%) - 215,000 = $105,000 p.a

Expected NPV

ENPV = 0.4 × (-4.84) + 0.4 × 124.76 + 0.2 × 254.36 = + 98.84

Comments

Based on ENPV the project should be accepted. However, there is still a 40% chance of making a slight loss rather than a gain.

Using EVs with decision matrices

EVs are also used to deal with situations where the same conditions are faced many times. The problems involve construction of a 'decision matrix'.

Illustration – Using expected values with decision matrices

A newsagent sells a weekly magazine which advertises local second-hand goods. The owner can buy the magazines for 15c each and sell them at the retail price of 25c. At the end of each week unsold magazines are obsolete and have no value.

The owner estimates a probability distribution for weekly demand which looks like this:

Weekly demand in units	Probability
10	0.20
15	0.55
20	0.25
	1.00

(a) What is the EV of demand?

(b) If the owner is to order a fixed quantity of magazines per week how many should that be? Assume no seasonal variations in demand.

Solution

(a) EV of demand = (10 × 0.20) + (15 × 0.55) + (20 × 0.25) = 15.25 units per week.

(b) **Step 1**: Set up a decision matrix of possible strategies (numbers bought) and possible demand, as follows:

	(Number demanded)		
Strategy (Number bought)	10	15	20
10			
15			
20			

Step 2: The 'payoff' from each combination of action and outcome is then computed:

No sale → loss of 15c per magazine.

Sale → profit of 25c − 15c = 10c per magazine.

- Payoffs are shown for each combination of strategy and outcome:

Workings

(i)   If 10 magazines are bought, then 10 are sold no matter how many are demanded and the payoff is always 10 × 10c = 100c.

(ii) If 15 magazines are bought and 10 are demanded, then 10 are sold at a profit of 10 × 10c = 100c, and 5 are scrapped at a loss of 5 × 15c = 75c, making a net profit of 25c.

(iii) The other contributions are similarly calculated.

Step 3: Probabilities are then applied to compute the expected value resulting from each possible course of action.

Alternatively, in the same matrix, probability × payoff can be inserted in each cell and totalled to give the expected payoff.

		(Number demanded)		
		p = 0.2	p = 0.55	p = 0.25
		10	15	20
Strategy					EV
	10	100	100	100	100
(Number bought)	15	25	150	150	125
	20	(50)	75	200	81.25

From this matrix we can see that the best alternative is to buy 15 magazines each week.

What does this EV mean?

It means that if the strategy is followed for many weeks, then on average the profit will be 125c per week.

What actually happens is that eight weeks out of ten the payoff is likely to be 150c and two weeks out of ten it drops to 25c.

This strategy produces the highest long-run profit for the firm.

Expandable text

A baker has determined the following probability distributions for daily demand for bread rolls.

Demand	Probability
300	0.2
400	0.3
500	0.3
600	0.1
700	0.1

The rolls must be baked first thing in the morning and any rolls not sold at the end of the day are given away.

Rolls cost 25c to make and are sold for 30c.

What is the optimal quantity of rolls the baker should bake each morning

Solution

Number demanded

Strategy	p = 0.2 300	p = 0.3 400	p = 0.3 500	p = 0.1 600	p=0.1 700	EV
			Payoff ($)			
300	15	15	15	15	15	15
400	(10)	20	20	20	20	14
500	(35)	(5)	25	25	25	4
600	(60)	(30)	0	30	30	(15)
700	(85)	(55)	(25)	5	35	(37)

The optimal quantity to bake is 300 rolls.

Strengths and weaknesses of EVs

Strengths

- Deals with multiple outcomes.
- Quantifies probabilities.
- Relatively simple calculation.
- Straightforward decision rule.

Weaknesses

- Subjective probabilities.
- Answer is only a long-run average.
- Ignores variability of payoffs.
- Risk neutral decision, i.e. ignores investor's attitude to risk.

The simple EV decision rule is appropriate if three conditions are met or nearly met:

- there is a reasonable basis for making the forecasts and estimating the probability of different outcomes

- the decision is relatively small in relation to the business, so risk is small in magnitude

- the decision is for a category of decisions that are often made.

 The EV technique is best suited to a problem which is repetitive and involves relatively small investments.

KAPLAN PUBLISHING

Expandable text

Advantages of EVs

- The technique recognises that there are several possible outcomes and is, therefore, more sophisticated than single value forecasts.
- Enables the probability of the different outcomes to be quantified.
- Leads directly to a simple optimising decision rule.
- Calculations are relatively simple.

Limitations of EVs

- By asking for a series of forecasts the whole forecasting procedure is complicated. Inaccurate forecasting is already a major weakness in project evaluation. The probabilities used are also usually very subjective.
- The EV is merely a weighted average of the probability distribution, indicating the average payoff if the project is repeated many times.
- The EV gives no indication of the dispersion of possible outcomes about the EV. The more widely spread out the possible results are, the more risky the investment is usually seen to be. The EV ignores this aspect of the probability distribution.
- In ignoring risk, the EV technique also ignores the investor's attitude to risk. Some investors are more likely to take risks than others.

Conclusions on EVs

The simple EV decision rule is appropriate if three conditions are met or nearly met:

- there is a reasonable basis for making the forecasts and estimating the probability of different outcomes
- the decision is relatively small in relation to the business. Risk is then small in magnitude
- the decision is for a category of decisions that are often made.

A technique which maximises average payoff is then valid.

4 Further techniques for adjusting for risk and uncertainty

Simulation

Sensitivity analysis considered the effect of changing one variable at a time. Simulation improves on this by looking at the impact of many variables changing at the same time.

Using mathematical models, it produces a distribution of the possible outcomes from the project. The probability of different outcomes can then be calculated.

Expandable text

There are four stages:

(1) Specify major variables, e.g.:

Market details:

- market size
- selling price
- market growth rate
- market share.

Investment costs:

- investment required
- residual value of investment.

Operating costs:

- variable costs
- fixed costs
- taxation
- useful life of plant.

(2) specify the relationships between variables to calculate an NPV, e.g.:

Sales revenue = market size × market share × selling price.

Net cash flow = sales revenue − (variable costs + fixed costs + taxation), etc.

(3) Simulate the environment:

- assign random numbers to represent the probability distribution for each variable

- draw a random number for each variable

- select the value of each variable corresponding with the selected random number and compute an NPV

- repeat the process many times to create a probability distribution of returns.

(4) The results of a simulation exercise will be a probability distribution of NPVs.

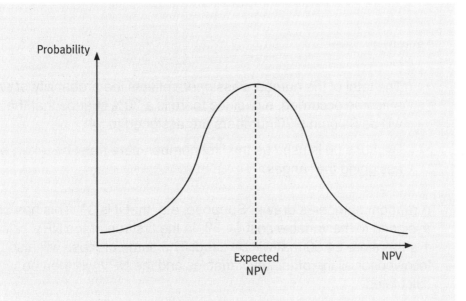

- Instead of choosing between expected values, decision makers can now take the dispersion of outcomes and the expected return into account.

Expandable text

Illustration – Simulation

The process of simulating the environment is illustrated below:

A firm has the following estimates of one major variable in the NPV calculation – variable cost:

Variable cost per unit ($)	4.00	4.50	5.00
Probability	0.3	0.5	0.2

Numbers between zero and 99 are then assigned to represent the distribution.

Calculating the cumulative probability makes the random numbers simpler to assign:

Variable cost per unit ($)	4.00	4.50	5.00
Probability	0.3	0.5	0.2
Cumulative probability	0.3	0.8	1.00
Random number range	00-29	30-79	80-99

Note that:

- The total of the numbers assigned reflects the probability of each outcome occurring, e.g. since there is a 30% chance that the cost will be $4 p/unit, 30 numbers are assigned to $4.

- Because 00 is used as the first number, care must be taken when assigning the ranges.

A random number is drawn. Suppose, e.g. that it is 33. This has been assigned to the variable cost $4.50. In the first run of the NPV calculation it is therefore $4.50 that will be used. The same process will also be followed for all the other key variables and the NPV will then be calculated.

A new batch of random numbers will then be drawn to do a second NPV, and the process will be continued until we have a probability distribution of returns.

Advantages of simulation

The major advantages of simulation are as follows:

- it includes all possible outcomes in the decision-making process
- it is a relatively easily understood technique
- it has a wide variety of applications (inventory control, component replacement, corporate models, etc.).

Drawbacks of simulation

However, it does have some significant drawbacks:

- models can become extremely complex and the time and costs involved in their construction can be more than is gained from the improved decisions
- probability distributions may be difficult to formulate.

Expandable text

Illustration – Simulation

A large chain of newsagents is reviewing the pattern of sales of a weekly magazine. The magazine sells for $3 per copy and costs $2 per copy from the publishers. There is a sale or return agreement whereby unsold copies can be returned to the publishers at cost price less a 40c per copy handling charge.

The demand pattern for a typical shop is as follows:

Average demand (copies)	Probability
50	0.07
150	0.12
250	0.14
350	0.19
450	0.18
550	0.09
650	0.07
750	0.07
850	0.05
950	0.02

and a typical shop orders 400 copies of the magazine a week.

Required:

(a) Allocate random numbers to the demand pattern for a typical shop.

(b) Using a tabular format and using the excerpt from the random number table given below, simulate 20 weeks' operations for a typical shop ordering 400 copies per week, showing weekly profit or loss. Also clearly show returns and lost sales for each week. **NB** Read horizontally across the random number table, i.e. number 00 for week 1, 27 for week 2 and so on.

(c) Interpret your results.

Random number table:

00	27	74	69	32	17	98	57	71	51
03	96	15	13	56	15	83	62	32	17

Expandable text

Solution

(a) It is helpful when assigning random numbers to calculate cumulative probabilities:

Demand	Probability	Cumulative probability	Random numbers
50	0.07	0.07	00-06
150	0.12	0.19	07-18
250	0.14	0.33	19-32
350	0.19	0.52	33-51
450	0.18	0.70	52-69
550	0.09	0.79	70-78
650	0.07	0.86	79-85
750	0.07	0.93	86-92
850	0.05	0.98	93-97
950	0.02	1.00	98-99

(b) The table can then be laid out to carry out the simulation where demand for each week is based upon the random number assigned.

C1	C2	C3	C4	C5	C6	C7	C8
Week	Ran. No.	Demand	Sales	Returns	Lost	Receipts	Profit/
1	00	50	50	350	–	710	(90)
2	27	250	250	150	–	990	190
3	74	550	400	–	150	1,200	400
4	69	450	400	–	50	1,200	400
5	32	250	250	150	–	990	190
6	17	150	150	250	–	850	50
7	98	950	400	–	550	1,200	400
8	57	450	400	–	50	1,200	400

9	71	550	400	–	150	1,200	400
10	51	350	350	50	–	1,130	330
11	03	50	50	350	–	710	(90)
12	96	850	400	–	450	1,200	400
13	15	150	150	250	–	850	50
14	13	150	150	250	–	850	50
15	56	450	400	–	50	1,200	400
16	15	150	150	250	–	850	50
17	83	650	400	–	250	1,200	400
18	62	450	400	–	50	1,200	400
19	32	250	250	150	–	990	190
20	17	150	150	250	–	850	50
		7,300	5,550	2,450	1,750	20,570	4,570
Weekly averages		365	277.5	122.5	87.5	1,028.50	228.50

Notes:

- C4 (sales) is the lower of demand (C3) and purchases (400 units).
- C5 (returns) is 400 less sales (C4).
- C6 (lost sales) is demand (C3) less sales (C4) where the answer is positive.
- C7 (receipts) is revenue ($3 × sales (C4)) plus returns payments ($1.60 × returns (C5)).
- C8 is receipts (C7) less costs of $800 (400 × $2).

(c) Interpretation of results

A typical shop will make an average daily profit of $228.50. The maximum profit in a day will be $400 and in any 20-day period a typical shop will make a loss of $90 on just 2 of the days.

Average daily returns were 122.5 copies. Since each return costs a net loss of 40c, this amounts to an average daily loss of $49.

Lost sales were 87.5 magazines on average. The opportunity cost of these lost sales is $1 or $87.50 in total. This outweighs the cost of returns and suggests a higher quantity should be ordered per day.

It would be useful to rerun the simulation at higher daily order volumes to identify the optimum level to order per day.

Expandable text

Mentor Products Co is considering the purchase of a new computer-controlled packing machine to replace the two machines which are currently used to pack product X. The new machine would result in reduced labour costs because of the more automated nature of the process and, in addition, would permit production levels to be increased by creating greater capacity at the packing stage. With an anticipated rise in the demand for product X, it has been estimated that the new machine will lead to increased profits in each of the next three years.

Due to uncertainty in demand however, the annual cash flows (including savings) resulting from the purchase of the new machine cannot be fixed with certainty and have therefore been estimated probabilistically as follows:

Year 1	Probability	Year 2	Probability	Year 3	Probability
$000		$000		$000	
10	0.3	10	0.1	10	0.3
15	0.4	20	0.2	20	0.5
20	0.3	40	0.3	30	0.2
		30	0.4		

Because of the overall uncertainty in the sales of product X, it has been decided that only three years' cash flows will be considered in deciding whether to purchase the new machine. After allowing for the scrap value of the existing machines, the net cost of the new machine will be $42,000.

The effects of taxation should be ignored.

(a) **Ignoring the time value of money, identify which combinations of annual cash flows will lead to an overall negative net cash flow, and determine the total probability of this occurring.**

(b) **On the basis of the average cash flow for each year, calculate the NPV of the new machine given that the company's cost of capital is 15%.**

Relevant DFs are as follows.

Year	DF
1	0.870
2	0.756
3	0.658

(c) **Analyse the risk inherent in this situation by simulating the NPV calculation. you should use the random numbers given at the end of the question to simulate five sets of cash flows. On the basis of your simulation results, what is the expected NPV and what is the probability of the new machine yielding a negative NPV?**

	Set 1	Set 2	Set 3	Set 4	Set 5
Year 1	4	7	6	5	0
Year 2	2	4	8	0	1
Year 3	7	9	4	0	3

Solution

(a) The combinations leading to a negative net cash flow are listed in the following table ($000):

Year				Probability		Net cash flow
0	1	2	3			
(42)	10	10	10	0.3 × 0.1 × 0.3	= 0.009	(12)
(42)	10	10	20	0.3 × 0.1 × 0.5	= 0.015	(2)
(42)	10	20	10	0.3 × 0.2 × 0.3	= 0.018	(2)
(42)	15	10	10	0.4 × 0.1 × 0.3	= 0.012	(7)
(42)	20	10	10	0.3 × 0.1 × 0.3	= 0.009	(2)
Total					0.063	

The total probability of a negative cash flow is 0.063.

Tutorial note: the probabilities are obtained using the multiplication law for mutually-exclusive outcomes:

P(A and B and C) = P(A) × P(B) × P(C)

(b) Calculation of average (expected) cash flows ($000s)

Year 1			Year 2			Year 3		
CF	Prob	CF × Prob	CF	Prob	CF × Prob	CF	Prob	CF × Prob
10	0.3	3	10	0.1	1	10	0.3	3
15	0.4	6	20	0.2	4	20	0.5	10
20	0.3	6	40	0.3	12	30	0.2	6
			30	0.4	12			
Expected cash flows		15			29			19

Discounting the expected CF to obtain present values ($000s):

Year	Expected cash flow	Discount Factor 15%	Present value
0	(42)	1.000	(42.000)
1	15	0.870	13.050
2	29	0.756	21.924
3	19	0.658	12.502
			5.476

The expected net present value is $5,476.

(c) Allocate the digits 0 to 9 to the cash flows each year such that the number of digits is proportional to the probability ($000s).

Year 1			Year 2			Year 3		
CF	Prob	digits	CF	Prob	digits	CF	Prob	digits
10	0.3	0-2	10	0.1	0	10	0.3	0-2
15	0.4	3-6	20	0.2	1-2	20	0.5	3-7
20	0.3	7-9	30	0.4	3-6	30	0.2	8-9
			40	0.3	7-9			

Select digits from the table of random numbers and record the corresponding cash flows ($000s).

Year	Year 1 DF = 0.870			Year 2 DF = 0.756			Year 3 DF = 0.658			NPV
Set 0	CF	RN	CF DCF		RN	CF DCF		RN	CF DCF	
1	(42)	4	15 13.05		2	20 15.12		7	20 13.16	(0.67)
2	(42)	7	20 17.40		4	30 22.68		9	30 19.74	17.82
3	(42)	6	15 13.05		8	40 30.24		4	20 13.16	14.45
4	(42)	5	15 13.05		0	10 7.56		0	10 6.58	(14.81)
5	(42)	0	10 8.70		1	20 15.12		3	20 13.16	(5.02)
										11.77

The average net present value is 11.77/5 ($'000s) = $2,354.

Three out of five outcomes are negative. The probability of a negative value is therefore 3/5 = 0.6.

However, probabilities are based on the relative frequency in a large number of trials. In practice, many hundreds of simulations would need to be carried out.

In comparing this result with part (a), it should also be remembered that the cash flows in part (a) are higher because they have not been discounted, leading to a lower probability of a negative net cash flow.

Adjusted payback

We looked at the payback form of investment appraisal in chapter 9. There are two ways in which risk can be incorporated into this method.

- Using payback as an addition to NPV analysis. Only projects with a positive NPV that also payback within a specified (usually short) period of time should be accepted.

- Discounting the cash flows using a risk-adjusted discount rate (see below) and calculating a discounted payback.
    - Only projects paying back within a specified period are accepted.
    - The discounted payback period represents the number of years required for the project to earn an NPV of zero.

Expandable text

Illustration – Adjusted payback

A project is expected to have the following cash flows:

Year	Cash flow $0000
0	(2,000)
1	500
2	500
3	400
4	600
5	350
6	400

Find

- the expected payback period
- the expected discounted payback period if the discount rate is 10%.

Solution

Year	Cash flow	Cumulative cash flow	DF at 10%	Discounted cash flow	Cumulative discounted cash flow
	$000	$000		$000	$000
0	(2,000)	(2000)	1	(2,000)	(2,000)
1	500	(1500)	0.909	454.5	(1,545.5)
2	2500	(1000)	0.826	413	(1,132.5)
3	3400	(600)	0.751	300.4	(832.1)
4	600	0	0.683	409.8	(422.3)
5	350	350	0.621	217.35	(204.95)
6	400	750	0.564	225.6	20.65

The standard payback period is exactly 4 years.

However when the flows are discounted the payback period becomes over 5 years.

Specifically $+ \dfrac{204.85}{225.6}$ or 6 years if the cash flows occur at year end.

Expandable text

Payback length

Discounting the cash flows takes account of the risks associated with inflation, interest loss and business variability. The discounted cash flows will be lower than the original values and therefore the payback period will be longer than with the simple method.

KAPLAN PUBLISHING

Projects should only be accepted if they pay back within the specified time frame even after the cash flows have been discounted.

Test your understanding 3

A project is expected to have the following cash flows:

Year	Cash flow
	$000
0	(1,700)
1	500
2	500
3	600
4	900
5	500

What is the expected discounted payback period if the discount rate is 12% and what is the NPV of the project?

Risk-adjusted discount rates

The discount rate we have assumed so far is the rate that reflects either:

- the cost of borrowing funds in the form of a loan rate or

- the underlying required return of the business (i.e. the return required by the shareholder),

- or a mix of both.

If an individual investment or project is perceived to be more risky than existing investments, the increased risk could be used as a reason to adjust the discount rate.

This is a key concept in investment appraisal. Applying the existing discount rate or cost of capital to an investment assumes that the existing business and gearing risk of the company will remain unchanged. If the project is significant in size and likely to result in additional risks then a project specific or risk-adjusted discount rate should be used.

The application of an increased discount rate is often successful in eliminating marginal projects. The addition to the usual discount rate is called the risk premium. The method used is examined further in chapter 19.

Chapter summary

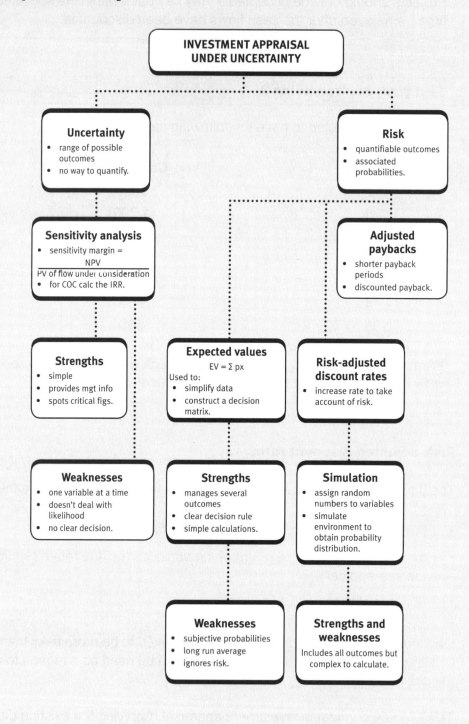

Test your understanding answers

Test your understanding 1

Although part (a) could be completed most efficiently by finding the PV of net annual inflows ($600,000 − $350,000 − $40,000), i.e. of $210,000, part (b) would be most effectively negotiated if the separate PVs were found.

NPV calculation

Time		Cash flow	15% DF	PV
		$000		$000
0	Equipment	(500)	1	(500)
1-3	Revenue	600	2.283	1,370
1-3	Variable costs	(350)	2.283	(799)
1-3	Fixed costs	(40)	2.283	(91)
3	Scrap value	80	0.658	53
				———
NPV ($000)				33
				———

The project should, on the basis of these estimates, be accepted.

(b) Sensitivity analysis

(i) Initial investment

For the decision to change, the NPV must fall by $33,000. For this to occur, the cost of the equipment must rise by $33,000.

This is a rise of: $\dfrac{33}{500} \times 100 = 6/6\%$

(ii) Scrap value

If the NPV is to fall by $33,000, the PV of scrap proceeds must fall by $33,000. The PV of scrap proceeds is currently $53,000. It must fall by: 33÷53 × 100 = 62.26%, say 62

(iii) Selling price

If sales price varies, sales revenue will vary (assuming no effect on demand). If the NPV of the project is to fall by $33,000, the selling price must fall by:

$$\frac{33}{1,370} \times 100 \qquad = 2.4\%$$

(iv) Unit variable cost

The project's NPV must fall by $33,000 therefore the PV of the variable costs must rise by $33,000. Since the PV of variable costs is $799,000, a rise of $33,000 is an increase of:

$$\frac{33}{799} \times 100 \qquad = 4.1\%$$

(v) Annual fixed costs

Since the PV of fixed costs is $91,000, a rise of $33,000 is an increase of:

$$\frac{33}{91} \times 100 \qquad = 3.6\%$$

(vi) Sales volume

If sales volume falls, revenue and variable costs fall (contribution falls). If the NPV is to fall by $33,000, volume must fall by:

$$\frac{33}{1,370 - 799} \times 100 = 5.8\%$$

(vii) Cost of capital

If NPV is to fall, cost of capital must rise. The figure which the cost of capital must rise to, that gives an NPV of zero, is the project's IRR.

NPV ($000) = − 500 + [210 × 2.210] + [80 × 0.624] = 14 The IRR is a little more than 17%, possibly 18%, but the formula can be used.

$$\text{IRR} \approx 15 + \frac{33}{33 - 14} \times (17 - 15)$$

≈ 18.47%, say 18.50%

To find the IRR, which is probably not much above 15%, the NPV at 17% can be found using the summarised cash flows.

The cost of capital would have to increase from 15% to 18½% before the investment decision changes

Test your understanding 2

Project A

State of the economy	Probability	Project NPV $(000)	EV $(000)
Recession	0.5	100	50
Stable	0.4	200	80
Growing	0.1	1,400	140
			270

Project B

State of the economy	Probability	Project NPV $(000)	EV $(000)
Recession	0.5	0	0
Stable	0.4	500	200
Growing	0.1	600	60
			260

Project C

State of the economy	Probability	Project NPV $(000)	EV $(000)
Recession	0.5	180	90
Stable	0.4	190	76
Growing	0.1	200	20
			186

On the basis of expected values Project A should be selected.

However it should be noted that Project A is also the most risky option as it has the widest range of potential outcomes.

Test your understanding 3

Year	Cash flow	DF at 12%	Discounted cash flow	Cumulative discounted cash flow
	$000		$000	$000
0	(1,700)	1	(1,700)	(1,700)
1	500	0.893	446.5	(1,253.5)
2	500	0.797	398.5	(855)
3	600	0.712	427.2	(427.8)
4	900	0.636	572.4	144.6
5	500	0.567	283.5	428.1

The discounted payback is between the end of year 3 and the end of year 4, i.e. during year 4. Assuming a constant rate of cash flow throughout the year, payback would be after 3.747 years or 3 years 9 months.

The NPV of the project will be $428,100 at the end of its life. It will have reached zero, i.e. the project will have broken even after, 3.7 years.

Asset investment decisions and capital rationing

Chapter learning objectives

Upon completion of this chapter you will be able to:

- evaluate the choice between leasing an asset and borrowing to buy using the before- and after-tax costs of debt

- define and calculate an equivalent annual cost (EAC)

- evaluate asset replacement decisions using EACs

- explain capital rationing in the context of capital budgeting

- define and distinguish between divisible and indivisible projects

- calculate profitability indexes for divisible investment projects and use them to evaluate investment decisions

- calculate the net present value (NPV) of combinations of non-divisible investment projects and use the results to evaluate investment decisions.

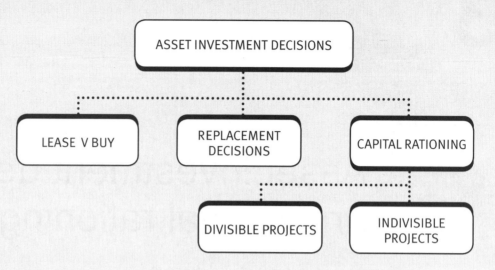

1 Lease versus buy

Once the decision has been made to acquire an asset for an investment project, a decision still needs to be made as to how to finance it. The choices that we will consider are:

- lease
- buy.

The NPVs of the financing cash flows for both options are found and compared and the lowest cost option selected.

The finance decision is considered separately from the investment decision. The operating costs and revenues from the investment will be common in each case.

Only the relevant cash flows arising as a result of the type of finance are included in the NPV calculation.

Leasing

The asset is never 'owned' by the user company from the perspective of the taxman.

Implications

- The finance company receives the WDAs as the owner of the asset.
- The user receives no WDAs but is able to offset the full rental payment against tax.

The relevant cash flows would thus be:

- the lease payments
- tax relief on the lease payments.

Buying

The assumption is that buying requires the use of a bank loan (for the sake of comparability). The user is the owner of the asset.

Implication

- The user will receive WDAs on the asset and tax relief for the interest payable on the loan.

The relevant cash flows would be:

- the purchase cost
- any residual value
- any associated tax implications due to WDAs.

 Do not include the interest payments or the tax relief arising on them in the NPV calculation, as this is dealt with via the cost of capital (see below).

Cost of capital

As the interest payments attract tax relief we must use the post-tax cost of borrowing as our discount rate. As all financing cash flows are considered to be risk-free, this rate is used for both leasing and buying.

 Post-tax cost of borrowing = Cost of borrowing × (1 − Tax rate).

(**Note:** in some questions you may find that a company is not paying tax and so the pre-tax rate would be appropriate.)

Expandable text

Illustration – Cost of capital

Walshey Co has already decided to accept a project and is now considering how to finance it.

For the four-year life of the project, the company can arrange a bank loan at an interest rate of 10% **after** corporation tax relief.

The asset cost (and hence loan size) would be $120,000 and the asset would be bought on 1 June 20X6, the first day of the company's tax year. The residual value of the equipment is $10,000 at the end of the fourth year.

An alternative would be to lease the asset over four years at a rental of $36,000 pa, payable at the start of each year.

Tax is payable at 33%, one year in arrears. Capital allowances are available at 25% on the written down value of the asset.

Required:

Determine whether it is better for the company to lease or buy the equipment.

Expandable text

Solution

WDA calculation **(W1):**

Year		$	Tax relief @ 33%	Timing
1	Initial investment	120,000	£	
	WDA	(30,000)	9,900	T_2
		————		
2	Book value	90,000		
	WDA	(22,500)	7,425	T_3
		————		
3	Book value	67,500		
	WDA	(16,875)	5,569	T_4
		————		
4	Book value	$	$	
		50,625		
	Residual value	(10,000)		
		————		

	40,625		
Balancing allowance (BA)/charge (BC)	(40,625)	13,406	T_5

Cost of borrowing to buy:

Time	0	1	2	3	4	5
	$	$	$	$	$	$
Initial investment	(120,000)					
Residual value					10,000	
Tax relief on WDAs (W1)			9,900	7,425	5,569	13,406
Net cash flows	(120,000)		9,900	7,425	15,569	13,406
DF @ 10%	1.000	0.909	0.826	0.751	0.683	0.621
PV	(120,000)	0	8,177	5,576	10,634	8,325

NPV (87,288)

Cost of leasing:

Year		Cash flows $	DF @10%	PV $
0-3	Rentals	(36,000)	1.000 + 2.487	(125,532)
2-5	Tax relief	11,880	3.791 – 0.909 = 2.882*	34,238

NPV (91,294)

*Or 3.170 × 0.909 = 2.882

Since the cost of buying is lower than the cost of leasing, the equipment should be bought

Expandable text

Where the use of an asset is required for a new project, there are effectively two decisions to be made:

- Is the project worth while?

- If so, should the asset be leased or bought with a loan?

If the project has been approved in principle then you need to calculate the NPVs of the two sets of financing cash flows for buying and leasing.

To be consistent with the earlier calculations, you could use the company's existing cost of capital to discount these cash flows. However, this is one of the areas where there is controversy. Once the asset has been bought or leased, then most of the cash flows listed above are reasonably certain. More specifically, the estimates are much less risky than those for the project's operating cash flows. One can argue, therefore, that a lower discount rate (to reflect the lower risk) should be used to evaluate the financing options. The usual alternative rate suggested is to use the post-tax cost of borrowing.

Test your understanding 1

A firm has decided to acquire a new machine to neutralise the toxic waste produced by its refining plant. The machine would cost $6.4 million and would have an economic life of five years.

Capital allowances (CAs) of 25% pa on a declining balance basis are available for the investment.

Taxation of 30% is payable on operating cash flows, one year in arrears.

The firm intends to finance the new plant by means of a five-year fixed interest loan at a pre-tax cost of 11.4% pa, principal repayable in five years' time.

As an alternative, a leasing company has proposed a finance lease over five years at $1.42 million pa payable in advance.

Scrap value of the machine under each financing alternative will be zero.

Evaluate the two options for acquiring the machine and advise the company on the best alternative.

Other considerations

There may be other issues to consider before a final decision is made to lease or buy, for example:

- Who receives the residual value in the lease agreement?

- Any restrictions associated with the taking on of leased equipment, e.g. leases may restrict a firm's borrowing capacity.

- Any additional benefits associated with lease agreement, e.g. maintenance or other support services.

See chapter 15 for further details.

2 Replacement decisions

Once the decision has been made to acquire an asset for a long-term project, it is quite likely that the asset will need to be replaced periodically throughout the life of the project.

Where there are competing replacements for a particular asset we must compare the possible replacement strategies available.

A problem arises where

- equivalent assets available are likely to last for different lengths of time or

- an asset, once bought, must be replaced at regular intervals.

The decision we are concerned with here is – how often should the asset be replaced?

EACs

In order to deal with the different time-scales, the NPV of each option is converted into an annuity or an EAC.

The EAC is the equal annual cash flow (annuity) to which a series of uneven cash flows is equivalent in PV terms.

The formula used is:

$$EAC = \frac{PV \text{ of costs}}{Annuity \text{ factor (AF)}}$$

The **optimum replacement period (cycle)** will be the period that has the lowest EAC, although in practice other factors may influence the final decision.

The method can be summarised as:

(1) calculate the NPV of each strategy or replacement cycle

(2) calculate the EAC for each strategy

(3) choose the strategy with the lowest EAC.

Key assumptions

- Cash inflows from trading are ignored since they will be similar regardless of the replacement decision. In practice using an older asset may result in lower quality, which in turn could affect sales.

- The operating efficiency of machines will be similar with differing machines or with machines of differing ages.

- The assets will be replaced in perpetuity or at least into the foreseeable future.

- In most questions tax and inflation are ignored.

- As with all NPV calculations non-financial aspects such as pollution and safety are ignored. An older machine may have a higher chance of employee accidents and may produce more pollution.

Expandable text

Within the UK, it is estimated that 50%-60% of total investment incorporates replacement. Yet the evidence also suggests that replacement appraisal is somewhat haphazard. In particular:

- there is a failure to take account of the timescale problems

- techniques such as payback and accounting rate of return are used, which are unsuitable for replacement decisions

- taxation and investment incentives are ignored

- inflation is ignored.

The factors to be considered when making replacement decisions are as follows:

- Capital cost of new equipment – the higher cost of equipment will have to be balanced against known or possible technical improvements.

- Operating costs – operating costs will be expected to increase as the machinery deteriorates over time. This is referred to as operating inferiority, and is the result of:
  - increased repair and maintenance costs
  - loss of production due to 'down time' resulting from increased repair and maintenance time
  - lower quality and quantity of output.

- Resale value – the extent to which old equipment can be traded in for new.

- Taxation and investment incentives.

- Inflation – both the general price level change, and relative movements in the prices of input and outputs.

Determining the optimum replacement period (cycle) will largely be influenced by:

- the capital cost/resale value of the asset – the longer the period, the less frequently these will occur

- the annual operating costs of running the asset – the longer the period, the higher these will become.

The timescale problems

A special feature of replacement problems is that it involves comparisons of alternatives with different timescales. If the choice is between replacing an item of machinery every two years or every three years, it would be meaningless simply to compare the NPV of the two costs.

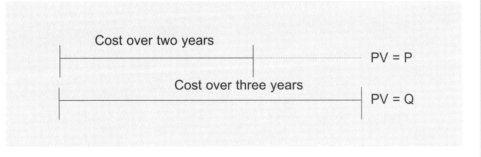

Almost certainly P < Q. However, this does not take account of the cost of providing an asset for the third year. One way of comparing asset replacement options is to convert the PV of cost over one replacement cycle to an equivalent annual PV of cost.

In other words, we compute the PV of costs over one cycle and then turn it into an EAC using the AF for the number of years in the replacement cycle.

Thus, the costs associated with any particular cycle can be considered as equivalent to having to pay this EAC every year throughout the cycle and throughout subsequent cycles.

Expandable text

Illustration – Key assumptions

A decision has to be made on replacement policy for vans. A van costs $12,000 and the following additional information applies:

Asset sold at end of year	Trade-in allowance	Asset kept for	Maintenance cost at end of year
	$		$
1	9,000	1 year	0
2	7,500	2 years	1,500 in 1st year
3	7,000	3 years	2,700 in 2nd year

Calculate the optimal replacement policy at a cost of capital of 15%. Note that the asset is only maintained at the end of the year if it is to be kept for a further year, i.e. there are no maintenance costs in the year of replacement. Ignore taxation and inflation.

Expandable text

Solution

The costs incurred over a single cycle are computed and the EAC is found as follows.

(1) Replace every year

	0	1	2	3
	$	$	$	$
Buy asset	(12,000)			
Maintenance costs		0		
Trade-in		9,000		
Net cash flow	(12,000)	9,000		
DF@15%	1	0.870		
PV	(12,000)	7,830		
NPV	(4,170)			

$$EAC = \frac{\text{PV of costs}}{\text{1 year AF}} = \frac{(4,170)}{0.870} = (\$4.793)$$

(2) Replace every two years

	0	1	2	3
Buy asset	(12,000)			
Maintenance costs		(1,500)		
Trade-in			7,500	
Net cash flow	(12,000)	(1,500)	7,500	
DF@15%	1	0.870	0.756	
PV	(12,000)	(1,305)	5,670	
NPV	(7,635)			

$$\text{EAC} = \frac{\text{PV of costs}}{\text{2 year AF}} = \frac{(7,635)}{1.626} = (\$4.696)$$

(3) Replace every three years

	0	1	2	3
Buy asset	(12,000)			
Maintenance costs		(1,500)	(2,700)	
Trade-in				7,000
Net cash flow	(12,000)	(1,500)	(2,700)	7,000
DF@15%	1	0.870	0.756	0.658
PV	(12,000)	(1,305)	(2,041)	4,606
NPV	(10,740)			

$$\text{EAC} = \frac{\text{PV of costs}}{\text{3 year AF}} = \frac{(10,740)}{2.283} = (\$4.704)$$

Here, the optimal replacement period is every two years.

> **Note** that the EAC is that sum that could be paid annually in arrears to finance the three replacement cycles. It is equivalent to the budget accounts that various public services encourage customers to open to spread the cost of those services more evenly. The PV of annual sums equal to the EAC is the same as the PV of the various receipts and payments needed to buy and maintain a van.

Test your understanding 2

A machine costs $20,000.

The following information is also available:

Running costs (payable at the end of the year):

Year 1	$5,000
Year 2	$5,500

Trade-in allowance

Disposal after 1 year:	$16,000
Disposal after 2 years:	$13,000

Calculate the optimal replacement cycle if the cost of capital is 10%.

Limitations of replacement analysis

The model assumes that when an asset is replaced, the replacement is in all practical respects identical to the last one and that this process will continue for the foreseeable future. However in practice this will not hold true owing to:

- changing technology
- inflation
- changes in production plans.

Expandable text

The replacement analysis model assumes that the firm replaces like with like each time it needs to replace an existing asset.

However this assumption ignores:

- Changing technology – machines fast become obsolete and can only be replaced with a more up-to-date model which will be more efficient and perhaps perform different functions.

- Inflation – the increase in prices over time alters the cost structure of the different assets, meaning that the optimal replacement cycle can vary over time.

- Changes in production plans – firms cannot predict with accuracy the market environment they will be facing in the future and whether they will even need to make use of the asset at that time.

3 Capital rationing

An introduction

Shareholder wealth is maximised if a company undertakes all possible positive NPV projects.

Capital rationing is where there are insufficient funds to do so.

There are two causes of this:

Hard capital rationing	Soft capital rationing

An absolute limit on the amount of finance available is imposed by the lending institutions. Reasons for hard capital rationing:
 	
• Industry-wide factors limiting funds.
• Company-specific factors, such as:
  – lack of or poor track record
  – lack of asset security
  – poor management team.
	A company may impose its own rationing on capital. This is contrary to the rational view of shareholder wealth maximisation. Reasons for soft capital rationing
	
	• Limited management skills available.
	• Desire to maximise return of a limited range of investments.
	• Limited exposure to external finance.
	• Encourages acceptance of only substantially profitable business.

Ensure you are able to discuss the difference between hard (external) and soft (internal) capital rationing.

Single and multi-period capital rationing

Single-period capital rationing: Shortage of funds for this period only.

Multi-period capital rationing: Shortage of funds in more than one period (outside syllabus)

The method for dealing with single-period capital rationing is similar to the limiting factor analysis used elsewhere in decision making.

Expandable text

A situation where there is a shortage of funds in more than one period is known as multi-period capital rationing. This makes the analysis more complicated because we have multiple limitations and multiple outputs. In such a situation we must employ a linear programming model to identify the profit maximising mix of investments.

Linear programming is beyond the scope of this syllabus.

The profitability index (PI) and divisible projects

If a project is divisible, any fraction of the project may be undertaken and the returns from the project are expected to be generated in exact proportion to the amount of investment undertaken. Projects cannot however be undertaken more than once.

The aim when managing capital rationing is to maximise the NPV earned per $1 invested in projects.

Where the projects:

*   are divisible (i.e. can be done in part)
*   earn corresponding returns to scale

it is achieved by:

(1) calculating a PI for each project

(2) ranking the projects according to their PI

(3) allocating funds according to the projects' rankings until they are used up.

The formula is:

$$PI = \frac{NPV}{Investment}$$

Illustration 1 – Capital rationing

A company has $100,000 available for investment and has identified the following 5 investments in which to invest. All investments must be started now (Yr 0).

Project	Initial investment (Yr 0) $000	NPV $000
C	40	20
D	100	35
E	50	24
F	60	18
G	50	(10)

Required:

Determine which projects should be chosen to maximise the return to the business.

Expandable text

Solution

Project	Working	PI	Ranking
C	20/40	= 0.5	1
D	35/100	= 0.35	3
E	24/50	= 0.48	2
F	18/60	= 0.3	4
G	Not worth while		

Funds available	Projects undertaken	NPV earned
$		$
100,000		
(40,000)	Project C	20,000
60,000		
(50,000)	Project E	24,000
10,000		
(10,000)	10/100 = 10% project D	3,500
Nil	Total NPV	47,500

Expandable text

C Co, with a cost of capital of 10%, has $40,000 available for investment in Year 0. Four divisible projects are available.

Project	Outlay	Receipts (cash flows)			
	Year 0	Year 1	Year 2	Year 3	Year 4
	$	$	$	$	$
1	100,000	40,000	100,000	80,000	60,000
2	30,000	40,000	40,000	40,000	40,000
3	20,000	40,000	30,000	40,000	50,000
4	40,000	20,000	30,000	30,000	30,000

Calculate the optimal investment policy.

Solution

Project	NPV at 10%	Profitability indices – NPV per $1 of outlay at 10%	Ranking
	$	$	
1	120,020	1.200	III
2	96,760	3.225	II
3	105,330	5.267	I
4	45,980	1.150	IV
	_____		
	368,090		
	_____		

Summary of optimal plan for C Co:

Project	Fraction of project accepted	Outlay at time 0	NPV
		$	$
3	1.00	20,000	105,330
2		20,000	64,507*
		_____	
Capital used and available		40,000	
			_____
NPV obtained			169,837
			_____

*Two-thirds of $96,760.

The opportunity cost of the capital rationing is $198,253 (368,090 − 169,837).

Indivisible projects – trial and error

If a project is indivisible it must be done in its entirety or not at all.

Where projects cannot be done in part, the optimal combination can only be found by trial and error.

Illustration 2 – Capital rationing

A Co has the same problem as before but this time the projects are indivisible.

The information is reproduced below:

A company has $100,000 available for investment and has identified the following 5 investments in which to invest. All investments must be started now (Yr 0).

Project	Initial investment (Yr 0) $000	NPV $000
C	40	20
D	100	35
E	50	24
F	60	18
G	50	(10)

Required:

Determine the optimal project selection.

Expandable text

Solution

Alternatives Mix	Investment	NPV earned
	$	$
C,F	100,000	38,000
D	100,000	35,000
C,E	90,000	44,000*

*C and E is the best mix. There is a problem however relating to the unused funds. The assumption is that the un-utilised funds will earn a return equivalent to the cost of capital and hence will generate an NPV of 0. This may or may not be the case.

Expandable text

PQ Co has $50,000 available to invest. Its cost of capital is 10%. The following indivisible projects are available:

Project	Initial outlay	Return pa to perpetuity
	$	$
1	20,000	1,500
2	10,000	1,500
3	15,000	3,000
4	30,000	5,400
5	25,000	4,800

Identify the optimal selection of projects for the firm to undertake.

Solution

The first stage is to calculate the NPV of the projects.

Project	Initial outlay	PV of cash flows **	NPV
	$	$	$
1	20,000	15,000	(5,000)
2	10,000	15,000	5,000
3	15,000	30,000	15,000
4	30,000	54,000	24,000
5	25,000	48,000	23,000

**PV of perpetuity = Annual receipt/Discount rate as a proportion

The approach is then one of considering all possible combinations of projects under the investment limit of $50,000. Project 1 is not worth while as it has a negative NPV.

Possible combinations are therefore: 2 and 4; 3 and 4; 3 and 5; 2,3 and 5.

The optimum selection of projects is as follows.

Projects	Initial outlay	NPV
	$	$
2	10,000	5,000
3	15,000	15,000
5	25,000	23,000
	50,000	43,000
Unused funds	Nil	
Funds available	50,000	

This may be compared to the ranking, if these were divisible projects:

Project	PI			Ranking	Fraction of project accepted	NPV
					$	$
1	− 5/20	=	− 0.25	V	–	
2	5/10	=	0.50	IV	–	
3	15/15	=	1.00	I	1.00	15,000
4	24/30	=	0.80	III	1/3	8,000
5	23/25	=	0.92	II	1.00	23,000
						46,000

The projects selected do not coincide with this ranking because of the fact that they are not divisible. Given there is this constraint, and also that finance is limited, no solution will give a higher NPV than $43,000.

The key in the examination is to ascertain whether or not the projects are divisible.

Divisible projects can be ranked using the PI. Combinations of indivisible projects must be considered on a trial and error basis.

Mutually-exclusive projects

Sometimes the taking on of projects will preclude the taking on of another, e.g. they may both require use of the same asset.

In these circumstances, each combination of investments is tried to identify which earns the higher level of returns.

Illustration 3 – Capital rationing

Using the same company information for A Co (divisible projects) the additional factor to be considered is that projects C and E are mutually exclusive.

The information is reproduced below.

A company has $100,000 available for investment and has identified the following 5 investments in which to invest. All investments must be started now (Yr 0).

Project	Initial investment (Yr 0) $000	NPV $000	PI NPV/$
C	40	20	0.5
D	100	35	0.35
E	50	24	0.48
F	60	18	0.3
G	50	(10)	not worth while

Required: Determine the optimal project selection.

Expandable text

Solution

Mix	Investment	NPV
	$	$
Project C mix	$100,000	$41,000 (20 + 0.6 × 35)
C, 60 % D		
Project E mix	$100,000	$41,500* (24 + 0.5 × 35)
E, 50%D		

* The best mix

Note that F is not considered as it ranks below project D according to the PI.

Expandable text

A firm has identified four possible projects, all of which are divisible:

Project	Initial investment (Yr 0)	NPV
	$000	$000
A	50	100
B	10	(50)
C	10	84
D	15	45

All must be started immediately but the firm has only $50,000 available for investment and C and D are mutually exclusive.

Determine the optimal project selection.

Solution

Project	NPV $000	Initial investment (Yr 0) $000	PI
A	100	50	100/50 = $2
B	(50)	10	Reject*
C	84	10	84/10 = $8.4
D	45	15	45/15 = $3

*B will be rejected, as the NPV is negative. As a result the calculation of the profitability index is unnecessary here since there is only one project (A) that can be mixed with either C or D.

Possible plans:

	NPV	Capital used
		50
Do C	84	(10)
		40
Do 40/50 =	80	(40)
80% A		
	___	___
	164	nil
	___	___

	NPV	Capital used
		50
Do D	45	(15)
		35
Do 35/50 =	70	(35)
70% A		
	___	___
	115	nil
	___	___

Therefore the optimal plan is to do project C and 80% of project A.

Chapter summary

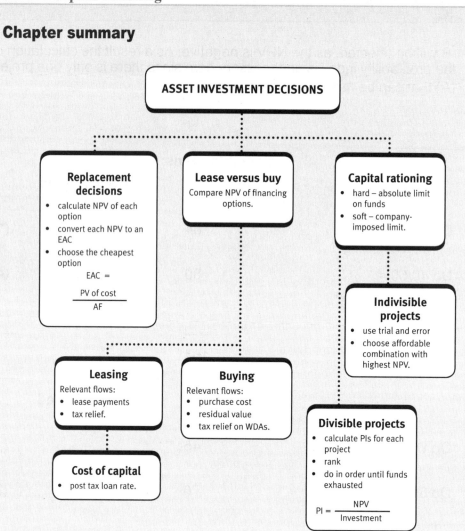

Test your understanding answers

Test your understanding 1

(W1) Calculation of the tax relief on WDAs if asset bought:

Year	Narrative	Written down value	Tax saved/ (extra tax paid) at 30%	Timing of tax flow
		$m	$m	
0	Cost	6.400		
1	CA	1.600	0.480	2
		────		
		4.800		
2	CA	1.200	0.360	3
		────		
		3.600		
3	CA	0.900	0.270	4
		────		
		2.700		
4	CA	0.675	0.203	5
		────		
		2.025		
5	Disposal proceeds	0.000		
		────		
	Balancing allowance	2.025	0.608	6
		────		

Note: The asset is bought at time t=0 as usual with the first CA in the year ended time one. Given the one-year time lag on the tax, the first tax effect is at time t=2.

(W2) Calculation of the post-tax cost of borrowing.

The pre-tax cost of borrowing is 11.4%.

The post-tax cost of borrowing can be approximated by multiplying this by (1 – tax rate), i.e. 11.4% × (1 – 0.3) = 7.98%, say 8% (strictly this ignores the impact of a one-year time delay on tax relief, but this is acceptable).

Cost of borrowing to buy:

Time	0	1	2	3	4	5	6
	$m	$m	$m	$m	$m	$m	$m
Asset	(6.400)						
Tax relief on CAs			0.480	0.360	0.270	0.203	0.608
	(6,400)	–	0.480	0.360	0.270	0.203	0.608
(W1)		–					
PV factor @ 8%	1	0.926	0.857	0.794	0.735	0.681	0.630
(W2)							
PV	(6.400)	0	0.411	0.286	0.198	0.138	0.383

NPV = $(4.984)m

Cost of leasing:

Timing	Narrative	Cash flow	DF @ 8%	PV
		$m		$m
0-4	Lease payments	(1.420)	1+ 3.312	(6.123)
2-6	Tax savings	0.426	3.993×0.926*	1.575
	NPV			(4.548)

* or AF 2-6 = 4.623 – 0.926

The cost of leasing is lower than the cost of buying and the asset should therefore be acquired under a finance lease.

Test your understanding 2

Note: in contrast to the maintenance costs in the above illustration, running costs (e.g. petrol) are incurred in every year of ownership.

One-year replacement cycle:

	0 $	1 $	2 $
Buy asset	(20,000)		
Running costs		(5,000)	
Trade-in		16,000	
Net cash flow	(20,000)	11,000	
DF@15%	1	0.909	
PV	(20,000)	9,999	
NPV	(10,001)		

$$\text{Annual equivalent} = \frac{\$10,001}{1 \text{ yr AF}} = \frac{\$10,001}{0.909} = \$11,002$$

Two-year replacement cycle:

	0 $	1 $	2 $
Buy asset	(20,000)		
Running costs		(5,000)	(5,500)
Trade-in			13,000
Net cash flow	(20,000)	(5,000)	7,500
DF@15%	1	0.909	0.826
PV	(20,000)	(4,545)	6,195
NPV	(18,350)		

$$\text{Annual equivalent} = \frac{\$18,350}{2 \text{ yr AF}} = \frac{\$18,350}{1.736} = \$10,570$$

The machine should therefore be replaced after two years.

14

The economic environment

Chapter learning objectives

Upon completion of this chapter you will be able to:

- explain the main objectives of macroeconomic policy

- explain the potential conflict between the main objectives of macroeconomic policy and its impact on policy targets

- explain the impact of general macroeconomic policy on planning and decision making in the business sector

- define monetary policy and explain the main tools used

- discuss the general role of monetary policy in the achievement of macroeconomic policy targets

- discuss use of interest rates in the achievement of macroeconomic policy targets

- define exchange rate policy and discuss its role in the achievement of macroeconomic policy targets

- explain the impact of specific economic policies on planning and decision making in the business sector

- define fiscal policy and explain the main tools used

- discuss the role of fiscal policy in the achievement of macroeconomic policy targets.

- explain the need for competition policy and its interaction with business planning and decision making

- explain the need for government assistance for business and its interaction with business planning and decision making

- explain the need for green policies and their interaction with business planning and decision making

- explain the need for corporate governance regulation and its interaction with business planning and decision making

- define financial intermediary and explain the role such intermediaries play in the UK financial system

- explain the role of financial markets in the UK financial system

- identify the nature and role of capital markets, both national and international, in the UK financial system

- identify the nature and role of money markets, both national and international, in the UK financial system

- explain the main functions of a stock market

- explain the main functions of a corporate bond market

- explain the relationship between risk and return in financial investments.

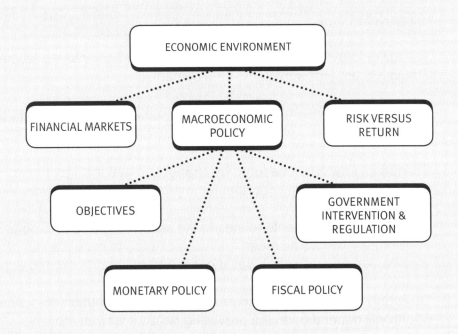

1 Macroeconomic policy

The objectives of macroeconomic policy

Macroeconomic policy is the management of the economy by government in such a way as to influence the performance and behaviour of the economy as a whole.

The principal objectives of macroeconomic policy will be to achieve the following:

- full employment of resources
- price stability
- economic growth
- balance of payments equilibrium
- an appropriate distribution of income and wealth.

Expandable text

The full employment of resources applies in particular to the labour force. The aim is both full and stable employment.

Price stability means little or no inflation putting upward pressure on prices.

Economic growth is measured by changes in national income from one year to the next and is important for improving living standards.

The balance of payments relates to the ratio of imports to exports. A payment surplus would mean the value of exports exceeds that of imports. A payment deficit would occur where imports exceed exports.

Obviously what is considered an appropriate distribution of income and wealth will depend upon the prevailing political view at the time.

Potential for conflict

The pursuit of macroeconomic objectives may involve trade-offs – where one objective has to be sacrificed for the sake of another, e.g.:

Full employment   **versus**   **Price stability**
Economic growth   **versus**   **Balance of payments**

Expandable text

Both economic theory and the experience of managing the economy suggest that the simultaneous achievement of all macroeconomic objectives may be extremely difficult. Two examples of possible conflict may be cited here.

There may be conflict between full employment and price stability. It is suggested that inflation and employment are inversely related. The achievement of full employment may therefore lead to excessive inflation through an excess level of aggregate demand in the economy.

Rapid economic growth may, in the short-term at least, have damaging consequences for the balance of payments since rapidly rising incomes may lead to a rising level of imports.

Government reputation and business confidence will both be damaged if the government is seen to be pursuing policy targets which are widely regarded as incompatible.

Policy objectives may conflict and hence governments have to consider trade-offs between objectives. The identification of targets for policy should reflect this.

Making an impact – how macroeconomic policy affects the business sector

In order for macroeconomic policy to work, its instruments must have an impact on economic activity. This means that it must affect the business sector. It does so in two broad forms:

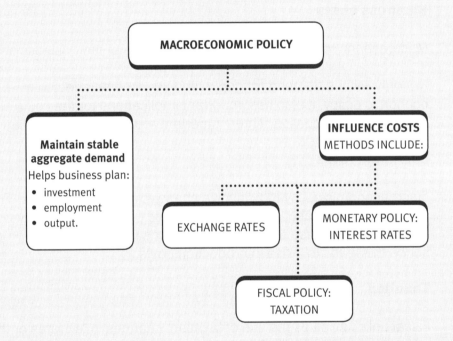

 Expandable text

AD

AD is the total demand for goods and services in the economy.

Note: National income is AD that has been satisfied by the provision of goods and services, etc.

The broad thrust of macroeconomic policy is to influence the level of AD in the economy. This is because the level of AD is central to the determination of the level of unemployment and the rate of inflation. If AD is too low, unemployment might result; if AD is too high, inflation induced by excess demand might result.

Changes in AD will affect all businesses to varying degrees.

Thus effective business planning requires that businesses can:

- predict the likely thrust of macroeconomic policy in the short- to medium-term
- predict the consequences for sales growth of the overall stance of macroeconomic policy and any likely changes in it.

The more stable government policy is, the easier it is for businesses to plan, especially in terms of investment, employment and future output capacity.

Business costs

Macroeconomic policy may influence the costs of the business sector.

Not only will the demand for goods and services be affected by macro-economic policy, it also has important implications for the costs and revenues of businesses. Three important areas may be identified:

Exchange rates

Macroeconomic policy may involve changes in exchange rates. This may have the effect of raising the domestic price of imported goods. Most businesses use some imported goods in the production process; hence this leads to a rise in production costs.

Taxation

Fiscal policy involves the use of taxation: changes in tax rates or the structure of taxation will affect businesses, e,g, a change in the employer's national insurance contribution (NIC) will have a direct effect on labour costs for all businesses. Changes in indirect taxes (e,g, a rise in sales tax or excise duties) will either have to be absorbed or the business will have to attempt to pass on the tax to its customers.

Interest rates

Monetary policy involves changes in interest rates. These changes will directly affect firms in two ways:

- Costs of servicing debts will change, especially for highly- geared firms.
- The viability of investment will be affected since all models of investment appraisal include the rate of interest as one, if not the main, variable.

2 Monetary policy

Monetary policy is concerned with influencing the overall monetary conditions in the economy in particular:

- the volume of money in circulation – the money supply
- the price of money – interest rates.

Governments cannot control both at once – in practice they:

- focus on interest rates – easier!
- monitor the money supply:

M0 – narrow measure:

M4 – broad measure:

Expandable text

It is clear that money is crucial to the way in which a modern economy functions. **Money** is any financial asset which has liquidity and fulfils the task of a medium of exchange.

Monetary policy is concerned with influencing the overall monetary conditions in the economy.

Two particular problems with the use of monetary policy are:

- the choice of targets
- the effects of interest rate changes.

The choice of targets

A fundamental problem of monetary policy concerns the choice of variable to operate on. The ultimate objective of monetary policy is to influence some important variable in the economy – the level of demand, the rate of inflation, the exchange rate for the currency, etc. However monetary policy has to do this by targeting some intermediate variable which, it is believed, influences, in some predictable way, the ultimate object of the policy.

The broad choice here is between targeting the **stock of money** or the **rate of interest:**

(a) The volume of money in circulation. The stock of money in the economy (the 'money supply') is believed to have important effects on the volume of expenditure in the economy. This in turn may influence the level of output in the economy or the level of prices.

(b) The **price** of money. The price of money is the rate of interest. If governments wish to influence the amount of money held in the economy or the demand for credit, they may attempt to influence the level of interest rates.

The monetary authorities may be able to control either the supply of money in the economy or the level of interest rates but cannot do both simultaneously. In practice, attempts by governments to control the economy by controlling the money supply have failed and have been abandoned. However, growth in the money supply is monitored, because excessive growth could be destabilising.

The measurement of the money supply (stock)

Currently, in the UK, two measures of money supply are monitored.

(a) **M0:** a **narrow** money measure, incorporating:

    (1) notes and coins in circulation with the public

    (2) till money held by banks and building societies

    (3) operational balances held by commercial banks at the Bank of England.

(b) **M4:** a **broad** money measure, incorporating:

   (1) notes and coins in circulation with the public

   (2) all sterling deposits held by the private sector at UK banks and building societies.

The effects of interest rate changes

Although easier to control than the money supply, the impact of any change in interest rates will be uncertain.

What will be most affected?

- Investment? or Consumption?
- Day to day purchases? or Consumer durables?

Will exchange rates be affected?

- High interest rates attract foreign investment and increase exchange rates.

In some countries, such as the UK, control of short-term interest rates has been given to the central bank. Control is achieved by setting commercial lending rates to the commercial banks, which in turn pass them on to their customers.

Expandable text

The effects of interest rates

The problem for the monetary authorities is that controlling the level of interest rates is rather easier than controlling the overall stock of money but the effects of doing so are less certain.

If governments choose to target interest rates as the principal means of conducting monetary policy, this may have a series of undesirable effects. These principally relate to the indiscriminate nature of interest rate changes and to the external consequences of monetary policy.

When interest rates are changed, it is expected that the general level of demand in the economy will be affected. Thus a rise in interest rates will discourage expenditure, by raising the cost of credit. However, the effects will vary:

(1) **Investment may be affected more than consumption.** The rate of interest is the main cost of investment whether it is financed by internal funds or by debt. However, most consumption is not financed by credit and hence is less affected by interest rate changes. Since the level of investment in the economy is an important determinant of economic growth and international competitiveness there may be serious long-term implications arising from high interest rates.

(2) Even where consumption is affected by rising interest rates, the **effects are uneven.** The demand for consumer durable goods and houses is most affected since these are normally credit-based purchases. Hence active interest policy may induce instability in some sectors of business.

The second problem arises from the openness of modern economies and their economic interdependence. There is now a very high degree of capital mobility between economies: large sums of short-term capital move from one financial centre to another in pursuit of higher interest rates. Changes in domestic interest rates relative to those in other financial centres will produce large inflows and outflows of short-term capital. Inflows of capital represent a demand for the domestic currency and hence push up the exchange rate. Outflows represent sales of the domestic currency and hence depress the exchange rate. This may bring about unacceptable movements in the exchange rate.

Monetary policy in the UK

It is useful to look at the current monetary policy in the UK. Similar policies are pursued in the US and the Euro-zone countries.

In the UK, the central bank has been given responsibility by the government for controlling short-term interest rates. Short-term interest rates are controlled with a view to influencing the rate of inflation in the economy, over the long-term. In broad terms, an increase in interest rates is likely to reduce demand in the economy and so lower inflationary pressures, whereas a reduction in interest rates should give a boost to spending in the economy, but could result in more inflation. The aim of economic policy is to find a suitable balance between economic growth and the risks from inflation.

Central governments can control short-term interest rates through their activities in the money markets. This is because the commercial banks need to borrow regularly from the central bank. The central bank lends to the commercial banks at a rate of its own choosing (a rate known in the UK as the repo rate). This borrowing rate for banks affects the interest rates that the banks set for their own customers. Action by a central bank to raise or lower interest rates normally results in an immediate increase or reduction in bank base rates.

Impact of monetary policy on business decision making

Factors affected	Achieved by controlling supply	Achieved by increasing interest rates
• Availability of finance	Credit restrictions ⇨small businesses struggle to raise funds	
• Cost of finance	Reduced supply pushes up the cost of funds ⇨ discourages expansion	S/hs require higher returns ⇨ if not met, share price falls
• Level of consumer demand	Too difficult to raisefunds to spend	Saving becomes more attractive
• Exchange rates		High interest rates attracts foreign investment ⇨ increase in exchange rates: • exports dearer • imports cheaper.

All the above factors will also therefore influence inflation, which has a significant impact on business cash flows and profits. Inflation may be:

- demand-pull inflation – excess demand
- cost-push inflation – high production costs.

Both can have negative impact on cash flows and profits.

Expandable text

Changes in monetary policy will influence the following factors.

The availability of finance. Credit restrictions achieved via the banking system or by direct legislation will reduce the availability of loans. This can make it difficult for small- or medium-sized new businesses to raise finance. The threat of such restrictions in the future will influence financial decisions by companies, making them more likely to seek long-term finance for projects.

The cost of finance. Any restrictions on the stock of money, or restrictions on credit, will raise the cost of borrowing, making fewer investment projects worth while and discouraging expansion by companies. Also, any increase in the level of general interest rates will increase shareholders' required rate of return so unless companies can increase their return, share prices will fall as interest rates rise. Thus, in times of 'tight' money and high interest rates, organisations are less likely to borrow money and will probably contract rather than expand operations.

The level of consumer demand. Periods of credit control and high interest rates reduce consumer demand. Individuals find it more difficult and more expensive to borrow to fund consumption, whilst saving becomes more attractive. This is another reason for organisations to have to contract operations.

The level of exchange rates. Monetary policy which increases the level of domestic interest rates is likely to raise exchange rates as capital is attracted into the country. Very many organisations now deal with both suppliers and customers abroad and thus cannot ignore the effect of future exchange rate movements. Financial managers must consider methods of hedging exchange rate risk and the effect of changes in exchange rates on their positions as importers and exporters.

The level of inflation. Monetary policy is often used to control inflation. Rising price levels and uncertainty as to future rates of inflation make financial decisions more difficult and more important. As prices of different commodities change at different rates, the timing of purchase, sale, borrowing and repayment of debt becomes critical to the success of organisations and their projects. This is discussed further below:

Impact of inflation on business cash flows and profits

The real effects on the level of profits and the cash flow position of a business of a sustained rate of inflation depend on the form that inflation is taking and the nature of the markets in which the company is operating. One way of analysing inflation is to distinguish between demand-pull inflation and cost-push inflation.

Demand-pull inflation might occur when excess aggregate monetary demand in the economy and hence demand for particular goods and services enable companies to raise prices and expand profit margins.

Cost-push inflation will occur when there are increases in production costs independent of the state of demand, e.g. rising raw material costs or rising labour costs. The initial effect is to reduce profit margins and the extent to which these can be restored depends on the ability of companies to pass on cost increases as price increases for customers.

One would expect that the effect of cost-push inflation on company profits and cash flow would always be negative, but that with demand-pull inflation, profits and cash flow might be increased, at least in nominal terms and in the short run. In practice, however, even demand-pull inflation may have negative effects on profits and cash flow.

Demand-pull inflation may in any case work through cost. This is especially true if companies use pricing strategies in which prices are determined by cost plus some mark-up.

- Excess demand for goods leads companies to expand output.

- This leads to excess demand for factors of production, especially labour, so costs (e.g. wages) rise.

- Companies pass on the increased cost as higher prices.

- In most cases inflation will reduce profits and cash flow, especially in the long run.

3 Fiscal policy

 Fiscal policy is the manipulation of the government budget in order to influence the level of aggregate demand and therefore the level of activity in the economy. It covers:

- government spending
- taxation
- government borrowing

which are linked as follows:

public expenditure = taxes raised + government borrowing (+ sundry other income)

The role of the Chancellor is to balance the budget:

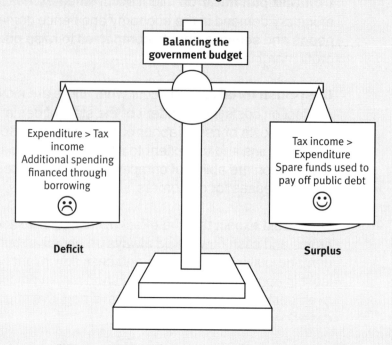

Expandable text

All governments engage in public expenditure, although levels vary somewhat from country to country. This expenditure must be financed either by taxation or by borrowing. Thus the existence of public expenditure itself raises issues of policy, notably how to tax and whom to tax. But, in addition, the process of expenditure and taxation permits the use of fiscal policy in a wider sense: the government budget can be manipulated to influence the level of AD in the economy and hence the level of economic activity.

The government budget (including central and local government) is a statement of public expenditure and income over a period of one year. Expenditure can be financed either by taxation or by borrowing. The relationship of expenditure to taxation indicates the state of the budget.

Three budget positions can be identified.

A **balanced budget:** total expenditure is matched by total taxation income.

A **deficit budget:** total expenditure exceeds total taxation income and the deficit must be financed by borrowing. In the UK the budget deficit was known as the public sector borrowing requirement (PSBR) but has been renamed to the (PSNCR) public sector net cash requirement.

A **surplus budget:** total expenditure is less than total taxation income and the surplus can be used to pay back public debt incurred as a result of previous deficits.

Taxation

Tax revenue is the main source of government spending. It is raised via:

- direct taxation – tax on income
- indirect taxation – tax on consumption.

It is important to pitch taxation at the correct level:

Too low = insufficient government income

Too high = disincentive effects = reduction in revenue raised.

Disincentive effects include reluctance to:

- work
- invest
- invest from overseas

and an increased keenness for:

- tax avoidance schemes.

Expandable text

Taxation

The obvious means by which public expenditure can be financed is by taxation. The government receives some income from direct charges in the public sector (e.g. health prescription charges) and from trading profits of some public sector undertakings, but the bulk of its income comes from taxation.

Taxes are divided into broad groups.

Direct taxes are taxes levied directly on income receivers whether they are individuals or organisations. These include income tax, NICs, corporation tax, and inheritance tax.

Indirect taxes are levied on one set of individuals or organisations but may be partly or wholly passed on to others and are largely related to consumption not income. These include VAT and excise duties. By their very nature, indirect taxes tend to be regressive which means they have a relatively greater impact on individuals with lower incomes.

Impacts of excessive taxation

Taxation can raise very large flows of income for the government. However excessive taxation may have undesirable economic consequences. Those most frequently cited are as follows

- Personal disincentives to work and effort: this may be related mainly to the form of taxation, e.g. progressive income tax (earn more, pay more), rather than the overall level of taxation.

- Discouragement to business, especially the disincentive to invest and engage in research and development (R&D), which results from high business taxation.

- Disincentive to foreign investment: multinational firms may be dissuaded from investing in economies with high tax regimes.

- A reduction in tax revenue may occur if taxpayers are dissuaded from undertaking extra income-generating work and are encouraged to seek tax-avoidance schemes.

If the tax rate exceeds a certain level, the total tax revenue falls. It should be noted that these disincentive effects, while apparently clear in principle, are difficult to identify in the real world and hence their impact is uncertain.

Government borrowing

Governments can borrow:

- Short-term, e.g. Treasury bills
- Long-term, e.g. National Savings certificates.

Expandable text

Government borrowing

Broadly the government can undertake two types of borrowing:

It can borrow directly or indirectly **from the public** by issuing relatively illiquid debt. This includes National Savings certificates, premium bonds, and long-term government stock. This is referred to as 'funding' the debt.

It can borrow **from the banking system** by issuing relatively liquid debt such as Treasury bills. This is referred to as 'unfunded' debt.

Long-term government stock is issued for long-term financing requirements, whereas Treasury bills are issued to fund short-term cash flow requirements.

Potential problems with fiscal policy

The risks associated with fiscal policy are related to the unintended effects:

- government borrowing 'crowding out' private investment by pushing up interest rates

  BUT: government spending can boost the economy

- changes in behaviour owing to taxation

  BUT: taxes can exert positive influences, e.g. excise duty on cigarettes.

Expandable text

Problems of fiscal policy

Two difficulties associated with fiscal policy have dominated debates about macroeconomic management in recent years:

- the problem of 'crowding out'
- the incentive effects of taxation.

Both have had a major impact on the way in which fiscal policy has been conducted, especially in the US and UK .

Crowding out

It is suggested that fiscal policy can lead to 'financial crowding out', whereby government borrowing leads to a fall in private investment. This occurs because increased borrowing leads to higher interest rates by creating a greater demand for money and loanable funds and hence a higher 'price'.

The private sector, which is sensitive to interest rates, will then reduce investment due to a lower rate of return. This is the investment that is crowded out. The weakening of fixed investment and other interest-sensitive expenditure counteracts the economy boosting benefits of government spending. More importantly, a fall in fixed investment by business can hurt long-term economic growth.

Doubts exist over the likely size of any crowding out effect of government borrowing on other borrowers but a very large PSBR may well lead to a fall in private investment.

However, when the economy is depressed, and there is not much new private sector investment, government spending programmes could help to give a boost to the economy.

Incentives

It is likely that all taxes have some effect. Indeed, the structure of taxes is designed to influence particular economic activities: in particular, taxes on spending are used to alter the pattern of consumption. Here are two examples.

- High excise duties on alcohol and tobacco products reflect social and health policy priorities.
- Policies to use excise duties to raise the real price of petrol over time is designed to discourage the use of private cars because of the environmental effects.

Thus taxes as instruments of fiscal policy can fulfil a variety of useful functions.

However, there has been a growing concern among some economists that taxes have undesirable side effects on the economy, notably on incentives. As we have seen, it is argued that high taxes, especially when they are steeply progressive, act as a disincentive to work.

Moreover some taxes have more specific effects. For example, employer national insurance (NI) payments raise the cost of labour and probably reduce employment.

Test your understanding 1

(1) What are the principal objectives of macroeconomic policy? How may these conflict?

(2) What implications does macroeconomic policy have for the costs of businesses?

(3) Define monetary policy and explain its principal elements.

(4) Discuss the possible impacts of excessive taxation.

(5) What is meant by 'financial crowding out'?

4 Government intervention and regulation

As well as the general measures to impact business operations discussed above, governments can also take more specific measures to regulate business.

Pricing restrictions

In the main, prices for goods and services are set by the market without government intervention.

However a market which lacks competition, e.g. one dominated by monopolies, creates disadvantages for the whole economy, e.g. the market may:

- produce inefficiently
- price discriminate
- fail to innovate
- price out any competition.

Test your understanding 2

Consider what benefits monopolies could bring to an economy.

Expandable text

It is not the government's place to set prices for goods and services provided by businesses in the private sector. In a competitive marketplace, prices will be set within the industry according to demand and supply. All producers have to accept the prevailing market price, unless they are able to add distinguishing features to their products (e.g. branding, superior technology) that enable them to charge higher prices.

However, some markets are characterised by various degrees of market power, in particular monopolies, whereby producers become price **makers** rather than price **takers.**

(A **monopoly** is where a firm has a sufficient share of the market to enable it to restrict output and raise prices.)

The absence of competition results in disadvantages to the economy as a whole.

- Economic inefficiency: output is produced at a higher cost than necessary. For example, there may be no incentive to reduce costs by improving technology used.

- Monopolies may be able to engage in price discrimination: charging different prices to different customers for the same good or service, e.g. peak and off-peak pricing. This may act against the interests of customers.

- Disincentive to innovate: the absence of competition may reduce the incentive to develop new products or new production processes.

- Pricing practices: monopolies may adopt pricing practices to make it uneconomic for new firms to enter the industry, thus reducing competition in the long run.

These potential problems of companies with monopoly power must be considered in the light of some possible advantages that may be associated with such firms:

- Large firms may secure economies of scale: it is possible that there are significant economies of scale, reducing production costs, but that these require large firms and hence the number of firms in an industry is restricted. In this case the benefits of economies of scale may offset the inefficiencies involved.

- The special case of natural monopolies: this is the case where the economies of scale in the provision of some basic infrastructure are so great that only one producer is feasible. This may be the case of the public utilities in energy and water.

- Research and development: it may be that monopoly profits are both the reward and the source of finance, for technological and organisational innovation. Thus some static welfare losses have to be accepted in order to ensure a dynamic and innovative business sector.

Economic theory concludes that, all other things being equal, economic welfare is maximised when markets are competitive.

Government responses

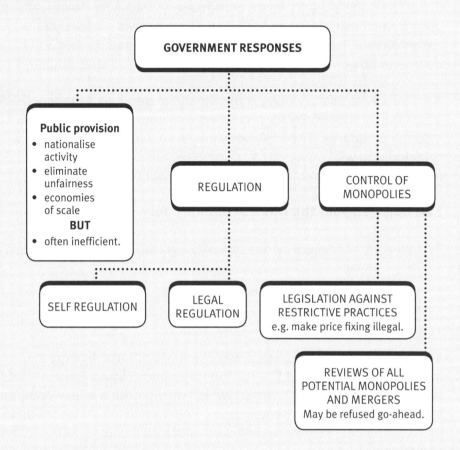

Fair competition: public provision and regulation

The response to the problems associated with monopoly power can take a variety of forms. The first of these is public provision. This is where an economic activity is nationalised. The advantages of this are as follows:

- unfair pricing practices and/or excessive prices can be eliminated

- cost advantages of economies of scale can be reaped.

Traditionally, public utilities have presented the most convincing case for nationalisation because they are natural monopolies. However, nationalised industries may have disadvantages, notably a greater potential for cost-inefficiency.

The alternative response to the dangers of monopoly is regulation.

Self-regulation is common in many professions where the profession itself establishes codes of conduct and rules of behaviour (e.g. the Law Society, the British Medical Association).

The alternative is some form of **public or legal regulation.** An example in the UK is the establishment of regulatory bodies for the privatised utilities such as OFTEL and OFGAS. These were established in recognition of the monopoly power of the privatised utilities and have a degree of power over both prices and services in these industries.

Another UK regulatory body is the Financial Services Authority (FSA) which has responsibility for regulating the financial services, banking and insurance markets. The FSA does not have to control monopolies, but it is concerned with ensuring fair competition and protecting the public against unfair treatment by financial organisations.

Fair competition: the control of monopoly

Formal competition policy has typically centred upon two broad issues.

- monopolies and mergers
- restrictive practices.

The concern for monopolies is with firms which have a degree of monopoly power (defined as having more than 25% of the market for a good or service) or with mergers which may produce a new company with more than 25% of market share. The underlying presumption is that monopolies are likely to be inefficient and may act against the interests of customers.

The concern over restrictive practices is with trading practices of firms which may be deemed to be uncompetitive and act against the interests of consumers.

Legislation typically prohibits:

(a) anti-competitive agreements (such as price-fixing cartels); and

(b) abuse of a dominant position in a market.

Government assistance

The political and social objectives of a government, as well as its economic objectives, could be pursued through official aid intervention such as grants and subsidies. The government provides support to businesses both financially, in the form of grants, and through access to networks of expert advice and information.

For example to:

- boost enterprise

- encourage innovation

- speed urban renewal

- revive flagging industries

- train labour force

- sponsor important research.

There is always strong competition for the grants and the criteria for awards are stringent. These vary but are likely to include the location, size and industry sector of the business.

Green policies

When a firm appraises a project it may, rationally, only include those costs it will itself incur. However, for the good of society, external costs (such as damage to wildlife) need to be taken into account.

This has led to:

- green legislation

- punitive taxation on damaging practices

- which force companies to consider the negative impacts of potential projects in any appraisals.

Test your understanding 3

Suggest ways in which government have attempted to impose consideration of 'green issues' onto business.

Expandable text

Externalities are costs (benefits) which are not paid (received) by the producers or consumers of the product but by other members of society.

The need for green policies arises from the existence of external environmental costs associated with some forms of production or consumption. An example of each is given below:

- production: river pollution from various manufacturing processes

- consumption: motor vehicle emissions causing air pollution and health hazards.

If external costs (and benefits) exist in the production or consumption process and if they are large in relation to private costs and benefits, the price system may be a poor mechanism for the allocation of resources. This is because private producers and consumers ignore (and indeed may be unaware of) the external effects of their activities.

Thus the price system, in which prices are determined by the interaction of supply and demand and which determines the allocation of resources, may lead to a misallocation of resources.

It is likely that policies to control damage to the environment will become more and more common as concern for the environment increases. Many countries already have a differential tax on leaded and unleaded petrol with governments taking the decision to use taxes to raise the real price of petrol each year. There is also a continuing debate in the EU over the possible introduction of a wider 'carbon tax'.

Externalities lead to a **misallocation of resources** and imply the need for policies to correct this. In particular, **green policies** are needed to tackle externalities that affect the **environment.**

Corporate governance

Corporate governance is defined as 'the system by which companies are directed and controlled' and covers issues such as ethics, risk management and stakeholder protection.

Regulation

Following the collapse of several large businesses and widespread concern about the standard of corporate governance across the business community, a new corporate governance framework was introduced.

A variety of rules have been introduced in different countries but the principles, common to all, contain regulations on:

- separation of the supervisory function and the management function

- transparency in the recruitment and remuneration of the board

- appointment of non-executive directors (NEDs)

- establishment of an audit committee

- establishment of risk control procedures to monitor strategic, business and operational activities.

Expandable text

A further constraint on a company's activities is the system of corporate governance regulation which has been introduced to improve the standard of corporate governance in companies. The framework was introduced following a series of high profile international business collapses. There was widespread belief that the traditional systems with the board of directors responsible for a company and the auditors appointed by the shareholders but remunerated by the directors, was insufficient to control modern companies.

Key issues in corporate governance

Governance reports, codes and legislation vary from country to country but typically cover the following:

- Membership of the board to achieve a suitable balance of power. The chairman and chief executive officer (CEO) should not be the same individual. There should be a sufficient number of non-executive directors on the board, and most of these should be independent.

- NEDs on the board should prevent the board from being dominated by the executive directors. The role of the NEDs is seen as critical in preventing a listed company from being run for the personal benefit of its senior executive directors.

- A remuneration committee to be established to decide on the remuneration of executive directors. Service contracts for directors should not normally exceed one year. There have also been efforts to give shareholders greater influence over directors' remuneration.

- The role of the audit committee of the board. This should consist of NEDs, and should work with the external auditors.

- The responsibility of the board of directors for monitoring all aspects of risk, not just the internal control system. For example, the Turnbull Committee was set up by the ICAEW to report on the risk management element of corporate governance.

The Turnbull report produced recommendations, and a risk report is now provided by listed companies in their annual report and accounts.

Audit committees

Many global listed companies now have an audit committee, or equivalent.

An audit committee:

- is a committee of the board of directors, normally three to five
- is made up of NEDs with no operating responsibility
- has a primary function to assist the board to fulfil its stewardship responsibilities by reviewing the:
  - systems of internal control
  - audit process
  - financial information which is provided to shareholders.

Test your understanding 4

List the advantages and disadvantages of audit committees.

5 The role of financial markets and institutions
Financial intermediation

Intermediation refers to the process whereby potential borrowers are brought together with potential lenders by a third party, the intermediary.

There are many types of institutions and other organisations that act as intermediaries in matching firms and individuals who need finance with those who wish to invest.

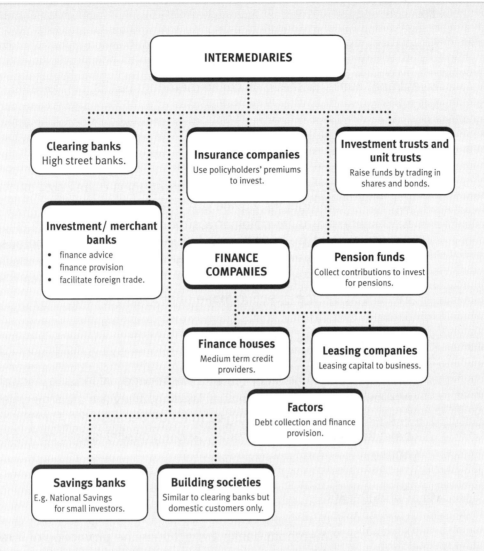

Clearing banks

The familiar high street banks provide a payment and cheque clearing mechanism. They offer various accounts to investors and provide large amounts of short- to medium-term loans to the business sector and the personal sector. They also offer a wide range of financial services to their customers.

Investment banks

Investment banks, sometimes called merchant banks, concentrate on the following.

(a) Financial advice to business firms

Few manufacturing or commercial companies of any size can now afford to be without the advice of a merchant bank. Such advice is necessary in order to obtain investment capital, to invest surplus funds, to guard against takeover, or to take over others. Increasingly, the merchant banks have themselves become actively involved in the financial management of their business clients and have had an influence over the direction these affairs have taken.

(b) Providing finance to business

Merchant banks also compete in the services of leasing, factoring, hire-purchase (HP) and general lending. They are also the gateway to the capital market for long-term funds because they are likely to have specialised departments handling capital issues as 'issuing houses'.

(c) Foreign trade

A number of merchant banks are active in the promotion of foreign trade by providing marine insurance, credits, and assistance in appointing foreign agents and arranging foreign payments.

Not all merchant banks are large and not all offer a wide range of services: the term is now rather misused. However, it is expected that a merchant bank will operate without the large branch network necessary for a clearing bank. It will work closely with its business clients, and will be more ready to take business risks and promote business enterprise than a clearing bank. It is probably fair to say that a merchant bank is essentially in the general business of creating wealth and of helping those who show that they are capable of successful business enterprise.

Savings banks

Public sector savings banks (e.g. the National Savings Bank in the UK) are used to collect funds from the small personal saver, which are then mainly invested in government securities.

Building societies

These take deposits from the household sector and lend to individuals buying their own homes. They also provide many of the services offered by the clearing banks. They are not involved, however, in providing funds for the business sector. Over recent years, many have converted to banks.

Finance companies

These come in three main varieties:

(a) Finance houses, providing medium-term instalment credit to the business and personal sector. These are usually owned by business sector firms or by other financial intermediaries. The trend is toward them offering services similar to the clearing banks.

(b) Leasing companies, leasing capital equipment to the business sector. They are usually subsidiaries of other financial institutions.

(c) Factoring companies, providing loans to companies secured on trade debtors, are usually bank subsidiaries. Other debt collection and credit control services are generally on offer.

Pension funds

These collect funds from employers and employees to provide pensions on retirement or death. As their outgoings are relatively predictable they can afford to invest funds for long periods of time.

Insurance companies

These use premium income from policyholders to invest mainly in long-term assets such as bonds, equities and property. Their outgoings from their long-term business (life assurance and pensions) and their short-term activities (fire, accident, motor insurance, etc.) are once again relatively predictable and therefore they can afford to tie up a large proportion of their funds for a long period of time.

Investment trusts and unit trusts

Investment trusts are limited liability companies collecting funds by selling shares and bonds and investing the proceeds, mainly in the ordinary shares of other companies. Funds at their disposal are limited to the amount of securities in issue plus retained profits, and hence they are often referred to as 'closed end funds'. Unit trusts on the other hand, although investing in a similar way, find that their funds vary according to whether investors are buying new units or cashing in old ones. Both offer substantial diversification opportunities to the personal investor.

The role of the financial markets

The financial markets, both capital and money markets, are places where those requiring finance (deficit units) can meet with those able to supply it (surplus units). They offer both primary and secondary markets

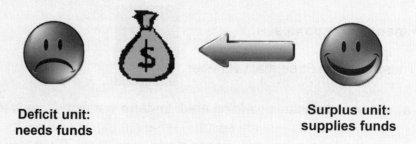

Deficit unit: needs funds   **Surplus unit: supplies funds**

Primary markets

Borrowers and lenders meet

Secondary markets

Lenders meet up with other investors to sell on their investments.

Provide opportunities to:

- diversify
- shift risk

- hedge
- arbitrage.

Expandable text

Primary markets provide a focal point for borrowers and lenders to meet. The forces of supply and demand should ensure that funds find their way to their most productive usage. Primary markets deal in new issues of loanable funds. They raise new finance for the deficit units.

Secondary markets allow holders of financial claims (surplus units) to realise their investments before the maturity date by selling them to other investors. They therefore increase the willingness of surplus units to invest their funds. A well-developed secondary market should also reduce the price volatility of securities, as regular trading in 'second-hand' securities should ensure smoother price changes. This should further encourage investors to supply funds.

Secondary markets help investors achieve the following ends.

(a) Diversification

By giving investors the opportunity to invest in a wide range of enterprises, it allows them to spread their risk. This is the familiar 'Don't put all your eggs in one basket' strategy.

(b) Risk shifting

Deficit units, particularly companies, issue various types of security on the financial markets to give investors a choice of the degree of risk they take. For example company loan stocks secured on the assets of the business offer low risk with relatively low returns, whereas equities carry much higher risk with correspondingly higher returns.

(c) Hedging

Financial markets offer participants the opportunity to reduce risk through hedging, which involves taking out counterbalancing contracts to offset existing risks, e.g. if a UK exporter is awaiting payment in euros from a French customer he is subject to the risk that the euro may decline in value over the credit period. To hedge this risk he could enter a counterbalancing contract and arrange to sell the euros forward (agree to exchange them for pounds at a fixed future date at a fixed exchange rate). In this way he has used the foreign exchange market to insure his future sterling receipt. Similar hedging possibilities are available on interest rates (see chapter 23).

(d) Arbitrage

Arbitrage is the process of buying a security at a low price in one market and simultaneously selling in another market at a higher price to make a profit.

Although it is only the primary markets that raise new funds for deficit units, well-developed secondary markets are required to fulfil the above roles for lenders and borrowers. Without these opportunities more surplus units would be tempted to keep their funds 'under the bed' rather than putting them at the disposal of deficit units.

However, the emergence of disintermediation (reduction in the use of intermediaries) and securitisation (conversion into marketable securities), where companies lend and borrow funds directly between themselves, has provided a further means of dealing with cash flow surpluses and deficits.

The capital markets

Capital markets deal in longer-term finance, mainly via a stock exchange.

The major types of securities dealt on capital markets are as follows:

- public sector and foreign stocks
- company securities
- Eurobonds.

 Eurobonds are bonds denominated in a currency other than that of the national currency of the issuing company (nothing to do with Europe or the Euro!). They are also called international bonds.

The money markets

Money markets deal in short-term funds and transactions are conducted by phone or telex. It is not one single market but a number of closely-connected markets.

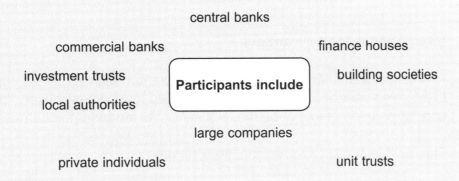

Division of sources of finance

Funds can be divided between short- and long-term funds:

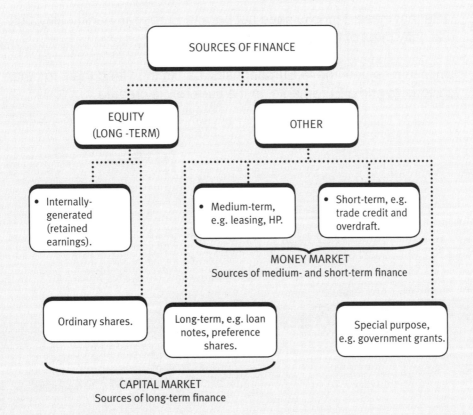

Durations of each are roughly:

Short-term	up to one year.
Medium-term	1-7 years
Long-term	7 years or more

International capital markets

An international financial market exists where domestic funds are supplied to a foreign user or foreign funds are supplied to a domestic user. The currencies used need not be those of either the lender or the borrower.

The most important international markets are:

- the Euromarkets
- the foreign bond markets.

Eurocurrency is money deposited with a bank outside its country of origin, e.g. money in a US dollar account with a bank in London is Eurodollars.

Note that these deposits need not be with European banks, although originally most of them were.

Once in receipt of these Eurodeposits, banks then lend them to other customers and a Euromarket in the currency is created.

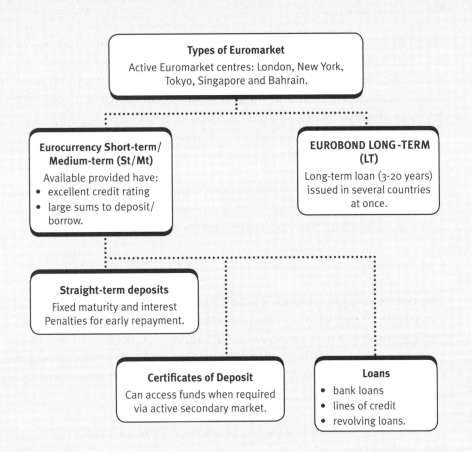

Expandable text

The Eurocurrency market

This incorporates the short- to medium-term end of the Euromarket. It is a market for borrowing and lending Eurocurrencies. Various types of deposits and loans are available.

Deposits vary from overnight to five years. Deposits can be in the form of straight-term deposits, with funds placed in a bank for a fixed maturity at a fixed interest rate. However, these carry the problem of interest rate penalties if early repayment is required.

Alternatively, deposits can be made in the form of negotiable Certificates of Deposit (CDs). There is an active secondary market in CDs and investors are therefore able to have access to their funds when required. Deposits can be made in individual currencies or in the form of 'currency cocktails' to allow depositors to take a diversified currency position. One common cocktail is the Special Drawing Right, consisting of US dollars, yen, Euros and sterling.

Euromarket loans may be in the form of straight bank loans, lines of credit (similar to overdraft facilities) and revolving commitments (a series of short-term loans over a given period with regular interest rate reviews). Small loans may be arranged with individual banks, but larger ones are usually arranged through syndicates of banks.

Much of the business on the Eurocurrency market is interbank, but there are also a large number of governments, local authorities and multinational companies involved. Firms wishing to use the market must have excellent credit standing and wish to borrow (or deposit) large sums of money.

The Eurobond market

A Eurobond is a bond issued in more than one country simultaneously, usually through a syndicate of international banks, denominated in a currency other than the national currency of the issuer.

This represents the long-term end of the Euromarket.

The bonds can be privately placed through the banks or quoted on stock exchanges. They may run for periods of between three and 20 years, and can be fixed or floating rate. Convertible Eurobonds (similar to domestic convertible loan stocks) and Option Eurobonds (giving the holder the option to switch currencies for repayment and interest) are also used.

The major borrowers are large companies, international institutions like the World Bank, and the EC. The most common currencies are the US dollar, the Euro, the Swiss franc, and to a lesser extent sterling.

Stock markets

The syllabus does not require you to have a detailed knowledge of any specific country's stock market or exchange. We may, however, make reference to the markets that operate in the UK for illustration purposes.

The role of the stock market is to:

- facilitate trade in stocks such as:
    - issued shares of public companies
    - corporate bonds
    - government bonds
    - local authority loans.
- allocate capital to industry
- determine a fair price for the assets traded.

Speculative trading on the market can assist by:

- smoothing price fluctuations
- ensuring shares are readily marketable.

Trading via a broker-dealer

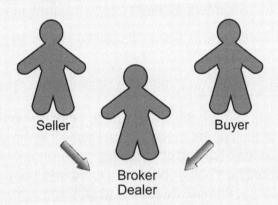

Trading via a broker and a market-maker

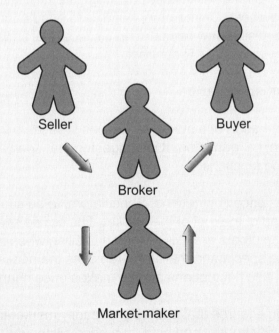

Market-makers:

- maintain stocks of securities in a number of quoted companies
- continually quote prices for buying and prices for selling the securities (bid and offer prices)

- generate income by the profits they make from the difference (or 'spread') between the bid and offer prices.

Countries may have more than one stock market. In the UK there are three:

(1) London Stock Exchange – main market

(2) Alternative Investment Market (AIM) – for smaller companies

(3) Ofex (off exchange) – trade via specialist brokers.

Expandable text

A country's stock market is the institution that embodies many of the processes of the capital market. Essentially it is the market for the issued securities of public companies, government bonds, loans issued by local authority and other publicly-owned institutions, and some overseas stocks. Without the ability to sell long-term securities easily, few people would be prepared to risk making their money available to business or public authorities.

A stock market assists the allocation of capital to industry; if the market thinks highly of a company, that company's shares will rise in value and it will be able to raise fresh capital through the new issue market at relatively low cost. On the other hand, less popular companies will have difficulty in raising new capital. Thus, successful firms are helped to grow and the unsuccessful will contract.

The role of speculation

Any consideration of a stock market has to face up to the problem of speculation, i.e. gambling. It is suggested that speculation can perform the following functions:

It smoothes price fluctuations. Speculators, to be successful, have to be a little ahead of the rest of the market. The skilled speculator will be buying when others are still selling and selling when others are still buying. The speculator, therefore, removes the peaks and troughs of inevitable price fluctuations and so makes price changes less violent.

Speculation ensures that shares are readily marketable. Almost all stock can be quickly bought and sold, at a price. Without the chance of profit there would be no professional operator willing to hold stock or agree to sell stock that is not immediately available. The fact that there are always buyers and sellers is of considerable importance to the ordinary individual investor, who may have to sell unexpectedly at any time with little warning.

Stock markets help in the determination of a fair price for assets, and ensure that assets are readily marketable.

Buying and selling shares or loan notes

An investor will contact a broker in order to buy and sell securities. The broker may act as agent for the investor by contacting a market-maker (see below) or he may act as principal if he makes a market in them himself (i.e. buys and sells on his own behalf). In the latter case he is a broker-dealer

Market-makers maintain stocks of securities in a number of quoted companies, appropriate to the level of trading in that security, and their income is generated by the profits they make by dealing in securities. A market-maker undertakes to maintain an active market in shares that it trades, by continually quoting prices for buying and prices for selling (bid and offer prices).

If security prices didn't move, their profits would come from the difference (or 'spread') between the bid and offer prices. This profit is approximately represented by the difference between the 'bid' and 'offered' price for a given security – the price at which a market-maker is prepared to buy the stock and the price at which he would be prepared to sell it.

For example, assume a quotation in respect of the shares of a fictitious company, Clynch Co.

The dealer might quote 145, 150.

This means he will buy the shares at $1.45 each and sell at $1.50 each.

Quotations are based on expectations of the general marketability of the shares and, as such, will probably vary constantly. For example, if an investor wants to buy 10,000 shares, the dealer might decide to raise his prices to encourage people to sell and thereby ensure that he will have sufficient shares to meet the order he has just received. Thus, his next quote might be 150, 155.

Conversely, if the investor wants to sell 10,000 shares, the dealer will be left with that number of additional shares, and he may wish to reduce his quotation to encourage people to buy; thus he may quote 140, 145.

If sufficient numbers of people wish to buy and sell the shares of Clynch Co, eventually a price will be found at which only marginal transactions are taking place.

If the general economic climate is reflected by each company's shares, it follows that there will be times when in general people wish to sell shares and hence prices drop, and other times when in general people are buying shares and prices rise.

Share prices are dictated by the laws of supply and demand. If the future return/risk profile of the share is anticipated to improve, the demand for that share will be greater and the price higher.

Broker-dealers in the UK act as both brokers for clients and trade on their own account as dealers. In the UK, their activities in share dealing are restricted largely to listed companies whose shares are traded on SETS, the electronic 'trading book' of the London Stock Exchange.

Types of stock market

A country may have more than one securities market in operation. For illustration, the UK has the following:

The London Stock Exchange – the main UK market for securities, on which the shares of large public companies are quoted and dealt. Costs of meeting entry requirements and reporting regulations are high.

The AIM – a separate market for the securities of smaller companies. Entry and reporting requirements are significantly less than those for the main market of the London Stock Exchange.

An 'Ofex' (off exchange) market in which shares in some public companies are traded, but through a specialist firm of brokers and not through a stock exchange.

6 The relationship between risk and return

Investment risk arises because returns are variable and uncertain. An increase in risk generally requires an increase in expected returns.

For example compare:

Building society investment versus Investment in equities

Investment in food retailing versus Investment in computer electronics

In each case we would demand higher returns from the second investment because of the higher risk.

KAPLAN PUBLISHING

Expandable text

Portfolio diversification

- Investors generally hold a portfolio of investments. A portfolio is simply a combination of investments.

- If an investor puts half of his funds into an engineering company and half into a retail shops' firm then it is possible that any misfortunes in the engineering company (e.g. a strike) may be to some extent offset by the performance of the retail investment. It would be unlikely that both would suffer a strike in the same period.

- This is discussed further in chapter 18.

Expandable text

(1) **Give three examples of intermediary institutions.**

(2) **Distinguish between money and capital markets.**

(3) **What is a Eurodollar?**

(4) **What is the difference between a broker-dealer and a market-maker?**

Solution

(1) Answers could include:

- Clearing banks.

- Investment/merchant banks.

- Savings banks.

- Building societies.

- Finance companies.

- Pension funds.

- Insurance companies.

- Investment and Unit Trusts.

(2) Money markets deal in short-term funds and have no physical location.

   Capital markets deal in long-term finance usually via a stock exchange.

(3) A Eurodollar is money in a US dollar account held in a bank outside the US.

(4)   A broker-dealer deals directly with buyers and sellers and creates a market in the shares himself.

A market-maker creates the market but trades only with brokers who make the deals on behalf of the investors.

Chapter summary

```
                        ┌─────────────────────────┐
                        │  ECONOMIC ENVIRONMENT   │
                        └─────────────────────────┘
```

| MACROECONOMIC POLICY | RISK VERSUS RETURN | FINANCIAL MARKETS |

| INTERMEDIARIES | STOCK MARKETS |

| CAPITAL MARKETS | MONEY MARKETS |

| OBJECTIVES & CONFLICTS | IMPACT ON BUSINESS | GOVERNMENT INTERVENTION AND REGULATION |

| GOVERNMENT ASSISTANCE | CORPORATE GOVERNANCE |

| POLICIES | Regulation
• price
• competition. | GREEN POLICIES |

| MONETARY POLICY | FISCAL POLICY |

| INTEREST RATE | TAX |

| IMPACT ON BUSINESS | GOVERNMENT BORROWING |

Test your understanding answers

Test your understanding 1

- employment of resources
- price stability
- economic growth
- balance of payments equilibrium
- an appropriate distribution of income and wealth.

(2) Will impact:

- Exchange rates – affecting importers (production costs) and exporters (competitive position and marketing).
- Tax rates – affecting costs such as labour (NI) and supplies (VAT) in addition to corporation tax.
- Interest rates – changing cost of debt and viability of investment plans.

(3) Monetary policy is concerned with influencing the overall monetary conditions in the economy in particular:

- the volume of money in circulation – the money supply
- the price of money – interest rates.

(4) Excessive taxation may bring about disincentive effects such as a personal reluctance to work harder, reluctance on the part of businesses to invest, and on overseas investors to invest in a high tax economy. There may also be an increase in attempts to create tax avoidance schemes.

(5) Government borrowing leads to a fall in private investment because it creates a greater demand for money and loanable funds:

- this increased borrowing leads to higher interest rates by creating a higher 'price'.
- the private sector will then reduce investment due to a lower rate of return. This is the investment that is crowded out.

Test your understanding 2

Monopolies are large-scale producers achieving significant economies of scale, which can be passed on to the customer in the form of cheaper prices.

The financial rewards from achieving a monopoly position may be the incentive for businesses to invest in R&D which benefits society as a whole.

Test your understanding 3

Methods include:

- tighter planning regulations
- more stringent testing regimes before licences are granted
- emissions targets backed up with fines
- taxes on damaging products, e.g. leaded petrol
- green targets for local authorities linked to funding.

Test your understanding 4

Advantages

- Increasing public confidence in the credibility and objectivity of published financial information (including unaudited interim statements).

- Assisting directors (particularly NEDs) in meeting their responsibilities in respect of financial reporting.

- Strengthening the independent position of a company's external auditor by providing an additional channel of communication.

- They may improve the quality of management accounting, being better placed to criticise internal functions.

- They should lead to better communication between the directors, external auditors and management.

Disadvantages

Audit committees may lead to:

- fear that their purpose is to catch management out
- NEDs being over-burdened with detail
- a 'two-tier' board of directors.

Finally, there is undoubtedly additional cost in terms of, at the least, time involved.

Sources of finance

Chapter learning objectives

Upon completion of this chapter you will be able to:

- discuss the criteria which may be used by companies to choose between sources of finance

- discuss the advantages and disadvantages of an overdraft as a source of short-term finance

- discuss the advantages and disadvantages of a short-term loan as a source of short-term finance

- discuss the advantages and disadvantages of trade credit as a source of short-term finance

- discuss increasing the efficiency of working capital management as a source of finance

- discuss the advantages and disadvantages of lease finance as a source of short-term finance

- suggest appropriate sources of short-term finance for a business in a scenario question

- define and distinguish between equity finance and other types of share capital

- explain the main sources of long-term debt finance available to a business

- discuss the advantages and disadvantages of debt finance as a source of long-term finance

- discuss the advantages and disadvantages of lease finance as a source of long-term finance

- discuss the advantages and disadvantages of venture capital as a source of long-term finance

- discuss the advantages and disadvantages of using retained earnings as a source of finance

- explain the benefits of a placing for an unlisted company

- describe the features and methods of a stock exchange listing including a placing and a public offer

- describe a rights issue

- calculate the theoretical ex-rights price (TERP) of a share

- demonstrate the impact of a rights issue on the wealth of a shareholder

- discuss the advantages and disadvantages of equity finance as a source of long-term finance

- identify and suggest appropriate methods of raising equity finance for a business in a scenario question

- suggest appropriate sources of long-term finance for a business in a scenario question

- explain the impact that the issue of dividends may have on a company's share price

- explain the theory of dividend irrelevance

- discuss the influence of shareholder expectations on the dividend decision

- discuss the influence of legal constraints on the dividend decision

- discuss the influence of liquidity constraints on the dividend decision

- define and distinguish between bonus issues and scrip dividends.

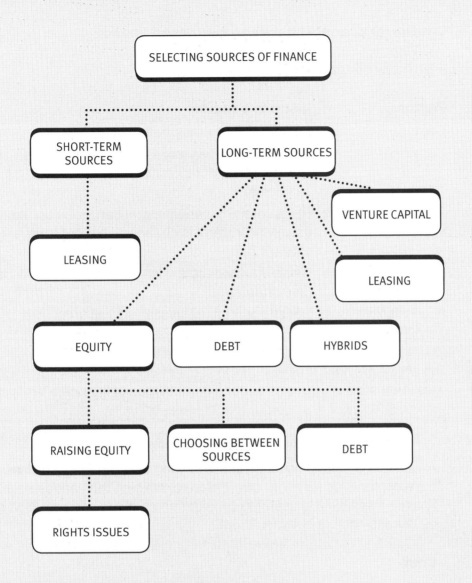

1 Selection of appropriate sources of finance

The need for finance

Firms need funds to:

* provide working capital
* invest in non-current assets.

The main source of funds available is retained earnings, but these are unlikely to be sufficient to finance all business needs.

Criteria for choosing between sources of finance

A firm must consider the following factors:

Factor	Issue to consider
Cost	Debt usually cheaper than equity.
Duration	Long-term finance more expensive but secure. Firms usually match duration to assets purchased (see chapter 8).
Term structure of interest rates	Relationship between interest and loan duration – usually short-term is cheaper – but not always! (see chapter 22).
Gearing	Using mainly debt is cheaper but high gearing is risky (see chapter 19).
Accessibility	Not all sources are available to all firms (see chapter 17).

The above provides a useful checklist of headings for an examinations question that asks you to consider different types of finance.

Expandable text

A vast range of funding alternatives is open to companies and new developments occur every day. Before examining the various sources of finance available it is useful to consider some of the criteria which may be used to choose between them.

Cost

The higher the cost of funding, the lower the firm's profit. Debt finance tends to be cheaper than equity. This is because providers of debt take less risk than providers of equity and therefore earn less return. Interest on debt finance is also normally corporation tax deductible, while returns on equity are not.

Duration

Finance can be arranged for various time periods. Normally, but not invariably, long-term finance is more expensive than short-term finance. This is because lenders normally perceive the risks as being higher on long-term advances. Long-term finance does, however, carry the advantage of security, whereas sources of short-term finance can often be withdrawn at short notice. You should remember 'The Matching Principle' that says:

'Long-term assets should be financed by long-term funds and short-term assets (to some extent) by short-term funds'.

KAPLAN PUBLISHING

We would generally expect to see working capital financed partly by short-term facilities such as overdraft, whilst fixed assets should be funded by long-term funds. This principle is commonly broken to gain access to cheap short-term funds but the risks involved should be appreciated.

Term structure of interest rates

The term structure of interest rates describes the relationship between interest rates charged for loans of differing maturities.

While short-term funds are usually cheaper than long-term funds, this situation is sometimes reversed and interest rates should be carefully checked.

Imagine the situation where the money markets expected interest rates to fall in the long-term but remain high in the short-term. In this situation borrowing short-term could prove quite expensive.

Gearing

Gearing is the ratio of debt to equity finance. Gearing will be investigated in depth later, but for now we should appreciate that although high gearing involves the use of cheap debt finance, it does bring with it the risk of having to meet regular repayments of interest and principal on the loans. If these are not met, the company could end up in liquidation.

On the other hand, too little debt could result in earnings dilution. For example the issue of a large amount of equity to fund a new project could result in a decrease in earnings per share (EPS), despite an increase in total earnings.

Accessibility

Not all companies have access to all sources of finance. Small companies traditionally have problems in raising equity and long-term debt finance. These problems are investigated later (chapter 17) but remember that many firms do not have an unlimited choice of funding arrangements.

A quoted company is one whose shares are dealt in on a recognised stock market, so shares in such a company represent a highly liquid asset. This, in turn, makes it much easier to attract new investors to buy new shares issued by the company because these investors know that they can always sell their shares if they wish to realise their investment.

Investment in shares of unquoted companies represents the acquisition of a highly illiquid investment. For this reason it is much more difficult for such a company to raise finance by new share issues.

2 Short-term sources of finance

As discussed earlier, working capital is usually funded using short-term sources of finance.

Sources of short-term finance include:

- bank overdrafts (see chapter 8)
- bank loans (see chapter 8)
- better management of working capital (see chapter 7)
- squeezing trade credit (see chapter 7)
- leasing.

Leasing as a source of short-term finance

Growing in popularity as a source of finance, a lease is:

- a contract between a lessor and a lessee for the hire of a particular asset
- lessor retains ownership of the asset
- lessor conveys the right to the use of the asset to the lessee for an agreed period
- in return lessor receives specified rentals.

Leasing is a means of financing the use of capital equipment, the underlying principle being that use is more important than ownership. It is a medium-term financial arrangement, usually from one to ten years.

There are two main types of lease agreement:

- operating leases – short-term
- finance leases – long-term.

This section will consider operating leases. Finance leases are considered below.

Conditions	Operating lease
Lease period	The lease period is less than the useful life of the asset. The lessor relies on subsequent leasing or eventual sale of the asset to cover his capital outlay and show a profit.
Lessor's business	The lessor may very well carry on a trade in this type of asset.
Risks and rewards	The lessor is normally responsible for repairs and maintenance.
Cancellation	The lease can sometimes be cancelled at short notice.
Substance	The substance of the transaction is the short-term rental of an asset.

Test your understanding 1

Identify the advantages and disadvantages of using an operating lease.

3 Long-term finance – equity

Types of share capital

Equity shareholders are the owners of the business and exercise ultimate control, through their voting rights.

The term equity relates to ordinary shares only.

Equity finance is the investment in a company by the ordinary shareholders, represented by the issued ordinary share capital plus reserves.

There are other types of share capital relating to various types of preference share. These are not considered part of equity, as their characteristics bear more resemblance to debt finance.

Expandable text

The main types of share capital are summarised in the table below:

Type of share capital	Security or voting rights	Income	Amount of capital
Ordinary shares	Voting rights in general meetings. Rank after all creditors and preference shares in rights to assets on liquidation.	Dividends payable at the discretion of the directors out of undistributed profits remaining after senior claims have been met.	The right to all surplus funds after prior claims have been met.
Cumulative preference shares	Limited right to vote at a general meeting (only when dividend is in arrears or when it is proposed to change the legal rights of the shares). Rank after all creditors but usually before ordinary shareholders in liquidation.	A fixed amount per year at the discretion of the directors. Arrears accumulate and must be paid before a dividend on ordinary shares may be paid. Dividend is not corporation tax deductible.	A fixed amount per share.
Non-cumulative preference shares	Typically acquire some voting rights if the dividend has not been paid for three years. Rank as cumulative in liquidation.	A fixed amount per year, as above. Arrears do not accumulate.	A fixed amount per share.

Ensure you are familiar with the key features of each type of share.

4 Long-term finance – debt

Long-term debt (loan notes), usually in the form of debentures or bonds, is frequently used as a source of long-term finance as an alternative to equity.

A loan note is a written acknowledgement of a debt by a company, normally containing provisions as to payment of interest and the terms of repayment of principal.

Loan notes are also known as corporate bonds or loan stock:

- traded on stock markets in much the same way as shares

- may be secured or unsecured

- secured debt will carry a charge over:
    - one or more specific assets, usually land and buildings, which are mortgaged in a fixed charge.
    - all assets – a floating charge.

    On default, the loan note holders can appoint a receiver to administer the assets until the interest is paid. Alternatively the assets may be sold to repay the principal.

- may be redeemable or irredeemable.

Irredeemable debt is not repayable at any specified time in the future. Instead, interest is payable in perpetuity. As well as some loan notes, preference shares are often irredeemable.

If the debt is redeemable the principal will be repayable at a future date.

Illustration 1 – Long-term finance debt

If a company has '5% 2015 loan notes redeemable at par, quoted at $95 ex-int', this description refers to loan notes that:

- pay interest at 5% on nominal value, i.e. $5 per $100 (this is known as the coupon rate)

- are redeemable in the year 2015

- will be repaid at par value, i.e. each $100 nominal value will be repaid at $100

- currently have a market value of $95 per $100, without rights to the current year's interest payment.

The terms 'loan notes' and 'bonds' are now used generally to mean any kind of long-term marketable debt securities.

5 Characteristics of loan notes and other long-term debt

Advantages:

From the viewpoint of the investor, debt:

- is low risk.

From the viewpoint of the company, debt:

- is cheap
- has predictable flows
- does not dilute control.

Disadvantages:

From the viewpoint of the investor, debt:

- has no voting rights.

- From the viewpoint of the company, debt:

- is inflexible
- increases risk at high levels of gearing (see chapter 18)
- must (normally) be repaid.

These are the key points for a discussion about the use of debt in an examination question.

Expandable text

Loan notes from the viewpoint of the investor

Debt is viewed as low risk because:

- it often has a definite maturity and the holder has priority in interest payments and on liquidation

- income is fixed, so the holder receives the same interest whatever the earnings of the company.

Debt holders do not usually have voting rights. Only if interest is not paid will holders take control of the company.

Loan note from the viewpoint of the company

Advantages of debt

- Debt is cheap. Because it is less risky than equity for an investor, loan note holders will accept a lower rate of return than shareholders. Also, debt interest is an allowable expense for tax. So if the cost of borrowing for a company is 6%, say, and the rate of corporation tax is 30%, the company can set the cost of the interest against tax, and the effective 'after-tax' cost of the debt would be just 4.2% (6% × 70%).

- Cost is limited to the stipulated interest payment.

- There is no dilution of control when debt is issued.

Disadvantages of debt

- Interest must be paid whatever the earnings of the company, unlike dividends which can be paid in good years and not in bad. If interest is not paid, the trustees for the loan note holders can call in the receiver.

- Shareholders may be concerned that a geared company cannot pay all its interest and still pay a dividend and will raise the rate of return that they require from the company to compensate for this increase in risk. This may effectively put a limit on the amount of debt that can be raised.

- With fixed maturity dates, provision must be made for the repayment of debt.

- Long-term debt, with its commitment to fixed interest payments, may prove a burden especially if the general level of interest rates falls.

Hybrids – convertibles

Some types of finance have elements of both debt and equity, e.g.:

- convertible loan notes.

Convertibles give the holder the right to convert to other securities, normally ordinary shares at either a:

- predetermined price
    - e.g. notes may be converted into shares at a value of 400c per share

- predetermined ratio
    - e.g. $100 of stock may be converted into 25 ordinary shares.

Conversion premium occurs if:

Market value convertible stock > Market price of shares the stock is to be converted into.

Stock trading at $102, to be converted into 10 shares currently trading at $9 each, has a conversion premium of :

$102 - (10 \times 9) = 12.

Hybrids – loan notes with warrants

Warrants give the holder the right to subscribe at a fixed future date for a certain number of ordinary shares at a predetermined price.

NB If warrants are issued with loan notes, the loan notes are **not** converted into equity. Instead bond holders:

- make a cash payment for the shares
- retain the loan notes until redemption.

Often used as sweeteners on debt issues:

- interest rate on the loan is low and loan may be unsecured
- right to buy equity set at an attractive price.

Attractions of convertibles and warrants

Advantage	Reason
Immediate finance at low cost	Because of the conversion option, the loans can be raised at below normal interest rates or with less security.
Attractive, if share prices are depressed	Where companies wish to raise equity finance, but share prices are currently depressed, convertibles offer a 'back-door' share issue method.
Self-liquidating	Where loans are converted into shares, the problem of repayment disappears.
Exercise of warrants related to need for finance.	Options would normally only be exercised where the share price has increased. If the options involve the payment of extra cash to the company, this creates extra funds when they are needed for expansion.

Expandable text

(1) Raybeck Co issues 8% unsecured loan notes 20X1/X5 as part of the consideration for the acquisition of companies. With the loan notes are subscription rights (warrants) on the basis that holders of $100 loan notes could subscribe for up to 30 ordinary shares in Raybeck at a price of $8.75 per share. The option could be exercised any time between 20X2 and 20X5. Irrespective of whether the option is exercised the loan notes are redeemable at par between 20X1 and 20X5.

(2) Associated Engineering Co issues 7% convertible loan notes 20X8/X9. The conversion option is 80 ordinary shares for each $100 loan note, and is exercisable between 20X1 and 20X5. If the option is not exercised, the loan notes are redeemable at par between 20X8 and 20X9.

Describe the nature of these securities and comment on the exercise decisions that must be made by the investor.

Solution

(1) **Note the difference between these two issues which is the key distinction between convertibles and warrants.**

In the Raybeck case, the option is separate from the loan notes, which continues to exist whether or not the option is exercised. Also, the exercise of the option costs money. On the other hand, conversion of Associated Engineering loan notes is an actual replacement of the loan notes by shares, with no cash effect.

The warrants issued by Raybeck Co are worth exercising if the share price of Raybeck is above $8.75. For example if the share price rose to $10 then the value of the warrant would be:

Current market price – Exercise price = $10 – $8.75 = $1.25.

If share prices fell below $8.75 the warrant would be worthless.

The above calculation is referred to as the **formula value of the warrant** or the **intrinsic value of the warrant**.

(2) The conversion option on Associated Engineering's convertible is worth exercising if the share price rises above:

Value of $100 loan stock /80 shares

Above this price, shareholders would receive equity of greater value than the $100 loan note. Unlike a warrant, however, below this share price the value of the convertible does not fall to zero, but would settle at the market value of the security as a straight debenture.

6 Long-term finance – leasing

Long-term lease arrangements likely to be a finance lease:

Conditions	Finance lease
Lease period	One lease exists for the whole useful life of the asset though may be a primary and secondary period.
Lessor's business	The lessor does not usually deal directly in this type of asset.
Risks and rewards	The lessor does not retain the risks or rewards of ownership. Lessee responsible for repairs and maintenance.
Cancellation	The lease agreement cannot be cancelled. The lessee has a liability for all payments.
Substance	The purchase of the asset by the lessee financed by a loan from the lessor, i.e. it is effectively a source of medium- to long-term debt finance.

Usually lease period is divided into two:

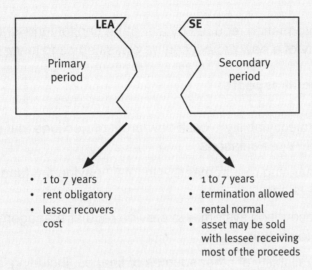

- 1 to 7 years
- rent obligatory
- lessor recovers cost

- 1 to 7 years
- termination allowed
- rental normal
- asset may be sold with lessee receiving most of the proceeds

Note: the key difference between an operating lease (short-term) and a finance lease (medium to long-term) is that the former equates to renting an asset whereas the latter equates to borrowing money in order to purchase the asset.

The decision whether to lease or buy is both a practical and financial one. The financial choice was discussed in chapter 13.

7 Venture capital

Venture capital is the provision of risk bearing capital, usually in the form of a participation in equity, to companies with high growth potential.

Venture capitalists provide start-up and late stage growth finance, usually for smaller firms.

Venture capitalists will assess an investment prospect on the basis of its:

- financial outlook
- management credibility
- depth of market research
- technical abilities
- degree of influence offered:
  - controlling stake?
  - board seat?
- exit route.

Expandable text

Evaluation of a new project by a venture capital fund

The information required by a venture capital fund when assessing the viability of a new project can be classified as follows:

Financial aspects

- project viability – cash flow/profit projections, net present value (NPV) calculations

- financing requirements – in total, leaving the fund to decide the best package

- accounting system – to provide regular management accounting information

- availability of other sources of finance, including loans and grants from government bodies and investment by the management

- future policy as regards dividends and retention of profits – with high growth being preferred

- the intention of eventually obtaining a quotation – usually within 3-5 years

- the percentage stake which is offered in the firm – indicating the degree of control and risk.

Additional information affecting the proposal

For most venture funds, evaluating financial information comes second to evaluating the credibility of the firm's management. A view must be formed as to whether the existing team has sufficient expertise to manage a growing firm, or whether specialist talent needs to be added.

The investor would then wish to see evidence that thorough studies of the firm's markets had been made, so that projected sales budgets were realistic. The single most common cause of failure in this sort of situation is over-optimism in sales projections. Relevant information includes market research, orders in hand, letters from potential customers and general projections of the market's prospects.

Information on technical aspects of the firm's products would then be useful, especially new designs which have not yet been tested.

The investor would also be interested in knowing how much influence it is envisaged it will have on the management decision making in the firm. Nearly all venture funds will want a seat on the board. Their aim is to provide advice and be able to influence management rather than to participate in the day-to-day running of the company.

Typically venture capitalists will provide finance in return for 20-49.9% of a company's shares. This allows them to exert control without becoming majority shareholders.

The venture capitalists may seek to exit (liquidate their investment) via a trade sale, flotation, redemption of preference shares at a premium or a buy-back of their shares on re-financing.

8 Raising equity

There are three main sources of equity finance:

- internally-generated funds – retained earnings
- rights issues
- new external share issues – placings, offers for sale, etc.

Expandable text

What would be the difference in terms of impact on shareholder base between raising equity finance through retained earnings and rights issues and raising equity finance via a new issue?

Solution

Equity finance raised through retained earnings and rights issues will principally be provided by existing shareholders; new issues will result in a wider shareholder base.

Note: legally a rights issue must be made before a company can undertake a new issue to the public.

Internally-generated funds

Internally-generated funds comprise:

- retained earnings (i.e. undistributed profits attributable to ordinary shareholders) plus
- non-cash charges against profits (e.g. depreciation).

For an established company, internally-generated funds can represent the single most important source of finance, for both short and long-term purposes.

Expandable text

What are the advantages of using retained earnings to finance the business?

Solution

Such finance is cheap and quick to raise, requiring no transaction costs, professional assistance or time delay.

Retained earnings are also a continual source of new funds, provided that the company is profitable and profits are not all paid out as dividends.

Of course, for major investment projects, a greater amount of equity finance may be required than that available from internal sources.

Expandable text

New share issues

There are several methods of issuing new shares, depending on the circumstances of the company:

Type of company	Company requirement	Method of issue	Type of investor
Unquoted	Finance without an immediate stock market quotation.	Private negotiation or placing. Enterprise investment scheme (EIS).	Individuals, merchant banks, finance corporations.
Unquoted or quoted	Finance with an immediate quotation. Finance with a new issue.	Stock exchange or small firm market placing. Offer for sale. Offer for sale by tender. Introduction.	The investing public, pension funds, insurance companies and other institutions.
Quoted or unquoted	Limited finance without offering shares to non-shareholders.	Rights issue.	Holders of existing shares.

KAPLAN PUBLISHING

Because of the relative issue costs and the ease of organisation, the most important source of equity is retained earnings, then rights issues, then new issues.

Placing

Unquoted companies may find it difficult to raise finance because:

- shares are not easily realisable
- it is cheaper to invest in large parcels of shares rather than in many companies
- small firms are regarded as more risky.

However, it is possible to arrange a **placing** of shares with an institution. Used for smaller issues of shares, the company's bank:

- selects institutional investors to buy a number of shares
- general public can then buy from the institutions.

There must usually be at least a prospect of eventually obtaining a quotation on the stock exchange.

Expandable text

In the modern business environment, it can be difficult for small unquoted companies to raise equity finance from outside shareholders. A country's tax system may channel individual investors' money into institutions, and institutions are generally unenthusiastic about investing in unquoted companies for the reasons outlined above.

Becoming quoted

A company will wish to become listed on the stock exchange to increase its pool of potential investors. Only by being listed can a company offer its shares to the public.

It may start with a quotation on a small firm stock market, such as the Alternative Investment Market (AIM) in the UK, followed by a full listing.

The possible methods of obtaining a stock exchange listing in the UK are:

Method   Conditions

Public offer Offered to public , either at a fixed price or via a tender process
             where investors 'bid' for shares.

A placing   Offered to institutions (see above).

Introduction No new issue of shares. Public already holds at least 25%.
             Shares become listed. Public can then buy on market.

Expandable text

Public offer

A public offer is an invitation to apply for shares in a company based upon information contained in a prospectus, either at a fixed price or by tender.

Fixed price offer

Shares are offered at a fixed price to the general public (including institutions). Details of the offer document are published in a prospectus for the issue. The prospectus contains information about the company's past performance and future prospects, as specified by the rules for stock exchange companies. The rule book for UK companies whose shares are listed on the main London Stock Exchange is the UK Listing Rules. These are overseen by the UK Listing Authority, a department of the Financial Services Authority (FSA).

Offer for sale by tender

Shares are offered to the general public (including institutions) but no fixed price is specified. Potential investors bid for shares at a price of their choosing. The 'striking price' at which the shares are sold is determined by the demand for shares.

The price will be either:

A   the highest price at which the entire issue is sold, all tenders at or above this being allotted in full, or

B   a price lower than in (a), but with tenders at or above this lower price receiving only a proportion of the shares tendered for, so as to avoid the concentration of ownership in the hands of a few.

Placing

A placing may be used for smaller issues of shares (up to $15 million in value). The bank advising the company selects institutional investors to whom the shares are 'placed' or sold. If the general public wish to acquire shares, they must buy them from the institutions.

Introduction

Introduction is a process that allows a company to join a stock exchange without raising capital. A company does not issue any fresh shares; it merely introduces its existing shares in the market.

It is used where the public already holds at least 25% of the shares in the company (the minimum requirement for a stock exchange listing). The shares become listed and members of the public can buy shares from the existing shareholders.

Institutional advisers on new share issues

As well as requiring the assistance of accountants in preparing the prospectus, new share issues may require the services of an **issuing house**. An issuing house is an investment bank specialising in new issue of shares.

Issuing houses

A company wishing to raise capital by offer for sale would first get in touch with one of the issuing houses which specialise in this kind of business.

In some cases, the issuing house earns a fee by organising public issues. In others, it purchases outright a block of shares from a company and then makes them an 'offer for sale' to the public on terms designed to bring in a profit to the issuing house.

There are between 50 and 60 members of the Issuing House Association, including all the important merchant banks. The fact that an issue is launched by one of these banks or other houses of high reputation is, in itself, a factor contributing to the chance of success of such a venture.

Investment banks

Investment banks also perform the functions of underwriting, marketing and pricing new issues.

- Underwriting: large share issues are usually underwritten which adds to the cost of raising finance but reduces the risk. An underwriter is someone (usually an investment institution) who is prepared to purchase shares in a share issue that other investors do not buy. For example, suppose that XYZ Co is issuing 50 million new shares at $2.50 each. If the issue is underwritten, the investment bank assisting the company with the issue will find one or more institutions that are prepared to buy up to a given quantity of the shares, if no one else wants them. In return for underwriting a portion of the new issue, an underwriter is paid a commission. If there are just one or two underwriters for an issue, the underwriters might offload some of their risk by getting other institutions to sub-underwrite the issue. Sub-underwriters are also paid a commission.

  The effect of underwriting is to ensure that all the shares in a new issue will find a buyer. However, if large quantities of the shares are left in the hands of the underwriters after the issue, the share price is likely to remain depressed until the underwriters have been able to sell off the shares they do not want in the secondary market.

- Marketing: the marketing and selling of a new issue is a business activity in its own right. The investment bank provides the expertise.

- Pricing: one of the most difficult decisions in making a new issue is that it should be priced correctly. If the price is too low, the issue will be over-subscribed, and existing shareholders will have had their holdings diluted more than is necessary. If the price is too high and the issue fails, the underwriters are left to subscribe to the shares. This will adversely affect the reputation of the issuing house and the company. Correct pricing is important, and the investment bank will be able to offer advice based on experience and expertise. One way round the issue price problem is an issue by tender.

9 Rights issues

A rights issue is an offer to existing shareholders to subscribe for new shares, at a discount to the current market value, in proportion to their existing holdings.

This right of pre-emption:

- enables them to retain their existing share of voting rights
- can be waived with the agreement of shareholders.

Shareholders not wishing to take up their rights can sell them on the stock market.

KAPLAN PUBLISHING

Advantages:

- it is cheaper than a public share issue
- it is made at the discretion of the directors, without consent of the shareholders or the Stock Exchange.
- it rarely fails.

TERP

The new share price after the issue is known as the **theoretical ex-rights price** and is calculated by finding the weighted average of the old price and the rights price, weighted by the number of shares.

The formula is:

Ex-rights price =

(Market value of shares already in issue) + (proceeds from new share issue)/Number of shares in issue after the rights issue ('ex rights')

Expandable text

Illustration – Rights issues

Babbel Co, which has an issued capital of 2 million shares, having a current market value of $2.70 each, makes a rights issue of one new share for every two existing shares at a price of $2.10.

Required:

Calculate the TERP.

Expandable text

Solution

Market value (MV) of shares in issue = 2m × $2.7 = $5.4m

Proceeds from new issue = $\dfrac{2m}{2} \times 1 = \$2.10 = \$2.1m$

Number of shares in issue ex-rights = $2m + (2m \times \dfrac{1}{2}) = \$3m$

TERP = $\dfrac{\$5.4m + \$2.1m}{3m}$ = $2.50/share

Note that the calculation can be done on the value of the whole equity or on the basis of the minimum shareholding needed to acquire one extra share:

TERP = $\dfrac{\$2.70 \times 2 + \$2.10 \times 1}{\$2.50/share}$

Test your understanding 2

ABC Co announces a 2 for 5 rights issue at $2 per share. There are currently 10 million shares in issue, and the current market price of the shares is $2.70.

What is the TERP?

The value of a right

To make the offer relatively attractive to shareholders, new shares are generally issued at a discount on the current market price.

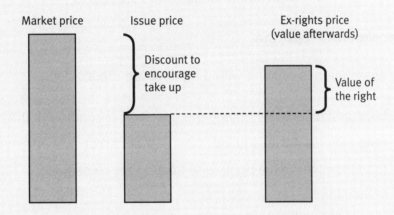

Value of a right = theoretical ex rights price – issue (subscription) price

Since rights have a value, they can be sold on the stock market in the period between:

- the rights issue being announced and the rights to existing shareholders being issued, and
- the new issue actually taking place.

Expandable text

Illustration – Rights issues

What is the value of the right in Babbel Co.

Expandable text

Solution

| Value of a right | = $2.50 – $2.10 |
| | = $0.40 per new share issued |

Test your understanding 3

What is the value of the right in ABC Co?

Shareholders' options

The shareholder's options with a rights issue are to:

(1) take up his rights by buying the specified proportion at the price offered

(2) renounce his rights and sell them in the market

(3) renounce part of his rights and take up the remainder

(4) do nothing.

Expandable text

Illustration – Rights issues

Using the information in Illustration 2, a shareholder B had 1,000 shares in Babbel Co before the rights offer. Calculate the effect on the net wealth of B of each of the following options:

(1) Take up the shares.

(2) Sell the rights.

(3) Do nothing.

The facts were:

Rights issue 2:1

Cum rights price:	$2.70
Ex-rights price:	$2.50
Issue price	$2.10
Value of right	$0.40

> **Note**:
>
> Cum rights price = market value of the share pre the rights issue.
>
> Buyers of shares quoted cum rights are entitled to forthcoming rights.

Expandable text

Solution

			$
Wealth before			
	Shares	1,000@$2.70	**2,700**
Wealth after			
1. Take up the shares			
	Shares	1,500@$2.50	3,750
	Less cash paid to buy shares	500 @$2.10	(1,050)
	Total wealth		**2700**
2. Sell the rights			
	Shares	1,000@$2.50	2,500
	Plus cash receivedfrom sale of rights	500 @$0.40	200
	Total wealth		2700
3. Do nothing			
	Shares	1,000@$2.50	2500
	Total wealth		2500
	Loss incurred		200
			2700

*By doing nothing you theoretically eventually forego the right to the new shares.

Note the wealth of the investor who takes up the rights appears to be unchanged at $2,700. In practice the funds raised would be used to invest in projects with positive NPVs so the wealth of the shareholder is likely to increase.

Test your understanding 4

Alpha Co has issued share capital of 100 million shares with a current market value of $1 each. It announces a 1 for 2 rights issue at a price of 40c per share. It therefore plans to raise $20 million in new funds by issuing 50 million new shares.

Calculate the ex-rights price and for a shareholder, B, holding 1,000 shares in Alpha, consider his wealth if he:

(1) takes up his rights

(2) sells his rights

(3) buys 200 shares and sells the rights to a further 300

(4) takes no action.

10 Choosing between sources of equity

When choosing between sources of equity finance, account must be taken of factors such as:

(1) the accessibility of the finance

(2) the amount of finance

(3) costs of the issue procedure

(4) pricing of the issue

(5) control

(6) dividend policy – using retained earnings could impact the share price (see below).

KAPLAN PUBLISHING

Expandable text

For items 1 to 5, consider the pros and cons of the alternative forms of raising equity finance.

Solution

Accessibility to finance

The ability of a company to raise equity finance is restricted by its access to the general market for funds. Thus, whilst **quoted** companies are able to use any of the sources, an **unquoted** company is restricted to rights issues and private placings. The problem of equity finance for smaller companies is examined later in chapter 17).

Furthermore, there are statutory restrictions, e.g. those in the UK imposed by the Companies Act 1985. Only public limited companies may offer shares to the general public.

Obviously, the need to raise finance could be combined with a **flotation** (i.e. a private company going public and having its shares quoted on a recognised stock exchange). However, flotations will incur significant costs.

Amount of finance

The amount of finance that can be raised by a **rights issue** from an **unquoted** company is limited by the number and resources of the existing shareholders. It is not possible to provide general estimates of the amounts that may be raised as the circumstances vary. For quoted companies, where rights may be sold, this is less problematic.

Larger sums can be raised by **placings**, but ultimately it is the offer of shares to the general public that opens up the full financial resources of the market.

Costs of issue procedures

Use of internally-generated funds is easily the cheapest and simplest method. For new issues, placings are the most attractive on cost grounds, followed by rights issues, with public offers being by far the most expensive.

However all new share issues will take management and administrative time within the company. This will be much greater for an offer for sale than for the other two alternatives.

Pricing of the issue

One of the most difficult problems in making a **new issue to the public** is setting the price correctly. If it is too high, the issue will not be fully taken up and will be left with the underwriters, and if it is underpriced some of the benefits of the project for which the finance is being raised will accrue to the new shareholders and not to the old.

The same pricing problem exists with a **placing** as with a new issue. There will be no danger of undersubscription, of course, because the placing is agreed before the issue is made. However, the price will have been negotiated so as to be attractive to the subscribing institutions. Almost inevitably, it will be below the issue price that it would obtain in the market, because of the attractions of lower issue costs.

A **rights issue**, on the other hand, completely by-passes the price problem. Since the shares are offered to existing shareholders, it does not matter if the price is well below the traded price. Indeed, it would be normal for this to be so. Any gain on the new shares would, by the nature of a rights issue, go to the existing shareholders.

The pricing of new issues is even more complex when the company is **unquoted**. A company coming to the market for the first time would have no existing market price to refer to and would have to value the shares from scratch.

Control

There is no change in the shareholders with internally-generated funds and rights issues, insofar as they are taken up by existing shareholders. On the other hand, **placings** and **sales** to the general public introduce new shareholders.

Which is preferable depends on the objectives of the fund-raising exercise. If the desire is to retain control for the existing shareholders, then a rights issue is preferable. If diversification of control is desired, then an issue to the public will be preferred.

There can be no rigid rules concerning the choice of finance. Use of internally-generated funds is the best choice, subject to sufficient availability and dividend policy considerations. Of the new issue options, the order of preference will generally be a rights issue, placing and offer for sale to the general public. As funds available are consumed, so the next source is utilised.

Expandable text

Bestlodge plc is planning to build production facilities to introduce a major new product at a cost of $12 million.

The board of directors has already approved the project on the basis that it will yield a positive NPV when discounted, over a ten-year period, at the company's market weighted average cost of capital. The investment is expected to increase profit before interest and tax by approximately 25%.

No internally-generated funds are available.

The finance director has suggested three possible sources of finance.

(1) A five-year $12 million floating rate term loan from a clearing bank, at an initial interest rate of 10%.

(2) A ten-year €16 million fixed-rate loan from the Euro-currency market at an interest rate of 7%.

(3) A rights issue at a discount of 10% on the current market price.

The company's share price is 170 cents.

The current summarised financial statements are shown below.

Summarised balance sheet(Statement of financial position) as at 31December 20X1

	$000
Non-current assets at NBV	38,857
Current assets	18,286
Total assets	57,143
Equity and liabilities	
Ordinary shares of 25 cents each	7,200
Reserves	19,863
	27,063
11% loan notes 20X4/20X7	13,166
Current liabilities	16,914
Total equity and liabilities	57,143

Summarised income statement for the year ended 31 December 20X1

	$000
Turnover	57,922
Profit before interest and taxation	7,744
Debenture interest	1,448
	6,296
Taxation	3,148
Profit available for ordinary shareholders	3,148
Ordinary dividend	2,250
Retained profits	898

Corporation tax is at 50%

Exchange rates (€1 = $...)

	$/€
Spot rate	1.2010 – 1.2028
1 year forward	1.2760 – 1.2785

Acting as a consultant to Bestlodge plc, prepare a report which:

Discusses the advantages and disadvantages of each of the three suggested sources of finance illustrating how the utilisation of each source might affect the various providers of finance. (Relevant calculations are an essential part of your report.)

Suggests other sources of finance that might be suitable for this investment.

Solution

Bestlodge plc

Report

To Managing Director, Bestlodge plc

From A Consultant

Date Today

Subject Evaluation of financing alternatives for Bestlodge plc

Contents

(1) Terms of reference

(2) Floating rate loan

(3) Euro currency loan

(4) Rights issue

(5) Alternative sources of finance

(6) Conclusions and recommendations

(1) **Terms of reference**

The following report will evaluate the impact of each source of finance in terms of its:

I   cost

II   risk

III   impact upon other suppliers of capital.

A number of alternative sources of finance are briefly discussed. I would be pleased to provide more details of these upon request. A recommendation is made on the most suitable of the sources of finance you are currently considering.

(2) **Floating rate loan**

1   **Cost**

Debt finance is relatively cheap particularly if the company is in a position to offset the interest charge against taxable profits.

2 Risk

The interest rate is variable and it could rise if general interest rates move upwards. On the other hand, if interest rates fall, it ensures that Bestlodge is not left with a high-cost loan. Floating rate loans make cash budgeting difficult, but as variation in interest rates tends to be related to inflation rates the firm should find that increases in interest costs are partly matched by increases in operating cash flows due to higher inflation.

The loan is only for five years. If the project has not generated sufficient cash to repay the principal in this time, a further source of finance will be required. The availability of further funds in five years' time should be considered.

The loan will, at least initially, substantially increase the firm's gearing. In book value terms the likely effect is as follows:

	Present	**After project**
Long-term debt	13,166	13,166 + 12,000
Equity	7,200 + 19,863	7,200 + 19,863
	= 48.6%	= 93.0%

Tutorial note

Other gearing measures would be acceptable. One particularly useful approach could be to calculate gearing on market values of debt and equity.

This increase in gearing is also reflected in the firm's interest coverage:

	Present	After project
Profit before interest after tax	7.744	19,680
Interest	1.448	1,448 + 1,200
	= 5.35	= 3.65

The acceptability of these increases will largely be determined by industry standards and the firm's debt capacity. However, the loan appears to increase significantly the financial risk of the firm.

The existing loan notes will need to be redeemed in the near future and the firm should consider how this is to be financed.

(3) **Impact upon other suppliers of capital**

Equity: The increase in gearing will increase the risks taken by equity holders.

Earnings per share (EPS) is, however, likely to increase. This would also improve dividend cover.

	Present	After project
	$	$
Profit before interest and tax	7,744	9,680
Interest	1,448	2,648
	6,296	7,032
Tax (50%)	(3,148)	(3,516)
Available to equity	3,148	3,516
Number of 25c shares	28,800	28,800
EPS	10.9c	12.2c

Debt: The increase in gearing, depending upon the quality of the assets supporting the new loan and the debt covenants involved, could increase the risks of the existing debenture holders.

(3) Euro currency loan

Many of the comments made regarding the above loan are also applicable. In addition, the following points should be considered.

Although this is a fixed rate loan, any changes in the €/$ exchange rate could significantly affect its cost. The $ appears to weaken on the forward market in the coming year by approximately

$$\frac{\text{Forward rate} - \text{Spot rate}}{\text{Spot rate}} = \frac{1.2760 - 1.2010}{1.2010} = 6.2\%$$

This would increase interest and principal repayments by 6% pa. If this trend continues it could add significantly to the cost of the loan. For example, if we assume a $ depreciation of 6% pa, then this would increase the actual pre-tax cost of the loan to

7% (1.06) + 6% = 13.42%

(Effect on interest) + (Effect on principal)

This would then be an expensive source of finance. It also adds foreign exchange risk to the substantial financial risk (gearing) being taken by the firm.

(4) Rights issue

To raise $12 million at current market prices the number of new shares required will be approximately

$$\frac{\$12m}{\$1.70(1 - 0.1)} = 7,840,000$$

1 Cost

As equity holders normally demand higher returns than debt investors, this will be a relatively expensive source of finance. If these returns are not earned, share price would fall.

Issue costs would probably be larger than the arrangement costs on the debt finance.

(2) Risk

This is permanent finance and will not bring the pressure of early repayment.

A rights issue should substantially reduce the firm's gearing level, from 48.9% to

$$\frac{13{,}166}{7{,}200 + 19{,}863 + 12{,}000} = 33.7\%$$

There is a risk of undersubscription.

(3) Impact upon other suppliers of capital

The EPS will change to approximately

	$000
Profits before interest and tax	9,680
Interest	(1,448)
Profits before tax	8,232
Tax (50%)	(4,116)
Available to equity	4,116
Number of shares (000)	36,640
EPS	11.23c

This represents only a marginal increase over existing EPS. This must be contrasted with the higher returns from the higher risk financing strategies

(5) Alternative sources of finance

This is a long-term investment and should normally be financed by long-term funds. Possible sources include:

I mortgage loan through an insurance company or pension fund

II debenture or convertible loan stock

III leasing, or sale and leaseback

IV venture capital

V Eurobond or foreign bonds.

(6) Conclusions and recommendations

- Each source of finance has its own advantages and disadvantages.

- Gearing would probably rule out a debt issue.

- On the figures available the rights issue looks the safest option. Much depends on the current state of the stock market, and the likely reception of a rights issue.

- A mixture of equity and debt could be raised to balance gearing and EPS.

- Plans for the redemption of the existing loan notes should be considered.

- Issue costs, particularly on a rights issue, should be considered.

11 The dividend decision

If a company chooses to fund a new investment by a cut in dividend what will the impact be on existing shareholders?

Dividend irrelevancy theory

The dividend irrelevancy theory argues that in a perfect capital market, existing shareholders will be indifferent about the pattern of dividend payouts, provided that all retained earnings are invested in positive NPV projects.

Expandable text

A firm pays out a constant dividend of 10c in perpetuity. Its cost of equity is 10%.

The value of the dividend stream to an investor is:

$$\frac{10}{0.1} = 100c$$

- They would need to cancel the T1 dividend of 10c to pay for it.
- The project should earn 10% return, i.e. the 10c would be worth 10 × 1.1 = 11c the following year.

Provided the firm then distributed the additional 11c, the shareholder would have:

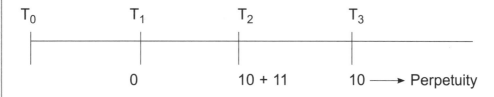

$$PV = 10 + 11/1.1^2 + \frac{10}{0.1} \times \frac{1}{1.1^2}$$

$$PV = 17.3554 + 82.6446 \qquad = 100c$$

So in theory, provided the firm invests the withheld dividend in projects that at least earn the shareholders' required return, the investors' wealth is unchanged and they will not object.

- Dividends become a residual – firms only pay a dividend if there are earnings remaining after all positive NPV projects have been financed.

Dividend relevance

However, practical influences, including market imperfections, mean that changes in dividend policy, particularly reductions in dividends paid, can have an adverse effect on shareholder wealth:

- reductions in dividend can convey 'bad news' to shareholders (dividend signalling)

- changes in dividend policy, particularly reductions, may conflict with investor liquidity requirements

- changes in dividend policy may upset investor tax planning (clientele effect).

As a result companies tend to adopt a stable dividend policy and keep shareholders informed of any changes.

Expandable text

In theory the level of dividend is irrelevant and in a perfect capital market it is difficult to challenge the dividend irrelevancy position. However, once these assumptions are relaxed, certain practical influences emerge and the arguments need further review.

Dividend signalling

In reality, investors do not have perfect information concerning the future prospects of the company. Many authorities claim, therefore, that the pattern of dividend payments is a key consideration on the part of investors when estimating future performance.

For example, an increase in dividends would signal greater confidence in the future by managers and would lead investors to increase their estimate of future earnings and cause a rise in the share price. A sudden dividend cut on the other hand could have a serious impact upon equity value.

This argument implies that dividend policy is relevant. Firms should attempt to adopt a stable (and rising) dividend payout to maintain investors' confidence.

Preference for current income

Many investors require cash dividends to finance current consumption. This does not only apply to individual investors needing cash to live on but also to institutional investors, e.g. pension funds and insurance companies, who require regular cash inflows to meet day-to-day outgoings such as pension payments and insurance claims. This implies that many shareholders will prefer companies who pay regular cash dividends and will therefore value the shares of such a company more highly.

The proponents of the dividend irrelevancy theory challenge this argument and claim that investors requiring cash can generate 'homemade dividends' by selling shares. This argument has some attractions but it does ignore transaction costs. The sale of shares involves brokerage costs and can therefore be unattractive to many investors.

Taxation

In many situations, income in the form of dividends is taxed in a different way from income in the form of capital gains. This distortion in the personal tax system can have an impact on investors' preferences.

From the corporate point of view this further complicates the dividend decision as different groups of shareholders are likely to prefer different payout patterns.

One suggestion is that companies are likely to attract a clientele of investors who favour their dividend policy (for tax and other reasons). E.g. higher rate tax payers may prefer capital gains to dividend income as they can choose the timing of the gain to minimise the tax burden. In this case companies should be very cautious in making significant changes to dividend policy as it could upset their investors.

Research in the US tends to confirm this 'clientele effect' with high dividend payout firms attracting low income tax bracket investors and low dividend payout firms attracting high income tax bracket investors.

Other practical constraints

Legal restrictions on dividend payments.

* Rules as to distributable profits that prevent excess cash distributions.

- Bond and loan agreements may contain covenants that restrict the amount of dividends a firm can pay.

Such limitations protect creditors by restricting a firm's ability to transfer wealth from bondholders to shareholders by paying excessive dividends.

Liquidity:

Consider availability of cash, not just to fund the dividend but also cash needed for the continuing working capital requirements of the company.

Alternatives to cash dividends

Share repurchase

- consider using cash to buy back shares as an alternative to a dividend, particularly if surplus cash available would distort normal dividend policy.
- alternative is to pay one-off surplus as a 'special dividend'.

Scrip dividends

A scrip dividend is where a company allows its shareholders to take their dividends in the form of new shares rather than cash.

- The advantage to the shareholder of a scrip dividend is that he can painlessly increase his shareholding in the company without having to pay broker's commissions or stamp duty on a share purchase.
- The advantage to the company is that it does not have to find the cash to pay a dividend and in certain circumstances it can save tax.

Do not confuse a scrip issue (which is a bonus issue) with a scrip dividend.

A bonus (scrip) issue is a method of altering the share capital without raising cash. It is done by changing the company's reserves into share capital.

The rate of a bonus issue is normally expressed in terms of the number of new shares issued for each existing share held, e.g. one for two (one new share for each two shares currently held).

Chapter summary

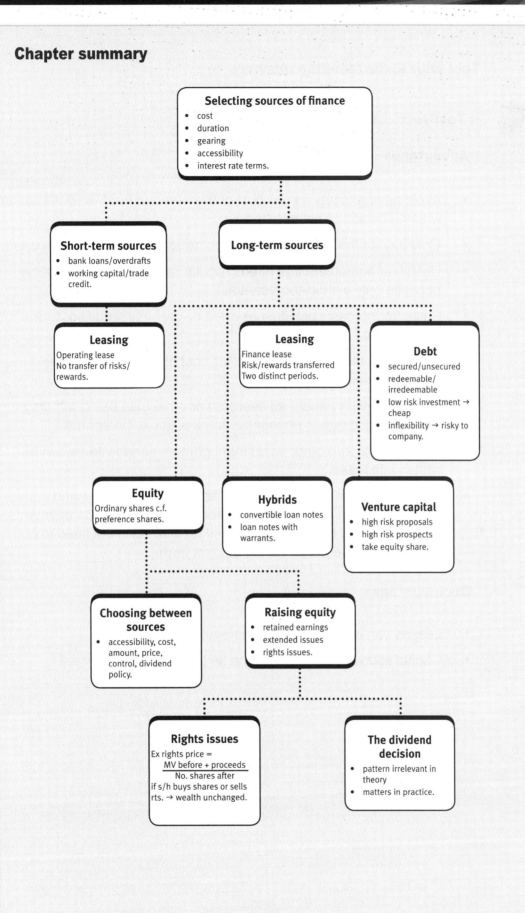

Selecting sources of finance
- cost
- duration
- gearing
- accessibility
- interest rate terms.

Short-term sources
- bank loans/overdrafts
- working capital/trade credit.

Long-term sources

Leasing
Operating lease
No transfer of risks/ rewards.

Leasing
Finance lease
Risk/rewards transferred
Two distinct periods.

Debt
- secured/unsecured
- redeemable/ irredeemable
- low risk investment → cheap
- inflexibility → risky to company.

Equity
Ordinary shares c.f. preference shares.

Hybrids
- convertible loan notes
- loan notes with warrants.

Venture capital
- high risk proposals
- high risk prospects
- take equity share.

Choosing between sources
- accessibility, cost, amount, price, control, dividend policy.

Raising equity
- retained earnings
- extended issues
- rights issues.

Rights issues
Ex rights price =
$$\frac{\text{MV before + proceeds}}{\text{No. shares after}}$$
if s/h buys shares or sells rts. → wealth unchanged.

The dividend decision
- pattern irrelevant in theory
- matters in practice.

Test your understanding answers

Test your understanding 1

Advantages

- Avoid having to pay the full cost of the asset up front, so don't use up working capital or have to borrow.

- Only pay for the asset over the fixed period of time that it is needed.

- Useful for equipment that needs regular replacement or updating because only a short-term contract.

- Easier to forecast cash flow as rates on monthly rental costs are usually fixed.

- Reduce tax bill by deducting the full cost of lease rentals from taxable income.

- No need to worry about an overdraft or other loan being withdrawn at short notice due to changes in bank policy or personnel.

- Maintenance and other asset management service items can be written into lease.

- Since the lessor will either sell the asset in the second-hand market or lease it again at the end of the agreed term, the lease payments can be kept low because the full asset value does not need to be recovered by the lessor during the first term.

Disadvantages

- Leases can be complex to understand.
- Capital allowances are foregone as the asset is not owned.

Test your understanding 2

MV of shares in issue = 10m × $2.70 = $27m

Proceeds from new issue = $\dfrac{10m}{5} \times 2 \times \$2.00 = \$8m$

Number of shares in issue ex-rights = 10m + $\dfrac{10m}{5} \times 2 = \$14m$

TERP = $\dfrac{\$27m + \$8m}{14m}$ = $2.50/share

Or TERP = $\dfrac{\$2.70 \times 5 + \$2.00 \times 2}{7}$ = $2.50/share

Test your understanding 3

$2.50 – $2.00 = 50c per new share issued

Test your understanding 4

The TERP is $0.80, calculated as follows:

$$\text{TERP} = 10m + \frac{\$1.00 \times 2 + \$0.40 \times 1}{3} = \$0.80/\text{share}$$

The value of each right is $0.40 per new share issued

($0.80 – $0.40 = $0.40)

Shareholder's choices:

(1) Take up his rights

Buy the new shares to which he is entitled. He can buy 500 new shares at $0.40, which will mean investing an additional $200 in the company.

	$
Current value of his 1,000 shares (1,000 × 1)	1,000
Additional investment to buy 500 new shares(500 × 0.4)	200
Total theoretical value of investment	1,200

Investor B will now have an investment of 1,500 shares that in theory will be worth $1,200 ($0.80 per share).

The value of the total investment has gone up by $200, but this is the amount of the additional investment he has made to acquire the new shares, so his wealth is unchanged.

(2) Sell his rights

	$
Current value of his 1,000 shares	1,000
Theoretical value of his shares after the rights issue (1000 × $0.80)	800
Theoretical loss in investment value	200
Sale value of rights (500 rights × $0.40)	200
Net gain/loss	0

By selling his rights, investor B receives $200, but the value of his investment is likely to fall by $200, leaving him no better and no worse off overall.

(3) **Buys 200 shares and sells 300 rights**

	$
Current value of his 1,000 shares	1,000
Theoretical value of shares after the rights issue (1,200 × $0.80)	960
Purchase price of 200 new shares (200 × $0.40)	(80)
	880
Sale value of rights (300 rights × $0.40)	120
Net wealth	1,000

Again his overall wealth is unchanged.

(4) **Take no action**

If investor B takes no action, the value of his shares is likely to fall from $1,000 before the rights issue to $800 after the rights issue. Taking no action is therefore an inadvisable option, because it results in a fall in investment value without any offsetting benefit from the sale of rights.

However, for those shareholders who do nothing, the company will try to sell the shares to which they are entitled, and if the shares can be sold for more than their rights issue price, the surplus will be paid to the 'do nothing' shareholders.

Capital structure and financial ratios

Chapter learning objectives

Upon completion of this chapter you will be able to:

- define, calculate and explain the significance to a company's financial position and financial risk of its level of the following ratios:
  - operating gearing
  - financial gearing
  - interest cover
  - interest yield
  - dividend cover
  - dividend per share
  - dividend yield
  - earnings per share (EPS)
  - price/earnings (PE) ratio

- assess a company's financial position and financial risk in a scenario by calculating and assessing appropriate ratios

- assess the impact of sources of finance on the financial position and financial risk of a company using cash flow forecasting

- assess the impact of sources of finance on the financial position and financial risk of a company by considering the effect on shareholder wealth.

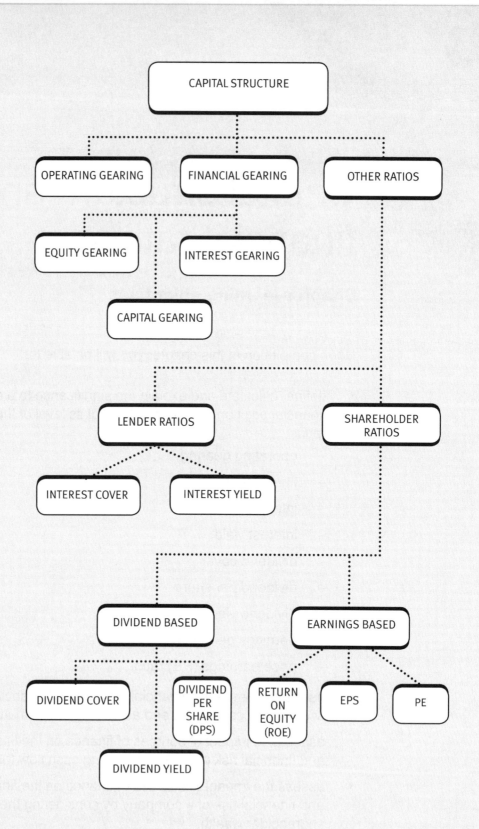

1 Operating gearing

Operating gearing is a measure of the extent to which a firm's operating costs are fixed rather than variable as this affects the level of business risk in the firm. Operating gearing can be measured in a number of different ways, including:

$$\frac{\text{Fixed costs}}{\text{Variable costs}} \quad \text{or} \quad \frac{\text{Fixed costs}}{\text{Total costs}} \quad \text{or even} \quad \frac{\text{\% change in EBIT}}{\text{\% change in turnover}}$$

Firms with a high proportion of fixed costs in their cost structures are known as having 'high operating gearing'.

Thus if the sales of a company vary:

The greater the operating gearing the greater the EBIT variability.

The level of operating gearing will be largely a result of the industry in which the firm operates.

Test your understanding 1

Two firms have the following cost structures:

	Firm A	Firm B
	$m	$m
Sales	5.0	5.0
Variable costs	(3.0)	(1.0)
Fixed costs	(1.0)	(3.0)
EBIT	1.0	1.0

What is the level of operating gearing in each and what would be the impact on each of a 10% increase in sales?

Expandable text

If a company were to automate its production line to replace the workers currently paid an hourly wage what would be the expected effect on its operating gearing?

Solution

Swapping variable costs for fixed would increase the level of operating gearing.

2 Financial gearing
The financial gearing ratios

Financial gearing is a measure of the extent to which debt is used in the capital structure.

Note that preference shares are usually treated as debt (see chapter 15 for logic).

It can be measured in a number of ways:

- Equity gearing:

$$\frac{\text{Preference share capital plus long-term debt}}{\text{Ordinary share capital and reserves}}$$

- Total or capital gearing:

$$\frac{\text{Preference share capital plus long-term debt}}{\text{Total long-term capital}}$$

Preference share capital plus long-term debt/

- Interest gearing:

$$\frac{\text{Debt interest}}{\text{Operating profits before debt interest and tax}}$$

NB Since preference shares are treated as debt finance, preference dividends are treated as debt interest in this ratio.

All three ratios measure the same thing, but

- for comparison purposes, the same ratio must be used consistently

- capital gearing is used more often than equity gearing

- interest gearing is an income statement measure rather than a balance sheet one. It considers the percentage of the operating profit absorbed by interest payments on borrowings and as a result measures the impact of gearing on profits. It is more normally seen in its inverse form as the interest cover ratio (see below).

Book or market values

The ratios can be calculated on either book or market values of debt and equity.

There are arguments in favour of both approaches:

Market values:

- are more relevant to the level of investment made

- represent the opportunity cost of the investment made

- are consistent with the way investors measure debt and equity.

Book values:

- are how imposed gearing restrictions are often expressed

- are not subject to sudden change due to market factors

- are readily available.

Illustration 1 – Book or market values

The following excerpt has been obtained from the financial statements of A Co.

Balance sheet(Statement of financial position) excerpt

	20X6	20X5
	$000	$000
Total assets less current liabilities	158	139
Creditors: amounts falling due beyond one year:		
5% secured loan notes	40	40
	118	99
Ordinary share capital (50c shares)	35	35
8% Preference shares ($1 shares)	25	25
Share premium account	17	17
Revaluation reserve	10	–
Income statement	31	22
	118	99

Income statement excerpt	20X6		20X5	
	$000		$000	
Gross profit		52		45
Interest	2		2	
Depreciation	9		9	
Sundry expenses	14		11	
		(25)		(22)
Net profit		27		23
Taxation		(10)		(10)
Net profit after taxation		17		13
Dividends:				
Ordinary shares	6		5	
Preference shares	2		2	
		(8)		(7)
Retained profit		9		6

The market values are/were as follows:	20X6	20X5
ordinary shares (per share)	204c	195c
preference shares (per share)	80c	102c
5% loan notes (per $100 nominal value)	$108	$116

Calculate the

A   equity gearing

B   capital gearing

C   interest gearing

for A Co using both balance sheet and market values

Expandable text

Solution

A. Equity gearing

	20X6	20X5

$$\text{Book values} = \frac{25 + 40}{118-25} \times 100 = 69.9\% \qquad \frac{25 + 40}{99-25} = 87.8\%$$

Market values

$$\frac{(0.8 \times 25) + (1.08 \times 40)}{2.04 \times 70} \times 100 = 44.3\% \qquad \frac{(1.02 \times 25) + (1.16 \times 40)}{1.95 \times 70} \times 100 = 52.7\%$$

Note: Since preference shares are treated as debt, equity gearing could also be described as the debt/equity ratio.

B. Capital gearing

	20X6	20X5

$$\text{Book values} = \frac{65}{158} \times 100 = 41.1\% \qquad \frac{65}{139} = 46.8\%$$

Market values

$$\frac{6.32 \quad 63.2}{142.8 + 63.2} \times 100 = 30.7\% \qquad \frac{71.9}{136.5 + 71.9} \times 100 = 34.5\%$$

C. Interest gearing

$$\frac{2 + 2}{27 + 2} \times 100 = 13.8\%$$

20X6

$$\frac{2 + 2}{23 + 2} \times 100 = 16.0\%$$

20X5

Note: that the results differ significantly depending on whether book or market values are used, which highlights the importance of consistency in the calculations.

Impact of financial gearing

Where two companies have the same level of variability in earnings, the company with the higher level of financial gearing will have increased variability of returns to shareholders.

Illustration 2 – Impact of financial gearing

Calculate the impact on Firm C of a 10% fall in sales and comment on your results:

	Firm C $000
Sales	10
Variable costs	(2)
Fixed costs	(5)
	—
EBIT	3
Interest	(2)
	—
EAIBT	1

Expandable text

Solution

	Firm C	Firm C – 10% decrease
	$000	$000
Sales	10	9
Variable costs	(2)	(1.8)
Fixed costs	(5)	(5)
	———	———
EBIT	3	2.2
Interest	(2)	(2)
	———	———
EAIBT	1	0.2

The impact of a 10% decrease in sales has reduced operating earnings by (3 – 2.2)/3 = 26.67%.

The increased volatility can be explained by the high operating gearing in C.

However, C also has debt interest obligations. This financial gearing has the effect of amplifying the variability of returns to shareholders. The 10% drop in sales has caused the overall return to fall by (1 – 0.2)/1= 80%. The additional 53.33% variation over and above the change in operating earnings is due to the use of debt finance.

Overall therefore there is a required trade-off between:

Overall therefore there is a required trade-off between:

Business risk
(associated with competing in the marketplace)

Operating gearing
(caused by the proportion of costs that are fixed)

Financial gearing
(caused by the proportion of debt in the structure)

A firm must consider the volatility it cannot avoid and ensure that the gearing decisions it takes avoid increasing risks to unacceptable levels.

Expandable text

Balance sheet for Redknapp Co

	$m	$m
Assets		
Non-current assets (total)		23.0
Current assets (total)		15.0

Total assets		38.0
		=====
Equity and liabilities:		
Ordinary share capital		10.0
Ordinary share premium		3.0
Preference share capital		1.5
Reserves		2.5

		17.0
Loan notes 10%		8.0
Current liabilities		
Trade payables	8.0	
Bank overdraft	5.0	

		13.0

Total equity and liabilities		38.0
		=====

Calculate the equity gearing and capital gearing of the business.

Solution

Debt	= $5m + $8m + $1.5m	= $14.5m
Equity	= $10m + $3m + $2.5m	= $15.5m
Equity gearing	= $14.5m/$15.5m × 100	= 93.5%
Capital gearing	= $14.5m/($14.5m + $15.5m)	= 48.3%

Note: strictly the overdraft is a short-term finance method whereas financial gearing looks at the mix of the company's medium to long-term finance. Where however a company were to consistently operate at an overdraft then there is an argument for including the core amount of the overdraft in long-term debt.

If we assume the overdraft is short-term finance, then the ratios become:

Debt	= $8m + $1.5m	= $9.5m
Equity	= $15.5m as before	
Equity gearing	= $9.5m/$15.5m × 100	= 61.3%
Capital gearing	= $9.5m/($9.5m + $15.5m)	= 38%

3 Other investor ratios

Other financial ratios that will be of interest to investors will relate to the level and safety of their income from the investment, and we shall now look at the following ratios:

- for debt holders:
    - interest cover
    - interest yield

- for shareholders:
    - dividend and earnings-related ratios.

KAPLAN PUBLISHING

To illustrate these, we shall use the account extracts from A Co. that were used earlier on gearing ratios.

Balance sheet (Statement of financial position) excerpt

	20X6	20X5
	$000	$000
Total assets less current liabilities	158	139
Creditors: amounts falling due beyond one year:		
5% secured loan notes	40	40
	118	99
Ordinary share capital (50c shares)	35	35
8% Preference shares ($1 shares)	25	25
Share premium account	17	17
Revaluation reserve	10	-
Retained profit	31	22
	118	99

Income statement excerpt	20X6	20X5
	$000	$000
Gross profit	52	45
Interest	2	2
Depreciation	9	9
Sundry expenses	14	11
	(25)	(22)
Net profit	27	23
Taxation	(10)	(10)
Net profit after taxation	17	13
Dividends:		
Ordinary shares	6	5
Preference shares	2	2
	(8)	(7)
Retained profit	9	6
The market values are/were as follows:	20X6	20X5
ordinary shares (per share)	204c	195c
preference shares (per share)	80c	102c
5% loan notes (per $100 nominal value)	$108	$116

Debt holder ratios: interest cover

Interest on loan stock (debenture stock) must be paid whether or not the company makes a profit.

 Interest cover is a measure of the adequacy of a company's profits relative to its interest payments on its debt:

$$\frac{\text{Operating profits before debt interest and tax}}{\text{Debt interest}}$$

The lower the interest cover, the greater the risk that profit (before interest and tax) will become insufficient to cover interest payments.

KAPLAN PUBLISHING

In general, a high level of interest cover is 'good' but may also be interpreted as a company failing to exploit gearing opportunities to fund projects at a lower cost than from equity finance.

Note: the interest cover ratio is the inverse of the interest gearing ratio (see above).

Expandable text

Illustration – Debt holder ratios: interest cover

Interest cover for A Co:

20X6

$$\frac{(52 - 9 - 14)}{2+2} = \frac{29}{4} \text{ i.e. 7.25 times}$$

20X5

$$\frac{(45 - 9 - 11)}{2+2} = \frac{25}{4} \text{ i.e. 6.25 times}$$

The company is in a strong position as regards the payment of interest. Profit would have to drop considerably before any problem of paying interest arose.

Debt holder ratios: interest yield

The interest yield is the interest or coupon rate expressed as a percentage of the market price:

$$\frac{\text{Interest rate}}{\text{Market value of debt}}$$

It is a measure of return on investment for the debt holder.

Expandable text

Illustration – Debt holder ratios: interest yield

On the 5% loan notes:

20X6		**20X5**	
$\dfrac{5}{108}$	= 4.6%	$\dfrac{5}{116}$	× 100 = 4.3%

Note this measure totally ignores whether the debt is redeemable and how close redemption might be. It is a reasonable approximation of return if the bond is irredeemable or has a long period to go to maturity.

Shareholder ratios

An investor is interested in:

- the income earned by the company for him
- the return on his investment.

For an ordinary shareholder the relevant information will be contained in the following ratios:

Dividends	**Earnings**
DPS	ROE
Dividend cover	EPS
Dividend yield	PE ratio

In general, the higher each of these ratios is, the more attractive the shares will be to potential investors, who will be increasingly confident about the return the shares will give.

With the exception of dividend cover, each of these was covered in chapter 3.

Illustration – Shareholder ratios

	20X6		20X5	

DPS $\dfrac{\$6,000}{70,000}$ = 8.6 cents per share $\dfrac{\$5,000}{70,000}$ = 7.1 cents per share

Dividend yield $\dfrac{8.6c}{204c}$ × 100 = 4.2% $\dfrac{7.1c}{195c}$ × 100 = 3.6%

ROE $\dfrac{(\$17,000 - \$2,000)}{(\$118,000 - \$25,000)}$ × 100 = 16% $\dfrac{(\$13,000 = \$2,000)}{(\$99,000 - \$25,000)}$ × 100 = 14.9%

EPS $\dfrac{(\$17,000 - \$2,000)}{70,000}$ = 21.4c per share $\dfrac{(\$13,000 - \$2,000)}{70,000}$ = 15.7c per share

PE ratio $\dfrac{204c}{21.4c}$ = 9.5 times $\dfrac{195c}{15.7c}$ = 12.4 times

Dividend cover

This is calculated as:

$$\frac{\text{Profit available for ordinary shareholders}}{\text{Dividend for the year (i.e. interim plus final)}}$$

It is a measure of how many times the company's earnings could pay the dividend.

It is a measure of how many times the company's earnings could pay the dividend.

The higher the cover, the better the ability to maintain dividends, if profits drop. This needs to be looked at in the context of how stable a company's earnings are: a low level of dividend cover might be acceptable in a company with very stable profits, but the same level of cover in a company with volatile profits would indicate that dividends are at risk.

Because buyers of high-yield shares tend to want a stable income, dividend cover is an important number for income investors.

Expandable text

20X6

$$\frac{\$17,000 - \$2,000}{\$6,000} = 2.5 \text{ times}$$

20X5

$$\frac{(\$13,000 - \$2,000)}{\$5,000} = 2.2 \text{ times}$$

The profits available for ordinary shareholders are taken after deduction of the preference dividend. The cover represents the 'security' for the ordinary dividend – in this company the cover is reasonable.

Test your understanding 2

Below are the summarised accounts for B Co, a company with an accounting year ending on 30 September:

Summarised balance sheets(Statement of financial position)

	20X5		20X6	
	$000	$000	$000	$000
Assets				
Tangible non-current assets – NBV		4,995		12,700
Current assets:				
Inventory	40,145		50,455	
Receivables	40,210		43,370	
Cash at bank	12,092		5,790	
		92,447		99,615
Total assets		97,442		112,315
Equity and liabilities				
Called up share capital of 25¢ per share		9,920		9,920
Retained profits		30,820		40,080
Shareholders' funds		40,740		50,000
10% loan notes 20Y6/20Y9		19,840		19,840
Current liabilities				
Trade payables	32,604		37,230	
Taxation	2,473		3,260	
Proposed dividend	1,785		1,985	
		36,862		42,475
		97,442		112,315

Summarised income statements

	20X5	20X6
	$000	$000
Revenue	486,300	583,900
Operating profit	17,238	20,670
Finance cost	1,984	1,984
Profit on ordinary activities before taxation	15,254	18,686
Tax on profit on ordinary activities	5,734	7,026
Profit for the financial year	9,520	11,660
Dividends	2,240	2,400
	7,280	9,260
Retained profit brought forward	23,540	30,820
Retained profit carried forward	30,820	40,080

(a) **Calculate, for each year, two ratios which are of particular significance to them, for each of the following user groups:**

(i) **shareholders**

(ii) **trade creditors.**

(b) **Make brief comments upon the changes, between the two years, in the ratios calculated in (a.) above.**

Expandable text

If for a given level of activity a firm's ratio of fixed to variable costs rose and at the same time its ratio of equity to debt fell, what would be the impact on its operating and financial risk?

Solution

Increasing fixed costs would cause operating risk to rise.

Reducing the proportion of equity in the capital structure would cause financial risk to rise.

Chapter summary

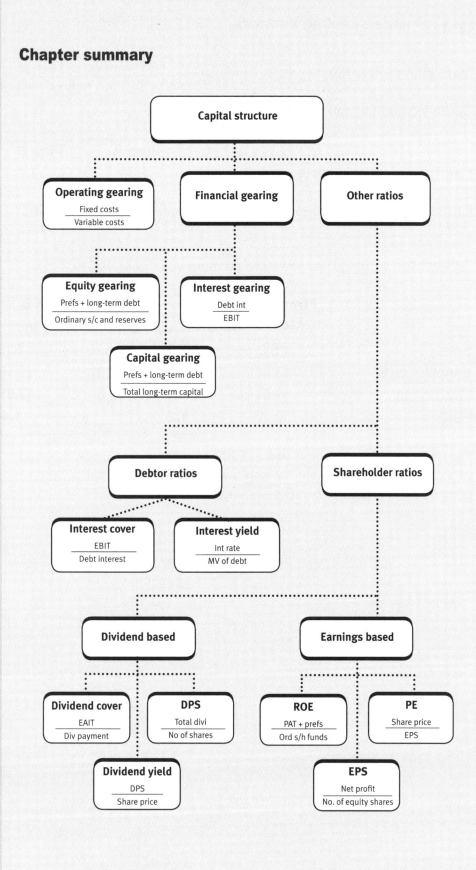

Test your understanding answers

Test your understanding 1

Operating gearing can be calculated as follows:

	Firm A	Firm B
Fixed costs/Variable costs	1/3 = 0.33	3/1 = 3

Firm B carries a higher operating gearing because it has higher fixed costs.

Its operating earnings will therefore be more volume-sensitive:

	Firm A $m	Firm A 10% inc	Firm B $m	Firm B 10% inc
Sales	5.0	**5.5**	5.0	5.5
Variable costs	(3.0)	**(3.3)**	(1.0)	**(1.1)**
Fixed costs	(1.0)	**(1.0)**	(3.0)	**(3.0)**
EBIT	1	**1.2**	1	**1.4**

Firm B has enjoyed an increase in EBIT of 40% whilst Firm A has had an increase of only 20%. In the same way a decrease in sales would bring about a greater fall in B's earnings than in A's.

Test your understanding 2

A i. Ratios of particular significance to shareholders

	20X5	20X6
EPS	$\dfrac{9{,}520}{39{,}680} \times 100 = 23.99c$	$\dfrac{11{,}660}{39{,}680} \times 100 = 29.39c$
Dividend cover	$\dfrac{9{,}250}{2{,}240} = 4.25 \text{ times}$	$\dfrac{11{,}660}{2{,}400} = 4.86 \text{ times}$

(ii) Ratios of particular significance for trade creditors

	20X5	20X6
Current ratio	$\dfrac{92{,}447}{36{,}862} = 2.51$	$\dfrac{99{,}615}{42{,}475} = 2.34$
Quick ratio	$\dfrac{92{,}447 - 40{,}145}{36{,}862} = 1.42$	$\dfrac{99{,}615 - 50{,}455}{42{,}475} = 1.16$

B EPS has increased by 22.5% due to improved profits. There has been no change in share capital. The dividend cover (the number of times the ordinary dividend is covered by the available profits) has increased because the percentage of profits paid out as a dividend has decreased. The dividend itself has gone up 7%, which is clearly not as much as the earnings improvement. The company is adopting a cautious policy but the dividend looks secure.

The current ratio is decreasing but it is still at an acceptable level. The quick ratio (measure of the company's liquidity) is also decreasing and at a faster rate due to the increasing investment in inventory (current ratio is down approximately 7% and the quick ratio about 18%). The quick ratio is above the generally desired level of 1 but the company should watch this area carefully.

Finance for small and medium enterprises

Chapter learning objectives

Upon completion of this chapter you will be able to:

- describe the financing needs of small businesses

- describe the nature of the financing problem for small businesses in terms of the funding gap, the maturity gap and inadequate security

- explain measures that may be taken to ease the financing problems of small and medium enterprises (SMEs), including the responses of government departments and financial institutions

- identify appropriate sources of finance for an SME in a scenario question and evaluate the financial impact of the different sources of finance on the business.

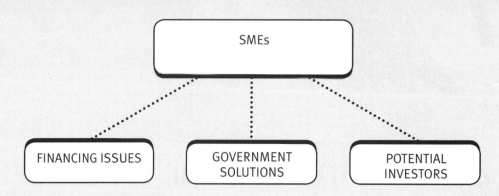

1 Specific financing issues for SMEs

The funding gap

As smaller companies tend to be unquoted, it is more difficult for equity investors to liquidate their investment. Typically therefore they rely on finance from retentions, rights issues and bank borrowings.

Initial ('seed') capital is often from family and friends, seriously limiting the scope for further rights issues.

A funding gap arises when they want to expand beyond these means of finance but are not yet ready for a listing on the Stock Exchange or Alternative Investment Market (AIM).

SMEs once got much of their expansion funding from equity stakes bought by wealthy individuals, but this is less common now because of:

- the increasing expense and difficulty of getting a stock market quote to provide an exit route

- tax incentives which encourage saving with large institutions.

> **Expandable text**
>
> Equity finance provided by wealthy individuals once formed an important source of expansion funds for the small business. More recently, however, SMEs have found themselves cut off from this source of capital for two main reasons:
>
> - The increasing expense and difficulty of obtaining a quotation on a stock market. The attractiveness of a speculative equity investment in a company is much increased if there is a reasonable chance of a quotation, which gives the opportunity of selling the shares.
>
> - In the UK the tax system has encouraged individuals to save with large institutions. These institutions prefer to invest in the shares of large companies rather than small ones or in non-corporate entities because of issues with marketability, risk and administrative costs.

Thus, wealthy individuals, who once provided a major source of venture capital (see below) for SMEs, have been persuaded by the tax system to channel their funds indirectly into large companies.

In addition:

- External equity may only be available on relatively unfavourable terms.

- Proprietors of small firms do not always have the same financial expertise as their larger competitors and information and advice about finance may not be easily accessible.

2 The financial investors

Other problems

Small firms are often considered to be more risky. This is a particular issue for newer businesses which may:

- lack proper financial control systems

- have inexperienced management teams

- not have an established track record

- lack sufficient good quality assets to offer as security (it is common for the owners of the business to be asked for personal guarantees).

Although banks remain reluctant to invest heavily in SMEs because of:

- the lack of security

- their risk-averse approach

investment has become more readily available from:

- venture capitalists – who provide risk-bearing capital to companies with high growth potential (see chapter 15)

- business angels – wealthy individuals investing in start-up, early stage or expanding firms, at lower levels than a venture capitalist (typically between £10,000 and £250,000 per deal).

Expandable text

Banks

Traditionally, small businesses have borrowed by means of loans and overdrafts from clearing banks. The main problems have always been the **security** required by the bank for granting the loan, and the **risk averse attitude of banks** when faced with a decision relating to a new and untested project. In the UK, the requirement for a personal guarantee from the proprietor to cover the loan or overdraft advance has inhibited the expansion of many small businesses and contributed towards the problem of British ideas being developed abroad.

Whilst the UK government has attempted to make debt investment in small businesses more attractive by the introduction of its Loan Guarantee Scheme, this has not proved very successful due to its relatively high interest rate.

Venture capital funds

The combination of increasing the prospective marketability of SME shares and tax relief schemes has led to the proliferation of venture capital funds, which provide equity capital for small and growing businesses.

One of the original, and still one of the best known, venture capital institutions in the UK is that forming part of the 3i Group. It takes a continuing interest in its client enterprises and does not require to withdraw the capital after, say, a five-year period.

However, in recent years, most major providers of business finance have in some way become involved in the provision of venture capital, usually by setting up or participating in specialist 'venture capital funds'. The main spur to their growth has come from the incentives described above.

The result is that there is now no real shortage of venture capital for viable projects. The range of possible funds includes those run by merchant and other banks, pension funds, individuals and local authorities

Business angels

Although venture capital companies are the main providers of equity finance to small businesses, they are highly selective and normally do not invest in amounts under £100,000 in the UK. An alternative source of smaller amounts of equity capital are private individuals, sometimes known as business angels, who normally have a business background.

Business angels are willing to make investments in small businesses in return for an equity stake. They can also offer the businesses the benefits of their own management expertise. A number of business angel networks operate in the UK to match businesses seeking equity finance with potential investors.

Test your understanding 1

Toogood Gardens is a private company that owns and operates a small chain of florists and garden centres in the south west. They have expanded rapidly since they opened 3 years ago, financing the expansion mainly through retained profits.

The directors are now considering a major expansion opportunity as a similar chain in a neighbouring area has become available for sale.

Advise the directors about the best way to raise funds to buy the chain, if a share-for-share deal is not available.

3 Government solutions

Governments have adopted a two-pronged response to increasing the attractiveness of SMEs:

- increasing marketability of shares
- tax incentives for investors.

In addition they have provided specific assistance in a range of areas (see below).

Making shares marketable

A number of SMEs that have good business ideas and growth potential do not fulfil the profitability/track record requirements to obtain a full stock exchange listing.

The development of small firm markets, such as the AIM in the UK and the Growth Enterprise Market (GEM) in Hong Kong, is designed to bridge this gap and provide both an exit ground and a venue for further fund-raising for investments.

In addition companies in the UK are now able to purchase their own shares, so a small investor can be bought out as needed.

Tax incentives

The following are the responses of the UK government which illustrate the types of incentives available:

- The Enterprise Investment Scheme (EIS) – tax incentives for individuals making equity investments in unquoted trading companies.

- Venture Capital Trusts (VCTs) – listed investment trust companies which invest their funds in a spread of small unquoted trading companies. Tax reliefs are granted to individuals who invest in VCTs.

- Employee share incentive schemes.

- Increasing profits and attractiveness by:
  - reducing rates of corporation tax for small companies
  - increasing the sales tax registration threshold.

Expandable text

The EIS

The Wilson Committee's recommendations led to the development of the current EIS which offers tax relief on investments in new ordinary shares in qualifying unlisted trading companies, including those traded on the AIM. There is a limit on the amount an individual may invest (currently up to £400,000 each tax year) and the investment qualifies for 20% income tax relief.

Any gain on disposing of EIS shares after 3 years is exempt from capital gains tax (CGT). Income tax or CGT relief is available on losses.

The scheme applies to any company carrying out a qualifying trade or business activity wholly or mainly in the UK, provided that the company's gross assets do not exceed £7 million immediately before the shares are issued. It enables companies to raise up to £1m a year. Participating investors may become paid directors of the company and in certain circumstances still qualify for the relief.

VCTs

VCTs are companies listed on the London Stock Exchange and are similar to investment trusts.

At least 70% of the underlying investments must be held in a spread of small unquoted trading companies within three years of the date of launch.

The aim is to encourage individuals to invest indirectly in a range of small higher-risk trading companies whose shares and securities are not listed on a recognised stock exchange. By investing through a VCT, the investment risk is spread over a number of companies.

Income tax relief is available at 30% on new subscriptions by individuals for ordinary shares in VCTs, to a maximum of £200,000 pa. In addition, subject to certain conditions, CGT relief is available on disposal of the shares.

Share incentive schemes

In the UK, there are schemes designed to encourage employees to hold shares in companies by which they are employed. All such schemes require HM Revenue and Customs (HMRC) approval.

Specific forms of assistance

This may take the form of:

- business links – a largely government-funded service that provides information, advice and support to those wishing to start, maintain and grow a business

- financial assistance:
  - loan guarantees
  - grants
  - loans.

Whilst you are not expected to have a detailed knowledge of particular government schemes, you should have a general awareness of the type of assistance offered.

Expandable text

Here we shall concentrate on the financial aspects of government assistance:

Small Firms Loan Guarantee Scheme (SFLGS)

This provides a government guarantee for loans by approved lenders. Loans are made to firms or individuals unable to obtain conventional finance because of a lack of track record or security. The guarantee generally covers 70% of the outstanding loan. This rises to 85% for established businesses trading for two years or more. Loans can be for amounts between £5,000 and £100,000 (£250,000 for established businesses) and over a period of two to ten years.

NB. Not all businesses are eligible for a loan and there are some restrictions on their use.

Regional Selective Assistance (RSA)

This is a discretionary scheme available in those parts of the UK designated as Assisted Areas. It takes the form of grants to encourage firms to locate or expand in these areas. Projects must either create new employment or safeguard existing jobs.

In England, for example, RSA is available for projects involving capital expenditure of at least £500,000.

Enterprise grants

This is a selective scheme for firms employing fewer than 250 people. It is available for high quality projects in designated areas. Businesses may only receive one such grant.

Regional innovation grants

This is available in certain areas of the UK to encourage the development of new products and processes. It is available to individuals or businesses employing no more than 50 people. The scheme provides a fixed grant of up to 50% of eligible costs up to a maximum of £25,000.

Small firms training loans

These are available through the Department for Education and Employment and eight major banks in the UK. The scheme helps businesses with up to 50 employees to pay for vocational education or training, by offering loans on deferred repayment terms:

- firms can borrow between £500 and £125,000 for between 1 and 7 years to cover education and training costs and, with restrictions, costs of consultancy advice on training matters

- the interest on the loan can be fixed or variable, and is paid by the Department for the first 6 to 12 months

- any education or training is eligible provided the firm can show that it will help them achieve their business objectives.

European Investment Bank (EIB) and European Investment Fund (EIF) schemes

The EIB provides loans to banks and leasing companies to help provide finance to small and medium-sized companies. The operators of EIB-supported schemes include finance organisations such as Barclays Mercantile, Lombard Business Finance and Forward Trust.

The EIF provides loan guarantees in conjunction with some finance organisations' own environmental loan facilities. These facilities are designed to assist business to finance investments that produce a quantifiable environmental benefit (energy usage, raw material usage, etc.).

Chapter summary

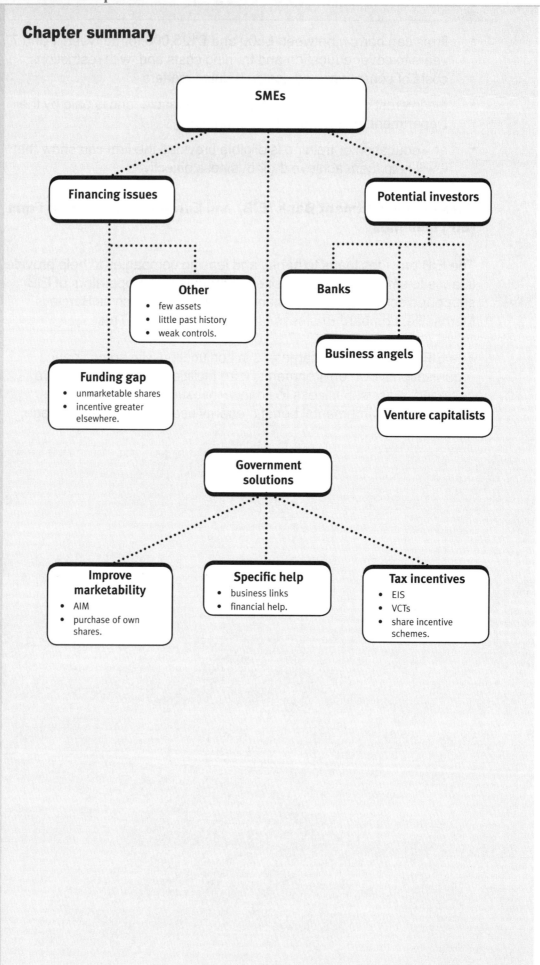

Test your understanding answers

Test your understanding 1

Rights issue

The easiest solution would be a rights issue to existing shareholders. It would:

- retain control
- not increase the financial risk.

However it may not be possible if existing shareholders:

- do not have further funds to invest
- are unwilling to invest further.

Venture capital

Since Toogoods Gardens has fast growth and a proven track record they may be able to attract venture capital funding. However they will need to provide the investors with an exit route, either by:

- agreeing to list on the AIM in the next few years
- buying back their shares at an agreed amount at a future date.

Bank loan

Assuming that the assets of Toogoods Gardens are not already being used as security, a bank loan would be a likely source of funds. It is relatively cheap because of the tax relief on the interest and is a predictable cash flow.

However, they would need to consider the level of financial gearing they have already, and the additional risk they face from business volatility and operating gearing. It would be unwise to take on debt finance if their risk profile was already high, as the increased gearing would amplify the issue.

Grants

If the area for the planned development is one where the government wants to encourage business, a grant may be available.

The cost of capital

Chapter learning objectives

Upon completion of this chapter you will be able to:

- explain the relationship between risk and return in financial investments

- explain the nature and features of different securities in relation to the risk/return trade-off

- explain the relative risk/return relationship of debt and equity and the effect on their relative costs

- describe the creditor hierarchy and its connection with the relative costs of sources of finance

- calculate a share price using the dividend valuation model (DVM)

- calculate cost of equity using the DVM

- calculate dividend growth using the dividend growth model (DGM)

- discuss the weaknesses of the DVM

- define and distinguish between systematic and unsystematic risk

- explain the relationship between systematic risk and return and describe the assumptions and components of the capital asset pricing model (CAPM)

- use the CAPM to find a company's cost of equity

- explain and discuss the advantages and disadvantages of the CAPM

- calculate the cost of finance for irredeemable debt, redeemable debt, convertible debt, preference shares and bank debt

- define and distinguish between a company's average and marginal cost of capital

- calculate the weighted average cost of capital (WACC) using book value (BV) and market value (MV) weightings

- calculate an appropriate WACC for a company in a scenario, identifying the relevant data.

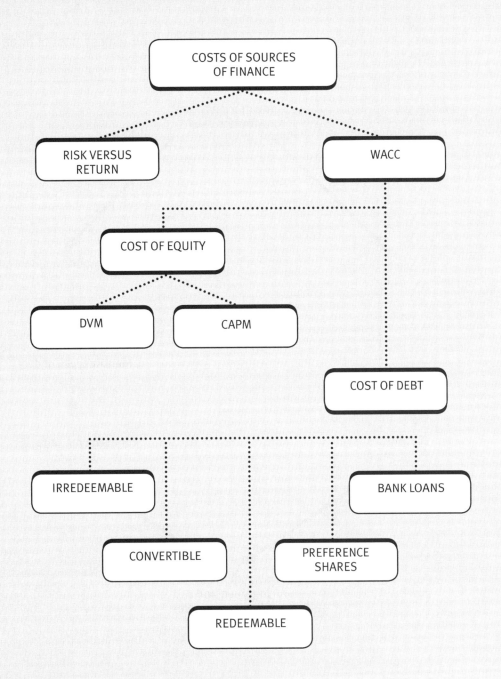

1 Relative costs of equity and debt

We have seen that when appraising investment projects, a firm may evaluate a project's returns using the company's cost of finance (also called the discount rate or cost of capital) to establish the net present value (NPV).

This cost of finance is dependent on two main factors:

- the prevailing risk-free rate (Rf) of return

- the reward investors demand for the risk they take in advancing funds to the firm.

This session will look at how a firm can identify their overall cost of finance using the technique below:

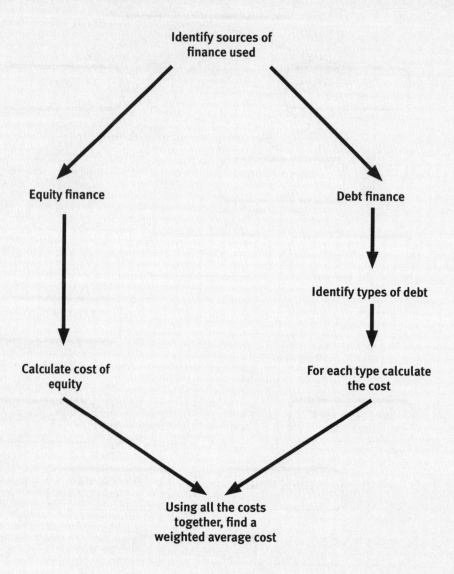

🔑 This is the key approach for finding a company's WACC in examination questions.

The relationship between risk and return

When considering the return investors require, the trade-off with risk is of fundamental importance. Risk refers not to the possibility of total loss, but to the likelihood of actual returns varying from those forecast.

Consider four investments opportunities: A, B, C and D shown on the risk/return chart below where:

The risk of project A = the risk of project B.

The return from B = the return from C.

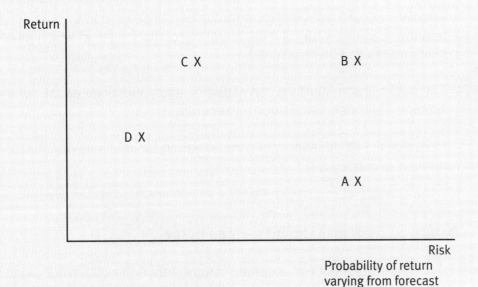

In choosing between the investment opportunities:

B is preferable to A – higher return for the same risk

C is preferable to B – same return for lower risk.

NB. The choice between D and C is less clear-cut. C pays higher returns but this is to compensate for the comparatively higher associated risk. The choice will therefore depend on the investor's attitude to risk and whether the increased return is seen by them as sufficient compensation for the higher level of risk.

The risk-free rate of return (Rf)

The Rf is the minimum rate required by all investors for an investment whose returns are certain.

It is given in questions as:

- the return on Treasury bills or
- the return on government gilts.

Expandable text

Once funds have been advanced to a company, an investor faces the risk that they will not be returned. However some investments are less risky than others. For example lending to a government is considered to be extremely low risk as governments are always able to raise funds via taxation to pay back the investor.

The risk is so minimal that government securities are known as risk-free and the return they pay is a minimum benchmark against which all other investments can be measured.

The return is sometimes given in examination questions as the return on Treasury Bills or gilts (gilt-edged securities).

Note that the Rf does include compensation for inflation – i.e. it is a nominal or money rate.

Return on risky investments – loan notes

A risk-free investment has a certain return. Although not risk-free, loan notes are lower risk investments than equities because the return is more predictable. This is because:

- interest is a legal commitment
- interest will be paid before any dividends
- loans are often secured.

If a company issues loan notes, the returns needed to attract investors will therefore be:

- higher than the Rf
- lower than the return on equities.

Expandable text

As companies have to make profits in order to honour their loan commitments, loan notes or corporate bonds are not risk-free. Since they are risky investments the company will need to offer a higher return/yield than is paid on gilts to entice investors. The investors will require both a risk-free return and a risk premium.

However as we saw in chapter 15 loan notes are a relatively low-risk investment. Since the loan commitments are legally binding and often secured on company assets they are considered to be less risky than equity investments.

Not all bonds have the same risk. There is a bond-rating system, which helps investors distinguish a company's credit risk. Below is the Fitch and Standard & Poor's bond-rating scales.

Fitch/S&P	Grade	Risk
AAA	Investment	Highest quality
AA	Investment	High quality
A	Investment	Strong
BBB	**Investment**	**Medium grade**
BB, B	Junk	Speculative
CCC/CC/C	Junk	Highly speculative
D	Junk	In default

Notice that if the company falls below a certain credit rating, its grade changes from investment quality to junk status. Junk bonds are aptly named: they are the debt of companies in some sort of financial difficulty. Because they are so risky they have to offer much higher yields than other debt. This brings up an important point: not all bonds are inherently safer than shares.

The minimum investment grade rating is BBB. Institutional investors may not like such a low rating. Indeed some will not invest below an A rating.

Return on risky investments – equities

Equity shareholders are paid only after all other commitments have been met. They are the last investors to be paid out of company profits.

The same pattern of payment also occurs on the winding up of a company. The order of priority is:

- secured lenders
- legally-protected creditors such as tax authorities
- unsecured creditors
- preference shareholders
- ordinary shareholders.

As their earnings also fluctuate, equity shareholders therefore face the greatest risk of all investors.

The level of risk depends on:

- volatility of company earnings
- extent of other binding financial commitments.

The return required to entice investors into risky securities can be shown as

> Required return = Risk-free return + Risk premium

Since ordinary shares are the most risky investments the company offer, they are also the most expensive form of finance for the company.

Expandable text

Equity shareholders are the last investors to be paid out of company profits or in the event of a winding up. The level of risk they face will depend on how volatile the company's earnings are to start with and how great its other commitments are (e.g. how much debt finance is to be serviced).

After contractual commitments such as debt interest, the profits available for distribution are then used to pay any preference shareholders, before the ordinary shareholders are finally able to participate in any remaining surplus.

What's more, dividends are paid only on the recommendation of the directors, and they may decide, if the business has not had a good year, to pay a reduced dividend or even to withhold a dividend altogether.

2 Estimating the cost of equity – the DVM

The cost of equity finance to the company is the return the investors expect to achieve on their shares.

One way to determine what return they expect to receive is to look at how much they are prepared to pay for a share.

Assumptions:

DVM states that:

- Share price = Future expected income stream from the share, discounted at the investor's required return

- Future income stream is the dividends paid out by the company

- Dividends will be paid in perpetuity

- Dividends will be constant or growing at a fixed rate.

Therefore:

- Share price = Dividends paid in perpetuity discounted at the shareholder's rate of return.

A discussion of the DVM and its assumptions is likely to be required in an examination question that asks you to calculate cost of equity.

DVM (no growth)

The formula for valuing a share is therefore:

$$P_0 = \frac{D}{r_e}$$

where:

D = constant dividend from year 1 to infinity

P_0 = share price now (year 0)

r_e = shareholders' required return, expressed as a decimal.

For a listed company, since the share price and dividend payment are known, the shareholder's required return can be found by rearranging the formula:

$$r_e = \frac{D}{P_0}$$

Expandable text

Illustration – DVM (no growth)

A company has paid a dividend of 20c for many years. The company expects to continue paying dividends at this level in the future. The company's cost of equity is 10%.

Required:

Calculate the market value of the share.

Expandable text

Solution

20 ÷ 0.10 = $2.00

Test your understanding 1

A company has paid a dividend of 30c for many years. The company expects to continue paying dividends at this level in the future. The company's current share price is $1.50 ex div (see below for explanation of ex div).

Calculate the cost of equity.

DVM (with growth)

Although in reality a firm's dividends will vary year on year, a practical assumption is to assume a constant growth rate in perpetuity.

The share valuation formula then becomes:

$$P_0 = \frac{D_0(1+g)}{r_e - g} = \frac{D_1}{r_e - g}$$

where:

g = constant rate of growth in dividends, expressed as a decimal

D_1 = dividend to be received in one year – i.e. at T_1

$D_0(1+g)$ = dividend just paid, adjusted for one year's growth.

Therefore to find the cost of equity the formula can be rearranged to:

$$r_e = \frac{D_0(1+g)}{P_0} + g = \frac{D_1}{P_0} + g$$

Expandable text

Illustration – DVM (with growth)

A company has just paid a dividend of 20c. The company expects dividends to grow at 7% in the future. The company's current cost of equity is 12%.

Required:

Calculate the market value of the share.

Solution

$$P_o = \frac{20(1 + 0.07)}{0.12 - 0.07} = 428 = \$4.28$$

Test your understanding 2

P Co has just paid a dividend of 10c. Shareholders expect dividends to grow at 5% pa. P Co's current share price is $1.05 ex div.

Calculate the cost of equity of P Co.

The ex-div share price

The DVM model is based on the perpetuity formula, which assumes that the first payment will arise in one year's time (i.e. at the end of year 1). A share price quoted on this basis is termed an ex div share price.

If the first dividend is receivable immediately, then the share is termed cum div. In such a case the share price would have to be converted into an ex div share price, i.e. by subtracting the dividend due for payment.

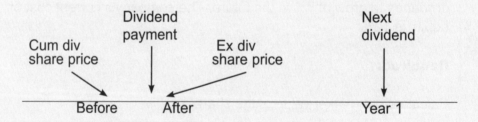

P_o represents the 'ex div' share price. A question may give you the cum div share price by stating that the dividend is to be paid shortly.

Cum div share price – dividend due = Ex div share price.

Expandable text

Dividends are paid periodically on shares. During the period prior to the payment of dividends, the price rises in anticipation of the payment. At this stage the price is **cum div**.

Some time after the dividend is declared the share becomes **ex div**, and the price drops. This may be expressed diagrammatically:

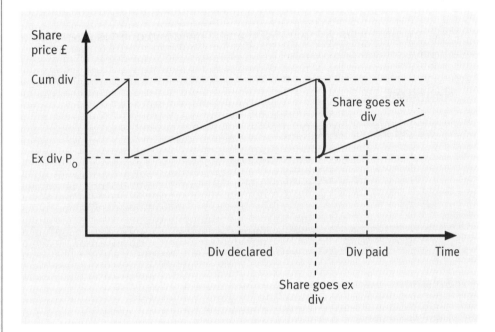

It will be noted that the share goes ex div shortly before the dividend is paid. Any person acquiring the share after this point in time will not receive the dividend, which will be paid to the original shareholder. The reason is that the time it takes for the company to amend its register of members requires a cut-off point somewhat before the dividend is paid.

Thus, when a share is quoted cum div, the price includes both the underlying ex div value of the share (P_o), and the dividend due shortly (D_o).

Use of the dividend valuation model and the formulae developed thus far requires an ex div share price to determine the P_0 value.

Expandable text

Illustration – The ex-div share price

The current share price is 140c and a dividend of 8c is due to be paid shortly.

Required:

Calculate the value of P_0.

Expandable text

Solution

140 – 8 = 132c.

Test your understanding 3

D Co is about to pay a dividend of 15c. Shareholders expect dividends to grow at 6% pa. D Co's current share price is $1.25.

Calculate the cost of equity of D Co.

Estimating growth

Two ways of estimating the likely growth rate of dividends are:

- extrapolating based on past dividend patterns

- assuming growth is dependent on the level of earnings retained in the business

A   Past dividends

This method assumes that the past pattern of dividends is a fair indicator of the future.

Expandable text

Illustration – Estimating growth

A company currently pays a dividend of 32c; five years ago the dividend was 20c.

Estimate the annual growth rate in dividends.

Expandable text

Solution

Since growth is assumed to be constant, the growth rate, g, can be assumed to have been the same in each of the 5 years, i.e. the 20c will have become 32c after 5 years of constant growth.

$20c \times (1 + g)^5 =$ 32c

or $(1 + g)^5 =$ 32/20

                                                        = 1.60

Therefore $1 + g = 1.6^{1/5} \approx 1.1$, so $g = 0.1$ or 10%

The formula for extrapolating growth can therefore be written as:

$$g = \sqrt[n]{\left(\frac{D_o}{\text{Dividend } n \text{ yrs ago}}\right)} - 1 = \left(\frac{D_o}{\text{Dividend } n \text{ yrs ago}}\right)^{1/n} - 1$$

where:

n = number of years of dividend growth.

Test your understanding 4

A company has paid the following dividends per share over the last five years.

20Y0	10.0c
20Y1	11.0c
20Y2	12.5c
20Y3	13.6c
20Y4	14.5c

Calculate the average annual historical growth rate.

B   The earnings retention model (Gordon's growth model)

Assumption

*   The higher the level of retentions in a business, the higher the potential growth rate.

The formula is therefore:

$g = br_e$

where:

r_e = accounting rate of return

b = earnings retention rate.

Expandable text

Illustration – Estimating growth

Consider the following summarised financial statement for XYZ Co

Balance sheet as at 31 December 20X5

	$		$
Assets	200	Ordinary shares	100
		Reserves	100
	200		200

Profits after tax for the year ended 31 December 20X6 $20

Dividend (a 40% payout) $8

Balance sheet as at 31 December 20X6

	$		$
Assets	212	Ordinary shares	100
		Reserves 100 + (20 – 8)	112
	212		212

If the company's return on equity and earnings retention rate remain the same, what will be the growth in dividends in the next year (20X7)?

Expandable text

Solution

Profit after tax as a % of capital employed will be 20 ÷ 200 = 10%.

10% × asset value at 31 December 20X6 = 10% × $212 = $21.20.

Dividends will therefore be 40% × $21.20 = $8.48.

This represents a growth of 6% on the year (8.48/8 = 1.06).

This is more directly calculated as:

Note: that the return on equity is calculated with reference to opening balance sheet values.

g = r (accounting rate of return) × b (the earnings retention rate)

= 10% × 60%

= 6%.

Test your understanding 5

A company is about to pay an ordinary dividend of 16c a share. The share price is 200c. The accounting rate of return on equity is 12.5% and 20% of earnings are paid out as dividends.

Calculate the cost of equity for the company.

Weaknesses of the DVM

The DVM has a sound basic premise. The weaknesses occur because:

- the input data used may be inaccurate:
  - current market price
  - future dividend patterns
- the growth in earnings is ignored.

Make sure you can challenge the assumptions of the DVM for an examination question.

Expandable text

Few would argue with the basic premise of the model that the value of a share is the present value of all its future dividends. Its major weakness stems from limitations in the input data.

Current market price

P_0 – this can be subject to other short-term influences, such as rumoured takeover bids, which considerably distort the estimate of the cost of equity.

Future dividends

For simplicity we usually assume no growth or constant growth. These are unlikely growth patterns. Further, growth estimates based on the past are not always useful; market trends, economic conditions, inflation, etc. need to be considered. In examination questions future dividends are often estimated rather mechanically but it is important to think about influences on future dividends other than past dividends.

Relevance of earnings in the DVM

Earnings do not feature as such in the DVM. However, earnings should be an indicator of the company's long-term ability to pay dividends and therefore in estimating the rate of growth of future dividends, the rate of growth of the underlying profits must also be considered. For example, if dividends grow at 10% whilst earnings grow at 5%, before long the firm will run out of funds with which to pay dividends. Similarly, if dividends grow at 5% and profits at 10%, the firm will soon accumulate excess funds.

3 Estimating the cost of equity – the CAPM

DVM assumes that an investor's current required return will remain unchanged for future projects. For projects with different risk profiles, this assumption may not hold true.

If an investor's required return reflects the risk they face, then one method of calculating the cost of equity involves looking more closely at the nature of the risk itself.

Expandable text

The DVM discussed above, assumes that the return currently being paid to ordinary shareholders will continue to be their required return in the future.

We have seen that the return required is a reflection of the risk the investor faces.

Therefore by using the DVM we are effectively assuming that all future investment projects will be subject to the same risk as those currently undertaken.

However, if the company is considering an investment project in a different business area, these assumptions may not be appropriate and an alternative approach to finding the cost of equity is needed.

Reducing risk by combining investments

An investor, knowing that a particular investment was risky, could decide to reduce the overall risk faced, by acquiring a second share with a different risk profile and so obtain a smoother average return.

Reducing the risk in this way is known as **diversification**.

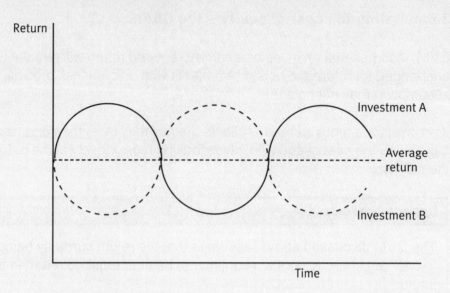

The diagram above is an exaggeration, as the returns from no two investments will ever move in completely opposite directions.

However an investor can reduce risk by diversifying to hold a portfolio of shareholdings, since shares in different industries will at least to some degree offer differing returns profiles over time.

Provided the returns on the shares are not perfectly positively correlated (that is they do not move in exactly the same way) then any additional investment brought into a portfolio (subject to a maximum point – see below) will reduce the overall risk faced.

Expandable text

In the diagram above, the investor has combined investment A (for example shares in a company making sunglasses) with investment B, (perhaps shares in a company making raincoats). The fortunes of both firms are affected by the weather, but whilst A benefits from the sunshine, B loses out and vice versa for the rain. Our investor has therefore smoother overall returns – i.e. faces less overall volatility/risk and will need a lower overall return.

The returns from the investments shown are negatively correlated – that is they move in opposite directions. In fact they appear to have close to perfect negative correlation – any increase in one is almost exactly matched by a decrease the other.

Obviously this example is over-simplified and it is unlikely that the returns of any two businesses would move in such opposing directions, but the principle of an investor diversifying a portfolio of holdings to reduce the risk faced is a good one. Provided the shares are not perfectly positively correlated (that is they do not move in exactly the same way) then any additional investment brought into a portfolio (subject to a maximum point – see below) will reduce the overall risk faced.

Initial diversification will bring about substantial risk reduction as additional investments are added to the portfolio.

However risk reduction slows and eventually stops altogether once 15-20 carefully selected investments have been combined.

This is because the total risk faced is not all of the same type.

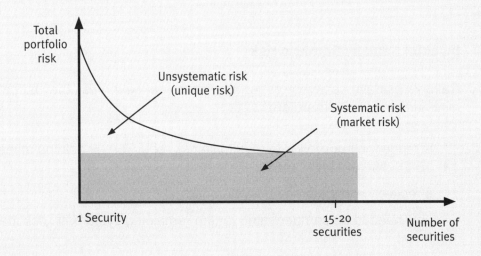

Systematic and non-systematic risk

The risk a shareholder faces is in large part due to the volatility of the company's earnings. This volatility can occur because of:

* systematic risk – market wide factors such as the state of the economy
* non-systematic risk – company/industry specific factors.

Systematic risk will affect all companies in the same way (although to varying degrees). Non-systematic risk factors will impact each firm differently, depending on their circumstances.

Diversification can almost eliminate unsystematic risk, but since all investments are affected in the same way by macro-economic i.e. systematic factors, the systematic risk of the portfolio remains.

Test your understanding 6

The following factors have impacted the volatility of the earnings of Chocbic Co, a manufacturer of chocolate biscuits and cereals:

- increase in interest rates

- increase in the price of cocoa beans

- legislation changing the rules on tax relief for investments in non-current assets

- growth in the economy of the country where Chocbic Co is based

- government advice on the importance of eating breakfast

- industrial unrest in Chocbic Co's main factory.

Are they examples of systematic or unsystematic risk?

Investors and systematic risk

Rational risk-averse investors would wish to reduce the risk they faced to a minimum and would therefore:

- arrange their portfolios to maximise risk reduction by holding at least 15-20 different investments

- effectively eliminate any unsystematic risk

- only need to be compensated for the remaining systematic risk they faced.

The CAPM

The CAPM shows how the minimum required return on a quoted security depends on its risk.

Assumptions:

- well-diversified investors

- perfect capital market

- unrestricted borrowing or lending at the risk-free rate of interest

- uniformity of investor expectations

- all forecasts are made in the context of one time period only.

The required return of a rational risk-averse well-diversified investor can therefore be found by returning to our original argument:

$$\text{Required return} = \text{Risk-free return} + \text{Risk premium}$$

The following additional points can now be added:

Required return = Risk-free return + relative level of systematic risk × market risk premium for a specific investment

2 The share of the premium an investor requires depends on how the risk of their investment compares to the average.

1 The overall average return on the market (Rm) paid by the stock market in excess of the risk-free rate (Rf) must represent a fair risk premium for systematic risk.

So the formula becomes:

Required return = Rf + β (Rm – Rf)

where:

Rf = risk-free rate

Rm = average return on the market

(Rm – Rf) = average market risk premium

β = systematic risk of the investment compared to market and therefore amount of the premium needed.

The required return of a rational risk-averse well-diversified investor can therefore be found by returning to our original argument:

Understanding beta:

If an investment is riskier than average (i.e. the returns more volatile than the average market returns) then the β > 1.

If an investment is less risky than average (i.e. the returns less volatile than the average market returns) then the β < 1.

If an investment is risk free then β = 0.

Expandable text

From the assumptions of CAPM it is deduced that all investors will hold a well-diversified portfolio of shares, known as the market portfolio, which is really a 'slice' of the whole stock market. Although the market portfolio is not really held by investors, in practice even a limited diversification will produce a portfolio which approximates its behaviour, so it is a workable assumption.

The attractiveness of any individual security is therefore judged in relation to its effect when combined with the market portfolio.

A security whose returns are highly correlated with fluctuations in the market is said to have a high level of systematic risk. It does not have much risk-reducing potential on the investor's portfolio and therefore a high return is expected of it. On the other hand, a security which has a low correlation with the market (low systematic risk) is valuable as a risk reducer and hence its required return will be lower.

The measure of the systematic risk of a security relative to that of the market portfolio is referred to as its beta factor. In practice industries such as construction are far more volatile than others such as food retailing and would have correspondingly higher betas.

The CAPM shows the linear relationship between the risk premium of the security and the risk premium of the market portfolio.

Risk premium of share = market risk premium β

i.e. Required return of share = Rf + market risk premium × β

or $Ry = R_f + (R_m - R_f)\beta$

The same formula can be applied to computing the minimum required return of a capital investment project carried out by a company, because the company is just a vehicle for the shareholders, who will view the project as an addition to the market portfolio.

The formula sheet expresses this as

$E(r_i) = R_f + \beta_i(E(r_m) - R_f)$

if an investment is risk free then β = 0

Illustration 1 – The CAPM

The current average market return being paid on risky investments is 12%, compared with 5% on Treasury bills. G Co has a beta of 1.2. What is the cost of equity of G Co?

Expandable text

Solution

Required return = Rf + β (Rm – Rf)

r_e = 5 + 1.2 (12 – 5) = 13.4%.

Test your understanding 7

B Co is currently paying a return of 9% on equity investment. If the return on gilts is currently 5.5% and the average return on the market is 10.5%, what is the beta of B Co and what does this tell us about the volatility of B's returns compared to those of the market on average?

The advantages and disadvantages of CAPM

Advantages:

*   works well in practice
*   focuses on systematic risk
*   is useful for appraising specific projects.

Disadvantages:

*   less useful if investors are undiversified
*   ignores tax situation of investors
*   actual data inputs are estimates and may be hard to obtain.

Expandable text

In practice, many of the assumptions underlying the development of CAPM are violated. However, rather than being overly critical, it is more sensible to ask 'does the theory work?', i.e. does it explain the returns on securities in the real world?

Fortunately, the answer is yes. Practical empirical tests, whilst showing that betas are not perfect predictors of rates of returns on investments, do show a strong correspondence between systematic risk and rate of return. Certainly CAPM outperforms other models in this area, and in particular it gives a far better explanation of the rate of return on a security than is obtained by looking at its total risk.

Advantages of CAPM

- It provides a market-based relationship between risk and return, and assessment of security risk and rates of return given that risk.

- It shows why only systematic risk is important in this relationship.

- It is one of the best methods of estimating a quoted company's cost of equity capital.

- It provides a basis for establishing risk-adjusted discount rates for capital investment projects.

Limitations of CAPM

By concentrating only on systematic risk, other aspects of risk are excluded; these unsystematic elements of risk will be of major importance to those shareholders who do not hold well-diversified portfolios, as well as being of importance to managers and employees. Hence it takes an investor-orientated view of risk.

The model considers only the level of return as being important to investors and not the way in which that return is received. Hence, dividends and capital gains are deemed equally desirable. With differential tax rates the 'packaging' of return between dividends and capital gain may be important.

It is strictly a one-period model and should be used with caution, if at all, in the appraisal of multi-period projects.

Some of the required data inputs are extremely difficult to obtain or estimate, for example:

R_f can be obtained from quoted rates. From the wide range of quoted interest rates, a relevant rate must be decided on. Ideally, the rate ought to relate to a security with the same duration as the project being appraised.

Beta – the measure of systematic risk. Here an estimate is usually required. Such estimates may be derived from subjective judgement, sensitivity analysis or, in some cases, by analysing (and, where necessary, adjusting) the beta coefficient of quoted firms which are thought to display the same risk characteristics as the project being appraised (see chapter 19). Use of regression analysis is subject to statistical error, the presence of unsystematic risk, and the effects of not having a perfect investment market – security prices not always simply reflecting underlying risk.

R_m is extremely difficult to determine as the market is volatile and the expected return is likely to vary with changes in the Rf. Hence, users often attempt to estimate (Rm – Rf), the excess return on the market. Historically in the UK this excess return has varied between 3% and 9% and similar figures may be used if:

I   it is felt that historic data is likely to be a good estimate of the future

II the expected excess return is thought to be a constant arithmetic amount above the Rf.

In practice there are certain instances when it is found that the CAPM does not perform as expected, e.g. investments with low betas, investments with low price/earnings (PE) ratios, investments with a strong seasonality.

Generally the basic CAPM is seen to overstate the required return for higher beta securities and understate the required return for low beta securities. However this problem mostly disappears when the effects of taxation are introduced to develop the basic model.

Similarly, CAPM does not seem to generate accurate forecasts for returns for companies with low price earnings ratios and is unable to account for seasonal factors observed in the UK stock market over the years.

January appears nearly always to be an outstandingly successful month for investing in UK shares, but no one can explain why this is the case.

4 Estimating the cost of debt

Types of debt

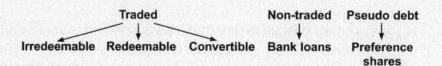

Terminology

- The terms loan notes, bonds, loan stock and marketable debt, are used interchangeably. Gilts are debts issued by the government.

- Irredeemable debt – no repayment of principal – interest in perpetuity.

- Redeemable debt – interest paid until redemption of principal.

- Convertible debt – may be later converted to equity.

Key points to note

- Debt is always quoted in $100 nominal value blocks.

- Interest paid on debt is stated as a percentage of nominal value – called the coupon rate.

Expandable text

The coupon rate is fixed at the time of issue, in line with the prevailing market interest rate. An 8% coupon rate means that $8 of interest will be paid on $100 nominal value block of debt.

The MV of loan notes may change daily. The main influence on the price of a loan note is the general level of interest rates for debt at that level of risk and for the same period to maturity.

Cost of debt and the impact of tax relief

A distinction must be made between the required return of debt holders and the company's cost of debt. Although in the context of equity the company's cost is equal to the investor's required return, the same is not true of debt. This is because of the impact of tax relief.

Expandable text

Consider two companies, identical apart from the choice of finance: A is all equity financed; B has $10,000 of 10% fixed interest debt.

	A	**B**
	$	$
Profits before interest and tax (PBIT)	10,000	10,000
Interest cost	–	(1,000)
Profits before tax	10,000	9,000
Tax @ 30%	3,000	2,700

B has paid $300 less tax because of the tax deductibility of the debt interest.

Therefore the net cost of the debt interest to B is:

	$
Interest cost	1,000
Less: Tax saving	(300)
Net cost	700

So B's actual cost of debt is 700/10,000 = 7%

i.e. $I(1 - T)$

where:

I = coupon rate

T = rate of corporation tax.

Consequently we will use separate terms to distinguish the two figures:

- r – the required return of the debt holder (pre-tax)
- K_d – the cost of the debt to the company (post-tax).

Irredeemable debt

The company does not intend to repay the principal but to pay interest forever.

Assumptions:

Market price = Future expected income stream from the debenture discounted at the investor's required return.

- expected income stream will be the interest paid in perpetuity.

The formula for valuing a loan note is therefore:

$$MV = \frac{I}{r}$$

where:

I = annual interest starting in one year's time

MV = market price of the loan note now (year 0)

r = debtholders' required return, expressed as a decimal.

The required return can be found by rearranging the formula:

$$r = \frac{I}{MV}$$

The cost of debt is found by adjusting the formula to take account of the tax relief on the interest:

$$K_d = \frac{I(1-T)}{MV}$$

where T = rate of corporation tax.

The MV of the loan notes is set by the investor, who does not get tax relief, and is therefore based on the interest before tax. The company gets corporation tax relief so the cost of debt calculation for the company is based on interest after tax.

Expandable text

Illustration – Irredeemable debt

A company has just issued 8% irredeemable loan notes. The required return of investors is 8%.

What is the MV of the loan notes?

Expandable text

Solution

$$MV \qquad \frac{I}{r}$$

$$MV = \frac{8}{0.08} = \$100$$

Expandable text

A company has in issue 10% irredeemable debt quoted at $80 ex interest.

What is the return required by the debt providers?

Solution

$$r = \frac{I}{MV}$$

$$r = \frac{10}{80} = 12.5\%$$

Test your understanding 8

A company has irredeemable loan notes currently trading at $40 ex interest. The coupon rate is 5% and the rate of corporation tax is 30%.

What is the cost of debt to the company?

Redeemable debt

The company will pay interest for a number of years and then repay the principal (sometimes at a premium or a discount to the original loan amount).

Assumptions:

- Market price = Future expected income stream from the loan notes discounted at the investor's required return.

- expected income stream will be:
  - interest paid to redemption
  - the repayment of the principal.

Hence the market value of redeemable loan notes is the sum of the PVs of the interest and the redemption payment.

Expandable text

Illustration – Redeemable debt

A company has in issue 12% redeemable loan notes with 5 years to redemption. Redemption will be at par. The investors require a return of 10%. What is the MV of the loan notes?

Expandable text

Solution

The MV is calculated by finding the PVs of the interest and the principal and totalling them as shown below.

Annuity Time		Cash flow	Discount Factor (DF) @ 10%	PV $
0	**MV**		Bal. fig	(107.59)
1-5	Interest payments	12	3.791	45.49
5	Capital repayment	100	0.621	62.10
	NPV			0

Note that for the investor the purchase is effectively a zero NPV project, as the present value of the income they receive in the future is exactly equivalent to the amount they invest today.

The investor's required return is therefore the internal rate of return (IRR) (breakeven discount rate) for the investment in the loan notes.

The return an investor requires can therefore be found by calculating the IRR of the investment flows:

T_o MV

T_{1-n} interest

T_n redemption payment.

Expandable text

Illustration – Redeemable debt

A company has in issue 12% redeemable debt with 5 years to redemption. Redemption is at par. The current market value of the debt is $107.59. The corporation rate is 30%.

What is the return required by the debt providers?

Expandable text

Solution

Annuity	Time		Cash flow	DF @ 5%	PV	DF @ 15%	PV
	0	MV	(107.59)	1	(107.59)	1	(107.59)
1-5		Interest payments	12.00	4.329	51.95	3.352	40.22
	5	Capital repayment	100.00	.784	78.40	.497	49.70
					_____		_____
		NPV			22.76		(17.67)
					_____		_____

$$IRR = 5 + \frac{(15 - 5) \times 22.76}{22.76 + 17.67} = 10.63$$

Therefore the required return of investors is 10.63%.

As the linear interpolation method used to estimate the IRR is an approximation, it does not reconcile back to the 10% required return per the illustration above.

Note that the rate of corporation tax has been ignored, as the question asked for the return required by the debt holders rather than the cost of debt to the company.

If it is the cost of debt to the company that is required, an IRR is still calculated but as the interest payments are tax-deductible, the IRR calculation is based on the following cash flows:

T_0	MV	(x)
T_{1-n}	Interest payments I (1 – T)	x
T_n	Capital repayment	x

Expandable text

Illustration – Redeemable debt

A company has in issue 12% redeemable debt with 5 years to redemption. Redemption is at par. The current MV of the debt is $107.59. The corporation rate is 30%.

What is the cost of debt?

Expandable text

Solution

As the linear interpolation method used to estimate the IRR in an approximation it does not back to the 10% required return per illustration in 8 above.

Time		Cash flow	DF @ 10%	PV	DF @ 5%	PV
0	MV	(107.59)	1	(107.59)	1	(107.59)
1-5	Interest payments	8.40	3.791	31.84	4.329	36.36
	$(12 \times (1 - 0.3))$					
Annuity 5	Capital repayment	100.00	0.621	62.10	0.784	78.40
	NPV			–13.65		7.17

$$IRR = 5\% + \left(\frac{7.17}{7.17 + 13.65} \times (10\% - 5\%) \right) = 6.72\%$$

Therefore the company's cost of debt is 6.72%.

Note that this Kd is lower than r (calculated in the previous example). This is to be expected because of the tax relief on the debt interest.

Test your understanding 9

A company has in issue 10% loan notes with a current MV of $98. The loan notes are due to be redeemed at par in five years time. If corporation tax is 30%, what is the company's cost of debt?

Debt redeemable at current market price

In this situation, where the debt is redeemable at its current market price, the position of the investor is the same as a holder of irredeemable debt.

Expandable text

Illustration – Debt redeemable at current market price

Consider the following investments:

A   an irredeemable loan note trading at $40 with a coupon rate of 5%

B   a redeemable loan note trading at $40 with a coupon rate of 5%, due to be redeemed at $40 in 3 years.

The return required by an investor in A can be calculated as:

$$r = \frac{I}{MV}$$

$$r = \frac{5}{40} = 12.5\%$$

If the investor was instead to invest in B, they would earn only 3 years of interest rather than receiving it in perpetuity.

The interest for 3 years (at a required return of 12.5%) would have a PV of:

= 3yr AF @ 12.5% × 5

$$r = \frac{5}{40} = 12.5\%$$

$$\frac{1}{0.125}\left(1 - \frac{1}{1.125^3}\right) = 2.3813 \times 5 = 11.9065$$

The $40 received at T3 (at a required return of 12.5%) would have a present value of:

$$\frac{40}{1.125^3} = 28.093$$

Therefore the PV of the overall return = 11.906 + 28.093 = $40.

This is the same return as received by the investor in the irredeemable debt!

Therefore where debt is redeemable at its current market price:

$$r = \frac{I}{MV}$$

$$K_d = \frac{I(1 - T)}{MV}$$

Convertible debt

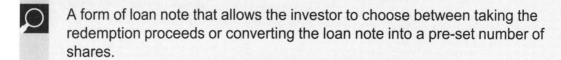

A form of loan note that allows the investor to choose between taking the redemption proceeds or converting the loan note into a pre-set number of shares.

Treated exactly the same as redeemable debt, except that the redemption value now equals the higher of

(1) the cash redemption and

(2) the future share value if converted.

Note: Terminology for convertibles

Floor value	= market value without the conversion option
	= PV of future interest and redemption value, discounted at the cost of debt.
Conversion premium	= market value - current conversion value.

Test your understanding 10

A company has issued convertible loan notes which are due to be redeemed at a 5% premium in five year's time. The coupon rate is 8% and the current MV is $85. Instead of the redemption payment, the investor can choose to convert each loan note into 20 shares on the same date.

The company pays tax at 30% per anum.

The company's shares are currently worth $4 and their value is expected to grow at a rate of 7% pa.

Find the cost of the convertible debt to the company.

Non-tradeable debt

Bank and other non-tradeable fixed interest loans simply need to be adjusted for tax relief:

Cost to company = Interest rate × (1 − T).

Alternatively, the cost of any 'normal' traded company debt could be used instead

> ### Illustration 2 – Non-tradable debt
>
> A firm has a fixed rate bank loan of $1million. It is charged 11% pa. The corporation tax rate is 30%.
>
> What is the cost of the loan?
>
> **Solution**
>
> 11 × 0.7 = 7.7%.

Preference shares

Although not strictly debt, the fixed rate of dividend and the fact that they are paid before ordinary shareholders, mean that preference shares are often treated as a form of lending similar to irredeemable debentures.

The main difference between preference shares and debt is that the preference dividend payments are not tax deductible.

The formulae are therefore:

$$K_p = \frac{D}{P_o} \qquad\qquad P_o = \frac{D}{K_p}$$

where:

D = the constant annual preference dividend

P_o = ex div MV of the share

K_p = cost of the preference share.

The fixed dividend is based on the nominal value of the preference share, which may vary. Do not assume the nominal value is always $1.

Test your understanding 11

A company has 50,000 8% preference shares in issue, nominal value $1. The current ex div MV is $1.20/share.

What is the cost of the preference shares?

5 Estimating the cost of capital

The need for a weighted average

In the analysis so far carried out, each source of finance has been examined in isolation. However, the practical business situation is that there is a continuous raising of funds from various sources.

These funds are used, partly in existing operations and partly to finance new projects. There is not normally any separation between funds from different sources and their application to specific projects:

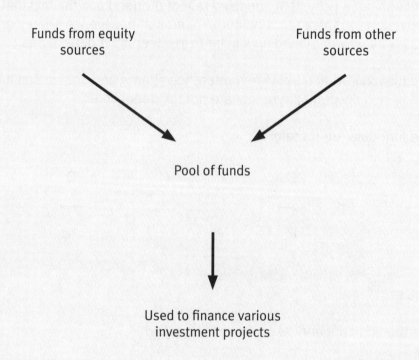

Even if a question tells you that a project is to be financed by the raising of a particular loan or through an issue of shares, in practice the funds raised will still be added to the firm's pool of funds and it is from that pool that the project will be funded.

It is therefore not the marginal cost of the additional finance, but the overall average cost of all finance raised, that is required for project appraisal.

The general approach is to calculate the cost of each individual source of medium-long term finance and then weight it according to its importance in the financing mix.

This average is known as the WACC.

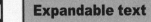

Expandable text

A firm's average cost of capital (ACC) is the average cost of the funds, normally represented by the WACC. The computed WACC represents the cost of the capital currently employed. This represents financial decisions taken in previous periods.

Alternatively, the cost of raising the next increment of capital can be determined – this is what is termed the marginal cost of capital (MCC). The firm's MCC is the additional cost the firm will pay to raise an additional dollar of capital, assuming the capital is raised using the optimal capital proportions (see chapter 19).

The relationship between MC and AC can be represented graphically, as indicated in the figure below.

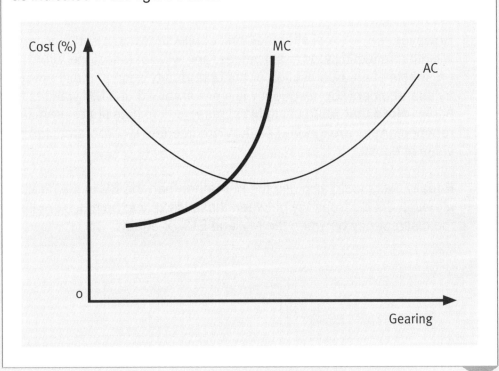

The relationship between ACC and MCC curves can be explained as follows: while the MCC is less than the ACC, the ACC will fall. Once the MCC rises above the ACC, however, the MCC will pull up the ACC, albeit at a slower rate than that at which MCC is rising.

Choice of weights

To find an average cost, the various sources of finance must be weighted according to the amount of each held by the company.

The weights for the sources of finance could be:

- book values (BVs) – represents historic cost of finance
- MVs – represent current opportunity cost of finance.

Wherever possible MVs should be used.

Expandable text

If we use the current proportions in which funds are raised, their weights may be measured by reference to BVs or MVs.

Note that when using BVs, reserves such as share premium and retained profits are included in the BV of equity, in addition to the nominal value of share capital.

However, the value of shareholders' equity shown in a set of accounts will often reflect historic asset values, and will not reflect the future prospects of an organisation or the opportunity cost of equity entrusted by shareholders. Consequently it is preferable to use MV weights for the equity. **Note** that when using MVs, reserves such as share premium and retained profits are ignored as they are in effect incorporated into the value of equity.

Equally, we should also use the MV rather than the BV of the debt, although the discrepancy between these is likely to be much smaller than the discrepancy between the MV and BVs of equity.

KAPLAN PUBLISHING

Expandable text

Illustration – Choice of weights

The accounts of Apollo Co reveal the following capital structure:

	$
$1 ordinary shares	2,000,000
Reserves	3,000,000
10% loan notes	1,000,000
	6,000,000

MVs of the above are as follows:

Ordinary shares	$3.75 each ex div
Loan notes	$80.

The cost of equity is estimated to be 20%, the cost of debt is 7.5% (after tax).

What is the WACC using

(1) BVs as weights?

(2) MVs as weights?

Expandable text

Solution

	$
Equity (ordinary shares + reserves)	
$2,000,000 + $3,000,000	5,000,000
Debt	1,000,000
Total	6,000,000

Proportions: $\dfrac{5}{6}$ Equity $\qquad \dfrac{1}{6}$ Debt

Combined cost of capital: $20 + \dfrac{5}{6} + 7.5 \times \dfrac{1}{6} = 17.92\%$

	$\$$
Equity 2,000,000 shares × $3.75/share	7,500,000
(see note below)	
Debt 1,000,000 × 80/100	800,000
Total	8,300,000

Proportions: $\dfrac{7,500,000}{8,300,000}$ Equity $\qquad \dfrac{800,000}{8,300,000}$ Debt

Combined cost of capital: $\dfrac{7,500,000}{8,300,000} \times 20\% \dfrac{800,000}{8,300,000} \times 7.5\% \ 18.79\%$

Note: when using MVs, reserves are ignored. They are in effect incorporated in the value of equity.

Book weights give a lower cost, as the proportion of equity is much smaller. Market weights are far more meaningful. Remember, the costs themselves are based on MVs. Book weights depend upon the historic accident of when the security was issued.

Therefore, the weightings used in the WACC calculation should be based on MVs whenever possible.

Note however that for non-quoted companies only BVs exist.

Calculating the WACC

The calculation involves a series of steps.

Step 1 Calculate weights for each source of capital.

Step 2 Estimate cost of each source of capital.

Step 3 Multiply proportion of total of each source of capital by cost of that source of capital.

Step 4 Sum the results of Step 3 to give the WACC.

Expandable text

Illustration – Calculating WACC

Butch Co has $1 million loan notes in issue, quoted at $50 per $100 of nominal value; $625,000 preference shares of $1 each quoted at 40c and 5 million ordinary $1 shares quoted at 25c. The cost of capital of these securities is 9%, 12% and 18% respectively. This capital structure is to be maintained.

Calculate the combined cost of capital.

Expandable text

Solution

S = step

Security	MV		Cost of capital (S2)	Weighted cost (S3)
	$000	Proportions (S1)	%	%
Loan notes	500	0.250	× 9.0 =	2.25
Preference shares	250	0.125	× 12.0 =	1.50
Ordinary shares	1,250	0.625	× 18.0 =	11.25
	2,000	1.000		15.00 (S4)

The weighted average cost of capital is therefore 15%. This figure represents an approximate cut-off rate of return on new investments.

Note that the relative costs of the various forms of finance reflect the risk to investors: Debt is cheapest at 9% because it is less risky for the investor and attracts tax relief for the company. Preference shares carry a risk and hence a return that is between that of debt and equity. The 18% return to the ordinary shareholders reflects the fact that their equity is most risky.

Test your understanding 12

Bacchante Co has a capital structure as follows:

	Cost of capital	BV	MV
	%	$m	$m
Bank loans	9	5	5
Loan notes	12	8	6
Ordinary shares	15	18	39

The company's current operations are carried out from two locations.

The Oxford factory shows a cash surplus of $1,750,000 on capital employed of $27.5 million, while the Cambridge factory produces a cash surplus of $640,000 on its capital of $3.5 million.

It is proposed to invest a further $1.5 million in facilities at Cambridge which will increase cash flow by $150,000 to perpetuity.

A   **Calculate Bacchante's weighted average cost of capital.**

B   **Comment on the proposed expansion.**

Ignore taxation.

Test your understanding 13

B Co has 10 million 25c ordinary shares in issue with a current price of 155c cum div. An annual dividend of 9c has just been proposed. The company earns an accounting rate of return to equity (ROE) of 10% and pays out 40% of the return as dividends.

The company also has 13% redeemable loan notes with a nominal value of $7 million, trading at par. They are due to be redeemed at par in five year's time.

If the rate of corporation tax is 33%, what is the company's WACC?

Chapter summary

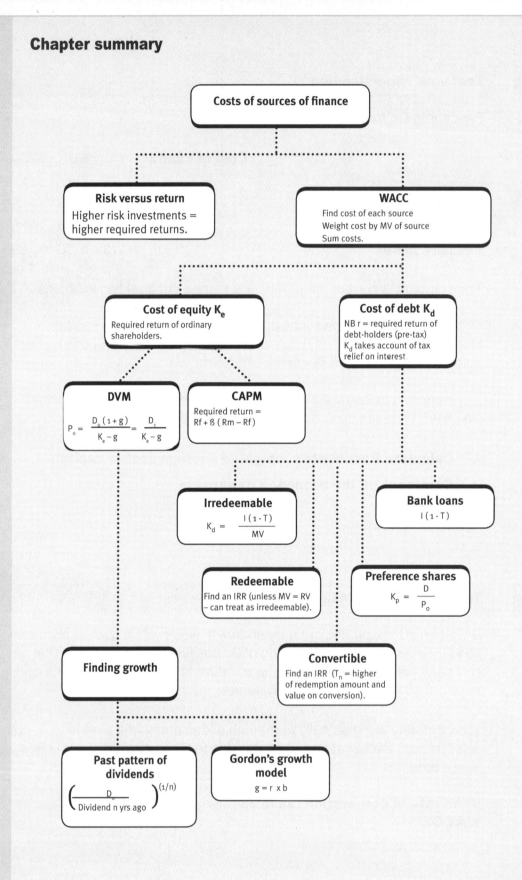

Test your understanding answers

Test your understanding 1

$30 \div 150 = 20\%$.

Test your understanding 2

$$r_e = \frac{10(1 + 0.05)}{105} + 0.05 = 15\%$$

Test your understanding 3

Since a dividend is about to be paid, the share price given must be cum div. The ex div price is therefore:

$125 - 15 = 110c$

$$r_e = \frac{15(1 + 0.06)}{110} + 0.06 = 20.5\%$$

Test your understanding 4

dividend with four years growth

20Y0	10.0c
20Y1	11.0c
20Y2	12.5c
20Y3	13.6c
20Y4	14.5c

The growth rate, g, is therefore:

$$g = \sqrt[4]{\left(\frac{14.5}{10}\right)} - 1 = \left(\frac{14.5}{10}\right)^{1/4} - 1 = 0.097 \text{ or } 9.7\%$$

This is also known as the geometric growth rate.

Test your understanding 5

$$K_e = \frac{16(1+0.1)}{184} + 0.1 = 19.6$$

P_0 ex div = 200 − 16 = 184

D_0 = 16

b = 1 − dividend payout % = 1 − 0.2 = 0.8

g = r × b = 0.125 × 0.8 = 0.1

Test your understanding 6

Factor	Type of risk
Increase in interest rates	Systematic
Increase in the price of cocoa beans	Unsystematic
Legislation changing the rules on tax relief for investments in non-current assets	Systematic
Growth in the economy of the country where Chocbic Co. is based	Systematic
Government advice on the importance of eating breakfast	Unsystematic
Industrial unrest in Chocbic Co's main factory	Unsystematic

Test your understanding 7

Required return = Rf + β (Rm – Rf)

9% = 5.5% + β (10.5 – 5.5)

3.5% = 5 β

β = 3.5/5 = 0.7

Since the beta is <1 the returns are less volatile than average.

Test your understanding 8

$$K_d = \frac{I(1 - T)}{MV}$$

$$K_d = \frac{5(1 - 0.3)}{40} = 0.0875 = 8.75\%$$

Test your understanding 9

Time		Cash flow	DF at 10%	PV	DF at 5%	PV
0	MV	(98)	1	(98)	1	(98)
1-5	Interest Payments	7	3.791	26.54	4.329	30.3
Annuity	(10 x (1 – 0.3))					
	Capital repayment	100	0.621	62.10	0.784	78.40
	NPV			-9.36		10.7

$$\text{IRR} = 5\% + \frac{10.7}{10.7 + 9.36} \times (10\% - 5\%) = 7.7\%$$

Therefore the company's cost of debt, Kd, is 7.7%.

Test your understanding 10

(1) Compare the redemption value (RV) with the value of the conversion option:

Cash RV = $100 × 1.05 = 105

Conversion value = 20 × 4$(1.07)^5$ = 20 × 5.61 = 112.20

(2) Select the highest of the two values as the amount to be received at T_n.

It is assumed that the investors will choose to convert the debenture and will therefore receive $112.20.

(3) Find the IRR of the cash flows to get the cost of debt as normal

Annuity	Time		Cash flow	DF@ 10%	PV	DF@ 5%	PV
	0	MV	(85)	1	(85)	1	(85)
	1-5	Interest payments $(8 × (1 – 0.3))$	5.6	3.791	21.23	4.329	24.24
	5	Conversion value	112.20	0.621	69.68	0.784	87.96
		NPV			5.91		27.2

$$IRR = 5\% + \frac{27.2}{27.2 - 5.91} × (10\% - 5\%) = 11.4\%.$$

KAPLAN PUBLISHING

Test your understanding 11

$$\text{Using } K_p = \frac{D}{P_o}, \quad K_p = \frac{8}{120} = 0.0667 \text{ or } 6.67\%$$

Test your understanding 12

x(S = Step)

A   Combined cost of capital is as follows:

Source	MV $m	Proportions (S1)	Cost of capital (S2) %	Weighted cost (S3) %
Bank loans	5	0.10	× 9 =	0.90
Loan notes	6	0.12	× 12 =	1.44
Ordinary shares	39	0.78	× 15 =	11.70
	50	1.00		14.04 (S4)

	Capital employed $m	Cash flow $000	Return %
Oxford	27.5	1,750	6.4
Cambridge	3.5	640	18.3
Total	31.0	2,390	7.7

The return on the additional facilities at Cambridge is estimated to be:

$$\frac{\$150,000}{\$1,500,000} = 10\% \ (= \text{project IRR})$$

Therefore:

(1) The proposal's return (IRR) is below current WACC and should be rejected.

(2) Note that current facilities at Oxford appear to yield a very low return, though without more data (e.g. is capital employed at current

valuation?) the significance of this fact is difficult to evaluate.

Alternatively the WACC could be used to discount the Cambridge project:

$$NPV = \frac{150,000}{0.1404 - 1,500,000} = (431,624).$$

Since the NPV is negative the project should be rejected.

Test your understanding 13

Information for step 1

MV of equity

10m × ($1.55 − $0.09) = $14.6m

MV of debt

Trading at par therefore $7m

Step 2

$$K_e = \frac{D_0(1 + g)}{P_0} + g$$

o

Po = 155 − 9 = 146

g = r × b where r = 0.1 and b = (1 − 0.4) g = 0.1 × 0.6 = 0.06

$$K_e = \frac{9\,(1.06)}{146} + 0.06 = 12.53\%.$$

Since the loan notes are redeemable at MV, the cost of debt is found using the formula:

$$K_d = \frac{I\,(1 − T)}{MV}$$

I = 13

T = 33%

MV = 100

$$K_d = \frac{13(1 - 0.33)}{100} = 8.71\%$$

Therefore the WACC = $\frac{7}{21.6} \times 8.71\% + \frac{14.6}{21.6} = 11.29\%$

Note:

Capital structure and the cost of capital

Chapter learning objectives

Upon completion of this chapter you will be able to:

- define company value

- explain the relationship between company value and cost of capital

- explain the traditional view of capital structure theory

- explain the underlying assumptions of the traditional view of capital structure theory

- interpret a graph demonstrating the traditional view of capital structure theory

- explain the assumptions of a perfect capital market

- describe the views and assumptions of Miller and Modigliani (M&M) on capital structure without corporate taxes

- interpret a graph demonstrating the views of M&M on capital structure without corporate taxes

- describe the views and assumptions of M&M on capital structure with corporate taxes

- interpret a graph demonstrating the views of M&M on capital structure with corporate taxes

- identify a range of capital market imperfections and describe their impact on the views of M&M on capital structure

- explain the relevance of pecking order theory to the selection of sources of finance

- discuss the circumstances under which weighted average cost of capital (WACC) can be used in investment appraisal

- identify in a scenario question whether WACC is appropriate for use by a company

- discuss the advantages of the capital asset pricing model (CAPM) over WACC in determining a project-specific cost of capital

- identify in a scenario where CAPM may be suitable to determine a project-specific cost of equity capital

- apply CAPM in calculating a project-specific discount rate.

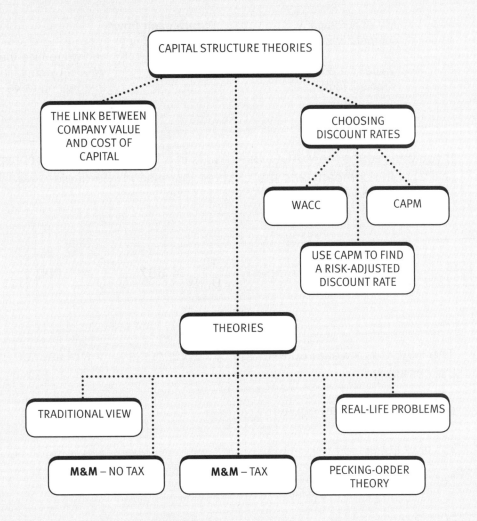

1 An optimal capital structure? – company value and the cost of capital

The objective of management is to maximise shareholder wealth. If altering the gearing ratio (the extent to which debt is used in the finance structure) could increase wealth, then finance managers would have a duty to do so.

Is it possible to increase shareholder wealth by changing the gearing ratio/level?

- The market value (MV) of a company is the sum of the MVs of its various forms of finance. This equates to the MV of the company's equity plus debt.

- The MV of each type of finance is known to be the PV of the returns to the investor, discounted at their required rate of return.

- If a company distributes all its earnings, it follows that the total MV of the company equates to the present value (PV) of the future cash flows available to investors, discounted at their overall required return or WACC.

MV of a company
(perpetuity formula)

Value of a company in its
simplest form

$= \dfrac{\text{Future cash flows}}{\text{WACC}}$

can we reduce the
WACC by changing
the gearing ratio?

If you can reduce the WACC, this results in a higher MV/net present value (NPV) of the company and therefore an increase in shareholder wealth as they own the company:

MV of a company $\quad \dfrac{100}{0.15} = \textbf{667} \quad \dfrac{100}{0.10} = \textbf{1,000}$

The WACC is a weighted average of the various sources of finance used by the company.

Debt is cheaper than equity:

- lower risk
- tax relief on interest

but:

increasing levels of debt make equity more risky:

- fixed commitment paid before equity – finance risk
- so increasing gearing increases the cost of equity and that would increase the WACC.

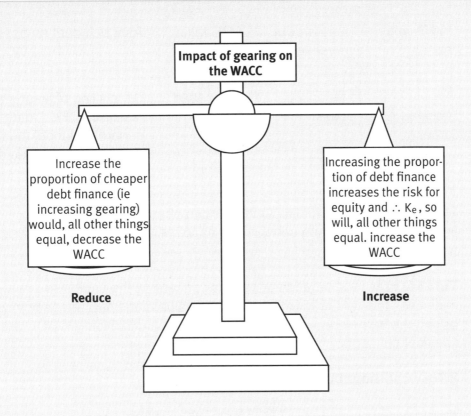

Various theories have attempted to answer the question:

Which has the greater effect on WACC?

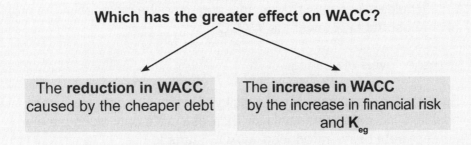

Gearing Theories:

Theory	Net effect as gearing increases	Impact on WACC	Optimal finance method
Traditional theory	The WACC is U-shaped.	At optimal point, WACC is minimised.	Find and maintain optimum gearing ratio.
M&M (no tax)	Cheaper debt = Increase in K_e.	WACC is constant.	Choice of finance is irrelevant – use any.

M&M (with tax)	Cheaper debt > Increase in K_e.	WACC falls.	As much debt as possible.
The pecking order	No theorised process.	No theorised process.	Simply line of least resistance. First internally-generated funds, then debt and finally new issue of equity.

Make sure you can explain clearly the two effects of introducing more debt finance and the differing conclusions as to the combined impact these may have on the WACC.

Tutorial note: examination questions concerning the capital structure that minimises the WACC, or maximises the value of the firm are basically asking the same question. Maximising MV and minimising WACC are identical concepts.

2 The traditional view of capital structure

Also known as the intuitive view, the traditional view has no theoretical basis but common sense. Taxation is generally ignored in this view.

At low levels of gearing:

Equity holders perceive risk as unchanged so the increase in the proportion of cheaper debt will lower the WACC

At higher levels of gearing:

Equity holders see increased volatility of returns as debt interest must be paid first increased financial risk increase in Ke outweighs the extra (cheap) debt being introduced WACC starts to rise.

At very high levels of gearing:

Serious bankruptcy risk worries equity and debt holders alike K_e and K_d rise WACC rises further.

This can be shown diagrammatically:

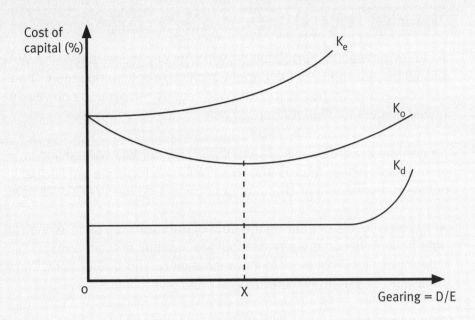

where:

K_e is the cost of equity

K_d is the cost of debt, and

K_o is the overall or WACC

Conclusion

There is an optimal level of gearing – point X. At point X the overall return required by investors (debt and equity) is minimised. It follows that at this point the combined market value of the firm's debt and equity securities will also be maximised.

Implication for finance

Company should gear up until it reaches optimal point and then raise a mix of finance to maintain this level of gearing.

Problem

There is no method, apart from trial and error, available to locate the optimal point.

Expandable text

As an organisation introduces debt into its capital structure, the WACC will fall because initially the benefit of cheap debt finance more than outweighs any increases in the cost of equity required to compensate equity holders for higher financial risk.

As gearing continues to increase the equity holders will ask for increasingly higher returns and eventually this increase will start to outweigh the benefit of cheap debt finance, and the WACC will rise.

At extreme levels of gearing the cost of debt will also start to rise (as debt holders become worried about the security of their loans), shareholders will continue to increase their required return and this will contribute to a sharply increasing WACC.

As a company begins to 'suffer' from high gearing, problems such as tax exhaustion, fewer assets left to offer for security on new loans, and restrictive terms from investors, become more likely. Key staff leave to avoid being tainted by a failed company. Uncertainties are placed in the minds of customers and suppliers, which may result in lost sales and more expensive trading terms. Shareholders refuse to invest new funds for positive NPV projects, as they do not wish 'to throw good money after bad'.

If a bankruptcy situation finally occurs, the assets may be sold off quickly and cheaply. A large proportion of management time is spent 'fire fighting', i.e. focusing on short-term cash flow rather than long-term shareholder wealth.

The traditional view therefore claims that there is an optimal capital structure where WACC is at a minimum. This is represented by point X on the above diagram.

At point X the overall return required by investors (debt and equity) is minimised. It follows that at this point the combined MV of the firm's debt and equity securities will also be maximised.

(If investors are offered the same $ return but the % return they require has fallen market pressures will make the value of the securities rise.)

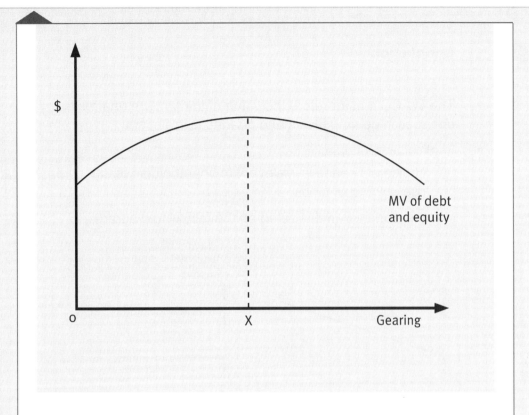

The main support for the traditional view is that it simply accords with 'common sense' and until 1958 it was not questioned.

To address this problem two economists attempted to find the optimal point in 1958.

3 M&M – no taxes

- there are no taxes.

A key part of **M&M**'s theories are the assumptions. Ensure you can discuss them.

The theory

M&M argued that:

- as investors are rational, the required return of equity is directly proportional to the increase in gearing. There is thus a linear relationship between K_e and gearing (measured as D/E)

- the increase in K_e exactly offsets the benefit of the cheaper debt finance and therefore the WACC remains unchanged.

Conclusion

- The WACC and therefore the value of the firm are unaffected by changes in gearing levels and gearing is irrelevant.

- Implication for finance:
  - choice of finance is irrelevant to shareholder wealth: company can use any mix of funds
  - this can be demonstrated on the following diagram:

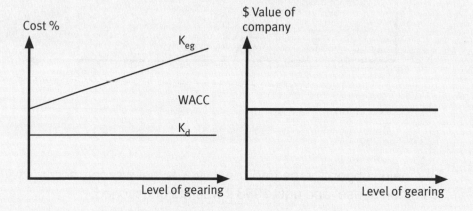

Note: in the above diagrams gearing is measured as:

$$\frac{Debt}{Equity}$$

Expandable text

The **M&M** view is that:

- companies which operate in the same type of business and which have similar operating risks must have the same total value, irrespective of their capital structures.

Their view is based on the belief that the value of a company depends upon the future operating income generated by its assets. The way in which this income is split between returns to debt holders and returns to equity should make no difference to the total value of the firm (equity plus debt). Thus, the total value of the firm will not change with gearing, and therefore neither will its WACC.

Their view is represented in the above diagrams.

If the WACC is to remain constant at all levels of gearing it follows that any benefit from the use of cheaper debt finance must be exactly offset by the increase in the cost of equity.

The essential point made by **M&M** is that a firm should be indifferent between all possible capital structures. This is at odds with the beliefs of the traditionalists.

M&M supported their case by demonstrating that market pressures (arbitrage) will ensure that two companies identical in every aspect apart from their gearing level, will have the same overall MV. This proof is outside the syllabus.

4 M&M – with tax

A number of practical criticisms were levelled at **M&M**'s no tax theory, but the most significant was the assumption that there were no taxes. Since debt interest is tax-deductible the impact of tax could not be ignored.

M&M therefore revised their theory (perfect capital market assumptions still apply):

In 1963, **M&M** modified their model to reflect the fact that the corporate tax system gives tax relief on interest payments.

The starting point for the theory is, as before, that:

- as investors are rational, the required return of equity is directly linked to the increase in gearing – as gearing increases, K_e increases in direct proportion.

However this is adjusted to reflect the fact that:

- debt interest is tax deductible so the overall cost of debt to the company is lower than in M&M – no tax

- lower debt costs less volatility in returns for the same level of gearing lower increases in K_e

- the increase in K_e does not offset the benefit of the cheaper debt finance and therefore the WACC falls as gearing increases.

Conclusion

Gearing up reduces the WACC and increases the MV of the company. The optimal capital structure is 99.9% gearing.

Implications for finance:

The company should use as much debt as possible.

This is demonstrated in the following diagrams:

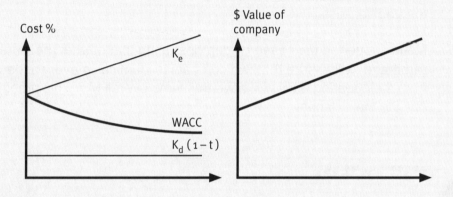

Note: Gearing is measured here using:

$$\frac{Debt}{Equity}$$

Expandable text

In their original model **M&M** ignored taxation. In 1963 they amended their model to include corporation tax. This alteration changes the implication of their analysis significantly.

Previously they argued that companies that differ only in their capital structure should have the same total value of debt plus equity. This was because it was the size of a firm's operating earnings stream that determined its value, not the way in which it was split between returns to debt and equity holders.

However, the corporation tax system carries a distortion under which returns to debt holders (interest) are tax deductible to the firm, whereas returns to equity holders are not. **M&M**, therefore, conclude that:

- geared companies have an advantage over ungeared companies, i.e. they pay less tax and will, therefore, have a greater MV and a lower WACC.

Once again they were able to produce a proof to support their arguments and show that as gearing increases, the WACC steadily decreases.

If the other implications of the M&M view are accepted, the introduction of taxation suggests that the higher the level of taxation, the lower the combined cost of capital.

More importantly for financial strategy, the higher the level of the company's gearing, the greater the value of the company. The logical conclusion is that companies should choose a 99.9% gearing level.

The problems of high gearing

In practice firms are rarely found with very high levels of gearing. This is because of:

- bankruptcy risk
- agency costs
- tax exhaustion
- the impact on borrowing/debt capacity
- differences in risk tolerance levels between shareholders and directors
- restrictions in the articles of association
- increases in the cost of borrowing as gearing increases.

As a result, despite the theories, gearing levels tend to be based on more practical concerns and companies will often follow the industry average gearing.

Expandable text

(1) Bankruptcy risk

As gearing increases so does the possibility of bankruptcy. If shareholders become concerned, this will increase the WACC of the company and reduce the share price.

(2) Agency costs: restrictive conditions

In order to safeguard their investments, lenders/debentures holders often impose restrictive conditions in the loan agreements that constrain management's freedom of action, e.g. restrictions:

(i) on the level of dividends

(ii) on the level of additional debt that can be raised

(iii) on management from disposing of any major fixed assets without the debenture holders' agreement.

(3) Tax exhaustion

After a certain level of gearing, companies will discover that they have no tax liability left against which to offset interest charges.

$K_d (1 - t)$ simply becomes K_d.

(4) Borrowing/debt capacity

High levels of gearing are unusual because companies run out of suitable assets to offer as security against loans. Companies with assets which have an active second-hand market, and with low levels of depreciation such as property companies, have a high borrowing capacity.

(5) Difference risk tolerance levels between shareholders and directors

Business failure can have a far greater impact on directors than on a well-diversified investor. It may be argued that directors have a natural tendency to be cautious about borrowing.

(6) Restrictions in the articles of association may specify limits on the company's ability to borrow.

(7) The cost of borrowing increases as gearing increases.

As a result debt becomes less attractive as it is no longer so cheap.

5 Pecking-order theory

In this approach, there is no search for an optimal capital structure through a theorised process. Instead it is argued that firms will raise new funds as follows:

- internally-generated funds

- debt
- new issue of equity.

Firms simply use all their internally-generated funds first then move down the pecking order to debt and then finally to issuing new equity. Firms follow a line of least resistance that establishes the capital structure.

Internally-generated funds – i.e. retained earnings

- Already have the funds.
- Do not have to spend any time persuading outside investors of the merits of the project.
- No issue costs.

Debt

- The degree of questioning and publicity associated with debt is usually significantly less than that associated with a share issue.
- Moderate issue costs.

New issue of equity

- Perception by stock markets that it is a possible sign of problems. Extensive questioning and publicity associated with a share issue.
- Expensive issue costs.

Expandable text

Issue cost

Internally-generated funds have the lowest issue costs, debt moderate issue costs and equity the highest. Firms issue as much as they can from internally-generated funds first then move on to debt and finally equity.

Asymmetric information

Myers has suggested asymmetric information as an explanation for the heavy reliance on retentions. This may be a situation where managers, because of their access to more information about the firm, know that the value of the shares is greater than the current MV (based on the weak and semi-strong market information: see chapter 21).

In the case of a new project, managers' forecasts may be higher and more realistic than that of the market. If new shares were issued in this situation, there is a possibility that they would be issued at too low a price, thus transferring wealth from existing shareholders to new shareholders. In these circumstances there might be a natural preference for internally-generated funds over new issues. If additional funds are required over and above internally-generated funds, then debt would be the next alternative.

If management is averse to making equity issues when in possession of favourable inside information, market participants might assume that management will be more likely to favour new issues when they are in possession of unfavourable inside information which leads to the suggestion that new issues might be regarded as a signal of bad news! Managers may therefore wish to rely primarily on internally-generated funds supplemented by borrowing, with issues of new equity as a last resort.

Myers and Majluf (1984) demonstrated that with asymmetric information, equity issues are interpreted by the market as bad news, since managers are only motivated to make equity issues when shares are overpriced. **Bennett Stewart** (1990) puts it differently: 'Raising equity conveys doubt. Investors suspect that management is attempting to shore up the firm's financial resources for rough times ahead by selling over-valued shares.'

Asquith and Mullins (1983) empirically observed that announcements of new equity issues are greeted by sharp declines in stock prices. Thus, equity issues are comparatively rare among large established companies.

Expandable text

Below is a series of graphs. Identify those that reflect:

- **the traditional view of capital structure**
- **M&M without tax**
- **M&M with tax.**

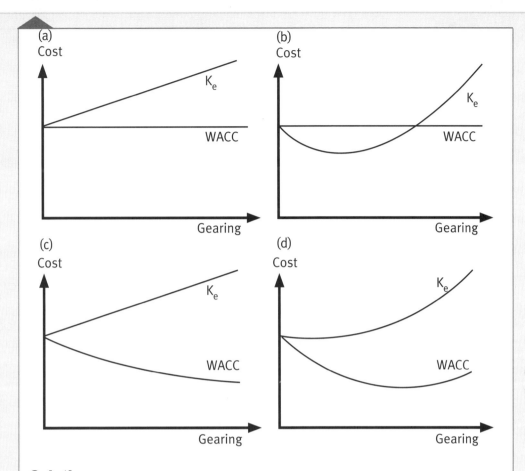

Solution

* the traditional view of capital structure – (d)
* M&M without tax – (a)
* M&M with tax – (c)

Tutorial note: Diagram (b) does not accord with any of the theories.

Test your understanding 1

Answer the following questions:

A   **If a company, in a perfect capital market with no taxes, incorporates increasing amounts of debt into its capital structure without changing its operating risk, what will the impact be on its WACC?**

B   **According to M&M why will the cost of equity always rise as the company gears up?**

C   **In a perfect capital market but with taxes, two companies are identical in all respects, apart from their levels of gearing. A has only equity finance, B has 50% debt finance. Which firm would M&M argue was worth more?**

> D   **In practice a firm which has exhausted retained earnings, is likely to select what form of finance next?**

6 Capital structure and the choice of discount rate
Use of the WACC in investment appraisal

In chapter 18 we learnt how to calculate WACC. It was based upon the firm's current costs of equity and debt. It is therefore appropriate for use in investment appraisal provided:

- the historic proportions of debt and equity are not to be changed

- the operating risk of the firm will not be changed

- the finance is not project-specific, i.e. projects are financed from a pool of funds.

or

- the project is small in relation to the company so any changes are insignificant.

Expandable text

In using the WACC to appraise projects we are implicitly making the following assumptions:

The historic proportions of debt and equity are not to be changed – the cost of equity and debt based on current market information reflects the firm's current gearing ratio. If the firm substantially changes the long-run proportions in which funds are raised, then the cost of equity and debt are likely to change, with a resultant change in the combined cost of capital.

The operating risk of the firm will not be changed – the firm's current cost of equity and debt also reflect its current area of operations. For example high risk electronics companies are likely to have higher costs of funds than, say, low risk food manufacturers. If a food manufacturing company were to diversify into electronics, its costs of finance would change. Current estimates of the cost of capital are therefore only suitable for appraising investments of similar operating risk. This problem is further investigated later.

The finance is not project specific – in some circumstances it is unwise to use the average cost of a pool of funds. Suppose a government offered a multinational company an interest-free loan to encourage it to invest in a particular country. In this situation it would be unwise to put the cheap loan into the pool of funds and spread its benefit over all projects as it is associated with only one specific project. In these circumstances we would need to credit the benefits of the cheap finance to the project.

The advantages of using CAPM in project appraisal

Unlike the WACC, the CAPM can be used to help find a discount rate, when the assumptions above do not hold, that is:

- the project risk is different from that of the company's normal business risk

and the shareholders of the company are well diversified.

The logic behind the CAPM is as follows:

- Objective is to maximise shareholder wealth
- Rational shareholders are well diversified
- Any new project is just another investment in a shareholder's portfolio
- CAPM can set the shareholders' required return on the project

It is important to understand that the CAPM equation only gives us the required return of the shareholders. If the project is to be equity financed, this can be used as the project discount rate. If the project is to be financed with both debt and equity, then the shareholders' required return will need to be combined with the cost of debt to find an appropriate discount rate.

Expandable text

Illustration – Advantages of using CAPM in project appraisal

Tussac Co is an all-equity company with a cost of capital of 15% pa.

It wishes to invest in a new project with an estimated beta of 1.2. If r_f = 10% and r_m = 18%, what is the minimum required return of the project?

Expandable text

Solution

The firm's cost of capital is probably irrelevant because the new project almost certainly has risk characteristics different from the firm's existing operations.

Using the project beta, its minimum required return is 10% + (8% × 1.2) = 19.6%.

Advantages of using CAPM in project appraisal

Comhampton Co is an all-equity company with a beta of 0.8. It is appraising a one-year project which requires an outlay now of $1,000 and will generate cash in one year with an expected value of $1,250. The project has a beta of 1.3. r_f = 10%, r_m = 18%.

(a) What is the firm's current cost of equity capital?

(b) What is the minimum required return of the project?

(c) Is the project worth while?

Expandable Text

Solution

(a) Cost of capital = 10% + (8% × 0.8) = 16.4%

(b) Project required return = 10% + (8% × 1.3) = 20.4%

(c) Expected project return:

$$= \text{Project IRR} \quad \frac{1{,}250 - 1{,}000}{1000} = 25\%$$

Thus the project is worth while because its expected rate of return is higher than its minimum required return. This again assumes investors will not want any returns to compensate for the unsystematic risk on the new project, i.e. that they are well diversified.

Alternatively, the NPV of the project at its minimum required return is:

$$ \$ \qquad -1{,}000 + 1{,}250 / 1.204 \qquad = \$38.20 $$

Expandable text

Kingswick Co is an all-equity financed company with a cost of capital of 18.5%.

The risk-free rate is 8% and the expected return on an average market portfolio is 15%.

It is considering the following capital investment projects:

Project	Outlay now	Expected receipt in one year	Beta factor
	$	$	
A	1,000	1,095	0.3
B	1,000	1,130	0.5
C	1,500	1,780	1.0
D	2,000	2,385	1.5
E	2,000	2,400	2.0

(a) **Calculate Kingswick's beta factor.**

(b) **Calculate the CAPM required return for each project.**

(c) **Calculate the expected rate of return of each project.**

(d) **Show which projects would be accepted and rejected if they were discounted at the firm's cost of capital, and highlight those projects where an incorrect decision would be made.**

Solution

(a) Since Kingswick is all equity financed its cost of capital is the same as its cost of equity.

Assuming that Kingswick's cost of capital properly reflects its beta factor:

$$ K_e = R_f + \beta (R_m - R_f) $$

therefore:

$18.5 = 8 + \beta(15 - 8)$

$10.5 = 7\beta$

$\beta = 10.5 \div 7 = 1.5$

(b) & (c)

Project	CAPM required return	Expected return		
A	$8\% + (7\% \times 0.3) = 10.1\%$	$\dfrac{95}{1,000}$	= 9.5%	Reject
B	$8\% + (7\% \times 0.5) = 11.5\%$	$\dfrac{130}{1,000}$	= 13%	Accept
C	$8\% + (7\% \times 1.0) = 15\%$	$\dfrac{280}{2,000}$	= 18.7%	Accept
D	$8\% + (7\% \times 1.5) = 18.5\%$	$\dfrac{385}{2,000}$	= 19.3%	Accept
E	$8\% + (7\% \times 2) = 22\%$	$\dfrac{400}{2,000}$	= 20%	Reject

(d) If the projects were discounted at the company's cost of capital, 18.5%, then only those with yield ≥ 18.5% would be accepted, i.e. the company would accept C, D and E and reject A and B.

Using the firm's cost of capital is clearly wrong because it does not allow for the different risks of the projects. It is simply a required rate of return given company risk at the time capital cost is evaluated. The projects where an incorrect decision would be made by using the firm's cost of capital are:

Project B a valuable low risk project is incorrectly rejected.

Project E this would be accepted despite the fact that its return is not high enough to compensate for its high systematic risk.

CAPM and gearing risk

When using betas in project appraisal, the impact of gearing must be borne in mind.

Finding betas

- to evaluate a project with a different risk profile, a company will select a suitable beta

- beta values are calculated with reference to existing companies operating in those business areas

- those companies paying above average returns are assumed to have a correspondingly higher than average systematic risk and their beta (the measure of the company's systematic risk compared to the market) is extrapolated accordingly

- the extrapolated beta is then considered a measure of the risk of that business area.

However:

Understanding betas

Firms must provide a return to compensate for the risk faced by investors, and even for a well-diversified investor, this systematic risk will have two causes:

- the risk resulting from its business activities

- the finance risk caused by its level of gearing.

Consider therefore two firms A and B:

- both are identical in all respects including their business operations but

- A has higher gearing than B:
    - A would need to pay out higher returns

    - any beta extrapolated from A's returns will reflect the systematic risk of both its business and its financial position and would therefore be higher than B's.

Therefore there are two types of beta:

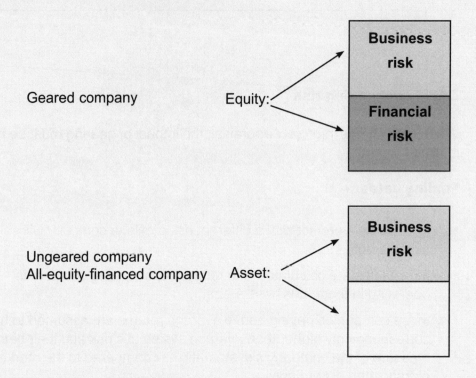

Geared company   Equity:

Ungeared company
All-equity-financed company   Asset:

β_{Asset} reflects purely the systematic risk of the business area.

β_{Equity} reflects the systematic risk of the business area and the company-specific gearing ratio.

It is critical in examination questions to identify which type of beta you have been given and what risk it reflects.

Choosing a beta

(1) Find an appropriate asset beta

(2) Adjust it to reflect its own gearing levels - gear the beta ro convert to an equity beta.

If the best beta available is from a geared company, let's call it Co A, i.e. it is an equity beta, the stages become:

(1) Find the appropriate equity beta.

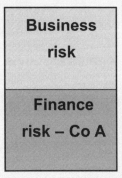

(2) Adjust the available equity beta to convert it to an asset beta – degear it.

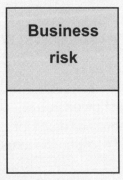

(3) Readjust the asset beta to reflect its own gearing levels – gear the beta.

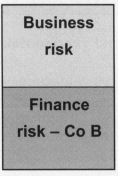

The formula to gear and degear betas is:

$$\beta_a = \beta_e \times \frac{V_e}{V_e + V_d(1 - T)}$$

where:

V_e = market value of equity

V_d = market value of debt

T = corporation tax rate.

NB1 This version of the formula assumes debt is risk-free.

NB2 In questions often just the ratio of V_e to V_d is given (see the illustration below).

Using the beta

Once an appropriate beta has been established, the company can proceed to evaluate its projects in the usual way.

- Use beta to find K_e.
- Use this K_e to find the risk-adjusted WACC.
- Evaluate the project.

Remember that CAPM just gives you K_e, so once you have found the relevant shareholders' required return for the project you need to combine it with the cost of debt if the company is to use a mix of funds.

Expandable text

Illustration – CAPM and gearing risk

B Co is a hot air balloon manufacturer whose equity:debt ratio is 5:2. The corporate debt, which is assumed to be risk-free, has a gross redemption yield of 11%. The beta value of the company's equity is 1.1. The average return on the stock market is 16%. The corporation tax rate is 30%.

The company is considering a water bed manufacturing project. S Co is a water bed manufacturing company. It has an equity beta of 1.59 and an E:D ratio of 2:1. B Co maintains its existing capital structure after the implementation of the new project.

What would be a suitable cost of capital to apply to the project?

Expandable text

Solution

Choose a beta.

Step 1

B Co has selected an appropriate equity beta for water bed manufacturing of 1.59.

Step 2

Based on new industry information:

- the ß equity (1.59)

- gearing ratio of the new industry (2:1)

- degear the ß equity of the company in the new industry and find the business risk ß asset of the new project/industry.

$$\beta_a = \beta_e \times \frac{V_e}{V_e + V_d(1 - T)}$$

$$= 1.59 \times \frac{2}{2 + 1(1 - 0.3)}$$

$$= 1.18$$

Step 3

Calculate the equity beta of the new project, by re-gearing:incorporate the financial risk of our company using our gearing ratio (5:2)

$$\beta_a = \beta_e \times \frac{V_e}{V_e + V_d(1 - T)}$$

$$1.18 = \beta_e \times \frac{5}{5 + 2(0.70)}$$

$$1.18 = 0.78\,\beta_e$$

$$\beta_e = \frac{1.18}{0.78} = 1.51$$

Now proceed as usual:

Calculate the cost of equity of the project based on CAPM:

$$Ke = R_F + \beta\,(R_M - R_F)$$

$$= 11\% + 1.51\,(16\% - 11\%) = 18.55\%$$

Find the cost of debt:

$$K_d = I\,(1 - T)$$

$$K_d = 11\%\,(1 - 0.3) = 7.70\%$$

Calculate the risk-adjusted WACC of the project.

(Use our company's D:E ratio)

$$WACC = 18.55\% \times \frac{5}{7 + 7.70} \times \frac{2}{7} = 15.45\%$$

We have calculated a discount rate, which reflects the systematic risk of this particular project and the gearing risk of the finance method chosen.

Test your understanding 2

Hubbard, an all-equity food manufacturing firm, is about to embark upon a major diversification in the consumer electronics industry. Its current equity beta is 1.2, whilst the average equity ß of electronics firms is 1.6. Gearing in the electronics industry averages 30% debt, 70% equity.

Corporate debt is considered to be risk free.

R_m = 25%, R_f = 10%, corporation tax rate = 30%

What would be a suitable discount rate for the new investment if Hubbard were to be financed in each of the following ways?

(a) **Entirely by equity.**

(b) **By 30% debt and 70% equity.**

(c) **By 40% debt and 60% equity.**

Suitable discount rates for the project should reflect both its systematic business risk and its level of gearing. As we are operating under an **M&M** 1963 world, the higher the level of gearing, the lower the discount rate.

Chapter summary

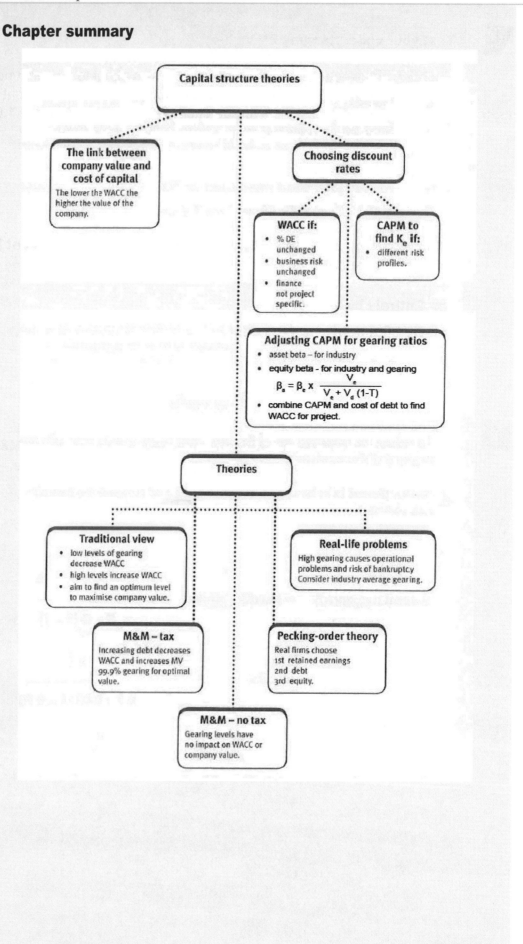

Test your understanding answers

A The WACC will remain the same M&M – no tax (see above).

B Because the returns to shareholders become more volatile. (Note: this is not just an M&M view but true of all the approaches to gearing).

C The company which had geared up M&M – with tax (see above).

D Debt Pecking-order theory (see 5 above).

Test your understanding 2

In all three situations the best approach is to treat the project as a 'mini-firm' and tailor the discount rate to reflect its level of systematic business risk and financial risk.

(a) Project financed entirely by equity

To reflect the business risk of the new venture we should start with the equity β of the electronics industry, i.e. 1.6.

As our project is to be ungeared we should then remove the financial risk element:

$$\beta_a = \beta_e \times \frac{V_e}{V_e + V_d(1 - T)}$$

$$= 1.6 \times \frac{0.7}{0.7 + 0.03\,(1 - 0.30)}$$

$$= 1.23$$

The pure cost of equity (and hence WACC in the all-equity case) would then be:

$k_e = R_f + \beta (R_m - R_f)$

$= 10\% + 1.23 (25\% - 10\%)$

$= 28.45\%$

The project should be evaluated at a rate of 28.45%.

(b) Project financed by 30% debt, 70% equity

In this case the observed equity beta of the electronics industry would reflect the level of business risk and financial risk of the project. No adjustments are therefore required.

To obtain a suitable discount rate we must simply weight the cost of equity and the cost of debt, hence:

$$\left(k_e \times \frac{V_e}{V_e + V_d} \right) \quad + \quad \left(kd \times \frac{V_d}{V_e + V_d} \right)$$

$$
\begin{aligned}
k_e \quad &= R_f + \beta (R_m - R_f) \\
&= 10\% + 1.6(25\% - 10\%) = 34\% \\
&= R_f (1 - t) \\
&= 10\% (1 - 0.30) = 7\%
\end{aligned}
$$

Suitable discount rate for project $= (34\% \times 0.7) + (7\% \times 0.3)$

$= 25.9\%$

Tutorial note: It is the WACC which is needed as the discount rate, not just the cost of equity, since the project is to be financed by a mix of debt and equity.

(c) **Project financed by 40% debt and 60% equity**

In this case the equity beta of the electronics industry reflects a lower level of gearing than that for the proposed project. The simplest procedure is to take a two-step approach to the gearing adjustment.

Step 1 Calculate the asset beta for the electronics company (as in (a)).

β asset = 1.23

This is a measure of the pure systematic risk of electronics companies. We now adjust this pure beta in the light of the given financial gearing ratio.

Step 2 Work out the equation 'backwards' to calculate the cost of equity for an electronics company with 60% equity and 40% debt.

$$\beta_a = \beta_e \times \frac{Ve}{Ve + Vd(1 - T)}$$

$$1.23 = \beta_e \times \frac{0.6}{0.6 + 0.4(1 - 0.39)}$$

$$1.23 \times \frac{1.23}{0.6818} = \beta_e$$

The cost of equity for such a firm would then be:

$$k_e = R_f + \beta (R_m - R_f)$$

$$= 10\% + 1.80 (25\% - 10\%)$$

$$= 37.0\%$$

The cost of debt would be as before.

$k_d = R_f (1 - t)$

$= 10\% (1 - 0.30)$

$= 7\%$

and a suitable discount rate for the project would be:

$$\left(k_e \times \frac{V_e}{V_e + V_d} \right) + \left(k_d \times \frac{V_d}{V_e + V_d} \right) = (37\% \times 0.6) + (7\% \times 0.4)$$

$= 25\%$

Business valuations

Chapter learning objectives

Upon completion of this chapter you will be able to:

- identify and discuss reasons for valuing businesses and financial assets

- identify information requirements for the purposes of carrying out a valuation in a scenario

- discuss the limitations of the different types of information available for valuing companies

- value a share using the dividend valuation model (DVM), including the dividend growth model

- define market capitalisation

- calculate the market capitalisation of a company using the DVM, including the dividend growth model

- use the capital asset pricing model (CAPM) to help value a company's shares

- explain the difference between asset- and income-based valuation models

- value a company using the balance sheet, net realisable value (NRV) and replacement cost asset-based valuation models

- discuss the advantages and disadvantages of the different asset-based valuation models

- value a company using the price/earnings (PE) ratio income-based valuation model

- value a company using the earnings yield income-based valuation model

- value a company using the discounted cash flow (DCF) income-based valuation model

- discuss the advantages and disadvantages of the different income-based valuation models

- value a company in a scenario question selecting appropriate valuation methods

- calculate the value of irredeemable debt, redeemable debt, convertible debt and preference shares.

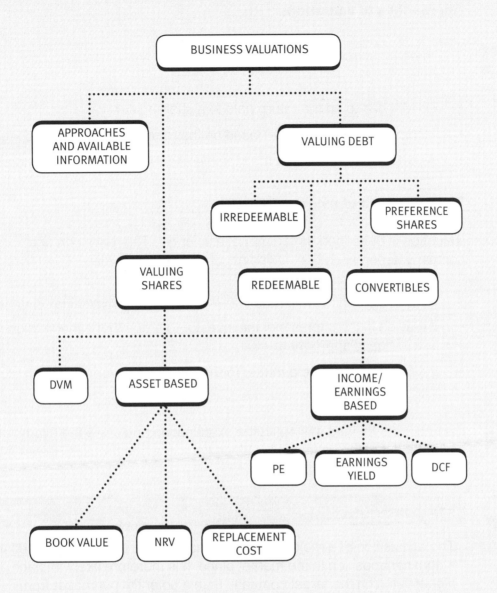

1 Valuing business and financial assets

Valuations of shares in both public and private companies are needed for several purposes by investors including:

- to establish terms of takeovers and mergers, etc.

- to be able to make 'buy and hold' decisions in general

- to value companies entering the stock market

- to establish values of shares held by retiring directors, which the articles of a company specify must be sold

- for fiscal purposes (capital gains tax (CGT), inheritance tax)

- divorce settlements, etc.

Approaches to valuations

The three main approaches are:

- DVM – based on the return paid to a shareholder.

- Income/earnings based – based on the returns earned by the company.

- Asset based – based on the tangible assets owned by the company.

The real worth of a company

Valuation is described as 'an art not a science'. The real worth of a company depends on the viewpoints of the various parties:

- the various methods of valuation will often give widely differing results

- it may be in the interests of the investor to argue that either a 'high' or 'low' value is appropriate

- the final figure will be a matter for negotiation between the interested parties.

It is important to bring this out in the examination and show the examiner you understand that the valuation is subjective and a compromise between two parties.

Expandable text

The acquisition of a major competitor may enable a company to secure a dominant position in the market place. It is therefore likely to place a higher value on the target company than a potential purchaser from outside the industry.

A realistic valuation will therefore require a full industry analysis rather than an isolated assessment of the business to be valued.

In some cases, the circumstances giving rise to the valuation may call for 'a value as would be agreed between a willing buyer and a willing seller' and may often be subject to independent arbitration.

KAPLAN PUBLISHING

2 Valuing shares – the DVM

The DVM was discussed in detail in chapter 18. It is summarised again here.

The method

- The value of the company/share is the present value (PV) of the expected future dividends discounted at the shareholders' required rate of return.

Either:

$$P_0 = \frac{D}{r_e}$$

or

$$P_0 = \frac{D_0(1 + g)}{r_e - g}$$

Assuming: a constant dividend **or** constant growth in dividends

r_e = shareholders' required return, expressed as a decimal

g = annual growth rate

P_0 = value of company, when D = Total dividend.

Strengths and weaknesses of the DVM

The model is theoretically sound and good for valuing a non-controlling interest but:

- there may be problems estimating a future growth rate
- it assumes that growth will be constant in the future, this is not true of most companies
- the model is highly sensitive to changes in its assumptions

- for controlling interests it offers few advantages over the earnings methods below.

To use this approach for valuation we need to be able to determine the cost of equity. The examiner will either give the cost of equity directly or give sufficient information so that you can use CAPM to determine the cost of equity.

Market capitalisation

A firm's market capitalisation is found by multiplying its current share price by the number of shares in issue.

NB1 The share prices of companies on stock exchanges move constantly in response to supply and demand, and as they move, so do market capitalisations.

NB2 The values calculated in this way do not necessarily reflect the actual market value of companies, as is shown when one company launches a takeover bid for another and (as frequently happens) pays a premium over the pre-bid price.

Illustration 1 – Market capitalisation

Company A has 120 million shares in issue. The current market price is 96c. What is the market capitalisation?

Expandable text

Solution

The market capitalisation is $115.2 million.

Test your understanding 1

A company has the following financial information available:

Share capital in issue: 4 million ordinary shares at a par value of 50c.

Current dividend per share (just paid) 24c.

Dividend four years ago 15.25c.

Current equity beta 0.8.

You also have the following market information:

Current market return 15%.

Risk-free rate 8%.

Find the market capitalisation of the company.

A company has the following financial information available:

Share capital in issue: 2 million ordinary shares at a par value of $1.

Current dividend per share (just paid) 18c.

Current EPS 25c.

Current return earned on assets 20%.

Current equity beta 1.1.

You also have the following market information:

Current market return 12%.

Risk-free rate 5%.

Find the market capitalisation of the company.

Solution

The formula

$$P_0 = D_0 \times \frac{(1 + g)}{r_e - g}$$

will provide the value of a single share. The market capitalisation can then be found by multiplying by the number of shares in issue.

$D_0 = 18c$

g using **Gordon's Growth Model**

$g = r \times b$

$r = 20\%$

If dividends per share of 18c are paid on EPS of 25c, then the payout ratio is 18/25 = 72%. The retention ratio is therefore 28%.

So b = 0.28

Therefore $g = 0.2 \times 0.28 = 0.056$.

r_e (using CAPM)

$R_f + ß (R_m - R_f) =$

$5 + 1.1 (12 - 5) = 12.7$

Therefore

$$P_0 = D_0 \times \frac{18(1 + 0.056)}{0.127 - 0.056} = 268c = 2.68$$

The market capitalisation is therefore:

2m × $2.68 = $5.36m

3 Asset-based valuations

Problems with asset-based valuations

The fundamental weakness:

- investors do not normally buy a company for its balance sheet assets, but for the earnings/cash flows that all of its assets can produce in the future
- we should value what is being purchased, i.e. the future income/cash flows.

Subsidiary weakness:

The asset approach also ignores non-balance sheet intangible 'assets', e.g.:

- highly-skilled workforce
- strong management team
- competitive positioning of the company's products.

It is quite common that the non-balance sheet assets are more valuable than the balance sheet assets.

When asset-based valuations are useful

- For asset stripping.
- To identify a minimum price in a takeover.
- To value property investment companies.

Asset stripping

Asset valuation models are useful in the unusual situation that a company is going to be purchased to be broken up and its assets sold off. In a break-up situation we would value the assets at their realisable value.

To set a minimum price in a takeover bid

Shareholders will be reluctant to sell at a price less than the net asset valuation even if the prospect for income growth is poor. A standard defensive tactic in a takeover battle is to revalue balance sheet assets to encourage a higher price. In a normal going-concern situation we value the assets at their replacement cost.

To value property investment companies

The market value of investment property has a close link to future cash flows and share values, i.e. discounted rental income determines the value of property assets and thus the company.

Tutorial Note: If we are valuing a profitable quoted company, in reality the minimum price that shareholders will accept will probably be the market capitalisation plus an acquisition premium and not the net asset valuation.

Types of asset-based measures

Measure	Strengths	Weaknesses
Book values	• None	• Historic cost value
NRV – assumes a break-up basis (NRV less liabilities)	• Minimum acceptable to owners	• Valuation problems especially if quick sale
	• Asset stripping	• Ignores goodwill

Measure	Strengths	Weaknesses
Replacement cost – going concern	• Maximum to be paid for assets by buyer	• Valuation problems – similar assets for comparison?
		• Ignores goodwill

Book value – this will normally be a meaningless figure as it will be based on historical costs.

Break-up value – the break-up value of the assets in the business will often be considerably lower than any other computed value. It normally represents the minimum price which should be accepted for the sale of a business as a going concern, since if the income based valuations give figures lower than the break-up value it is apparent that the owner would be better off by ceasing to trade and selling off all the assets piecemeal.

Replacement cost and deprival value – this should provide a measure of the maximum amount that any purchaser should pay for the whole business, since it represents the total cost of forming the business from scratch. However, a major element of any business as a going concern is likely to be the 'goodwill'. Since this can only be defined by determining the 'income-based value of business less tangible assets' it may be seen that there is no real way of applying a pure 'asset-based value' to a business – it is always necessary to consider an 'income-based value' as well.

Expandable text

The following is an abridged version of the balance sheet of Grasmere Contractors Co, an unquoted company, as at 30 April X6:

	$
Non-current assets (carrying value)	450,000
Net current assets	100,000
	550,000
Represented by	
$1 ordinary shares	200,000
Reserves	250,000
6% loan notes Z1	100,000
	550,000

You ascertain that:

- loan notes are redeemable at a premium of 2%

- current market value of freehold property exceeds book value by $30,000

- all assets, other than property, are estimated to be realisable at their book value.

Calculate the value of an 80% holding of ordinary shares, on an assets basis.

Solution

Calculation of value of 200,000 shares on an assets basis, as at 30 April year 20X6

	$
Non-current assets per balance sheet	450,000
Add: Undervalued freehold property	30,000
Adjusted value of fixed assets	480,000
Net current assets	100,000
Net assets	580,000
Less: Payable to loan note holders on redemption	(102,000)
	478,000
Valuation of 80% holding = 80 ÷ 100 × 478,000	382,400

4 Income/earnings-based methods

Income-based methods of valuation are of particular use when valuing a majority shareholding:

- ownership bestows additional benefits of control not reflected in the DVM model
- majority shareholders can influence dividend policy and therefore are more interested in earnings.

PE method

PE ratios are quoted for all listed companies and calculated as:

Price per share/Earnings per share (EPS)

This can then be used to value shares in unquoted companies as:

Value of company = Total earnings × PE ratio

Value per share = EPS × PE ratio

using an adjusted PE multiple from a similar quoted company (or industry average).

Problems with the PE ratio valuation

- It may be necessary to make an adjustment(s) to the PE ratio of the similar company to make it more suitable, e.g. if the company being valued:

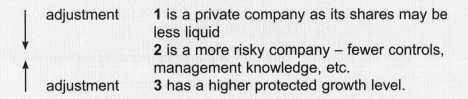

adjustment **1** is a private company as its shares may be less liquid

2 is a more risky company – fewer controls, management knowledge, etc.

adjustment **3** has a higher protected growth level.

Ensure that you explain the reasons why an adjustment is needed. This is essential as it shows you have an understanding of the bigger picture.

Arbitrary rule: Adjusted by 10% per reason – but amounts are less important than the explanation.

- It can be difficult to estimate the maintainable or normal ongoing level of earnings of the company being valued. It may be necessary to adjust these earnings to obtain a maintainable figure, e.g. change a director's emoluments from an abnormal to normal level.

 Remember to adjust for tax as the PE ratio is applied to profits after tax.

- PE ratios are in part based upon historical accounting information (the EPS) whereas the valuation should reflect future earnings prospects.

Expandable text

The basic choice for a suitable PE ratio will be that of a quoted company of comparable size in the same industry.

However, since share prices are broadly based on expected future earnings a PE ratio – based on a single year's reported earnings – may be very different for companies in the same sector, carrying the same systematic risk.

For example a high PE ratio may indicate:

- growth stock – the share price is high because continuous high rates of growth of earnings are expected from the stock

- no growth stock – the PE ratio is based on the last reported earnings, which perhaps were exceptionally low yet the share price is based on future earnings which are expected to revert to a 'normal' relatively stable level

- takeover bid – the share price has risen pending a takeover bid

- high security share – shares in property companies typically have low income yields but the shares are still worth buying because of the prospects of capital growth and level of security.

Similarly a low PE ratio may indicate:

- losses expected – future profits are expected to fall from their most recent levels

- share price low – as noted previously, share prices may be extremely volatile – special factors, such as a strike at a manufacturing plant of a particular company, may depress the share price and hence the PE ratio.

Consequently the main difficulty in trying to apply the model is finding a similar company, with similar growth prospects.

A further difficulty is that the reported earnings are based on historical cost accounts, which in general makes a nonsense of trying to compare two companies. Also it is important to ensure that the earnings in the victim company reflect future earnings prospects. It would be unwise to value a company on freakishly high earnings.

Expandable text

Illustration – Problems with the PE ratio valuation

You are given the following information regarding Accrington Co, an unquoted company:

(a) Issued ordinary share capital is 400,000 25c shares.

(b) Extract from profit and loss account for the year ended 31 July 20X4

	$	$
Profit before taxation		260,000
Less: Corporation tax	120,000	
	———	
Profit after taxation		140,000
Less: Preference dividend	20,000	
Ordinary dividend	36,000	
	———	(56,000)
		———
Retained profit for the year		84,000
		———

(c) The PE ratio applicable to a similar type of business (suitable for an unquoted company) is 12.5.

> You are required to value 200,000 shares in Accrington Co on a PE basis.

Expandable text

Solution

Valuation of 200,000 shares = 200,000 × [PE ratio × EPS]

$$= 200{,}000 \times \left[12.5 \times \frac{(140{,}000 - 20{,}000)}{400{,}000} \right]$$

$$= \$750{,}000$$

Or 50% (12.5 x $120,000) = $750,000.

Earnings yield

The earnings yield is simply the inverse of the PE ratio:

$$\frac{EPS}{Price\ per\ share}$$

It can therefore be used to value the shares or market capitalisation of a company in exactly the same way as the PE ratio:

Value of company	= Total earnings	×	$\dfrac{1}{earnings\ yield}$
Value per share	= EPS	×	$\dfrac{1}{earnings\ yield}$

KAPLAN PUBLISHING

Test your understanding 2

Company A has earnings of $300,000. A similar listed company has an earnings yield of 12.5%.

Company B has earnings of $420,500. A similar listed company has a PE ratio of 7.

Estimate the value of each company.

Discounted cash flow basis

A buyer of a business is obtaining a stream of future operating cash flows.

The maximum value of the business is:

PV of future cash flows

A discount rate reflecting the systematic risk of the flows should be used.

Method:

(1) Identify relevant 'free' cash flows (i.e. excluding financing flows)

    – operating flows

    – revenue from sale of assets

    – tax

    – synergies arising from any merger.

(2) Select a suitable time horizon.

(3) Calculate the PV over this horizon. This gives the value to all providers of finance, i.e. equity + debt.

(4) Deduct the value of debt to leave the value of equity.

Expandable text

Illustration – Earnings yield

The following information has been taken from the income statement and balance sheet of B Co:

Revenue	$350m
Production expenses	$210m
Administrative expenses	$24m
Tax allowable depreciation	$31m
Capital investment in year	$48m
Corporate debt	$14m trading at 130%

Corporation tax is 30%.

The WACC is 16.6%. Inflation is 6%.

These cash flows are expected to continue every year for the foreseeable future.

Required:

Calculate the value of equity.

Expandable text

Solution

Operating profits = $350m – $210m – $24m = $116m

Tax on operating profits = $116m × 0.3 = $34.8m

Allowable depreciation = $31m (assumed not included in production or administration expenses)

Tax relief on depreciation = $31m × 0.3 = $9.3

Therefore net cash flow = $116 – $34.8 + $9.3 – $48 = $42.5

The real discount rate is:

$$\frac{1.166}{1.06} = 10\%$$

The corporate value is =

$$\frac{\$42.5m}{0.10} = \$425m$$

Equity = \$425m − (\$14m × 1.3) = \$406.8m.

Note: because the cash flow is a perpetuity we have used the real (uninflated) cash flow and the real discount rate (see chapter 11).

Test your understanding 3

A company's current revenues and costs are as follows: sales \$200 million, cost of sales \$110 million, distribution and administrative expenses are \$20 million, tax allowable depreciation \$40 million and annual capital spending is \$50 million. Corporation tax is 30%. The current value of debt is \$17 million.

The WACC is 14.4%. Inflation is 4%.

These cash flows are expected to continue every year for the foreseeable future.

Calculate the value of equity.

Advantages

- theoretically the best method.
- can be used to value part of a company.

Weaknesses

- it relies on estimates of both cash flows and discount rates – may be unavailable
- difficulty in choosing a time horizon
- difficulty in valuing a company's worth beyond this period
- assumes that the discount rate, tax and inflation rates are constant through the period.

5 Valuation of debt and preference shares

In chapter 18 we looked at using the DVM to determine costs of capital and saw that many of the equations could be rearranged to give market value. These are summarised below:

Type of finance   **Market value**

Preference shares $P_o = D/K_p$

Irredeemable debt $MV = I/r$

Redeemable debt $MV = $ PV of future interest and redemption receipts, discounted at investors' required returns

where:

D = the constant annual preference dividend

P_o = ex-div market value of the share

K_p = cost of the preference share.

I = annual interest starting in one year's time

MV = market price of the debenture now (year 0)

r = debt holders' required return, expressed as a decimal

K_d = company's cost of debt, expressed as a decimal

Test your understanding 4

A firm has in issue $112% preference shares. Currently the required return of preference shareholders is 14%.

What is the value of a preference share?

Test your understanding 5

A company has issued irredeemable loan notes with a coupon rate of 7%. If the required return of investors is 4%, what is the current market value of the debt?

Test your understanding 6

A company has in issue 9% redeemable debt with 10 years to redemption. Redemption will be at par. The investors require a return of 16%.

What is the market value of the debt?

Expandable text

Convertible debt

The value of a convertible is the higher of its value as debt and its converted value. This is known as its **formula value.**

Expandable text

Illustration – Convertible debt

Rexel Co has in issue convertible loan notes with a coupon rate of 12%. Each $100 loan note may be converted into 20 ordinary shares at any time until the date of expiry and any remaining loan notes will be redeemed at $100.

The loan notes have five years left to run. Investors would normally require a rate of return of 8% pa on a five-year debt security.

Should investors convert if the current share price is:

(a) $4.00.

(b) $5.00.

(c) $6.00.

Expandable text

Solution

Value as debt

If the security is not converted it will have the following value to the investor:

	PVF @ 8%	PV
		$
Interest $12/year for 5 years	3.993	47.916
Redemption $100 in 5 years	0.681	68.100
		116.016

Note the PV is calculated at 8% – the required rate of return on a straight debt security.

Value as equity

Market price	Value as equity
	$
4.00	$80 (i.e. 20 × $4)
5.00	$100
6.00	$120

If the market price of equity rises to $6.00 the security should be converted, otherwise it is worth more as debt. The 'breakeven' conversion price is $5.80 per share ($116/20 shares).

The value of the convertible will therefore be $116, unless the share price rises above $5.80 at which point it will be the value of the equity received on conversion.

Expandable text

Rexel Co has in issue convertible loan notes with a coupon rate of 4%.

Each $100 loan note may be converted into 12 ordinary shares at any time until the date of expiry and any remaining loan notes will be redeemed at $100 in four years time.

Investors would normally require a rate of return of 5% pa on a four-year debt security.

Should investors convert if the current share price is:

(a) $7.00.

(b) $8.00.

(c) $9.00.

Solution

Value as debt

If the security is not converted it will have the following value to the investor:

	PVF @ 5%	PV
		$
Interest $4/year for 4 years	3.546	14.184
Redemption $100 in 4 years	0.823	82.300
		─────
		96.484
		─────

Note the present value is calculated at 5% – the required rate of return on a straight debt security.

Value as equity

Market price	Value as equity
	$
7.00	$84 (i.e. 12 × $7)
8.00	$96
9.00	$108

If the market price of equity rises to $9.00 the security should be converted, otherwise it is worth more as debt. The 'break-even' conversion price is $8.04 per share ($96.484/12 shares).

The value of the convertible will therefore be $96.48, unless the share price rises past $8.04 at which point it will be the value of the equity received on conversion.

Chapter summary

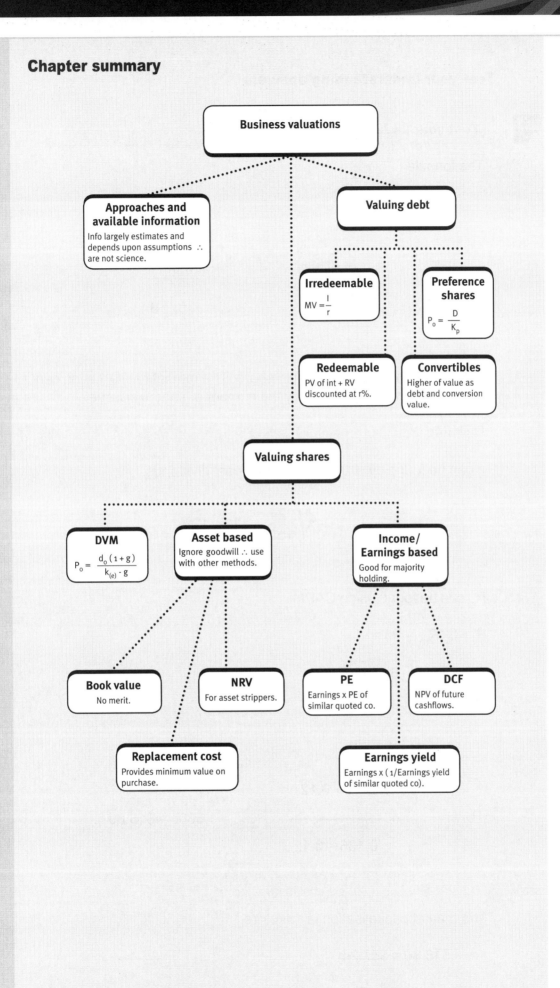

Test your understanding answers

Test your understanding 1

The formula

$$P_o = D_o \frac{(1 + g)}{r_e - g}$$

will provide the value of a single share. The market capitalisation can then be found by multiplying by the number of shares in issue.

$D_o = 24c$

g can be found by extrapolating from past dividends:

$$\sqrt[4]{\frac{24}{15.25}} - 1 = 12\%$$

R_e can be found using CAPM

$R_f + ß (R_m - R_f) =$

$8 + 0.8 (15 - 8) = 13.6$

Therefore

$$P_o = \frac{24(1 + 0.12)}{0.136 - 0.12} = 1{,}680c = \$16.80$$

The market capitalisation is therefore:

4m × \$16.80 = \$67.2m

Test your understanding 2

Company A: $300,000 × $\dfrac{1}{0.125}$ = \$2,4000,000

Company B: \$420,500 × 7 = \$2,943,500

Test your understanding 3

Operating profits = \$200m − \$110m − \$20m = \$70m

Tax on operating profits = \$70m × 0.3 = \$21m

Allowable depreciation = \$40m

Tax relief on depreciation = \$40m × 0.3 = \$12

Therefore net cash flow = \$70 − \$21 + \$12 − \$50 = \$11

$$1 + r = \dfrac{(1 + i)}{(1 + h)} = \dfrac{1.144}{1.04} = 1.10$$

The real discount rate is: 10%

The corporate value is = $\dfrac{\$11m}{0.10}$ = \$110m

Equity = \$110m − \$17m = \$93m.

Test your understanding 4

$$\text{Using } P_o = \frac{D}{K_p}, \quad P_o = \frac{12}{0.14} = 85.71\text{cents}$$

Test your understanding 5

$$MV = \frac{7}{0.04} = \$175$$

Test your understanding 6

The market value is calculated by finding the PVs of the interest and the principal and totalling them as shown below.

	Time		Cash flow	DF @ 16%	PV
Annuity →	0	**MV**		**Bal fig**	**$(66.20)**
	1-10	Interest payments	9	4.833	$43.50
	10	Capital repayment	$100	0.227	$22.70

Market efficiency

Chapter learning objectives

Upon completion of this chapter you will be able to:

- explain the concept of market efficiency

- distinguish between and discuss markets that are not efficient at all, weak form efficient, semi-strong form efficient and strong form efficient

- evaluate the efficiency of a market in a scenario

- describe the significance of investor speculation and the explanations of investor decisions offered by behavioural finance

- discuss the impact of the marketability and liquidity of shares in reaching a valuation

- discuss the impact of availability and sources of information in reaching a valuation

- discuss the impact of market imperfections and pricing anomalies in reaching a valuation.

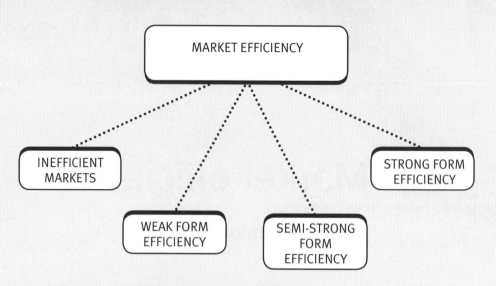

1 The efficient market hypothesis (EMH)

The concept of market efficiency

Opening question:

*   If N plc shares are valued at $1.30, is this value reliable (fair, true, accurate)?

Or put another way:

*   How efficient is the stock market at valuing the shares of a company?

*   An efficient market is one in which security prices fully reflect all available information.

*   In an efficient market, new information is rapidly and rationally incorporated into share prices in an unbiased way.

Current position

In the sophisticated financial markets of today, there are

*   cheap electronic communications
*   large numbers of informed investors.

Conclusion

New information is rapidly (in minutes not days) incorporated into share prices.

Benefits of an efficient market

We need an efficient stock market to

- ensure investor confidence
- reflect directors' performance in the share price.

Expandable text

Investor confidence

Investors need to know that they will pay and receive a fair price when they buy and sell shares. If shares are incorrectly priced, many savers would refuse to invest, thus seriously reducing the availability of funds and inhibiting growth. Investor confidence in the pricing efficiency is essential.

Motivation and control of directors

The primary objective of directors is the maximisation of shareholder wealth, i.e. maximise the share price. In implementing a positive net present value (NPV) decision, directors can be assured that the decision once communicated to the market will result in an increased share price. Conversely if directors make sub-optimal decisions then the share price will fall. Like all feedback systems the stock market has a dual function. It motivates directors to maximise share price, whilst providing an early warning system of potential problems.

The EMH

The EMH states that it is not possible to consistently outperform the market by using any information that the market already knows, except through luck.

The idea is that new information is quickly and efficiently incorporated into asset prices at any point in time, so that old information cannot be used to foretell future price movements.

Three levels of efficiency are distinguished, depending on the type of information available to the majority of investors and hence already reflected in the share price.

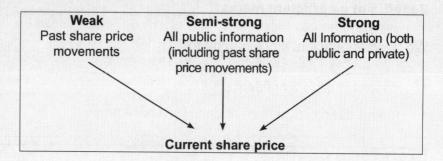

Weak	Semi-strong	Strong
Past share price movements	All public information (including past share price movements)	All Information (both public and private)

Current share price

The forms of efficiency are cumulative, so that if the market is semi-strong it is also weak.

2 Types of efficiency

Market inefficiency

An inefficient market is one in which the value of securities is not always an accurate reflection of the available information. Markets may also operate inefficiently, e.g. due to low volumes of trade.

In an inefficient market, some securities will be overpriced and others will be underpriced, which means some investors can make excess returns while others can lose more than warranted by their level of risk exposure.

Weak form efficiency

Information

Information In a weak form efficient market **all past price movements** are already incorporated into the share price.

Evidence

Share prices follow a random walk:

- there are no patterns or trends

- prices rise or fall depending on whether the next piece of news is good or bad

- tests show that only 0.1% of a share price change on one day can be predicted from knowledge of the change on the previous day.

Conclusion

The stock market is weak form efficient and so:

- future price movements cannot be predicted from past price movements

- chartism/technical analysis cannot help make a consistent gain on the market.

Expandable text

Random walks

In 1953 **Kendall** presented a paper which examined share price movements over time. He concluded that the prices of shares followed a random walk, i.e. there are no patterns or trends. Any apparent pattern or trend purely occurs by chance.

Why does the random walk occur?

Prices change because of new information. New information is by definition independent of the last piece of new information and thus the resulting share price movements are independent of each other, i.e. the next piece of new information has equal chance of being good or bad, nobody knows.

If a pattern is identified from historical share price movements and this information becomes known in the market, the pattern disappears, as the market buys and sells shares accordingly to take advantage of the pattern.

The market is weak form efficient, as the study of the history of share prices cannot be used to predict the future in any abnormally profitable way.

Semi-strong efficiency

Information

In a semi-strong efficient market the share price incorporates **all publicly-available** information.

Evidence

Share prices react within 5-10 minutes of any new information being released and:

- rise in response to breaking good news
- fall in response to breaking bad news.

Conclusion

The stock market is (almost) semi-strong form efficient and so:

- fundamental analysis – examining publicly-available information will not provide opportunities to consistently beat the market
- only those trading in the first few minutes after the news breaks can beat the market
- since published information includes past share prices a semi- strong form efficient market is also weakly efficient.

Strong form efficiency

Information

In a strongly efficient market the share price incorporates **all information**, whether public or private, including information which is as yet unpublished.

Evidence

Insiders (directors for example) have access to unpublished information. If the market was strong form

- the share price wouldn't move when, e.g. news broke about a takeover, as it would have moved when the initial decision was made – in practice they do!

- there would be no need to ban 'insider dealing' as insiders couldn't make money by trading before news became public– it is banned because they do!

Conclusion

The stock market is not strong form efficient and so:

- insider dealers have been fined and imprisoned for making money trading in shares before the news affecting them went public

- the stock exchange encourages quick release of new information to prevent insider trading opportunities

- insiders are forbidden from trading in their shares at crucial times.

Expandable text

It is well-known that shares can be traded on the basis of information not in the public domain and thereby make abnormal profits. Stock markets are not strong form efficient. The engineer who discovers gold may buy shares before the discovery is made public. The merchant banker who hears a colleague is assisting in a surprise takeover bid has been known to purchase shares in the target firm.

A breakdown in the fair game perception will damage investor confidence and reduce investment. To avoid a loss of confidence **most stock markets have codes of conduct and most countries have introduced legislation to curb insider dealing**. Insider dealing became a criminal offence in the UK in 1980. However British regulators tend to be less effective than some of their foreign counterparts. American and French regulators rely initially on civil law where the burden of proof is lower than in a criminal case.

Another weapon against insiders is to **make companies release price-sensitive information quickly**. The London Stock Exchange has strict guidelines to encourage companies to make announcements to the market as early as possible, on such matters as current trading conditions and profit warnings. Therefore there is a mechanism to force private information into the public arena to attempt to ensure that share prices are reasonably accurate.

A third approach is to completely prohibit certain individuals from dealing in a company shares at crucial time periods. The stock exchange **Model Code for Directors Dealings** precludes directors of quoted companies (and indeed other employees in the possession of price-sensitive information) from trading shares for a period of two months before the announcement of the annual results. The Code also precludes dealing before the announcement of matters of an exceptional nature involving unpublished information, which is potentially price sensitive.

Conclusions for the market

If the market is semi-strong then a number of key conclusions can be drawn:

- shares are fairly priced – the purchase is a zero NPV transaction (unless you are an insider dealer!)

- managers can improve shareholders' wealth by investing in positive NPV projects and communicating this to the market

- most investors (including professional fund managers) cannot consistently beat the market without inside information.

KAPLAN PUBLISHING

Expandable text

In an efficient market, shares are priced to give investors the exact return to reward them for the level of (systematic) risk in their shares. As a result the purchase of shares is a zero NPV transaction because the price paid for the share is an accurate reflection of its worth i.e. shares are fairly priced and the concept of an over- or under-valued security does not apply. Therefore the rationale behind mergers and takeovers must be questioned. Semi-strong efficiency implies that mergers could only be successful if synergies can be created, i.e. economies of scale or rationalisation.

Given the fact that well-developed stock markets are weak and semi-strong market efficient most of the time, once new information is communicated to the market it is rapidly reflected in the share price. Thus managers can achieve the overall objective of maximising shareholder wealth by making good decisions and communicating them to the market.

Is it worth acquiring and analysing public information?

If semi-strong efficiency is true, it undermines the work of millions of fundamental (professional and amateur) analysts, whose work cannot be used to produce abnormal returns because all public information is already reflected in the share price.

These analysts study the fundamental factors that underpin the share price, i.e. revenues, costs and risk associated with the company as well as many other sources of public information such as macroeconomic and industry conditions, details of the company personnel, technological changes and so on.

They will then use this information, together with a share valuation model (e.g. like the dividend valuation model – DVM), to estimate the true or intrinsic value of the shares. This value is then compared with the current market price of shares to see if the shares are over- or under-valued (mispriced).

The fundamental analyst is attempting to beat the market to earn an abnormal return by:

- buying under-valued shares before the prices rise.
- selling over-valued shares before the prices fall.

But in an efficient market mis-priced shares do not exist.

Given that there are thousands of sophisticated investors examining the smallest piece of information about each company and its environment, it would seem reasonable to postulate that the semi strong form of EMH is a reality in well-developed stock markets.

Conclusion:

The vast majority of investors (including professional fund managers) cannot consistently beat the market by analysing the information they have available to them, as this public information is already reflected in the share price. So long as the market remains efficient, fundamental analysis is a waste of money and the average investor would be better off by simply selecting a diversified portfolio, thereby avoiding costs of analysis. This message has struck a chord with millions of investors who have placed billions of pounds in low cost Index Tracking Funds, which merely replicate a stock market index, rather than an actively managed fund which tries to pick winners.

The market paradox

In order for the market to remain efficient, investors must believe there is value in assessing information.

Because they assess it continuously the information is reflected in the share price as soon as it is released and an investor cannot beat the market.

Expandable text

The paradox of the EMH is that large numbers of investors have to disbelieve the hypothesis in order to maintain efficiency. The continuous collective actions of fundamental analysts ensure that the market reacts almost instantaneously to the disclosure of new information. Their actions safeguard market efficiency and are thus self-defeating, as they cannot then individually beat the market. Their collective value to the market is that they guarantee its efficiency.

Investor behaviour

Despite the evidence in support of the theory, some events seem to contradict it:

- significant share price volatility
- boom/crash patterns.

e.g. the **stock market crash of October 1987** where most stock exchanges crashed at the same time. It is virtually impossible to explain the scale of those market falls by reference to any news event at the time.

An explanation has been offered by the science of behavioural finance:

- naïve investors see high-performing shares (for example) and rush to buy
- this noise inflates the share price artificially
- informed investors then buy, planning to sell before the inevitable crash.

Expandable text

Events such as significant share price volatility and boom/crash patterns seem at odds with the theory of efficient markets because prices are not supposed to deviate markedly from their fundamental value.

One theory behind this seemingly irrational behaviour of the markets is called noise trading by naïve investors. According to this theory there are two types of investors, the informed and uninformed. The informed trade shares to bring them to their fundamental value. The uninformed act irrationally. Perhaps they noticed that certain shares have made investors high returns over the last number of years. So they rush out and buy these shares to get their piece of the action i.e. they chase the trend.

The uninformed investors create lots of noise and push the market up and up. The informed investor often tries to get in on the act. Despite knowing it will end in disaster, the informed investor buys in the hope of selling before the crash. This is based on the idea that the price an investor is willing to pay for a share today is dependent on the price the investor can sell it for at some point in the future and not necessarily at its fundamental value.

Can you remember the opening question?

The shares in N plc are probably correctly valued at $1.30 as stock markets are at least semi-strong market efficient most of the time.

Expandable text

In summary:

 Weak form   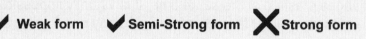 Semi-Strong form   ✗ Strong form

Means that the current share price reflects all information that could be obtained from studying and analysing past share price movements.	Means that the current share price reflects all publicly-available information.	Means that the current share price reflects all information, including that which is privately held.
Evidence: overwhelming in support.	Evidence: substantial in support.	Evidence: stock markets are **not** strong form efficient.

KAPLAN PUBLISHING

Conclusion: a technical analyst/chartist who studies trends and patterns in past share movements will not make an abnormal gain.

Conclusion: a fundamental analyst will generally not make an abnormal gain, i.e. from analysing publicly-available information.

The vast majority of investors cannot consistently beat the market (i.e. earn an abnormal return), as they only have public information available to them and this information is already reflected in the share price.

Conclusion: If the market were strong form efficient an investor could only make abnormal gains by luck. Because the market is only semi-strong efficient, abnormal gains can be made from analysing 'inside information'. Hence the need for legislation to prevent insider dealing, i.e. the 1985 Company Securities (Insider Dealing) Act.

Conclusion:

The stock exchanges of all developed nations are regarded as at least semi-strong efficient for the shares traded actively on those markets.

Test your understanding 1

What would you believe about the efficiency of the market if you thought you could make money by:

(1) **insider dealing**

(2) **analysing past price movements**

(3) **only by pure luck**

(4) **analysing financial statements, directors' statements, company activities, etc.?**

To beat the market you need to possess information which is not available to the majority of investors.

Expandable text

Consider the following comments and explain the theoretical errors they contain.

The EMH says that share prices are always right. This is because shares move in a random fashion when new information is made public. The only reason prices move randomly is because of the new information contained in the accounts when they are published.

Both technical and fundamental analysis serve no function and cannot predict future share prices. Corporate fund managers cannot predict share prices either.

Solution

The accuracy of each statement depends on which view of market efficiency is considered:

The EMH says that share prices are always right.

If 'right' means at a true value – an equilibrium price incorporating all information available, then this is mainly true in a strong form efficient market. However, since the reaction to new information would not be instant, there will be a short period even in a strong market when the price is not 'right'.

In a semi-strong market the price will be fair (reflecting all publicly-available information) rather than right.

In a weak form efficient market, the price does not include all information.

This is because shares move in a random fashion when new information is made public.

Share prices do not move randomly when new information is announced – they move in a predictable fashion – up for good news and down for bad. However they follow a 'random walk' in that each price change is independent of the one that went before and it is not possible to predict the content of the new information without insider information.

In a strong form market, shares would not move just because the information had been publicly announced – the information would be incorporated as soon as the content of the news arose, e.g. at the point the directors decided to embark upon a particular investment.

The only reason prices move randomly is because of the new information contained in the accounts when they are published.

New information impacting share movements when announced can come from a variety of sources including announcements by management, changes in interest rates or exchange rates, dividend announcements, etc. In a semi-strong market it is likely that the majority of information contained in the published accounts is already known to the market and therefore reflected in the share price. In this case, the share price would only react if the published accounts contained new or unexpected information.

Both technical and fundamental analysis serve no function

In fact the analysts play a key role in reviewing information and communicating it quickly to the market. They therefore help ensure the market remains efficient.

technical and fundamental analysis ... cannot predict future share price

It is true that, in an efficient market, analysing information already in the public domain cannot help predict the future share price, as the share price will already reflect all the information being analysed.

Corporate fund managers cannot predict share prices either

There is a possibility that fund managers could predict future share prices in a semi-strong efficient market but only if they are operating with inside information.

Expandable text

Other factors to take into account when considering the value of shares

Marketability and liquidity of shares

As discussed in chapter 20, the shares in a private company are often valued by using measures based on the 'fair' share prices of similar listed companies.

However buying a share in an unlisted company is more of a gamble, as the share cannot be easily sold.

This is why the values given by methods such as price/earnings (PE) ratio and earnings yield, are often downgraded.

Available information

We discussed above the importance of information concerning a company being fully available if the share is to be fairly priced.

In unlisted companies, information may be less readily available for a number of reasons such as:

- a weaker control environment
- unaudited financial statements
- fewer compliance regulations apply
- no tradition of sharing information so channels of communication not set up
- less detailed record keeping.

The relative shortage of information in unlisted companies may also cause the initial valuation to be downgraded.

Equilibrium prices

In practice, as discussed above, the market does show sudden price fluctuations that cannot be explained simply by the information being newly released. If a share price is highly volatile, then it is considered not in equilibrium.

Prices used to provide data for the valuation of unlisted shares need to be in equilibrium if meaningful values are to be obtained.

If only a few similar companies exist, and their shares are **not in equilibrium**, any share price calculated must be treated with caution.

Chapter summary

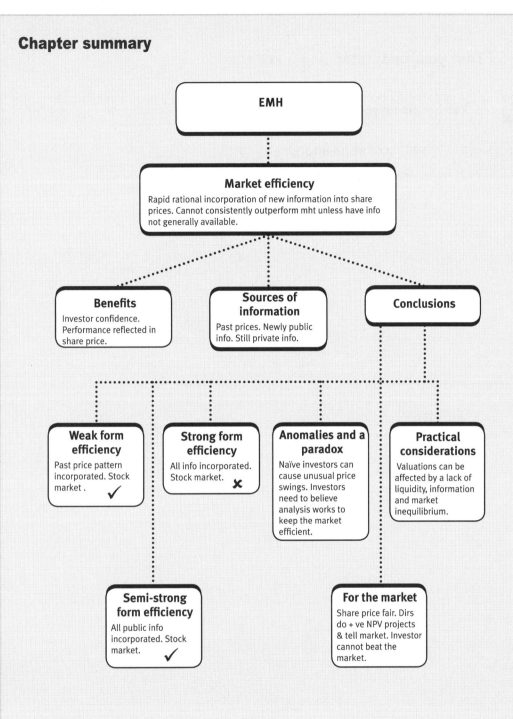

Test your understanding answers

Test your understanding 1

(1) It is at most semi-strong.

(2) It is not efficient at all.

(3) It is strong form.

(4) It is at most weak form.

Foreign exchange risk

Chapter learning objectives

Upon completion of this chapter you will be able to:

- explain the meaning and causes of translation risk

- explain the meaning and causes of transaction risk

- explain the meaning and causes of economic risk

- describe how the balance of payments can cause exchange rate fluctuations

- explain the impact of purchasing power parity on exchange rate fluctuations

- explain the impact of interest rate parity on exchange rate fluctuations

- use purchasing power parity theory (PPPT) to forecast exchange rates

- use interest rate parity theory (IRPT) to forecast exchange rates

- explain the principle of four-way equivalence and the impact on exchange rate fluctuations

- explain the significance of the currency of an invoice on foreign currency risk management

- discuss and apply netting and matching as a form of foreign currency risk management

- discuss and apply leading and lagging as a form of foreign currency risk management

- define a forward exchange contract

- calculate the outcome of a forward exchange contract

- define money market hedging

- calculate the outcome of a money market hedge used by an exporter

- calculate the outcome of a money market hedge used by an importer

- explain the significance of asset and liability management on foreign currency risk management

- compare and evaluate traditional methods of foreign currency risk management

- define the main types of foreign currency derivates and explain how they can be used to hedge foreign currency risk.

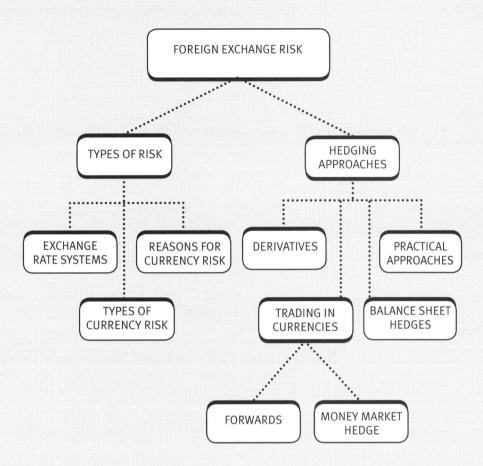

1 Foreign currency risk

Unlike when trading domestically, foreign currency risk arises for companies that trade internationally.

In a floating exchange rate system:

- the authorities allow the forces of supply and demand to continuously change the exchange rates without intervention
- the future value of a currency vis-à-vis other currency is uncertain
- the value of foreign trades will be affected.

Expandable text

Depreciation and appreciation of a foreign currency

If a foreign currency depreciates it is now worth less in our home currency.

- Receipt – adverse movement – will receive less in your home currency.

- Payment – favourable movement – will end up paying less in your home currency.

If a foreign currency appreciates it is simply worth more in our home currency.

- Receipt – favourable movement – will receive more in your home currency.
- Payment – adverse movement – will end up paying more in your home currency.

The comfort table

	Sell fewer $s to get a pound.	Sell more $s to get a pound.	
	$ appreciates (0.10c)	$10m 0.10c	$ depreciates
Rates – $/£ =	$1.5 <--------------------	$1.6 ------------------>	$1.7
£ Cash flow	£6.67m	£6.25m	£5.88m
Receipts	√		
Payments			√

Test your understanding 1

What would a strong pound mean for companies in the UK pricing transactions in foreign currency?

- **UK exporters**
- **UK importers.**

What would a weak Euro mean for companies in the Eurozone pricing transactions in foreign currency?

- **European exporters**
- **European importers.**

KAPLAN PUBLISHING

The currency blues

'If a currency appreciates, companies complain that they cannot sell their goods abroad and workers agitate about losing their jobs.

If a currency depreciates, consumers are unhappy because inflation is imported and their money travels less far when they go abroad.'

Exchange rate systems

The world's leading currencies such as:

- US dollar
- Japanese yen
- British pound
- European Euro

float against each other. However only a minority of currencies use this system.

Other systems include.

- Fixed exchange rates
- Freely floating exchange rates
- Managed floating exchange rates.

Expandable text

Although the world's leading trading currencies, like the US dollar, Japanese yen, British pound and European Euro are floating against the other currencies, a minority of countries use floating exchange rates. The main exchange rate systems include:

(a) **Fixed exchange rates**

This involves publishing the target parity against a single currency (or a basket of currencies), and a commitment to use monetary policy (interest rates) and official reserves of foreign exchange to hold the actual spot rate within some trading band around this target.

Fixed against a single currency

This is where a country fixes its exchange rate against the currency of another country's currency. More than 50 countries fix their rates in this way, mostly against the US dollar. Fixed rates are not permanently fixed and periodic revaluations and devaluations occur when the economic fundamentals of the country concerned strongly diverge (e.g. inflation rates).

Fixed against a basket of currencies

Using a basket of currencies is aimed at fixing the exchange rate against a more stable currency base than would occur with a single currency fix. The basket is often devised to reflect the major trading links of the country concerned.

Historical perspective: British pound previously used a fixed rate system

The pound was fixed against the US dollar from 1945 to 1972, and more recently was part of the European Exchange Rate Mechanism (ERM) between 1990 and 1992. The rules of the ERM were complicated, UK membership of the ERM involved a target rate of 2.95 DM against the DM with a +/– 6% trading band: in other words, a minimum spot rate of around 2.77DM. To hold sterling above this rate in 1992, the government used a significant amount of the UK's foreign currency reserves and a high interest rate policy. Following its failure to defend the pound within the system, the UK left the ERM in September 1992.

(b) Freely floating exchange rates (sometimes called a 'clean float')

A genuine free float would involve leaving exchange rates entirely to the vagaries of supply and demand on the foreign exchange markets, and neither intervening on the market using official reserves of foreign exchange nor taking exchange rates into account when making interest rate decisions. The Monetary Policy Committee of the Bank of England clearly takes account of the external value of sterling in its decision-making process, so that although the pound is no longer in a fixed exchange rate system, it would not be correct to argue that it is on a genuinely free float.

(c) **Managed floating exchange rates (sometimes called a 'dirty float')**

The central bank of countries using a managed float will attempt to keep currency relationships within a predetermined range of values (not usually publicly announced), and will often intervene in the foreign exchange markets by buying or selling their currency to remain within the range.

2 Types of foreign currency risk

Since firms regularly trade with firms operating in countries with different currencies, and may operate internationally themselves, it is essential to understand the impact that foreign exchange rate changes can have on the business.

Transaction risk

Transaction risk is the risk of an exchange rate changing between the transaction date and the subsequent settlement date, i.e. it is the gain or loss arising on conversion.

It arises primarily on imports and exports.

> **Expandable text**
>
> On 1 January a UK firm enters into a contract to buy a piece of equipment from the US for $300,000. The invoice is to be settled on 31 March.
>
> The exchange rate on 1 January is $1.6/£ (i.e. $1.6 = £1).
>
> However by 31 March, the pound may have
>
> (1) strengthened to $1.75/£ or
>
> (2) depreciated to $1.45/£.
>
> Explain the risk faced by the UK firm.

Expandable Text

Solution

The UK firm faces uncertainty over the amount of sterling they will need to use to settle the US dollar invoice.

The cost of the equipment on 1 January is $\dfrac{\$300,000}{1.6} = £187,500$

However on settlement, the cost may be:

1. $= \dfrac{\$300,000}{1.75} = £171,429$

2. $= \dfrac{\$300,000}{1.45} = £206,897$

This uncertainty is the transaction risk.

A firm may decide to hedge – take action to minimise – the risk, if it is:

- a material amount
- over a material time period
- thought likely exchange rates will change significantly.

Expandable text

This type of risk is primarily associated with imports and exports. If a company exports goods on credit then it has a figure for receivables in its accounts. The amount it will finally receive depends on the foreign exchange movement from the transaction date to the settlement date.

As transaction risk has a potential impact on the cash flows of a company, most companies choose to hedge against such exposure. Measuring and monitoring transaction risk is normally an important component of treasury management.

The degree of exposure involved is dependent on:

- the size of the transaction, is it material?

- the hedge period, the time period before the expected cash flows occurs

- the anticipated volatility of the exchange rates during the hedge period.

The corporate risk management policy should state what degree of exposure is acceptable. This will probably be dependent on whether the treasury department has been established as a cost or profit centre.

Economic risk

Economic risk is the variation in the value of the business (i.e. the present value of future cash flows) due to unexpected changes in exchange rates. It is the long-term version of transaction risk.

For an export company it could occur because:

- the home currency strengthens against the currency in which it trades

- a competitor's home currency weakens against the currency in which it trades.

Expandable text

Illustration – Economic risk

A US exporter sells one product in Europe on a cost plus basis.

The selling price is based on a US price of $16 to cover costs and provide a profit margin.

The current exchange rate is €1.26/$.

What would be the effect on the exporter's business if the dollar strengthened to €1.31/$?

Expandable text

Solution

The product was previously selling at $16 × 1.26 = €20.16. After the movement in exchange rates the exporter has an unhappy choice:

Either they must

- raise the price of the product to maintain their profits: 16 × 1.31 = €20.96 but risk losing sales as the product is more expensive and less competitive, or

  maintain the price to keep sales volume but risk eroding profit margins as €20.16 is now only worth €20.16 ÷ 1.31 = $15.39.

The exporter is facing economic risk.

A favoured but long-term solution is to diversify all aspects of the business internationally so the company is not overexposed to any one economy in particular.

Expandable text

Economic risk

Transaction exposure focuses on relatively short-term cash flows effects; economic exposure encompasses these, plus the longer-term effects of changes in exchange rates on the market value of a company. Basically this means a change in the present value of the future after-tax cash flows due to changes in exchange rates.

There are two ways in which a company is exposed to economic risk

Directly: If your firm's home currency strengthens then foreign competitors are able to gain sales at your expense because your products have become more expensive (or you have reduced your margins) in the eyes of customers both abroad and at home.

Indirectly: Even if your home currency does not move vis-à-vis your customer's currency, you may lose competitive position. For example suppose a South African firm is selling into Hong Kong and its main competitor is a New Zealand firm. If the New Zealand dollar weakens against the Hong Kong dollar the South African firm has lost some competitive position.

Economic risk is difficult to quantify but a favoured strategy is to diversify internationally, in terms of sales, location of production facilities, raw materials and financing. Such diversification is likely to significantly reduce the impact of economic exposure relative to a purely domestic company, and provide much greater flexibility to react to real exchange rate changes.

Translation risk

Where the reported performance of an overseas subsidiary in home-based currency terms is distorted in consolidated financial statements because of a change in exchange rates.

NB. This is an accounting risk rather than a cash-based one.

Expandable text

The financial statements of overseas subsidiaries are usually translated into the home currency in order that they can be consolidated into the group's financial statements. Note that this is purely a paper-based exercise – it is the translation not the conversion of real money from one currency to another.

The reported performance of an overseas subsidiary in home-based currency terms can be severely distorted if there has been a significant foreign exchange movement.

'If initially the exchange rate is given by $1/£ and an American subsidiary is worth $500,000, then the UK parent company will anticipate a balance sheet value of £500,000 for the subsidiary. A depreciation of the US dollar to $2/£ would result in only £250,000 being translated.'

Unless managers believe that the company's share price will fall as a result of showing a translation exposure loss in the company's accounts, translation exposure will not normally be hedged. The company's share price, in an efficient market, should only react to exposure that is likely to have an impact on cash flows.

Make sure you are able to distinguish between the three types of foreign currency risk: transaction, economic and translation.

Expandable text

Why exchange rates fluctuate

Changes in exchange rates result from changes in the demand for and supply of the currency. These changes may occur for a variety of reasons, e.g. due to changes in international trade or capital flows between economies.

Balance of payments

Since currencies are required to finance international trade, changes in trade may lead to changes in exchange rates. In principle:

- demand for imports in the US represents a demand for foreign currency or a supply of dollars

- overseas demand for US exports represents a demand for dollars or a supply of the currency.

Thus a country with a current account deficit where imports exceed exports may expect to see its exchange rate depreciate, since the supply of the currency (imports) will exceed the demand for the currency (exports).

Any factors which are likely to alter the state of the current account of the balance of payments may ultimately affect the exchange rate.

Capital movements between economies

There are also **capital movements between economies**. These transactions are effectively switching bank deposits from one currency to another. These flows are now more important than the volume of trade in goods and services.

Thus supply/demand for a currency may reflect events on the capital account. Several factors may lead to inflows or outflows of capital:

- changes in interest rates: rising (falling) interest rates will attract a capital inflow (outflow) and a demand (supply) for the currency

- inflation: asset holders will not wish to hold financial assets in a currency whose value is falling because of inflation.

These forces which affect the demand and supply of currencies and hence exchange rates have been incorporated into a number of formal models.

3 Purchasing Power Parity Theory (PPPT)

PPPT claims that the rate of exchange between two currencies depends on the relative inflation rates within the respective countries.

PPPT is based on:

'the law of one price'.

In equilibrium, identical goods must cost the same, regardless of the currency in which they are sold.

Expandable text

Illustration – Why exchange rates fluctuate

An item costs $3,000 in the US.

Assume that sterling and the US dollar are at PPPT equilibrium, at the current spot rate of $1.50/£, i.e. the sterling price x current spot rate of $1.50 = dollar price.

The spot rate is the rate at which currency can be exchanged today.

	The US market		The UK market
Cost of item now	$3,000	$1.50	£2,000
Estimated inflation	5%		3%
Cost in one year	$3,150		£2,060

The 'law of one price' states that the item must always cost the same. Therefore in one year:

$3,150 must equal £2,060

and so the expected future spot rate can be calculated:

$3,150/2,060 = $1.5291

Rule: PPPT predicts that the country with the higher inflation will be subject to a depreciation of its currency.

If you need to estimate the expected future spot rates, simply apply the following formula:

$$S_1 = S_0 \times \frac{(1+h_c)}{(1+h_b)}$$

Where:

S_0 = Current spot

S_1 = Expected future spot

h_b = Inflation rate in country for which the spot is quoted (base currency)

h_c = Inflation rate in the other country. (counter currency)

Expandable text

Illustration – Why exchange rates fluctuate

So where inflation in the US is expected to be 5% and in the UK 3%, the future expected spot is:

$$1.50 \times \frac{1.05}{1.03} = \$1.5291$$

Test your understanding 2

The dollar and sterling are currently trading at \$1.72/£.

Inflation in the US is expected to grow at 3% pa, but at 4% pa in the UK.

Predict the future spot rate in a year's time.

PPPT can be used as our best predictor of future spot rates; however it suffers from the following major limitations:

- the future inflation rates are only estimates

- the market is dominated by speculative transactions (98%) as opposed to trade transactions; therefore purchasing power theory breaks down

- government intervention: governments may manage exchange rates, thus defying the forces pressing towards PPPT.

Expandable text

The main function of an exchange rate is to provide a means of translating prices expressed in one currency into another currency. The implication is that the exchange will be determined in some way by the relationship between these prices. This arises from the law of one price.

The law of one price states that in a free market with no barriers to trade and no transport or transactions costs, the competitive process will ensure that there will only be one price for any given good. If price differences occurred they would be removed by arbitrage; entrepreneurs would buy in the low market and resell in the high market. This would eradicate the price difference.

If this law is applied to international transactions, it suggests that exchange rates will always adjust to ensure that only one price exists between countries where there is relatively free trade.

Thus if a typical set of goods cost $1,000 in the USA and the same set cost £500 in the UK, free trade would produce an exchange rate of £1 to $2.

How does this result come about?

Let us suppose that the rate of exchange was $1.5 to £1: the sequence of events would be:

- US purchasers could buy UK goods more cheaply (£500 at $1.5 to £1 is $750).

- There would be a flow of UK exports to the US: this would represent demand for sterling.

- The sterling exchange rate would rise.

- When the exchange rate reached $2 to £1, there would be no extra US demand for UK exports since prices would have been equalised: purchasing power parity would have been established.

The clear prediction of the purchasing power parity model of exchange rate determination is that if a country experiences a faster rate of inflation than its trading partners, it will experience a depreciation in its exchange rate. It follows that if inflation rates can be predicted, so can movements in exchange rates.

In practice the purchasing power parity model has shown some weaknesses and is a poor predictor of short-term changes in exchange rates.

- It ignores the effects of capital movements on the exchange rate.

- Trade and therefore exchange rates will only reflect the prices of goods which enter into international trade and not the general price level since this includes non-tradeables (e.g. inland transport).

- Governments may 'manage' exchange rates, e.g. by interest rate policy.

- It is likely that the purchasing power parity model may be more useful for predicting long-run changes in exchange rates since these are more likely to be determined by the underlying competitiveness of economies, as measured by the model.

4 Interest Rate Parity Theory (IRPT)

The IRPT claims that the difference between the spot and the forward exchange rates is equal to the differential between interest rates available in the two currencies.

The forward rate is a future exchange rate, agreed now, for buying or selling an amount of currency on an agreed future date.

Expandable text

Illustration – Why exchange rates fluctuate

UK investor invests in a one-year US bond with a 9.2% interest rate as this compares well with similar risk UK bonds offering 7.12%. The current spot rate is $1.5/£.

When the investment matures and the dollars are converted into sterling, IRPT states that the investor will have achieved the same return as if the money had been invested in UK government bonds.

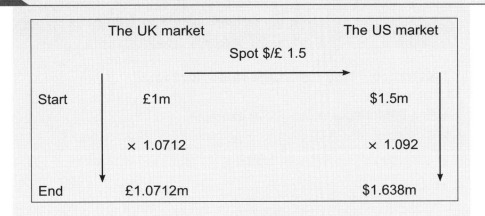

In 1 year, £1.0712 million must equate to $1.638 million so what you gain in extra interest, you lose on an adverse movement in exchange rates.

Any attempt to 'fix' the future exchange rate by locking into an agreed rate now (for example by buying a forward (see chapter 23 for details)), will also fail.

The forward rates moves to bring about interest rate parity amongst different currencies:

$$\frac{\$1.638}{£1.0712} = \$1.5291$$

Rule: IRPT predicts that the country with the higher interest rate will see the forward rate for its currency subject to a depreciation.

If you need to calculate the forward rate in one year's time:

$$F_0 = S_0 \times \frac{(1+i_c)}{(1+i_b)}$$

F_0 = Forward rate

i_b = interest rate for base currency

i_c = interest rate for counter currency

Illustration – Why exchange rates fluctuate

Using the formula in the above example:

$$1.50 \times \frac{1.092}{1.0712} = \$1.5291$$

The IRPT generally holds true in practice. There are no bargain interest rates to be had on loans/deposits in one currency rather than another.

However it suffers from the following limitations:

- government controls on capital markets
- controls on currency trading
- intervention in foreign exchange markets.

Test your understanding 3

A treasurer can borrow in Swiss francs at a rate of 3% pa or in the UK at a rate of 7% pa. The current rate of exchange is 10SF/£.

What is the likely rate of exchange in a year's time?

The interest rate parity model shows that it may be possible to predict exchange rate movements by referring to differences in nominal exchange rates . If the forward exchange rate for sterling against the dollar was no higher than the spot rate but US nominal interest rates were higher, the following would happen:

- UK investors would shift funds to the US in order to secure the higher interest rates, since they would suffer no exchange losses when they converted $ back into £.
- the flow of capital from the UK to the US would raise UK interest rates and force up the spot rate for the US$.

Expandable text

Expectations theory

The expectations theory claims that the current forward rate is an unbiased predictor of the spot rate at that point in the future.

If a trader takes the view that the forward rate is lower than the expected future spot price, there is an incentive to buy forward. The buying pressure on the forward raises the price, until the forward price equals the market consensus view on the expected future spot price.

In practice, it is a poor unbiased predictor – sometimes it is wide of the mark in one direction and sometimes wide of the mark in the other.

The International Fisher Effect

The International Fisher Effect claims that the interest rate differentials between two countries provide an unbiased predictor of future changes in the spot rate of exchange.

The International Fisher Effect assumes that all countries will have the same real interest rate, although nominal or money rates may differ due to expected inflation rates. Thus the interest rate differential between two countries should be equal to the expected inflation differential. Therefore, countries with higher expected inflation rates will have higher nominal interest rates, and vice versa.

In practice interest rate differentials are a poor unbiased predictor of future exchange rates.

Factors other than interest differentials influence exchange rates such as government intervention in foreign exchange markets.

Four-way equivalence

The four theories can be pulled together to show the overall relationship between spot rates, interest rates, inflation rates and the forward and expected future spot rates. As shown above, these relationships can be used to forecast exchange rates.

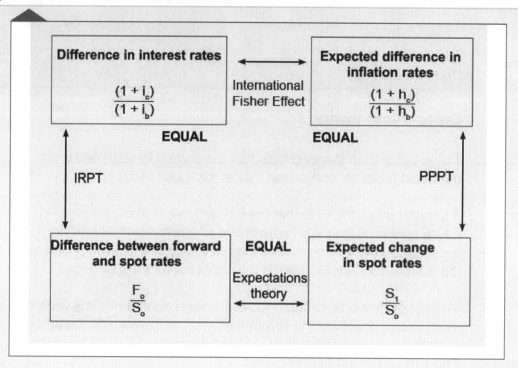

5 Managing foreign currency risk

When currency risk is significant for a company, it should do something to either eliminate it or reduce it.

Taking measures to eliminate or reduce a risk is called:

- hedging the risk or
- hedging the exposure.

Practical approaches

Deal in home currency

Insist all customers pay in your own home currency and pay for all imports in home currency.

This method:

- transfers risk to the other party
- may not be commercially acceptable.

KAPLAN PUBLISHING

Do nothing

In the long run, the company would 'win some, lose some'.

This method:

* works for small occasional transactions
* saves in transaction costs
* is dangerous!

Leading

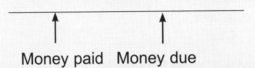

Receipts – If an exporter expects that the currency it is due to receive will depreciate over the next few months it may try to obtain payment immediately.

This may be achieved by offering a discount for immediate payment.

Lagging

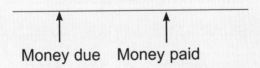

Payments – If an importer expects that the currency it is due to pay will depreciate, it may attempt to delay payment.

This may be achieved by agreement or by exceeding credit terms.

Note: If the importer expects that the currency will in fact appreciate, then it should settle the liability as soon as possible (leading).

NB Strictly this is not hedging – it is speculation – the company only benefits if it correctly anticipates the exchange rate movement!

Matching

When a company has receipts and payments in the same foreign currency due at the same time, it can simply match them against each other. It is then only necessary to deal on the foreign exchange (forex) markets for the unmatched portion of the total transactions.

Suppose that ABC plc has the following receipts and payments in three months time:

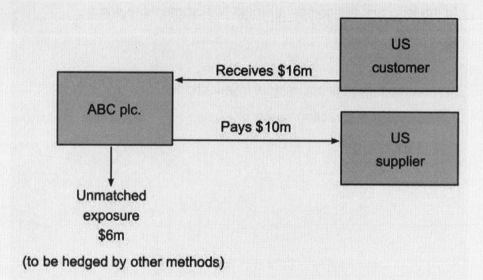

Foreign currency bank accounts

Where a firm has regular receipts and payments in the same currency, it may choose to operate a foreign currency bank account.

This operates as a permanent matching process.

The exposure to exchange risk is limited to the net balance on the account.

Test your understanding 4

Certain organisational and policy adjustments may be made internally by a business for the purpose of minimising the effects of transactions in foreign currencies.

A group of companies controlled from the UK includes subsidiaries in India, Hong Kong and the US. It is forecast that at the end of the current month, intercompany indebtedness will be as follows:

- the Indian subsidiary will be owed 144,381,000 Indian rupees by the Hong Kong subsidiary and will owe the USA subsidiary $1,060,070

- the Hong Kong subsidiary will be owed 14,438,000 Hong Kong dollars by the USA subsidiary and will owe it US$800,000.

It is a function of the central treasury department to net off inter-company balances as far as possible and to issue instructions for settlement of the net balances. For this purpose the relevant exchange rates in terms of £1 are US$1.415; Hong Kong $10.215; Indian rupees 68.10.

(a) **Calculate the net payments to be made in respect of the above balances and state the possible advantages of such netting.**

(b) **Explain the terms 'leading' and 'lagging' in relation to foreign currency settlements and state the circumstances under which this technique might be used.**

(c) **Explain the procedures for matching foreign currency receipts and payments, having regard to the possibility that these might be on different time scales, and state their possible advantages.**

Trading in currencies

The foreign exchange market

The foreign exchange or forex market is an international market in national currencies. It is highly competitive and virtually no difference exists between the prices in one market (e.g. New York) and another (e.g. London).

Bid and offer prices

Banks dealing in foreign currency quote two prices for an exchange rate:

- a lower 'bid' price
- a higher 'offer' price.

For example, a dealer might quote a price for US$/£ of 1.4325 – 1.4330:

- The lower rate, 1.4325, is the rate at which the dealer will sell the variable currency (US$) in exchange for the base currency (sterling).

- The higher rate, 1.4330, is the rate at which the dealer will buy the variable currency (US$) in exchange for the base currency (sterling).

To remember which of the two prices is relevant to any particular foreign exchange (FX) transaction, remember the bank will always trade at the rate that is more favourable to itself.

Expandable text

Illustration – Trading currencies

Suppose that the US$ rate per £ is quoted as 1.4325 – 1.4330.

If a company wants to buy $100,000 in exchange for sterling (so that the bank will be selling dollars):

- If we used the lower rate of 1.4325, the bank would sell them for £69,808

- If we used the higher rate of 1.4330, the bank would sell them for £69,784.

Clearly the bank would be better off selling them at the lower rate

RULE => Bank sells lower.

If a company wants to sell $200,000 in exchange for sterling (so the bank would be buying dollars):

- If we used the lower rate of 1.4325, the bank would buy them for £139,616

- If we used the higher rate of 1.4330, the bank would buy them for £139,567

The bank will make more money buy at the higher rate:

RULE => Bank buys high.

If in doubt, work out which rate most favours the bank or remember the rules:

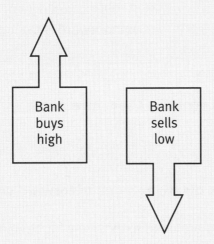

The spot market

The spot market is where you can buy and sell a currency now (immediate delivery), i.e. the spot rate of exchange.

The forward market

The forward market is where you can buy and sell a currency, at a fixed future date for a predetermined rate, i.e. the forward rate of exchange.

Hedging with forwards

Although other forms of hedging are available, forward cover represents the most frequently employed method of hedging.

Expandable text

Illustration – Forward contract

It is now 1 January and Y plc will receive $10 million on 30 April.

It enters into a forward contract to sell this amount on the forward date at a rate of $/£1.60. On 30 April the company is guaranteed £6.25 million.

The risk has been completely removed.

In practice, the forward rate is quoted as a margin on the spot rate. In the exam you will be given the forward rate.

Advantages and disadvantages of forward contracts

Forward contracts are used extensively for hedging currency transaction exposures.

Advantages include:

- flexibility with regard to the amount to be covered
- relatively straightforward both to comprehend and to organise.

Disadvantages include:

contractual commitment that must be completed on the due date

- (option date forward contract can be used if uncertain)
- no opportunity to benefit from favourable movements in exchange rates.

Expandable text

Disadvantages of a forward

It is a contractual commitment which must be completed on the due date.

This means that if a payment from the overseas customer is late, the company receiving the payment and wishing to convert it using its forward contract will have a problem. The existing forward contract must be settled, although the bank will arrange a new forward contract for the new date when the currency cash flow is due.

To help overcome this problem an 'option date' forward contract can be arranged. This is a forward contract that allows the company to settle a forward contract at an agreed fixed rate of exchange, but at any time between two specified dates. If the currency cash flow occurs between these two dates, the forward contract can be settled at the agreed fixed rate.

Inflexible

It eliminates the downside risk of an adverse movement in the spot rate, but also prevents any participation in upside potential of any favourable movement in the spot rate. Whatever happens to the actual exchange rate, the forward contract must be honoured, even if it would be beneficial to exchange currencies at the spot rate prevailing at that time.

A money market hedge

The money markets are markets for wholesale (large-scale) lending and borrowing, or trading in short-term financial instruments. Many companies are able to borrow or deposit funds through their bank in the money markets.

Instead of hedging a currency exposure with a forward contract, a company could use the money markets to lend or borrow, and achieve a similar result.

Since forward exchange rates are derived from spot rates and money market interest rates (see chapter 23), the end result from hedging should be roughly the same by either method.

NB Money market hedges are more complex to set up than the equivalent forward.

Hedging a payment

If you are hedging a future payment:

- buy the present value of the foreign currency amount today at the spot rate:
    - this is, in effect, an immediate payment in sterling
    - and may involve borrowing the funds to pay earlier than the settlement date
- the foreign currency purchased is placed on deposit and accrues interest until the transaction date.
- the deposit is then used to make the foreign currency payment.

Expandable text

Illustration – A money market hedge

Liverpool plc must make a payment of US $450,000 in 3 months' time. The company treasurer has determined the following:

Spot rate $1.7000 – $1.7040

3-months forward $1.6902 – $1.6944

6-months forward $1.6764 – $1.6809

Money market rates: 3-mth Borrowing 3-mth Deposit

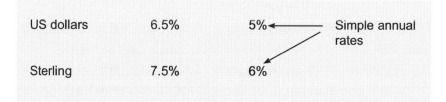

	3-mth Borrowing	3-mth Deposit	
US dollars	6.5%	5%	Simple annual rates
Sterling	7.5%	6%	

Decide whether a forward contract hedge or a money market hedge should be undertaken.

Money market rates vary according to the length of time the funds are borrowed or lent (see chapter 23).

Here the rates quoted apply to a loan or deposit taken out for a 3 month period. However the interest rates are quoted as simple annual interest. In the examination, don't forget to adjust these for the period of the loan or deposit. (See step 1 below.)

Expandable text

Solution

Money market hedge:

(1) Create an equal and opposite asset to match the $ liability. Calculate the amount the company needs to deposit now, so that with interest it will generate $450,000 to make the payment in three months' time.

If annual interest rate for a three-month $ deposit is 5%, then interest for three months is 5 × 3 ÷ 12 = 1.25%. The company will want to put 450,000 ÷ 1.0125 = $444,444 on deposit now, so that it will mature to match the payment in three months' time.

(2) The company needs to purchase the required amount of dollars now, at the spot rate, at a cost of $444,444 ÷ $1.70 = £261,438.

(3) In order to compare the money market hedge (MMH) with a forward contract we assume that the company will borrow this money today and repay it in three months' time, with interest.

If annual interest rate for a three-month £ borrowing is 7.5%, then interest for three months is 7.5 × 3 ÷ 12 = 1.875%. So the company will have to repay £261,438 × 1.01875 = £266,340 in three months' time.

Overall result: Liverpool knows today that it will cost £266,340 to settle the $ liability in three month's time.

	Now		**3 mths**	
MMH				
Payment		3 m rates	($450,000)	**Buy $**
		US deposit rate		
Deposit	$444,444	1.0125 ←	$450,000	
			0	
Buy $ at spot.	1.7000	↕		
Immediate payment	(£261,438)	1.01875 →	= **£266,340**	
		UK borrowing rate		
				Payment
Forward contract:			$450,000/ 1.6902	
			= **£266,241**	√

The cost of a forward contract is marginally cheaper though this is largely due to rounding differences. In practice because of IRPT, the result should be very similar.

Note that:

- as the payment has been made today, all forex risk is eliminated
- the method presupposes the company can borrow funds today.

Test your understanding 6

Bolton, a UK company, must make a payment of US$230,000 in three months' time. The company treasurer has determined the following:

Dollar: Sterling Spot rate $1.8250 – $1.8361.

3-months forward $1.8338 - $1.8452

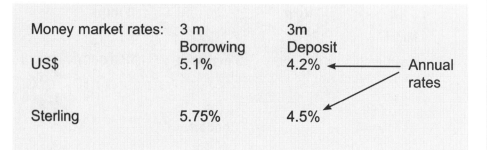

Money market rates:	3 m Borrowing	3m Deposit	
US$	5.1%	4.2%	Annual rates
Sterling	5.75%	4.5%	

Ascertain the cost of the payment using a forward contract hedge and a money market hedge.

Hedging a receipt

If you are hedging a receipt:

- borrow the present value of the foreign currency amount today:
    - sell it at the spot rate
    - this results in an immediate receipt in sterling
    - this can be invested until the date it was due
- the foreign loan accrues interest until the transaction date
- the loan is then repaid with the foreign currency receipt.

Illustration – Managing foreign currency risk

Liverpool plc is now expecting a receipt of US$900,000 in six months' time. The company treasurer has determined the following:

Spot rate $1.7000 – $1.7040.

3-months forward $1.6902 – $1.6944

6-months forward $1.6764 – $1.6809

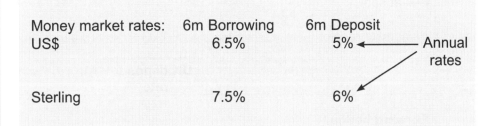

Money market rates:	6m Borrowing	6m Deposit	
US$	6.5%	5%	Annual rates
Sterling	7.5%	6%	

Decide whether a forward contract hedge or a money market hedge should be undertaken.

Money market rates vary according to the length of time the funds are borrowed or lent (see chapter 22).

Here the rates quoted apply to a loan or deposit taken out for a 3 month period. However the interest rates are quoted as simple annual interest. In the examination, don't forget to adjust these for the period of the loan or deposit. (See step 1 below.)

Solution

Money market hedge:

(1) Create a liability to match the receipt: borrow an amount now, ($900,000 ÷ 1.0325 = $871,671) so that with interest, $900,000 is owing in 6 months' time.

(2) Convert the $871,671 borrowed into sterling immediately to remove the exchange risk ($871,671 ÷ 1.7040) and deposit the £511,544.

(3) In 3 months the $ loan is paid off by the $ received from the customer and Liverpool plc realises the £526,890 deposit (£511,544 × 1.03).

Overall result: Liverpool knows today that it will effectively exchange the $900,000 received for £526,890 in 6 months' time.

	Now	6m rate	**6 mths**
Receipt			$900,000 receipt
		US loan rate	
Loan	$871,671	1.0325 →	($900,000)
			0
Sell at spot	1.7040		
Immediate receipt	£511,544	1.03	£526,890
		UK deposit rate →	
Forward hedge:			
	$900,000/1.6809 =		£535,427

The forward hedge is the recommended hedging strategy.

Test your understanding 7

Bolton is now to receive US$400,000 in 3 months' time. The company treasurer has determined the following:

Spot rate $1.8250 – $1.8361

3-months forward 1.8338 - 1.8452

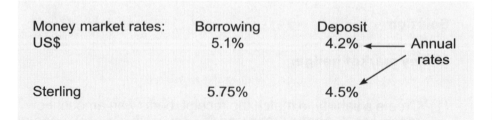

Money market rates: US$	Borrowing 5.1%	Deposit 4.2%	← Annual rates
Sterling	5.75%	4.5%	

Decide whether a forward contract hedge or a money market hedge should be undertaken.

Balance sheet hedging

All the above techniques are used to hedge transaction risk.

Sometimes transaction risk can be brought about by attempts to manage translation risk.

Translation exposure:

*   arises because the financial statements of foreign subsidiaries must be restated in the parent's reporting currency, for the firm to prepare its consolidated financial statements

*   is the potential for an increase or decrease in the parent's net worth and reported income caused by a change in exchange rates since the last transaction.

A balance sheet hedge involves matching the exposed foreign currency assets on the consolidated balance sheet with an equal amount of exposed liabilities, i.e.:

*   a loan denominated in the same currency as the exposed assets and for the same amount is taken out

*   a change in exchange rates will change the value of exposed assets but offset that with an opposite change in liabilities.

This method eliminates the mismatch between net assets and net liabilities denominated in the same currency, but may create transaction exposure.

As a general matter, firms seeking to reduce both types of exposure typically reduce transaction exposure first. They then recalculate translation exposure and decide if any residual translation exposure can be reduced, without creating more transaction exposure.

Foreign currency derivatives

Foreign currency risk can also be managed by using derivatives:

Futures

Futures are like a forward contract in that:

*   the company's position is fixed by the rate of exchange in the futures contract

*   it is a binding contract.

A futures contract differs from a forward contract in the following ways:

- futures are for standardised amounts
- futures can be traded on currency exchanges.

Because each contract is for a standard amount and with a fixed maturity date, they rarely cover the exact foreign currency exposure.

Expandable text

Effectively a future works like a bet. If a company expects a US$ receipt in 3 month's time, it will lose out if the US$ depreciates relative to sterling. Using a futures contract, the company 'bets' that the US$ will depreciate. If it does, the win on the bet cancels out the loss on the transaction. If the US$ strengthens, the gain on the transaction covers the loss on the bet.

Ultimately futures ensure a no win/no loss position.

Currency options

Options are similar to forwards but with one key difference.

They give the right but not the obligation to buy or sell currency at some point in the future at a predetermined rate.

A company can therefore:

- exercise the option if it is in its interests to do so
- let it lapse if:
    - the spot rate is more favourable
    - there is no longer a need to exchange currency.

The option therefore eliminates downside risk but allows participation in the upside.

Options are most useful when there is uncertainty about the timing of the transaction or when exchange rates are very volatile.

KAPLAN PUBLISHING

Options may be:

PUT   **CALL**

Right to sell   Right to buy
currency   currency

The catch:

The additional flexibility comes at a price – a premium must be paid to purchase an option, whether or not it is ever used.

Chapter summary

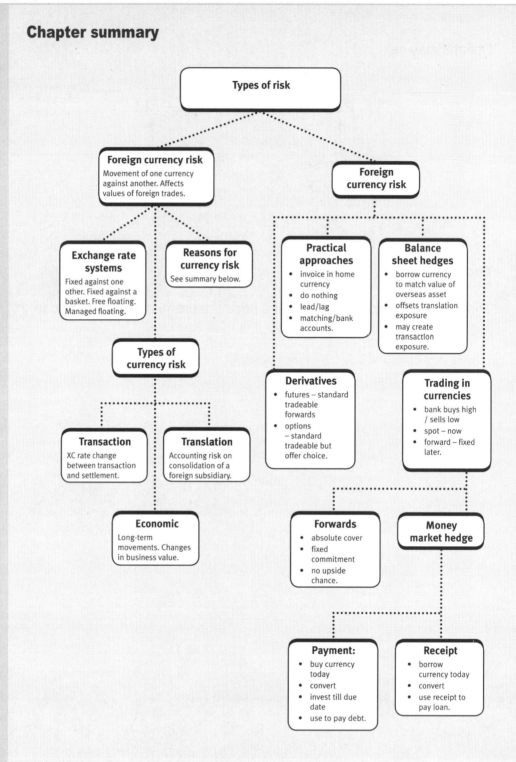

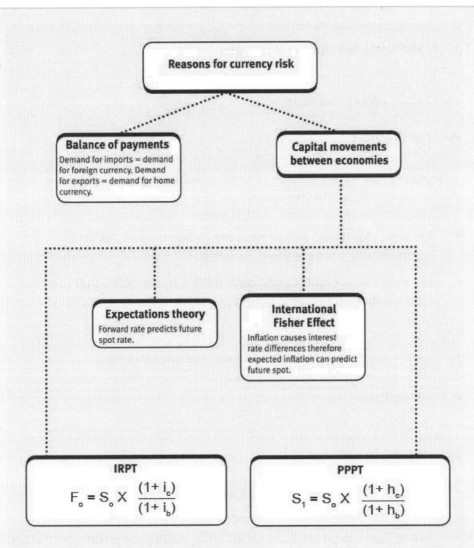

Test your understanding answers

Test your understanding 1

A strong pound

The pound has appreciated – therefore other foreign currencies have depreciated relative to the pound:

- UK exporters: Bad news; receipts in currencies that are depreciating; receive fewer pounds.
- UK importers: Good news; payments in currencies that are depreciating; pay fewer pounds.

Notethe alternative for the UK exporter is to put the price up in the foreign currency, but exports then become uncompetitive.

A weak Euro

The Euro has depreciated – therefore other foreign currencies have appreciated relative to the Euro.

- European exporters: Good news; receipts in currencies that are appreciating; receive more Euros.
- European importers: Bad news – payments in currencies that are appreciating – pay more Euros.

Test your understanding 2

$$1.72 \times \frac{1.03}{1.0} = \$1.7035$$

Test your understanding 3

$$10 \times \frac{1.03}{1.07} = \$9.6262$$

Test your understanding 4

Tutorial note: the best approach is to set up a matrix in a common currency – usually US$ or sterling.

(a) Net payments: advantages and disadvantages of multilateral netting.

Conversion rates are £1 = US$1.415

= Hk$10.215

= IRu68.10

	India £	Hong Kong £	US £
Indian subsidiary owes			749,166
Hong Kong subsidiary owes	2,120,132		565,371
US subsidiary owes		1,413,412	
Indian subsidiary owes £749,166 and is owed	£2,120,132		

Net receipts   £1,370,966

	India £	Hong Kong £	US £
Hong Kong subsidiary owes £2,685,503 and is owed £1,413,412		Net payment	(£1,272,091)
		Net payment	(£98,875)

The central treasury department should issue instructions for the Hong Kong subsidiary to pay the Indian subsidiary £1,272,091 and the US subsidiary to pay the Indian subsidiary £98,875.

Possible advantages

Fewer transactions – less administration

– lower transaction costs.

(b) 'Leading' and 'lagging'

'Leading' and 'lagging' are terms relating to the speed of settlement of debts.

'Leading' refers to an immediate payment or the granting of very short-term credit, whereas 'lagging' refers to the granting (or taking) of long-term credit.

Leading and lagging are a form of speculation. In relation to foreign currency settlements, additional benefits can be obtained by the use of these techniques when currency exchange rates are fluctuating (assuming one can forecast the changes).

If a company is due to make a payment to a supplier in a foreign currency, then 'leading' the liability, i.e. settling as quickly as possible, would be beneficial to the payer if this currency were strengthening against his own. 'Lagging' would be appropriate for the payer if the currency were weakening.

In either case, the supplier's view would be the opposite.

(c) Matching

Matching of foreign currency receipts and payments is common in multi-national enterprises. Assuming a foreign subsidiary has both payments and receipts from a third country, then payments and settlements are made directly by the subsidiary.

For example, a South African subsidiary makes purchases from, and sales to, the US. It may open a currency account into which it receives dollars, and from which it makes payments in dollars, without converting into rand.

Where the timescale is significant, care must be exercised to ensure that large balances are not left idle, or unnecessary and expensive overdrafts incurred.

Possible advantages

Transaction costs are virtually eliminated.

Transaction exposure is eliminated, except for any balancing figure.

Test your understanding 5

The exporter will be selling his dollars to the bank and the bank buys high at 1.4565.

The exporter will therefore receive = 400,000 ÷ 1.4565 = £274,631.

Test your understanding 6

	Now		**3 mths**	
Payment			($230,000)	**Buy $**
		US deposit rate		
Deposit	$227,610	1.0105	$230,000	
		←	0	
Buy $ at spot	1.8250			
Immediate payment	(£124,718)	1.014375 =	**£126,511**	
		→	Payment	
		UK borrowing rate		

Forward market hedge: $230,000/1.8338

                    =   **£125,423**

Test your understanding 7

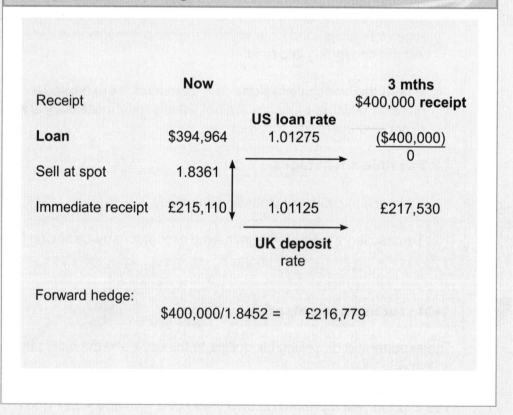

	Now		**3 mths**
Receipt			$400,000 **receipt**
		US loan rate	
Loan	$394,964	1.01275	($400,000)
		→	0
Sell at spot	1.8361		
Immediate receipt	£215,110	1.01125	£217,530
		→	
		UK deposit rate	

Forward hedge:

          $400,000/1.8452 =   £216,779

Interest rate risk

Chapter learning objectives

Upon completion of this chapter you will be able to:

- describe and discuss gap exposure as a form of interest rate risk

- describe and discuss basis risk as a form of interest rate risk

- define the term structure of interest rates

- explain the features of a yield curve

- explain expectations theory and its impact on the yield curve

- explain liquidity preference theory and its impact on the yield curve

- explain market segmentation theory and its impact on the yield curve

- discuss and apply matching and smoothing as a method of interest rate risk management

- discuss and apply asset and liability management as a method of interest rate risk management

- define a forward rate agreement

- use a forward rate agreement as a method of interest rate risk management

- define the main types of interest rate derivatives and explain how they can be used to hedge interest rate risk.

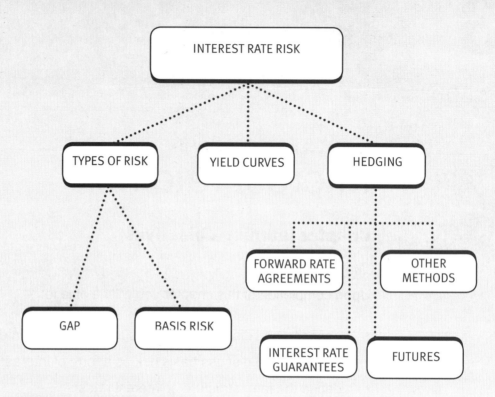

1 Interest rate risk

Financial managers face risk arising from changes in interest rates as well as exchange rates, i.e. a lack of certainty about the amounts or timings of cash payments and receipts. These arise whether or not financial managers trade internationally.

Many companies borrow, and if they do they have to choose between borrowing at a fixed rate of interest (usually by issuing bonds) or borrow at a floating (variable) rate (possibly through bank loans). There is some risk in deciding the balance or mix between floating rate and fixed rate debt. Too much fixed-rate debt creates an exposure to falling long-term interest rates and too much floating-rate debt creates an exposure to a rise in short-term interest rates.

Managers are normally risk-averse, so they will look for techniques to manage and reduce these risks.

Gap/interest rate exposure

Interest rate risk refers to the risk of an adverse movement in interest rates and thus a reduction in the company's net cash flow.

Adverse Interest Rate Movements

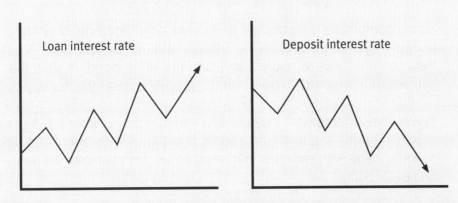

Compared to currency exchange rates, interest rates do not change continually:

* currency exchange rates change throughout the day
* interest rates can be stable for much longer periods

but changes in interest rates can be substantial.

It is the duty of the corporate treasurer to reduce (hedge) the company's exposure to the interest rate risk.

Expandable text

Basis risk

There are a number of ways in which a corporate treasurer can hedge exposure to interest rate risk. One method (discussed further in section 'Interest rate futures' below) is to lock the company into an agreed interest rate by buying **futures.**

However, normally these futures do not completely eliminate interest rate exposure and the remaining exposure is known as basis risk.

Even non-bank companies can have substantial exposures to interest rate risk.

A company might borrow at a variable rate of interest, with interest payable every six months and the amount of the interest charged each time varying according to whether short-term interest rates have risen or fallen since the previous payment.

Some companies borrow by issuing bonds. If a company foresees a future requirement to borrow by issuing bonds, it will have an exposure to interest rate risk until the bonds are eventually issued.

Some companies also budget to receive large amounts of cash, and so budget large temporary cash surpluses that can be invested short-term. Income from those temporary investments will depend on what the interest rate happens to be when the money is available for depositing.

Some investments earn interest at a variable rate of interest (e.g. money in bank deposit accounts) and some short-term investments go up or down in value with changes in interest rates (for example, Treasury bills and other bills).

Some companies hold investments in marketable bonds, either government bonds or corporate bonds. These change in value with movements in long-term interest rates.

Interest rate risk can be significant. For example, suppose that a company wants to borrow $10 million for one year, but does not need the money for another three weeks. It would be expensive to borrow money before it is needed, because there will be an interest cost. On the other hand, a rise in interest rates in the time before the money is actually borrowed could also add to interest costs. For example, a rise of just 0.25% (25 basis points) in the interest rate on a one-year loan of $10 million would cost an extra $25,000 in interest over the course of a year.

2 Why interest rates fluctuate

The yield curve

The **term structure of interest rates** refers to the way in which the yield of a debt security or bond varies according to the term of the security, i.e. to the length of time before the borrowing will be repaid.

The yield curve is an analysis of the relationship between the yields on debt with different periods to maturity.

A yield curve can have any shape, and can fluctuate up and down for different maturities.

There are three main types of yield curve shapes: normal, inverted and flat (or humped):

- normal yield curve – longer maturity bonds have a higher yield compared with shorter-term bonds due to the risks associated with time

- inverted yield curve – the shorter-term yields are higher than the longer-term yields, which can be a sign of upcoming recession

- flat (or humped) yield curve – the shorter- and longer-term yields are very close to each other, which is also a predictor of an economic transition.

The slope of the yield curve is also seen as important: the greater the slope, the greater the gap between short- and long-term rates.

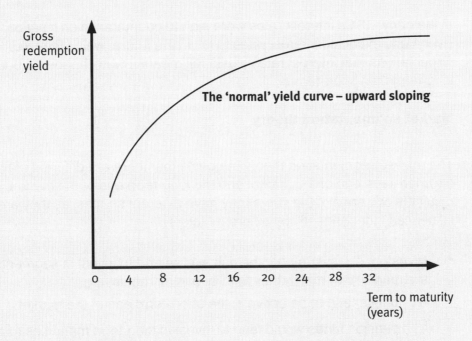

The shape of the yield curve at any point in time is the result of the three following theories acting together:

- liquidity preference theory

- expectations theory

- market segmentation theory.

Liquidity preference theory

Investors have a natural preference for more liquid (shorter maturity) investments. They will need to be compensated if they are deprived of cash for a longer period.

Therefore the longer the maturity period, the higher the yield required leading to an upward sloping curve, assuming that the interest rates were not expected to fall in the future.

Expectations theory

The normal upward sloping yield curve reflects the expectation that inflation levels, and therefore interest rates will increase in the future.

Note: Downward sloping yield curve.

In the early 1990s interest rates were high to counteract high inflation. Everybody expected interest rates to fall in the future, which they did. Expectations that interest rates would fall meant it was cheaper to borrow long-term than short-term.

Market segmentation theory

The market segmentation theory suggests that there are different players in the short-term end of the market and the long-term end of the market. As a result the two ends of the curve may have different shapes, as they are influenced independently by different factors.

- Investors are assumed to be risk averse and to invest in segments of the market that match their liability commitments, e.g.
    - banks tend to be active in the short-term end of the market
    - pension funds would tend to invest in long-term maturities to match the long-term nature of their liabilities.

- The supply and demand forces in various segments of the market in part influence the shape of the yield curve.

If there is an increased supply in the long-term end of the market because the government needs to borrow more, this may cause the price to fall and the yield to rise and may result in an upward sloping yield curve.

The significance of the yield curve

Financial managers should inspect the current shape of the yield curve when deciding on the term of borrowings or deposits, since the curve encapsulates the market's expectations of future movements in interest rates.

For example, a normal upward sloping yield curve suggests that interest rates will rise in the future. The manager may therefore:

- wish to avoid borrowing long-term on variable rates, since the interest charge may increase considerably over the term of the loan

- choose short-term variable rate borrowing or long-term fixed rate instead.

Expandable text

Analysis of term structure is normally carried out by examining risk-free securities such as UK government stocks (gilts). Newspapers such as the Financial Times show the gross redemption yield (i.e. interest yield plus capital gain/loss to maturity) and time to maturity of each gilt on a daily basis.

The return for each instrument is plotted on a graph where the y axis represents the annual return and the x axis represents the instrument's remaining term to maturity. The points plotted on the graph are then joined up to produce a yield curve.

This term structure of interest rates might be shown as a yield curve, as follows.

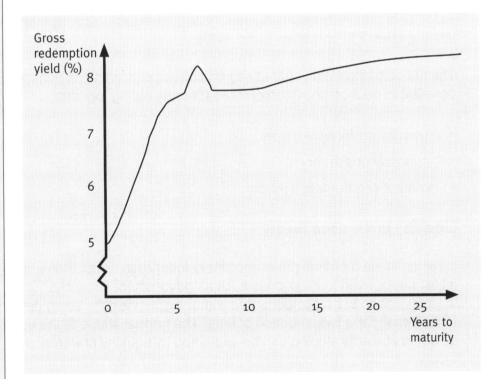

The redemption yield on shorts is less than the redemption yield of mediums and longs, and there is a 'wiggle' on the curve between 5 and 10 years.

A yield curve can have any shape, and can fluctuate up and down for different maturities.

Generally however, yield curves fall into one of three typical patterns.

Normal. A normal yield curve is upward sloping, so that the yield is higher on instruments with a longer-remaining term to maturity. The higher yield compensates the investor for tying up capital for a longer period. Although the yield curve slopes upwards, the gradient of the curve is not steep. A normal yield curve might be expected when interest rates are not expected to change.

Inverse. An inverse yield curve is downward sloping, so that the yield is lower on instruments with a longer-remaining term to maturity. An inverse yield curve might be expected when interest rates are currently high but are expected to fall.

Steep upward-sloping curve. When interest rates are expected to rise, the yield curve is likely to have a steep upward slope, with yields on longer-term investments much higher than the yield on shorter-dated investments.

Yield curves are usually drawn for 'benchmark' investments that are either risk free (government securities) or low risk (such as yields on interest rate swaps). However, they are representative of the slope of the yield curve generally for all other financial instruments, such as inter-bank lending rates and corporate bond yields.

The shape of the yield curve at any particular point in time is generally believed to be a combination of three theories acting together:

- liquidity preference theory
- expectations theory
- market segmentation theory.

Liquidity preference theory

Investors have a natural preference for holding cash rather than other investments, even low-risk ones such as government securities. They therefore need to be compensated with a higher yield for being deprived of their cash for a longer period of time. The normal shape of the curve as being upwards sloping can be explained by liquidity preference theory.

Expectations theory

This theory states that the shape of the yield curve varies according to investors' expectations of future interest rates. A curve that rises steeply from left to right indicates that rates of interest are expected to rise in the future. There is more demand for short-term securities than long-term securities since investors' expectation is that they will be able to secure higher interest rates in the future so there is no point in buying long-term assets now. The price of short-term assets will be bid up, the price of long-term assets will fall, so the yields on short-term and long-term assets will consequently fall and rise.

A falling yield curve (also called an inverted curve, since it represents the opposite of the usual situation) implies that interest rates are expected to fall. For much of the period of sterling's membership of the Exchange Rate Mechanism (ERM), for instance, high short-term rates were maintained to support sterling and the yield curve was often inverted since the market believed that the long-term trend in interest rates should be lower than the high short-term rates.

A flat yield curve indicates expectations that interest rates are not expected to change materially in the future.

Market segmentation theory

Market segmentation theory explains the 'wiggle' seen in the middle of the curve where the short end of the curve meets the long end – it is a natural disturbance where two different curves are joining and the influence of both the short-term factors and the long-term factors are weakest.

Significance of yield curves to financial managers

Expectations of future interest rate movements are monitored closely by the financial markets, and are important for any organisation that intends to borrow heavily or invest heavily in interest-bearing instruments. A company might use a 'forward yield curve' to predict what interest rates might be in the future. For example, if we know the current interest rate on a two-month and a six-month investment, it is possible to work out what the market expects the four-month interest rate to be in two months' time.

A corporate treasurer might analyse a yield curve to decide for how long to borrow. For example, suppose a company wants to borrow $20 million for five years and would prefer to issue bonds at a fixed rate of interest. One option would be to issue bonds with a five-year maturity. Another option might be to borrow short-term for one year, say, in the expectation that interest rates will fall, and then issue a four-year bond. When borrowing large amounts of capital, a small difference in the interest rate can have a significant effect on profit. For example, if a company borrowed $20 million, a difference of just 25 basis points (0.25% or one quarter of one per cent) would mean a difference of $50,000 each year in interest costs. So if the yield curve indicates that interest rates are expected to fall then short-term borrowing for a year, followed by a 4-year bond might be the cheapest option.

Expandable text

(1) **What is gap exposure?**

(2) **What are the three determinants of the yield curve?**

Solution

(1) Gap exposure refers to the risk of an adverse movement in interest rates and thus a reduction in the company's net cash flow.

(2) The shape of the yield curve at any point in time is the result of the three following theories acting together:

    – liquidity preference theory

    – expectations theory

    – market segmentation theory.

3 Hedging interest rate risk

Forward rate agreements (FRAs)

The aim of an FRA is to:

- lock the company into a target interest rate

- hedge both adverse and favourable interest rate movements.

The company enters into a normal loan but independently organises a forward with a bank:

- interest is paid on the loan in the normal way

- if the interest is greater than the agreed forward rate, the bank pays the difference to the company

- if the interest is less than the agreed forward rate, the company pays the difference to the bank.

Expandable text

Illustration – Hedging interest rate risk

Enfield plc's financial projections show an expected cash deficit in two months' time of $8 million, which will last for approximately three months. It is now 1 November 20X4. The treasurer is concerned that interest rates may rise before 1 January 20X5. Protection is required for two months.

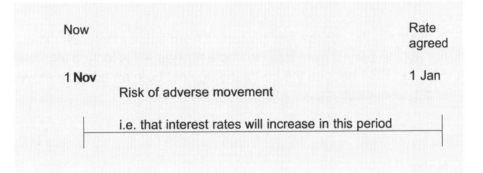

The treasurer can lock into an interest rate today, for a future loan. The company takes out a loan as normal, i.e. the rate it pays is the going market rate at the date the loan is taken out. It will then receive or pay compensation under the separate FRA to return to the locked-in rate.

A 2-5 FRA at 5.00 – 4.70 is agreed.

This means that:

- The agreement starts in 2 months time and ends in 5 months' time.

- The FRA is quoted as simple annual interest rates for borrowing and lending, e.g. 5.00 – 4.70.

- The borrowing rate is always the highest.

Required:

Calculate the interest payable if in two months' time the market rate is:
(a) 7% or (b) 4%.

Expandable text

Solution

The FRA:		7%	4%
interest payable: 8m × .07 × 3/12	=	(140,000)	
8m × .04 × 3/12	=		(80,000)
compensation receivable	=	40,000	
payable	=		(20,000)
Locked into the effective interest rate of 5%.		(100,000)	(100,000)

In this case the company is protected from a rise in interest rates but is not able to benefit from a fall in interest rates – it is locked into a rate of 5% – an FRA hedges the company against both an adverse movement and a favourable movement.

Note:

- The FRA is a totally separate contractual agreement from the loan itself and could be arranged with a completely different bank.
- They can be tailor-made to the company's precise requirements.

- Enables you to hedge for a period of one month up to two years.

- Usually on amounts > £1 million. The daily turnover in FRAs now exceeds £4 billion.

Test your understanding 1

Able Plc needs to borrow £30 million for eight months, starting in three months' time.

A 3-11 FRA at 2.75 – 2.60 is available.

Show the interest payable if the market rate is (a) 4%, (b) 2%.

Interest rate guarantees (IRGs)

An IRG is an option on an FRA. It allows the company a period of time during which it has the option to buy an FRA at a set price.

IRGs, like all options, protect the company from adverse movements and allow it to take advantage of favourable movements.

Decision rules:

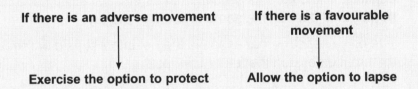

IRGs are more expensive than the FRAs, as one has to pay for the flexibility to be able to take advantage of a favourable movement.

If the company treasurer believes that interest rates will rise:

- he will use an FRA, as it is the cheaper way to hedge against the potential adverse movement.

If the treasurer is unsure which way interest will move:

- he may be willing to use the more expensive IRG to be able to benefit from a potential fall in interest rates.

Interest rate futures

The target of a future is to

*   lock the company into the effective interest rate
*   hedge both adverse and favourable interest rate movements.

Futures can be used to fix the rate on loans and investments. We will look here at loans.

How they work

As with an FRA, a loan is entered into in the normal way. Suitable futures contracts are then entered into.

A futures contract is a promise, e.g.:

*   if you sell a futures contract you have a contract to borrow money – what you are selling is the promise to make interest payments.

However the borrowing is only notional.

*   We close out the position by reversing the original deal, before the real borrowing starts, i.e. before the expiry date of the contract.
*   This means buying futures, if you previously sold them, to close out the position. The contracts cancel each other out, i.e. we have contracts to borrow and deposit the same amount of money.
*   The only cash flow that arises is the net interest paid or received, i.e. the profit or loss on the future contracts.

The price of futures moves inversely to interest rates therefore:

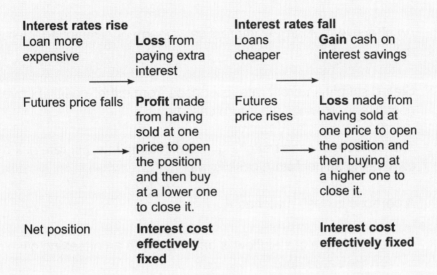

Interest rates rise		Interest rates fall	
Loan more expensive	**Loss** from paying extra interest	Loans cheaper	**Gain** cash on interest savings
Futures price falls	**Profit** made from having sold at one price to open the position and then buy at a lower one to close it.	Futures price rises	**Loss** made from having sold at one price to open the position and then buying at a higher one to close it.
Net position	**Interest cost effectively fixed**		**Interest cost effectively fixed**

Basis risk

The gain or loss on the future may not exactly offset the cash effect of the change in interest rates, i.e. the hedge may be imperfect. This is known as basis risk.

Options

Borrowers may additionally buy options on futures contracts. These allow them to enter into the future if needed, but let it lapse if the market rates move in their favour.

Swaps

An interest rate swap is an agreement whereby the parties agree to swap a floating stream of interest payments for a fixed stream of interest payments and vice versa. There is no exchange of principal.

Swaps can be used to hedge against an adverse movement in interest rates. Swaps may also be sought by firms that desire a type of interest rate structure that another firm can provide less expensively.

Say a company has a $200 million floating loan and the treasurer believes that interest rates are likely to rise over the next five years. He could enter into a five-year swap with a counter-party to swap into a fixed rate of interest for the next five years. From year six onwards, the company will once again pay a floating rate of interest.

Expandable text

Cash flow matching

An effective, but largely impractical, means of eliminating interest rate risk.

Stated simply, interest rate risk arises from either positive (invested) or negative (borrowed) net future cash flows.

The concept of cash matching is to eliminate interest rate risk by eliminating all net future cash flows.

A portfolio is cash matched if :

- every future cash inflow is balanced with an offsetting cash outflow on the same date
- every future cash outflow is balanced with an offsetting cash inflow on the same date.

The net cash flow for every date in the future is then zero, and there is no risk of interest rate exposure.

Whilst clearly not achievable, it does provide a broad goal that businesses can work towards.

Asset and liability management

Problems arise if interest rates are fixed on liabilities for periods that differ from those on offsetting assets.

Suppose a company is earning 6% on an asset supported by a liability on which it is paying 4%. The asset matures in two years while the liability matures in ten.

- In two years, the firm will have to reinvest the proceeds from the asset.
- If interest rates fall, it could end up reinvesting at 3%. For the remaining eight years, it would earn 3% on the new asset while continuing to pay 4% on the original liability.

To avoid this, companies attempt to match the duration of their assets and liabilities.

Interest rate smoothing

Interest rate smoothing is the policy of some central banks to move official interest rates in a sequence of relatively small steps in the same direction, rather than waiting until making a single larger change.

This is usually for the following reasons:

- economic (e.g. to avoid instability and the need for reversals in policy) and
- political (e.g. higher rates are broken to the electorate gently).

Chapter summary

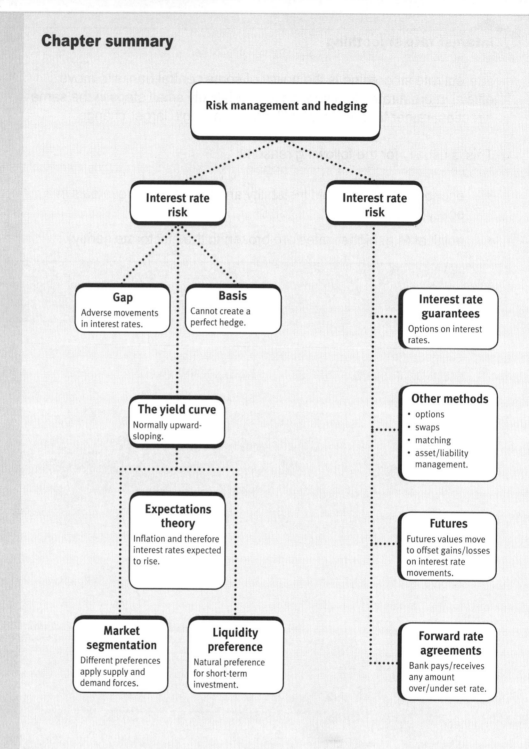

Test your understanding answers

Test your understanding 1

The FRA:		4%	2%
Interest payable: 30m × 0.04 × 8 12	=	(800,000)	
30m × 0.02 × 8/12	=		(400,000)
Compensation receivable	=	250,000	
payable	=		(150,000)
Locked into the effective interest rate of 2.75%.		(550,000)	(550,000)

Questions & Answers

1 Management and the achievement of stakeholder objectives

Stakeholders

Question 1

Private sector companies have multiple stakeholders who are likely to have divergent interests.

Required:

A   Identify five stakeholder groups and briefly discuss their financial and other objectives.

(12 marks)

B   Examine the extent to which good corporate governance procedures can help manage the problems arising from the divergent interests of multiple stakeholder groups in private sector companies.

(13 marks)

(Total: 25 marks)

2 Measuring achievement of corporate objectives

Wide-ranging review

Question 1

The directors of PDQ Inc have commissioned a firm of consultants to conduct a wide-ranging review of the company's public image and market position. Although this is not predominantly a financial review, the consultants need to examine the company's financial performance.

The company has the following summary information for the last five years:

	Year 1 $m	Year 2 $m	Year 3 $m	Year 4 $m	Year 5 $m
Turnover	51.2	58.3	63.9	75.2	78.2
Cost of sales	20.5	22.2	24.3	30.1	30.5
Salaries and wages	15.4	16.8	17.2	15.8	15.2
Other costs	6.1	7.9	9.9	16.3	17.9
Profit before interest and tax	9.2	11.4	12.5	13.0	14.6
Interest	1.5	1.6	1.3	0.3	0.2
Tax	2.5	3.2	3.7	4.2	4.8
Profit after interest and tax	5.2	6.6	7.5	8.5	9.6
Dividends payable	2.1	2.6	3.0	3.4	4.8
Average receivables	10.5	11.7	13.3	14.8	15.2
Average payables	3.8	4.2	5.1	6.7	6.9
Average total assets	41.2	45.2	46.7	63.3	67.1
Shareholders' funds	26.2	30.2	34.7	59.8	64.6
Long-term debt	15.0	15.0	12.0	3.5	2.5
Number of shares in issue (millions)	6.0	6.0	6.0	8.0	8.0
P/E ratio:					
Company	8.0	8.5	9.0	9.2	9.5
Industry	8.5	9.0	9.1	9.0	9.1
Number of employees	1,720	1,750	1,820	1,720	1,690

Notes

(1) Each P/E ratio is the average for the year.

(2) The increased equity in year 4 was partly the result of a share issue which took place at the beginning of the year. Some of the $20m raised was used to reduce debt.

For the past five years, PDQ Inc has stated its objectives as: 'To maximise shareholder wealth whilst recognising the responsibility of the company to its other stakeholders'.

As one of the consultants working on this assignment, you have been asked to assess whether the company has achieved its objectives in the five-year period under review and to discuss the key factors which have determined your assessment.

You are required:

A   to discuss whether the company has met its objectives, based solely on the information available

(15 marks)

B   to comment on what other financial information you would need in order to provide your client with a more accurate assessment.

(10 marks)

(Total:25 marks)

3 Financial and other objectives in not-for-profit organisations

Private and public

Question 1

This question concerns two organisations, one in the private sector and one in the public sector.

Organisation 1

This is a listed company in the electronics industry. Its stated financial objectives are:

*   'to increase earnings per share year-on-year by 10% per annum'
*   'to achieve a 25% per annum return on capital employed'.

This company has an equity market capitalisation of $600 million. It also has a variety of debt instruments trading at a total value of $150 million.

Organisation 2

This organisation is a newly-established purchaser and provider of healthcare services in the public sector. The organisation's legal status is a Trust.

Its total income for the current year will be almost $100 million. The Trust's sole financial objective states simply 'to achieve financial balance during the year'. Its other objectives are concerned with qualitative factors such as 'providing high quality healthcare'.

Required:

Discuss:

I   the reasons for the differences in the financial objectives of the two types of organisation given above

II   the main differences in the risks involved in the achievement of their financial objectives and how these risks might be managed.

        Use the scenario details given above to assist your answer wherever possible.

(Total: 15 marks)

4 Working capital management

Hottubes Co

Question 1:

Hottubes Co is a small company specialising in the supply of high quality amplifier do-it-yourself kits for sale to Hi-Fi enthusiasts. These include superior electronic components, circuit boards and detailed instructions. Promotion is carried out through adverts in electronics and Hi-Fi magazines. The company buys most of its components from a specialist supplier in Hong Kong and the remainder from a few local suppliers.

The CEO (and founder) is very proud of the company's performance and recently made the following comment.

'We have excellent products as seen in the recent rave reviews in a major consumer electronics magazine. Our business has grown rapidly over recent years and we have good profitability. We also have good liquidity with current assets easily covering current liabilities. This is partly due to improved credit control over receivables. However, our Hong Kong supplier demands payment at the end of each month for all items shipped in that month…'

As with many other small businesses, Hottubes uses its bank overdraft to finance working capital and has no other longer term funding. The current overdraft rate is 1.0% per month on the monthly outstanding balance.

Extracts from the management accounts for the last two years are as follows.

31 December

	20X2	20X1
	$000	$000
Sales	1,024	640
Cost of sales	640	400
Other expenses	132	81
Inventories		
Components	300	208
Finished kits	220	96
Trade receivables	320	204
Trade payables	135	104
Other payables	31	30
Corporation tax due	63	40
Purchases for the year	776	490
Bank overdraft	180	100

Requirement

Prepare briefing notes for a meeting with the CEO analysing the company's working capital management and suggesting how Hottubes may improve its working capital position. Include in your answer a calculation of the cash operating cycle and any other calculations you feel are appropriate.

(Total: 15 marks)

5 Working capital management – inventory control

TNG

Question 1

TNG Co expects annual demand for product X to be 255,380 units. Product X has a selling price of $19 per unit and is purchased for $11 per unit from a supplier, MKR Co. TNG places an order for 50,000 units of product X at regular intervals throughout the year. Because the demand for product X is to some degree uncertain, TNG maintains a safety (buffer) inventory of product X which is sufficient to meet demand for 28 working days. The cost of placing an order is $25 and the storage cost for Product X is 10 cents per unit per year.

TNG normally pays trade suppliers after 60 days but MKR has offered a discount of 1% for cash settlement within 20 days.

TNG Co has a short-term cost of debt of 8% and uses a working year consisting of 365 days.

Required:

A Calculate the annual cost of the current ordering policy. Ignore financing costs in this part of the question.

(4 marks)

B Calculate the annual saving if the economic order quantity model is used to determine an optimal ordering policy. Ignore financing costs in this part of the question.

(5 marks)

C Determine whether the discount offered by the supplier is financially acceptable to TNG Co.

(4 marks)

D Critically discuss the limitations of the economic order quantity model as a way of managing inventory.

(4 marks)

E   Discuss the advantages and disadvantages of using just-in-time inventory management methods.

(8 marks)

(Total: 25 marks)

6 Working capital management – accounts receivable and payable

Velm Inc

Question 1:

Velm Inc sells stationery and office supplies on a wholesale basis and has an annual turnover of $4,000,000. The company employs four people in its sales ledger and credit control department at an annual salary of $12,000 each. All sales are on 40 days' credit with no discount for early payment. Irrecoverable debts represent 3% of turnover and Velm plc pays annual interest of 9% on its overdraft. The most recent accounts of the company offer the following financial information:

Velm Inc: Balance Sheet(Statement of financial position) as at 31 December 20X2

	$000	$000
Non-current assets		17,500
Current assets		
Inventory of goods for resale	900	
Receivables	550	
Cash	120	
	———	
		1,570
		———
Total assets		19,070
		———
Equity and liabilities		
Ordinary shares		3,500
Reserves		11,640
		———
		15,140

Non-current liabilities		
12% loan notes due 20X9		2,400
Current liabilities		
Trade payables	330	
Overdraft	1,200	
	———	
		1,530
		———
		19,070
		=====

Velm Inc is considering offering a discount of 1% to customers paying within 14 days, which it believes will reduce irrecoverable debts to 2.4% of turnover. The company also expects that offering a discount for early payment will reduce the average credit period taken by its customers to 26 days. The consequent reduction in the time spent chasing customers where payments are overdue will allow one member of the credit control team to take early retirement. Two -thirds of customers are expected to take advantage of the discount.

Required:

A   Using the information provided, determine whether a discount for early payment of one per cent will lead to an increase in profitability for Velm Inc.

(Total: 5 marks)

7 Working capital management: cash and funding strategies

Thorne

Question 1:

Thorne Co values, advertises and sells residential property on behalf of its customers. The company has been in business for only a short time and is preparing a cash budget for the first four months of 2006. Expected sales of residential properties are as follows.

Month	2005 December	2006 January	2006 February	2006 March	2006 April
Units sold	10	10	15	25	30

The average price of each property is $180,000 and Thorne Co charges a fee of 3% of the value of each property sold. Thorne Co receives 1% in the month of sale and the remaining 2% in the month after sale. The company has nine employees who are paid on a monthly basis. The average salary per employee is $35,000 per year. If more than 20 properties are sold in a given month, each employee is paid in that month a bonus of $140 for each additional property sold.

Variable expenses are incurred at the rate of 0.5% of the value of each property sold and these expenses are paid in the month of sale. Fixed overheads of $4,300 per month are paid in the month in which they arise. Thorne Co pays interest every three months on a loan of $200,000 at a rate of 6% per year. The last interest payment in each year is paid in December.

An outstanding tax liability of $95,800 is due to be paid in April. In the same month Thorne Co intends to dispose of surplus vehicles, with a net book value of $15,000, for $20,000. The cash balance at the start of January 2006 is expected to be a deficit of $40,000.

Required:

A   Prepare a monthly cash budget for the period from January to April 2006. Your budget must clearly indicate each item of income and expenditure, and the opening and closing monthly cash balances.

(10 marks)

KAPLAN PUBLISHING

> B Discuss the factors to be considered by Thorne Co when planning ways to invest any cash surplus forecast by its cash budgets.
>
> **(5 marks)**
>
> C Discuss the advantages and disadvantages to Thorne Co of using overdraft finance to fund any cash shortages forecast by its cash budgets.
>
> **(5 marks)**
>
> D Explain how the Baumol model can be employed to reduce the costs of cash management and discuss whether the Baumol cash management model may be of assistance to Thorne Co for this purpose.
>
> **(5 marks)**
>
> **(Total: 25 marks)**

8 Capital budgeting and basic investment appraisal techniques

Armcliffe

Question 1

Armcliff Inc. is a division of Sherin Inc., which requires each of its divisions to achieve a rate of return on capital employed of at least 10 per cent per annum. For this purpose, capital employed is defined as fixed capital and investment in inventories. This rate of return is also applied as a hurdle rate for new investment projects. Divisions have limited borrowing powers and all capital projects are centrally funded.

The following is an extract from Armcliff's divisional accounts.

Income statement for the year ended 31 December 20X4

	$m
Turnover	120
Cost of sales	(100)
Operating profit	20

Assets employed as at 31 December 20X4

	$m	$m
Non-current assets (net)		75
Current assets (including inventories $25m)	45	
Current liabilities	(32)	
		13
Net capital employed		88

Armcliff's production engineers wish to invest in a new computer-controlled press. The equipment cost is $14 million. The residual value is expected to be $2 million after four years operation, when the equipment will be shipped to a customer in South America.

The new machine is capable of improving the quality of the existing product and also of producing a higher volume. The firm's marketing team is confident of selling the increased volume by extending the credit period. The expected additional sales are as follows.

Year 1	2,000,000 units
Year 2	1,800,000 units
Year 3	1,600,000 units
Year 4	1,600,000 units

Sales volume is expected to fall over time because of emerging competitive pressures. Competition will also necessitate a reduction in price by $0.5 each year from the $5 per unit proposed in the first year. Operating costs are expected to be steady at $1 per unit, and allocation of overheads (none of which are affected by the new project) by the central finance department is set at $0.75 per unit.

Higher production levels will require additional investment in inventories of $0.5 million, which would be held at this level until the final stages of operation of the project. Customers at present settle accounts after 90 days on average.

Required:

A   Determine whether the proposed capital investment is attractive to Armcliff Inc, using the average rate of return on capital method, defined as average profit to average capital employed, ignoring receivables and payables.

   Note. Ignore taxes

(7 marks)

(b)

   I   Suggest three problems which arise with the use of the average return method for appraising new investment.

(6 marks)

   II   In view of the problems associated with the ARR method, why do companies continue to use it in project appraisal?

(3 marks)

C   Briefly discuss the dangers of offering more generous credit, and suggest ways of assessing customers' creditworthiness.

(9 marks)

(Total: 25 marks)

9 Investment appraisal: discounted cash flow techniques

Wotton Inc

Question 1:

Wotton Inc is a small company specialising in the manufacture of high quality machine components using the latest techniques and materials. Sue, the owner, is a keen cyclist and has been considering the possibility of making very strong lightweight sets of bicycle gears out of titanium. Research and development costs of $20,000 have been incurred, which indicate that the cycle parts can be manufactured to the required quality and weight and that a market would exist for the sets of gears.

As an outside consultant you have been asked to appraise the venture, and are supplied with the following information.

(1) Sales are anticipated to be 500 sets per annum for the next five years. Ignoring inflation, the sets should sell for $600 each to enthusiasts.

(2) Advertising costs would be $5,000 in the first year and $1,000 per annum thereafter.

(3) Each set of gears requires 0.5 kg of titanium at $600/kg, 10 hours of skilled labour, 4 hours of unskilled labour and 2 hours in the automated finishing room.

(4) Skilled workers are paid $10 per hour with time and a half for overtime. They are guaranteed 2,000 hours per annum; however, at present the 15 workers are only 90% utilised. No further skilled workers will be recruited. Unskilled workers are paid $7 per hour and are only hired when needed.

(5) The finishing room incurs variable costs of $10 per hour when in use. At present the production of Wotton Inc's existing machine components fully utilises the room, generating contribution of $5 per hour. For the first two years Sue will have to cut back on this production in order to have sufficient capacity to finish the new product. However, in two years' time the finishing room will be expanded at a cost of $2,000 in order that production of the old product can be brought back up to its current levels.

(6) The cycle parts venture would also require the use of an existing machine (net book value = $40,000) which would otherwise be sold for $60,000. The asset is expected to be worthless in five years' time.

(7) Wotton Inc currently absorbs fixed overheads at $6 per direct labour hour.

(8) In the past Sue has used a required return of 20% to assess projects.

Requirements

Write a report to Miss Wotton advising her on whether she should go ahead with the bicycle parts project. Your report should include the following.

A   An evaluation of the project using return on capital employed (ROCE) based on the initial capital employed.

(6 marks)

B   An evaluation of the project based on its net present value (NPV).

(7 marks)

C   An explanation of any figures treated differently in the two calculations above.

(6 marks)

D   Any reservations you have concerning your recommendation.

(6 marks)

Ignore taxation.

(Total: 25 marks)

10 Investment appraisal – further aspects of discounted cash flows (DCF)

Howden plc

Question 1:

A   Explain how inflation affects the rate of return required on an investment project, and the distinction between a real and a nominal (or 'money terms') approach to the evaluation of an investment project under inflation.

(6 marks)

B   Howden plc is contemplating investment in an additional production line to produce its range of compact discs. A market research study, undertaken by a well-known firm of consultants, has revealed scope to sell an additional output of 400,000 units p.a. The study cost $0.1 m but the account has not yet been settled.

The price and cost structure of a typical disc (net of royalties), is as follows:

	$	$
Price per unit	12.00	
Costs per unit of output		
Material cost per unit	1.50	
Direct labour cost per unit	0.50	
Variable overhead cost per unit	0.50	
Fixed overhead cost per unit	1.50	
		(4.00)
Profit		8.00

The fixed overhead represents an apportionment of central administrative and marketing costs. These are expected to rise in total by $500,000 pa as a result of undertaking this project. The production line is expected to operate for five years and require a total cash outlay of $11m, including $0.5m of materials inventories. The equipment will have a residual value of $2m. Because the company is moving towards a JIT inventory management policy, it is expected that this project will involve steadily reducing working capital needs, expected to decline at about 3% pa by volume. The production line will be accommodated in a presently empty building for which an offer of $2m has recently been received from another company. If the building is retained, it is expected that property price inflation will increase its value to $3m after five years.

KAPLAN PUBLISHING

While the precise rates of price and cost inflation are uncertain, economists in Howden's corporate planning department make the following forecasts for the average annual rates of inflation relevant to the project:

Retail Price Index	6% pa
Disc prices	5% pa
Material prices	3% pa
Direct labour wage rates	7% pa
Variable overhead costs	7% pa
Other overhead costs	5% pa

Note: you may ignore taxes and capital allowances in this question.

Required:

Given that Howden's shareholders require a real return of 8.5% for projects of this degree of risk, assess the financial viability of this proposal.

(13 marks)

C   Briefly discuss how inflation may complicate the analysis of business financial decisions.

(6 marks)

(Total: 25 marks)

11 Investment appraisal under uncertainty

Sludgewater plc

Question 1

Sludgewater plc, a furniture manufacturer, has been reported to the anti-pollution authorities on several occasions in recent years, and fined substantial amounts for making excessive toxic discharges into the air. Both the environmental lobby and Sludgewater's shareholders have demanded that it clean up its operations.

If no clean up takes place, Sludgewater estimates that the total fines it would incur over the next three years can be summarised by the following probability distribution (all figures are expressed in present values).

Level of fine	Probability
$1.0m	0.3
$1.8m	0.5
$2.6m	0.2

A firm of environmental consultants has advised that spray painting equipment can be installed at a cost of $4m to virtually eliminate discharges. Unlike fines, expenditure on pollution control equipment is tax-allowable via a 25% writing-down allowance (reducing balance, based on gross expenditure).

The rate of corporation tax is 30%, paid with a one-year delay. The equipment will have no scrap or resale value after its expected three year working life. The equipment can be in place ready for Sludgewater's next financial year.

A European Union grant of 25% of gross expenditure is available, but with payment delayed by a year. The consultant's charge is $200,000 and the new equipment will raise annual production costs by 2% of sales revenue. Current sales are $15 million per annum, and are expected to grow by 5% per annum compound. No change in working capital is envisaged.

Sludgewater applies a discount rate of 10% after tax on investment projects of this nature. All cash inflows and outflows occur at year ends.

Required:

A   Calculate the expected net present value of the investment. Briefly comment on your results.

(15 marks)

B   Write a memorandum to Sludgewater's management in respect of the potential investment taking into account both financial and non-financial criteria.

(10 marks)

(Total: 25 marks)

12 Asset investment decisions and capital rationing

Capital rationing

Question 1:

Basril Inc is reviewing investment proposals that have been submitted by divisional managers. The investment funds of the company are limited to $800,000 in the current year. Details of three possible investments, none of which can be delayed, are given below.

Project 1

An investment of $300,000 in work station assessments. Each assessment would be on an individual employee basis and would lead to savings in labour costs from increased efficiency and from reduced absenteeism due to work-related illness. Savings in labour costs from these assessments in money terms are expected to be as follows:

Year	1	2	3	4	5
Cash flows ($000)	85	90	95	100	95

Project 2

An investment of $450,000 in individual workstations for staff that is expected to reduce administration costs by $140,800 per annum in money terms for the next five years.

Project 3

An investment of $400,000 in new ticket machines. Net cash savings of $120,000 per annum are expected in current price terms and these are expected to increase by 3.6% per annum due to inflation during the five-year life of the machines.

Basril plc has a money cost of capital of 12% and taxation should be ignored.

Required:

A   Determine the best way for Basril plc to invest the available funds and calculate the resultant NPV:

  I   on the assumption that each of the three projects is divisible;

  II   on the assumption that none of the projects are divisible.

(10 marks)

B   Explain how the NPV investment appraisal method is applied in situations where capital is rationed.

(3 marks)

C   Discuss the reasons why capital rationing may arise.

(7 marks)

D   Discuss the meaning of the term 'relevant cash flows' in the context of investment appraisal, giving examples to illustrate your discussion.

(5 marks)

(Total: 25 marks)

13 Sources of finance

QueTirwen plc

Question 1

Tirwen Inc is a medium-sized manufacturing company which is considering a 1 for 5 rights issue at a 15% discount to the current market price of $4.00 per share. Issue costs are expected to be $220,000 and these costs will be paid out of the funds raised. It is proposed that the rights issue funds raised will be used to redeem some of the existing loan notes at par. Financial information relating to Tirwen Inc is as follows:

Current balance sheet(statement of financial position)

	$000	$000
Non-current assets		6,550
Current assets		
Inventory	2,000	
Receivables	1,500	
Cash	300	
	─────	
		3,800

Total assets	10,350
Equity and liabilities	
Ordinary shares (per value 50p)	2,000
Reserves	1,500
	3,500
12% loan notes 2012	4,500
Current liabilities	
Trade creditors	1,100
Overdraft	1,250
	2,350
	10,350

Other information:

Price/earnings ratio of Tirwen Inc:	15.24
Overdraft interest rate:	7%
Corporation tax rate:	30%
Sector advantages: debt/equity ratio (book value):	100%
interest cover:	6 times

Required:

A Ignoring issue costs and any use that may be made of the funds raised by the rights issue, calculate:

   I   the theoretical ex rights price per share;

   II the value of rights per existing share.

(3 marks)

B What alternative actions are open to the owner of 1,000 shares in Tirwen Inc as regards the rights issue? Determine the effect of each of these actions on the wealth of the investor.

(6 marks)

C   Calculate the current earnings per share and the revised earnings per share if the rights issue funds are used to redeem some of the existing loan notes.

(6 marks)

D   Evaluate whether the proposal to redeem some of the loan notes would increase the wealth of the shareholders of Tirwen Inc. Assume that the price/earnings ratio of Tirwen Inc remains constant.

(3 marks)

E   Discuss the reasons why a rights issue could be an attractive source of finance for Tirwen Inc. Your discussion should include an evaluation of the effect of the rights issue on the debt/equity ratio and interest cover.

(7 marks)

(Total: 25 marks)

14 Business valuations

Predator Co

Question 1

The board of directors of Predator Co, a listed company, is considering making an offer to purchase Target Co, a private limited company in the same industry. If Target Co is purchased it is proposed to continue operating the company as a going concern in the same line of business.

Summarised details from the most recent set of financial statements for Predator and Target are shown below:

	Predator Balance sheet as at 31 March		Target Balance sheet as at 31 March	
	$m	$m	$'000	$'000
Freehold property		33		460
Plant & equipment		58		1,310
Inventory	29		330	
Receivables	24		290	
Cash	3		20	
less current liabilities	(31)	25	(518)	122
		116		1,892
Financed by:				
Ordinary shares		35		160
Reserves		43		964
Shareholders' funds		78		1,124
Medium-term bank loans		38		768
		116		**1,892**

Predator Co 50 cents ordinary shares, Target Co, 25 cents ordinary shares.

	Predator Co		Target Co	
Year	PAT	Dividend	PAT	Dividend
	$m	$m	$'000	$'000
T5	14.30	9.01	143	85.0
T4	15.56	9.80	162	93.5
T3	16.93	10.67	151	93.5
T2	18.42	11.60	175	102.8
T1	20.04	12.62	183	113.1

T5 is five years ago and T1 is the most recent year.

Target's shares are owned by a small number of private individuals. Its managing director who receives an annual salary of $120,000 dominates the company. This is $40,000 more than the average salary received by managing directors of similar companies. The managing director would be replaced, if Predator purchases Target.

The freehold property has not been revalued for several years and is believed to have a market value of $800,000.

The balance sheet value of plant and equipment is thought to reflect its replacement cost fairly, but its value if sold is not likely to exceed $800,000. Approximately $55,000 of inventory is obsolete and could only be sold as scrap for $5,000.

The ordinary shares of Predator are currently trading at 430 cents ex-div. A suitable cost of equity for Target has been estimated at 15%.

Both companies are subject to corporation tax at 33%.

Required:

Estimate the value of Target Co using the different methods of valuation and advise the board of Predator as to how much it should offer for Target's shares.

25 marks

15 Market efficiency

Tagna

Question 1

Tagna is a medium-sized company that manufactures luxury goods for several well-known chain stores. In real terms, the company has experienced only a small growth in turnover in recent years, but it has managed to maintain a constant, if low, level of reported profits by careful control of costs. It has paid a constant nominal (money terms) dividend for several years and its managing director has publicly stated that the primary objective of the company is to increase the wealth of shareholders.

Tagna is financed as follows:

	$m
Overdraft	1.0
10 year fixed-interest bank loan	2.0
Share capital and reserves	4.5
	7.5

Tagna has the agreement of its existing shareholders to make a new issue of shares on the stock market but has been informed by its bank that current circumstances are unsuitable. The bank has stated that if new shares were to be issued now they would be significantly under-priced by the stock market, causing Tagna to issue many more shares than necessary in order to raise the amount of finance it requires. The bank recommends that the company waits for at least six months before issuing new shares, by which time it expects the stock market to have become strong-form efficient.

The financial press has reported that it expects the Central Bank to make a substantial increase in interest rate in the near future in response to rapidly increasing consumer demand and a sharp rise in inflation. The financial press has also reported that the rapid increase in consumer demand has been associated with an increase in consumer credit to record levels.

Required:

A   Discuss the meaning and significance of the different forms of market efficiency (weak, semi-strong and strong) and comment on the recommendation of the bank that Tagna waits for six months before issuing new shares on the stock market.

(9 marks)

B   On the assumption that the Central Bank makes a substantial interest rate increase, discuss the possible consequences for Tagna in the following areas:

   I   sales

   II   operating costs, and

   III earnings (profit after tax).

(10 marks)

C   Explain and compare the public sector objective of 'value for money' and the private sector objective of 'maximisation of shareholder wealth'.

(6 marks)

(Total: 25 marks)

16 Foreign exchange risk

Exchange rate systems

Question 1

Discuss the possible foreign exchange risk and economic implications of each of the following types of exchange rate system for multinational companies with subsidiaries located in countries with these systems:

A   a managed floating exchange rate

B   a fixed exchange rate linked to a basket of currencies, and

C   a fixed exchange rate backed by a currency board system.

(Total: 15 marks)

Test your understanding answers

Stakeholders

Answer 1

A   Stakeholders in a company include amongst others: shareholders, directors/managers, lenders, employees, suppliers and customers. These groups are likely to share in the wealth and risk generated by a company in different ways and thus conflicts of interest are likely to exist. Conflicts also exist not just between groups but within stakeholder groups. This might be because sub-groups exist, for example preference shareholders and equity shareholders within the overall category of shareholders.

Alternatively individuals within a stakeholder group might have different preferences (e.g. to risk and return, short term and long term returns). Good corporate governance is partly about the resolution of such conflicts. Financial and other objectives of stakeholder groups may be identified as follows:

Shareholders

Shareholders are normally assumed to be interested in wealth maximisation. This, however, involves consideration of potential return and risk. For a listed company, this can be viewed in terms of the changes in the share price and other market-based ratios using share price (e.g. price/earnings ratio, dividend yield, earnings yield).

Where a company is not listed, financial objectives need to be set in terms of other financial measures, such as return on capital employed, earnings per share, gearing, growth, profit margin, asset utilisation, and market share. Many other measures also exist which may collectively capture the objectives of return and risk.

Shareholders may have other objectives for the company and these can be identified in terms of the interests of other stakeholder groups. Thus, shareholders as a group may be interested in profit maximisation; they may also be interested in the welfare of their employees, or the environmental impact of the company's operations.

Directors and managers

While executive directors and managers should attempt to promote and balance the interests of shareholders and other stakeholder groups, it has been argued that they also promote their own individual interests and should be seen as a separate stakeholder group.

This problem arises from the divorce between ownership and control. The behaviour of managers cannot be fully observed by the shareholders, giving them the capacity to take decisions which are consistent with their own reward structures and risk preferences. Directors may therefore be interested in their own remuneration package. They may also be interested in building empires, exercising greater control, or positioning themselves for their next promotion. Non-financial objectives of managers are sometimes inconsistent with what the financial objectives of the company ought to be.

Lenders

Lenders are concerned to receive payment of interest and eventually re-payment of the capital at maturity. Unlike the ordinary shareholders, they do not share in the upside (profitability) of successful organisational strategies. They are therefore likely to be more risk averse than shareholders, with an emphasis on financial objectives that promote liquidity and solvency with low risk (e.g. low gearing, high interest cover, security, strong cash flow).

Employees

The primary interests of employees are their salary/wage and their security of employment. To an extent there is a direct conflict between employees and shareholders as wages are a cost to the company and income to employees.

Performance-related pay based on financial or other quantitative objectives may, however, go some way toward drawing the divergent interests together.

Suppliers and customers

Suppliers and customers are external stakeholders with their own set of objectives (profit for the supplier and, possibly, customer satisfaction with the good or service from the customer) that, within a portfolio of businesses, are only partly dependent on the company in question. Nevertheless it is important to consider and measure the relationship in term of financial objectives relating to quality, lead times, volume of business, price and a range of other variables in considering any organisational strategy.

B Corporate governance is the system by which organisations are directed and controlled.

Where the power to direct and control an organisation is given, a duty of accountability exists to those who have devolved that power. Part of that duty of accountability is discharged by disclosure of both performance in the annual report and accounts and also the governance procedures themselves.

Corporate governance codes are usually voluntary, and operate on a comply or explain basis. Thus, any requirements are to disclose governance procedures in relation to best practice, rather than comply with best practice, and to explain/justify any divergence from best practice.

The decision-making powers in a company rest mainly with the board of directors. Much of corporate governance regulation has therefore focused on governance principles and best practice relating to this stakeholder group. The principles and guidelines in the UK Combined Code, for example, are aimed largely at trying to ensure that the directors act responsibly and in the interests of the other stakeholder groups, particularly the shareholders, rather than themselves. Ideally, the interests of directors and other stakeholders should be aligned and consistent with each other.

Some companies, such as those in the UK, have a unitary board structure, with one board consisting of both executive and non-executive directors. This contrasts with the two-tier board structure in Germany for instance where there is more independence between the two groups of directors. In a two-tier structure, non-executives on a supervisory board and executive directors on a management board which reports to the supervisory board.

Typical corporate governance proposals (such as those written into the UK Combined Code) include the following:

(1) Independence of the board with no covert financial reward

(2) Adequate quality and quantity of non-executive directors to act as a counterbalance to the power of executive directors.

(3) Remuneration committee controlled by non-executives, to decide the remuneration of the executive directors.

(4) Appointments committee consisting of non-executives, to recommend new appointments to the board.

(5) Audit committee consisting of non-executives, with responsibilities for audit matters, including negotiating the fee of the external auditors.

(6) Separation of the roles of chairman and chief executive to prevent concentration of power in one person.

(7) Full disclosure of all forms of director remuneration including shares and share options.

(8) Better communication between the board of directors and the shareholders, particularly institutional investors.

(9) Greater prominence for risk management, which is specified as a particular board responsibility.

Overall, the visibility given by corporate governance procedures goes some way toward discharging the directors' duty of accountability to stakeholders and makes more transparent the underlying incentive systems of directors.

Wide-ranging review

Answer 1

A   The company states its objectives as 'to maximise shareholder wealth whilst recognising the responsibility of the company to its other stakeholders.' Since we are only given financial information in the question, we can only assess whether the company has met its objectives with respect to its shareholders and other financial stakeholders (suppliers, customers, employees, loan creditors and the government) and not to its non-financial stakeholders (journalists, the public, etc).

Consider first the shareholders.

	Year 1	Year 2	Year 3	Year 4	Year 5
Market capitalisation ($m)	41.6	56.1	67.5	78.2	91.2
(Profit after tax × P/E ratio)					
Earnings per share (cents)	87c	110c	125c	106c	120c
(Profit after tax × number of shares)					
Dividends per share (cents)	35c	43c	50c	43c	60c
(Total dividends × number of shares)					

The share issue of $20m at the start of year 4 seems to have disturbed the favourable trends in earnings and dividends per share for that year. However the overall pattern looks very satisfactory over the 5 year period; the company has succeeded in increasing shareholder wealth as it hoped.

By year 5 the share price stands at $91.2m/8m = $11.40 per share compared with only $41.6m/6m = $6.93 in year 1.

The other financial stakeholders can see their shares in the company's results as follows:

	Year 1 $m	Year 2 $m	Year 3 $m	Year 4 $m	Year 5 $m
Employees Wages and salaries	15.4	16.8	17.2	15.8	15.2
Loan creditors Interest	1.5	1.6	1.3	0.3	0.2
Government Tax	2.5	3.2	3.7	4.2	4.8
Shareholders Dividends	2.1	2.6	3.0	3.4	4.8

We can see that payments to employees fell substantially after year 3, together with the absolute number of employees. The average wages per employee has fallen since year 2, suggesting that the mix of employees is shifting towards less-skilled workers which could bring problems in the future.

	Year 1	Year 2	Year 3	Year 4	Year 5
Average wages per employee ($)	8,950	9,600	9,450	9,190	9,000

The loan creditors have received less interest payments in years 4 and 5, but this arises purely because of the reduction in long-term debt made possible by the rights issue at the start of year 4.

Conclusion

It appears that individual employees have received less of the financial benefits accruing to the company than the shareholders. While the average wages per employee has fallen over the last four years (suggesting perhaps that certain senior employees have been made redundant), dividends per share have risen substantially over the same period.

It is not possible to judge, purely from the information available, whether the company has or has not met its objectives. The additional information that would be helpful is discussed below.

B   Other financial information which would be needed to assess more accurately whether the company has met its objectives includes the following:

–   What investment possibilities were rejected by management? The analysis above seemed to show that shareholders did well over the period, but was their return maximised, i.e. the best possible? To decide this it would be necessary to assess the alternative courses of action that were rejected during the course of the year; if any of these would have been more profitable than what was actually decided, then the shareholders' return was not the maximum possible.

–   How did securities markets in general fare over the period? A shareholder should view his investment in shares in the company in the light of other returns available on similarly risked securities in the market. If better returns were available elsewhere at no more risk then the rational risk averse investor should dispose of their shares.

–   What was the inflation rate over the period? Growth in money amounts of dividends and earnings might look less impressive if the trend is deflated by the inflation rate and only real increases are examined.

–   Details of the company's workforce. Why has the payroll cost reduced in the last two years, by cutting wage rates or by losing high-paid employees? If there has been a formal programme of rationalisation and redundancies, an assessment of future prospects would be valuable.

–   Volatility of share prices. We are given an average P/E ratio for each year, but how volatile has this and the share price been during each year? Companies should seek to reduce volatility by keeping markets informed so that analysts appreciate what the management are trying to do. This should support the share price.

–   Amounts spent on environmental and social issues. A progressive company in today's business environment recognises its responsibilities to society on top of its other duties. Projects to ensure the minimum of pollution and support of local communities will serve to discharge these responsibilities.

–   Amounts spent on employee communications and staff welfare would similarly support the good reputation of the company.

Private and public

Answer 1

A Introduction

There has been a convergence in the objectives of public and private sector organisations.

- Private sector organisations increasingly need to take notice of the views of a wider group of stakeholders in addition to shareholders.

- On the other side, the public sector has increasingly adopted management and financial practices based upon private sector models and there has been an increased focus on the need for accountability.

It is still the case, however, that private sector companies have as a central responsibility the need to maximise shareholder wealth.

EPS in the private sector

- EPS and growth in EPS has been used by private sector organisations as a measure of success and EPS growth can be compared with other organisations.

- Growth in EPS is seen as an important means of assessing company performance both by the market and by shareholders.

- However, organisational decisions need to be based upon a broader set of criteria.

- EPS is not appropriate to the public sector where there is more attention on issues such as economy, efficiency and effectiveness and obtaining value for money.

Returns and investment

- Private sector organisations will need to set targets in terms of the return on capital employed in order to ensure that the needs of shareholders are met. The latter will expect a return which adequately compensates them for the risks which they are taking.

- Public sector organisations may set targets in terms of a required return on capital but ultimately other factors are more important in assessing their success and the acquisition of resources may be more closely linked to political issues than purely financial ones.

- Most private sector organisations will use investment decision criteria based upon investment appraisal, calculating NPV's. The cost of capital for public sector organisations is effectively fixed by the Government. It is unlikely to be risk adjusted and any public sector evaluation may take into consideration social costs and benefits. Taxation will be of less significance in a public sector appraisal.

- While private sector companies can freely borrow funds in the marketplace, subject to the normal market judgements of their ability to repay and use the money effectively, public sector organisations normally work within a cash limited budget within a single financial year. This sometimes means that there are difficulties in adequately funding long term investments as there is a pre-occupation with staying within short term financial limits.

Risk management

There is a difference between the Private and Public sectors in terms of the management of risk.

- Private sector organisations generally have to compete for customers and ensure that they charge a price which covers cost, generates a profit, but is nevertheless competitive with other suppliers. The main risk they face is a loss of customer demand.

- Public sector services are often provided free of charge to the user. Some areas of the public sector (especially health) have the problem of managing capacity to meet demand and this can lead to prioritisation and effectively rationing, with waiting lists as a consequence. Other areas of the public sector may need to have contingency plans for sudden changes in state funding, which will impact upon financial viability. The public sector may thus face risks of both excess demand and reduced funding because of demand changes or changes in political priorities.

Managing risk in the private sector may therefore entail:

– meeting the needs of customers and of stakeholders

– undertaking market research to get a better understanding of customers and markets

– taking steps to assess and manage risks via insurance, hedging of foreign exchange and interest rate risks.

Managing risks in the public sector may therefore entail:

– monitoring of economy, efficiency and effectiveness and value for money

– using internal markets to purchase services and establish 'fair' transfer prices

– using private sector funds where appropriate to give longer term investment horizons.

Hottubes Co

Answer 1

Tutorial note: detailed discussions of receivables, payables and inventories policies are covered in later chapters. However, you should still be able to use some common sense to comment on the reasonableness of Hottubes' figures, especially given the description of its products, customers, suppliers and market.

Briefing Notes

(1) **Introduction – the profitability v liquidity trade-off**

  – Sales have grown 60% over the last year, reflecting increasing customer awareness of a quality product.

  – However, the overdraft has increased by $80,000 suggesting that there may be problems with working capital management.

  – Has growth been pursued at the expense of liquidity?

  – Over-trading is common in small companies with high growth.

(2) **Overview – Liquidity ratios**

  – Current ratio is 2.05 and growing. This is >1 and, viewed in isolation, suggests that there are few short term liquidity problems (as indicated by the CEO).

  – However, the quick ratio is only 0.78. This is <1 suggesting potential problems.

  – In particular the company would struggle to repay its overdraft should the bank recall the facility for any reason.

  – The current ratio appears healthy only because of the very high levels of inventory.

(3) **Overview – The cash operating cycle**

  – The operating cycle has increased from 282 to 317 days and seems excessively high at over ten months.

  – This means that more funds are tied up in working capital and is a concern, given the high growth rates of Hottubes.

  – New business will result in increased cash outflows with resulting increased inflows delayed a further ten months. This is likely to result in the overdraft increasing in the short term.

(4) Specific issues – Receivables

–   Credit control does appear to have improved as receivables days has fallen from 116 to 114 days.

–   However, this still seems excessively high given that most customers are individual enthusiasts and not major corporations.

–   Given the specialist nature of the product would it be possible to insist on payment up front before kits are despatched? It is unlikely that such a policy would lose sales. There is no reason for the firm to offer credit.

–   Note: even halving receivables would free up $160,000 cash – this would reduce the overdraft significantly.

(5) Specific issues – Inventories

–   Hottubes is holding over 4 months' worth of kits and the figure seems to be rising.

–   It is difficult to justify why such high kit inventory levels are being held. Presumably the production period is quite short (components simply need to be placed in boxes) and, in any case, customers will probably be happy to wait for kits should there be production delays.

–   The holding period of components has fallen but, as with kits, seems excessive. The time period could be justified if certain components are rare and difficult to source but there is no suggestion that the Hong Kong supplier could not send additional components at short notice if the need arose (e.g. by airmail?)

(6) Specific issues – Payables

–   Hottubes is currently taking two months to pay suppliers. This seems high given the Hong Kong supplier's insistence that goods are paid for in the month they are shipped.

–   While delaying payment is good for Hottubes' liquidity, there is a danger that the Hong Kong supplier will respond through some or all of the following:

  –   Price rises.

  –   Refusing to supply.

  –   Refusing to allow further credit.

  –   Sending Hottubes lower grade components.

–   It appears that Hottubes is dependent on the supplier for its competitive advantage and would thus be advised to ensure this relationship does not deteriorate due to late payment.

(7) Specific issues - Overdraft

- Hottubes is dependent on its overdraft for financing. Unless working capital policies change, the overdraft looks set to increase.

- The firm should do detailed cash flow forecasts to identify how large it will grow, to ensure that any limits are not breached.

- The possibility of consolidating part of the overdraft into a loan should also be considered.

Appendix – Key Figures

	20X2	20X1
Receivables credit period	114	116
Components holding period	141	155
Finished kits holding period	125	88
Trade payables period	(63)	(77)
Length of operating cycle	317	282
Current ratio(840/409 and 508/274)	2.67	2.49
Quick ratio(320/409 and 204/274)	1.02	1

TNG

Answer 1

A   TNG has a current order size of 50,000 units.

Average number of orders per year = demand/order size = 255,380/50,000 = 5.11 orders.

Annual ordering cost = 5.11 × 25 = $127.75

Buffer inventory held = 255,380 × 28/365 = 19,591 units.

Average inventory held = 19,591 + (50,000/2) = 44,591 units.

Annual holding cost = 44,591 × 0.1 = $4,459.10.

Annual cost of current ordering policy = 4,459.10 + 127.75 = $4,587.

B   We need to calculate the economic order quantity:

EOQ = ((2 × 255,380 × 25)/0.1)0.5 = 11,300 units.

Average number of orders per year = 255,380/11,300 = 22.6 orders.

Annual ordering cost = 22.6 × 25 = $565.00.

Average inventory held = 19,591 + (11,300/2) = 25,241 units.

Annual holding cost = 25,241 × 0.1 = $2,524.10.

Annual cost of EOQ ordering policy = 2,524.10 + 565.00 = $3,089.

Saving compared to current policy = 4,587 − 3,089 = $1,498.

C   Annual credit purchases = 255,380 × 11 = $2,809,180.

Current payables = 2,809,180 × 60/365 = $461,783.

Payables if discount is taken = 2,809,180 × 20/365 = $153,928.

Reduction in payables = 461,783 − 153,928 = $307,855.

Finance cost increase = 307,855 × 0.08 = $24,628.

Discount gained = 2,809,180 × 0.01 = $28,09.

Net benefit of taking discount = 28,092 – 24,628 = $3,464.

The discount is financially acceptable.

An alternative approach is to calculate the annual percentage benefit of the discount.

This can be done on a simple interest basis: $(1/(100 – 1)) \times (365/40)$ = 9.2%.

Alternatively, the equivalent annual rate can be calculated: $(100/(100 – 1))^{365/40} – 1 = 9.6\%$.

Both methods indicate that the annual percentage benefit is greater than the current cost of short-term debt (8%) of TNG and hence can be recommended on financial grounds.

D   The economic order quantity (EOQ) model is based on a cost function for holding inventories which has two terms: holding costs and ordering costs. With the EOQ, the total cost of having inventory is minimised when holding cost is equal to ordering cost. The EOQ model assumes certain knowledge of the variables on which it depends and for this reason is called a deterministic model. Demand for inventory, holding cost per unit per year and order cost are assumed to be certain and constant for the period under consideration. In practice, demand is likely to be variable or irregular and costs will not remain constant. The EOQ model also ignores the cost of running out of inventory (stockouts). This has caused some to suggest that the EOQ model has little to recommend it as a practical model for the management of inventory.

The model was developed on the basis of zero lead time and no buffer inventory, but these are not difficulties that prevent the practical application of the EOQ model. As our earlier analysis has shown, the EOQ model can be used in circumstances where buffer inventory exists and provided that lead time is known with certainty it can be ignored.

The EOQ model also serves a useful purpose in directing attention towards the costs that arise from holding inventory. If these costs can be reduced, working capital tied up in inventory can be reduced and overall profitability can be increased.

If uncertainty exists in terms of demand or lead time, a more complex inventory management model using probabilities (a stochastic model) such as the Miller-Orr model can be used. This model calculates control limits that give guidance as to when an order should be placed.

E   Just-in-time (JIT) inventory management methods seek to eliminate any waste that arises in the manufacturing process as a result of using inventory. JIT purchasing methods apply the JIT principle to deliveries of material from suppliers. With JIT production methods, inventory levels of raw materials, work-in-progress and finished goods are reduced to a minimum or eliminated altogether by improved work-flow planning and closer relationships with suppliers.

Advantages

•   JIT inventory management methods seek to eliminate waste at all stages of the manufacturing process by minimising or eliminating stock, defects, breakdowns and production delays. This is achieved by improved workflow planning, an emphasis on quality control and firm contracts between buyer and supplier.

•   One advantage of JIT inventory management methods is a stronger relationship between buyer and supplier. This offers security to the supplier, who benefits from regular orders, continuing future business and more certain production planning. The buyer benefits from lower inventory holding costs, lower investment in inventory and work in progress, and the transfer of inventory management problems to the supplier. The buyer may also benefit from bulk purchase discounts or lower purchase costs.

•   The emphasis on quality control in the production process reduces scrap, reworking and set-up costs, while improved production design can reduce or even eliminate unnecessary material movements. The result is a smooth flow of material and work through the production system, with no queues or idle time.

Disadvantages

•   A JIT system may not run as smoothly in practice as theory may predict, since there may be little room for manoeuvre in the event of unforeseen delays. There is little room for error, for example, on delivery times.

•   The buyer is also dependent on the supplier for maintaining the quality of delivered materials and components. If delivered quality is not up to the required standard, expensive downtime or a production standstill may arise, although the buyer can protect against this eventuality by including guarantees and penalties in to the supplier's contract. If the supplier increases prices, the buyer may find that it is not easy to find an alternative supplier who is able, at short notice, to meet his needs.

Velm Inc

Answer 1

A The benefits of the proposed policy change are as follows.

Trade terms are 40 days, but customers are taking 365 × 550,000/4 million = 50 days.

Current level of receivables = $550,000.

Cost of 1% discount = 0.01 × 4m × 2/3 = $26,667.

Proposed level of receivables = (4,000,000 – 26,667) × (26/365) = $283,032.

Reduction in receivables = 550,000 – 283,032 = $266,968.

Receivables appear to be financed by the overdraft at an annual rate of 9%.

		$
Reduction in financing cost	$266,968 × 9%	24,027
Reduction of 0.6% in bad debts	0.6% × $4 million	24,000
Salary saving from early retirement		12,000
Total benefits		60,027
Cost of 1% discount (see above)		(26,667)
Net benefit of discount		33,360

A discount for early payment of one per cent will therefore lead to an increase in profitability for Velm Inc.

Thorne

Answer 1

A   Cash Budget for Thorne Co:

	January $	February $	March $	April $
Receipts				
Cash fees	18,000	27,000	45,000	54,000
Credit fees	36,000	36,000	54,000	90,000
Sale of assets				20,000
Total receipts	54,000	63,000	99,000	164,000
Payments				
Salaries	26,250	26,250	26,250	26,250
Bonus			6,300	12,600
Expenses	9,000	13,500	22,500	27,000
Fixed overheads	4,300	4,300	4,300	4,300
Taxation				95,800
Interest			3,000	
Total payments	39,550	44,050	62,350	165,950
Net cash flow	14,450	18,950	36,650	(1,950)
Opening balance	(40,000)	(25,550)	(6,600)	30,050
Closing balance	(25,550)	(6,600)	30,050	28,100

Workings

Month	December	January	February	March	April
Units sold	10	10	15	25	30
Sales value ($000)	1,800	1,800	2,700	4,500	5,400
Cash fees at 1% ($)	18,000	18,000	27,000	45,000	54,000
Credit fees at 2% ($)	36,000	36,000	54,000	90,000	108,000
Variable costs at 0·5% ($)		9,000	13,500	22,500	27,000

Monthly salary cost = (35,000 × 9)/12 = $26,250

Bonus for March = (25 – 20) × 140 × 9 = $6,300 Bonus for April = (30 – 20) × 140 × 9 = $12,600.

B   The number of properties sold each month indicates that Thorne Co experiences seasonal trends in its business. There is an indication that property sales are at a low level in winter and increase as spring approaches. A proportion of any cash surplus is therefore likely to be short-term in nature, since some cash will be required when sales are at a low level. Even though net cash flow is forecast to be positive in the January, the month with the lowest level of property sales, the negative opening cash balance indicates that there may be months prior to December when sales are even lower.

Short-term cash surpluses should be invested with no risk of capital loss. This limitation means that appropriate investments include treasury bills, short-dated gilts, public authority bonds, certificates of deposit and bank deposits. When choosing between these instruments Thorne Co will consider the length of time the surplus is available for, the size of the surplus (some instruments have minimum investment levels), the yield offered, the risk associated with each instrument, and any penalties for early withdrawal. A small company like Thorne Co, with an annual turnover slightly in excess of $1m per year, is likely to find bank deposits the most convenient method for investing short-term cash surpluses.

The company must also consider how to invest longer-term surpluses. As a new company Thorne Co is likely to want to invest surplus funds in expanding its business, but as a small company it is likely to find few sources of funds other than bank debt and retained earnings. There is therefore a need to guard against capital loss when investing cash that is intended to fund expansion at a later date. As the retail property market is highly competitive, investment opportunities must be selected with care and retained earnings must be invested on a short- to medium-term basis until an appropriate investment opportunity can be found.

C   In two of the four months of the cash budget Thorne Co has a cash deficit, with the highest cash deficit being the opening balance of $40,000. This cash deficit, which has occurred even though the company has a loan of $200,000, is likely to be financed by an overdraft. An advantage of an overdraft is that it is a flexible source of finance, since it can be used as and when required, provided that the overdraft limit is not exceeded. In addition, Thorne Co will only have to pay interest on the amount of the overdraft facility used, with the interest being charged at a variable rate linked to bank base rate. In contrast, interest is paid on the full $200,000 of the company's bank loan whether the money is used or not. The interest rate on the overdraft is likely to be lower than that on long-term debt.

A disadvantage of an overdraft is that it is repayable on demand, although in practice notice is given of the intention to withdraw the facility. The interest payment may also increase, since the company is exposed to the risk of an interest rates increase. Banks usually ask for some form of security, such as a floating charge on the company's assets or a personal guarantee from a company's owners, in order to reduce the risk associated with their lending.

D   The Baumol model is derived from the EOQ model and can be applied in situations where there is a constant demand for cash or cash disbursements. Regular transfers are made from interest-bearing short-term investments or cash deposits into a current account. The Baumol model considers the annual demand for cash (D), the cost of each cash transfer (C), and the interest difference between the rate paid on short-term investments (r_1) and the rate paid on a current account (r_2), in order to calculate the optimum amount of funds to transfer (F). The model is as follows.

$$F = ((2 \times D \times C)/(r_1 - r_2))^{0.5}$$

By optimising the amount of funds to transfer, the Baumol model minimises the opportunity cost of holding cash in the current account, thereby reducing the costs of cash management.

However, the Baumol model is unlikely to be of assistance to Thorne Co because of the assumptions underlying its formulation. Constant annual demand for cash is assumed, whereas its cash budget suggests that Thorne Co has a varying need for cash. The model assumes that each interest rate and the cost of each cash transfer are constant and known with certainty. In reality interest rates and transactions costs are not constant and interest rates, in particular, can change frequently. A cash management model which can accommodate a variable demand for cash, such as the Miller-Orr model, may be more suited to the needs of the company.

Armcliffe

Answer 1

A Current ROCE

$$= \frac{\text{Operating profit}}{\text{Capital employed}} = \frac{\text{Operating profit}}{\text{(Non-current assets + inventories)}} = \frac{20}{(75 + 25)} = 20\%$$

Sales

		$000
Year 1	2m × $5	10,000
Year 2	1.8m × $4.50	8,100
Year 3	1.6m × $4.00	6,400
Year 4	1.6m × $3.50	5,600
Operating costs @ $1/unit (2m + 1.8m + 1.6m + 1.6m) × $1		(7,000)
Fixed costs @ $0.75/unit (2m + 1.8m + 1.6m + 1.6m) × $0.75		(5,250)
Depreciation ($14m − $2m)		(12,000)
		5,850
Project life		4 years
Average profit per year		$1,462,500

Capital employed

Initial	$= \dfrac{\$14m + \$0.5m}{\text{Non-current assets + inventories}}$	= $14.5m
Closing	= $2m + $0.5m	= $2.5m
Average	= ($14.5m + $2.5m)/2	$8.5m
ROCE	$= \dfrac{\$1,462,500}{\$8,500,000}$	= 17.2%

There is here a conflict between Armcliff Inc and Sherin Inc

From Sherin's point of view, the project should be accepted in that it achieves the 10 per cent hurdle required for the ROCE of new projects.

However, Armcliff Inc will not want the project because, although it passes the 10 per cent hurdle, its ROCE of 17.2 per cent is lower than the current 20 per cent and therefore the overall average will fall.

B.

I   Problems of ARR

– ARR is based on accounting profits and is therefore vulnerable to accounting standards. Profit is a subjective concept and cannot be said to be absolute but only 'true and fair'.

– More than one definition of ARR exists and it is therefore important that the exact definition used is highlighted to avoid misrepresentation.

– The ARR can improve over time as the asset base is depreciated. More importantly in later years of a project's life we are comparing current profits (with many years of inflation) with a historical cost base.

II   Why is it used?

– ARR is a familiar concept to users of financial statements. The figures needed are available in published accounts and are easily calculated.

– ARR is very common in practice.

– As a result, managers appraise projects with ARR because it is common in practice and also because shareholders will often calculate the ARR of the company as a whole.

C **The dangers of Armcliff Inc extending credit are as follows.**

- **Risk of default** – older debts are more difficult to pursue as paperwork becomes mislaid etc. There is also the difficulty that any problems may not be identified until much later than currently may be the case.

- **Opportunity cost** – capital tied up in debtors cannot be employed elsewhere.

- **Administration** – the older debts will also require more administration effort.

- Assessing credit worthiness

- **References** – these may be taken up from bankers and trade references. New customers are likely, however to provide bad referees.

- **Credit reports** – agencies like Dun & Bradstreet can provide up-to-date credit reports on any UK company.

- **Analysis of published accounts** – ratio analysis of financial statements can prove useful. However the data will be historical and potentially out-of-date.

- **Trade journals** – these can often give insight into a given industry and information can be gleaned from significant events such as expansion plans or redundancy announcements.

- **Word of mouth** – it is likely that sales representatives within the industry are knowledgeable about a given company's financial health.

- Even if no information can be gleaned from any research, this does not rule out trading with a new customer. Safeguards must be put into place initially such as a 'cash on delivery' policy.

Wotton Inc

Answer 1

	REPORT
To	Miss Sue Wotton, Managing Director, Wotton Inc
From	A Consultant
Date	30 June 20X7
Re	Proposed expansion into the manufacture of bicycle parts ('Bicycle Project')

Introduction

We have appraised the Bicycle Project by calculating its return on capital employed ('ROCE') and its net present value ('NPV') using figures supplied by yourself.

Recommendation

Despite the project ROCE of 17% (see Appendix 1) being less than your usual required return of 20%, we recommend that you do accept the project, since it gives a positive NPV of $211,700 (see Appendix II).

The differences between these two approaches are detailed below, together with reservations we hold concerning the project.

Differences between the two approaches used.

The main difference is that ROCE looks at accounting revenues and expenses whereas NPV uses only relevant incremental cash flows, i.e. it shows the real benefit of undertaking the project as opposed to not undertaking it.

In particular:

- NPV ignores the development costs of $20,000, since they have already been incurred (they are sunk) and are not affected by the decision.

- ROCE includes the full 1,000 hours per annum of skilled labour required to make the sets. The NPV approach recognises that 600 hours spare capacity exist, so only 400 extra hours are paid for.

- The NPV approach recognises that in the first two years the true cost of using the coating room is not only the $10/hour variable cost but also the contribution lost of $5/hour, giving a total cost of $15/hour.

- The NPV approach recognises that the $2,000 cost of expanding the coating room would not be incurred were it not for the new product and therefore includes this cost. ROCE ignores this cost as it would be allocated to the old product.

- Depreciation and amortisation are not cash flows, so are not to be included in the NPV calculation.

- The fixed overheads will be incurred whether or not the project is undertaken, so are not to be included in the NPV calculation.

- ROCE brings in the asset transferred at its existing book value, whereas the NPV approach recognises that the true cost of undertaking the project is the "opportunity" cost of the sale of proceeds forgone.

Reservations

Subject to the reliability of the estimates supplied, the project does appear to be worthwhile. However, we do suggest that the following factors are considered before the decision is finalised.

- Presumably the 20% required return is a reflection of the cost of Wotton Inc's finance and of the risk associated with the company's existing business. Given the increase risk of branching out into a completely new market, a higher return may be required.

- The likely effects of inflation on both the selling price and costs need to be considered.

- Given that the high price is linked to the improved performance of the sets, the sales estimate is very dependent upon even better, lighter sets not coming to the market for five years. This may be too optimistic and a shorter lifetime may be more realistic.

- An advertising budget of $5,000 seems rather low if it is to generate sales of $300,000 in the first year.

- It is difficult to estimate whether spare capacity for skilled labour would still exist in the future. Presumably workers would be laid off if the project were not undertaken, in which case redundancy costs, etc would have to be included.

- Metal prices can be very volatile and it is unlikely that the price of $600/kg will remain constant for the duration of the project.

Appendix 1: ROCE

Initial capital employed

	$
Asset transferred at NBV	40,000
Development costs	20,000
	60,000

Accounting return

		$000
Total sales	(5 × 500 units × $600)	1,500
Materials	(5 × 500 units × $300)	(750)
Skilled labour	(5 × 300 units × 10 hrs × $10)	
	(5 × 200 units × 10 hrs × $15)	(300)
Unskilled labour	(5 × 500 units × 4 hrs × $7)	(70)
Variable overheads	(5 × 500 units × 2 hrs × $10)	(50)
		330
Depreciation of asset		(40)
Amortisation of development costs		(20)
Advertising (5,000) + (4 × 1,000)		(9)
Fixed overheads		(210)
(5 × 500 units × 14 hrs × $6)		
Total project profit		51

$$\text{Therefore Average return} = \frac{\$51,000}{5 \text{ years}} = \$10,200 \text{ pa}$$

$$\text{ROCE} = \frac{10,200}{60,000} \times 100\% = 17\% < \text{required return of } 20\% \text{ -therefore: Reject}$$

Appendix II: NPV

$000	t_0	t_1	t_2	t_3	t_4	t_5
Sales		300	300	300	300	300
Advertising		(5)	(1)	(1)	(1)	(1)
Materials		(150)	(150)	(150)	(150)	(150)
Skilled labour**		(30)	(30)	(30)	(30)	(30)
Unskilled labour		(14)	(14)	(14)	(14)	(14)
Finishing time		(15)	(15)	(10)	(10)	(10)
Machine cost	(60)					
Expansion of finishing room			(2)			
Net relevant cash flow	(60)	86	88	95	95	95
Discount factor@20%	1	0.833	0.694	0.579	0.482	0.402
Present value	(60)	71.6	61.1	55.0	45.8	38.2

NPV = $211,700 > 0 therefore Accept

** Spare capacity = 15 × 2,000 × 10% = 3,000 hours pa

Therefore: Relevant cost = 2,000 hours pa @ Overtime rates of $15/hour = $30,000 pa

Howden plc

Answer 1

Key answer tips

In part (a) the answer implies that it is possible to determine a 'real' rate of return which can then be adjusted in the light of estimated future rates of inflation. The most likely method of calculating a company's required rate of return will actually produce a 'money cost of capital'. To produce a 'real' cost of capital requires some tinkering with this initial calculation.

In part (b) a clear lay out will greatly assist both you and the marker. With projects of short time span, up to, say, five years, a horizontal tabulation is generally best. Where various annuities in real terms are inflating at different rates the best approach is to split them into single year flows and inflate each separately.

Note that in (c), the consideration is not limited to investment decisions – take care to read the requirements carefully.

A   Investors invest capital in companies expecting a reward for both the delay in waiting for their returns (time value of money) and also for the risks to which they expose their capital (risk premium). In addition, if prices in general are rising, shareholders require compensation for the erosion due to inflation in the real value of their capital.

   For example, suppose that in the absence of inflation, shareholders require a company to offer a return of 10%. The need to cover price inflation of, say, 5% will raise the overall required return to about 15%. If people in general expect a particular rate of inflation, the structure of interest rates in the capital market will adjust to incorporate these inflationary expectations. This is known as the 'Fisher effect'.

   More precisely, the relationship between the real required return (r) and the nominal or money rate of return (i), i.e. the rate which includes an allowance for inflation, is given by: $(1 + r) \times (1 + h) = (1 + i)$, where h is the expected rate of price inflation.

It is essential when evaluating an investment project under inflation that future expected price level changes are treated in a consistent way. Companies may correctly allow for inflation in two ways each of which computes the real value of an investment project:

I   Inflate the future expected cash flows at the expected rate of inflation (allowing for inflation rates specific to the project), and discount these cash flows at a discount rate of at i. This is the fully-inflated rate or 'money terms' approach.

II   Strip out the inflation element from the market-determined rate and apply the resulting real rate of return, r, to the stream of project cash flows expressed in today's or constant prices. This is the 'real terms' approach.

B   First, the relevant set-up cost needs identification. The offer of $2m for the building, if rejected, represents an opportunity lost, although this appears to be compensated by its predicted eventual resale value of $3m.

The cost of the market research study has to be met irrespective of the decision to proceed with the project or not and is thus not relevant.

Secondly, incremental costs and revenues are identified. All other items are avoidable except the element of apportioned overhead, leaving the incremental overhead alone to include in the evaluation.

Thirdly, all items of incremental cash flow, including this additional overhead, must be adjusted for their respective rates of inflation. Because (with the exception of labour and variable overhead) the inflation rates differ, a disaggregated approach is required.

The appropriate discount rate is given by:

$(1 + h) \times (1 + r) - 1 = i$

$= (1.06) \times (1.085) - 1$

$= 15\%$

Assuming that the inflated costs and prices apply from and including the first year of operation, the cash-flow profile is as follows:

Cash flow profile	Year					
Item	0	1	2	3	4	5
	$m	$m	$m	$m	$m	$m
Equipment	(10.50)					2.00
Forgone sale of buildings	(2.00)					
Residual value of building						3.00
Working capital*	(0.50)					0.50
Revenue		5.04	5.29	5.56	5.83	6.13
Materials		(0.62)	(0.64)	(0.66)	(0.68)	(0.70)
Labour and variable overhead		(0.43)	(0.46)	(0.49)	(0.52)	(0.56)
Relevant fixed overhead	–	(0.53)	(0.55)	(0.58)	(0.61)	(0.64)
Net cash flows	(13.00)	3.46	3.64	3.83	4.02	9.73
Discount factor at 15%	1.000	0.870	0.756	0.658	0.572	0.497
Present value	(13.00)	3.01	2.75	2.52	2.30	4.84

NPV = +$2.42m, i.e. positive, therefore, the project appears to be acceptable.

However, the financial viability of the project depends quite heavily on the estimate of the residual value of the building and equipment.

*Note: The working capital cash recovery towards the end of the project is approximately equal to the initial investment in inventory, because the rate of material cost inflation tends to cancel out the JIT-induced reduction in volume, leading to roughly constant stock-holding in value terms throughout most of the project life-span.

C   Inflation adds an extra element of uncertainty into forecasting future cash flows, because it becomes more difficult to estimate what future prices and costs will be. This extra uncertainty means that financial evaluations will be less reliable.

In addition to the problems offered for investment appraisal such as forecasting the various rates of inflation relevant to the project, inflation poses a wider range of difficulties in a variety of business decision areas.

Inflation may pose a problem for businesses if it distorts the signals transmitted by the market. In the absence of inflation, the price system should translate the shifting patterns of consumer demand into price signals to which producers respond in order to plan current and future output levels. If demand for a product rises, the higher price indicates the desirability of switching existing production capacity to producing the goods or of laying down new capacity.

Under inflation, however, the producer may lose confidence that the correct signals are being transmitted, especially if the prices of goods and services inflate at different rates. He may thus be inclined to delay undertaking new investment. This applies particularly if price rises are unexpected and erratic.

Equally, it becomes more difficult to evaluate the performance of whole businesses and individual segments when prices are inflating. A poor operating performance may be masked by price inflation, especially if the price of the product sold is increasing at a rate faster than prices in general or if operating costs are inflating more slowly. The rate of return on capital achieved by a business is most usefully expressed in real terms by removing the effect on profits of generally rising prices (or better still, the effect of company-specific inflation). The capital base of the company should also be expressed in meaningful terms. A poor profit result may translate into a high ROI if the capital base is measured in historic terms. Unless these sorts of adjustment are made, inflation hinders the attempt to measure company performance on a consistent basis and thus can cloud the judgement of providers of capital in seeking out the most profitable areas for investment.

Sludgewater plc

Answer 1

A   The expected present value of the fines is equal to:

EV = (0.3 × $1.0m) + (0.5 × $1.8m) + (0.2 × $2.6m) = $0.3m + $0.9m + $0.52m = $1.72 million.

Calculation of the net present value of the investment requires computation of the capital cost plus incremental production costs as set out in the following table:

Year	0	1	2	3	4
	$m	$m	$m	$m	$m
Equipment purchase	(4.0)				
European Union grant (25% of cost)		1.000			
Increased production costs		(0.315)	(0.331)	(0.347)	
Tax saving at 30%			0.095	0.099	0.104
Tax saving on WDA (see note 3 below)		0.300	0.225	0.169	0.506
Net cash flow	(4.0)	0.985	(0.011)	(0.079)	0.610
Discount factor at 10%	1.000	0.909	0.826	0.751	0.683
Present value of cash flow	(4.0)	0.895	(0.009)	(0.059)	0.417
Net Present Value = ($2.756m)					

Notes:

(1) The consultant's charge has already been incurred and (as a committed cost) is therefore irrelevant to the current decision. The consultant's charge has already been incurred, and as a committed or sunk cost, it is not relevant to the current decision.

(2) Increased production costs

Year	Sales	Extra production costs (2%)
	$m	$m
1	15.750	0.315
2	16.538	0.331
3	17.364	0.347

(3) Writing down allowances:

Year	Written down value	Writing down allowance (25%)	Tax saved (one year in arrears, at 30%)
0	4.00	1.000	0.300
1	3.00	0.750	0.225
2	2.25	0.563	0.169
3	1.687 (balance)	0.506	

The negative NPV on the investment in spray painting equipment exceeds the present value of the fines which Sludgewater might expect to pay. It therefore seems that the project is not viable in financial terms, and it would be cheaper to risk payment of the fines. However, the company must accept that to do so might risk incurring the wrath of both shareholders and the environmental lobby.

B   Memorandum

To: Sludgewater Board

From: Accountant

Subject: Air pollution

On purely non-financial criteria, it can be argued that our company has a moral and community responsibility to install anti-pollution equipment as long as the cost of installation does not jeopardise the long-term survival of the company.

However, the figures attached suggest that the project is not wealth-creating for Sludgewater's shareholders, because the value of the expected saving in fines ($1.72 million) is below the expected cost of the project ($2.756 million). The difficulty is that this conclusion is dependent on the current size of the fines payable, and if they were to rise substantially, then the optimal choice (in financial terms) might change. The difference between the expected value of the fines and the cost of the project is currently just over $1 million. This means that the fines would need to rise by nearly 60% (1/1.72 × 100) before the project becomes financially worthwhile. Changes in the size of the fines would be very difficult to predict as it is a political issue. However, since the company is a persistent offender, and the green lobby is becoming more influential, it is not unreasonable to anticipate that the fines will rise in the future as a result of political pressure.

It would be advisable, from a public relations perspective, for the Board to consider alternative and perhaps less expensive anti-pollution measures. It is also possible that the market for this company's products might increase if it is perceived to be more environmentally friendly, and if customers are sensitive to this. It is even possible that the company's share price might benefit from managers of 'ethical' investment funds deciding to include Sludgewater shares in their portfolio.

In addition, the company needs to think about its long-term strategic objectives, and its stance on anti-pollution systems in relation to these objectives. The market positioning of the company over the longer term is likely to be affected by decisions made in the short term, and so even if not investing in the project makes short-term financial sense, it may be more attractive from a long-term viewpoint. It is also possible that technological and legal circumstances will change over time, and such changes need to be anticipated in current decisions.

Capital rationing

Answer 1

Key answer points

You need to start your answer in part (a) by calculating the NPV of each project. Having calculated the NPVs, you can (1) work out an NPV per unit of limiting factor (per $1 invested) to answer the question assuming that projects are divisible, and (2) compare the feasible combinations of projects if they are not divisible, within the constraints imposed by limited capital to invest.

Unless you are aware of 'hard' and 'soft' capital rationing, you might struggle to provide a complete answer to part (c).

It is worth noting that although parts (b) and (d) should be straightforward, you need to make your points clearly and briefly.

A (i)

Analysis of projects assuming they are divisible

		Project 1		Project 3	
	Discount factor at 12%	Cash flow	PV	Cash flow	PV
		$	$	$	$
Initial investment	1.000	(300,000)	(300,000)	(400,000)	(400,000)
Year 1	0.893	85,000	75,905	124,320	111,018
Year 2	0.797	90,000	71,730	128,795	102,650
Year 3	0.712	95,000	67,640	133,432	95,004
Year 4	0.636	100,000	63,600	138,236	87,918
Year 5	0.567	95,000	53,865	143,212	81,201
PV of savings			332,740		477,791
NPV			32,740		77,791
Profitability index			332,740 /300,000 = 1.11		477,791 /400,000 = 1.19

		Project 2	
	Discount factor at 12%	Cash flow	PV
		$	$
Initial investment	1.000	(450,000)	(450,000)
Annual cash flows, years 1 – 5	3.605	140,800	507,584
Net present value			57,584
Profitability index		507,584 /450,000	= 1.13

Order of preference (in order of profitability index) = Project 3 then Project 2 then Project 1.

Project	Profitability index	Ranking	Investment	NPV
			$	$
3	1.19	1st	400,000	77,791
2	1.13	2nd	400,000	51,186 (= 57,584 x 400/450)
			800,000	128,977

(ii)

Analysis of projects assuming they are indivisible

If the projects are assumed to be indivisible, the total NPV of combinations of projects must be considered.

Projects	Investment	NPV
	$	$
1 and 2	750,000	90,324 $(32,740 + 57,584)
1 and 3	700,000	110,531 $(32,740 + 77,791)
2 and 3	850,000	not feasible, too much investment

The optimum combination is now projects 1 and 3.

B The NPV decision rule requires that a company invest in all projects that have a positive net present value. This assumes that sufficient funds are available for all incremental projects, which is only true in a perfect capital market. When insufficient funds are available, that is when capital is rationed, projects cannot be selected by ranking by absolute NPV. Choosing a project with a large NPV may mean not choosing smaller projects that, in combination, give a higher NPV. Instead, if projects are divisible, they can be ranked using the profitability index in order make the optimum selection. If projects are not divisible, different combinations of available projects must be evaluated to select the combination with the highest NPV.

C The NPV decision rule, to accept all projects with a positive net present value, requires the existence of a perfect capital market where access to funds for capital investment is not restricted. In practice, companies are likely to find that funds available for capital investment are restricted or rationed.

Hard capital rationing is the term applied when the restrictions on raising funds are due to causes external to the company. For example, potential providers of debt finance may refuse to provide further funding because they regard a company as too risky. This may be in terms of financial risk, for example if the company's gearing is too high or its interest cover is too low, or in terms of business risk if they see the company's business prospects as poor or its operating cash flows as too variable. In practice, large established companies seeking long-term finance for capital investment are usually able to find it, but small and medium-sized enterprises will find raising such funds more difficult.

Soft capital rationing refers to restrictions on the availability of funds that arise within a company and are imposed by managers. There are several reasons why managers might restrict available funds for capital investment. Managers may prefer slower organic growth to a sudden increase in size arising from accepting several large investment projects. This reason might apply in a family-owned business that wishes to avoid hiring new managers. Managers may wish to avoid raising further equity finance if this will dilute the control of existing shareholders. Managers may wish to avoid issuing new debt if their expectations of future economic conditions are such as to suggest that an increased commitment to fixed interest payments would be unwise.

One of the main reasons suggested for soft capital rationing is that managers wish to create an internal market for investment funds. It is suggested that requiring investment projects to compete for funds means that weaker or marginal projects, with only a small chance of success, are avoided. This allows a company to focus on more robust investment projects where the chance of success is higher. This cause of soft capital rationing can be seen as a way of reducing the risk and uncertainty associated with investment projects, as it leads to accepting projects with greater margins of safety.

D When undertaking the appraisal of an investment project, it is essential that only relevant cash flows are included in the analysis. If non-relevant cash flows are included, the result of the appraisal will be misleading and incorrect decisions will be made. A relevant cash flow is a differential (incremental) cash flow, one that changes as a direct result of an investment decision.

If current fixed production overheads are expected to increase, for example, the additional fixed production overheads are a relevant cost and should be included in the investment appraisal. Existing fixed production overheads should not be included.

A new cash flow arising as the result of an investment decision is a relevant cash flow. For example, the purchase of raw materials for a new production process and the net cash flows arising from the production process are both relevant cash flows.

The incremental tax effects arising from an investment decision are also relevant cash flows, providing that a company is in a tax-paying position. Direct labour costs, for example, are an allowable deduction in calculating taxable profit and so give rise to tax benefits: tax liabilities arising on incremental taxable profits are also a relevant cash flow.

One area where caution is required is interest payments on new debt used to finance an investment project. They are a differential cash flow and hence relevant, but the effect of the cost of the debt is incorporated into the discount rate used to determine the net present value. Interest payments should not therefore be included as a cash flow in an investment appraisal.

Market research undertaken to determine whether a new product will sell is often undertaken prior to the investment decision on whether to proceed with production of the new product. This is an example of a sunk cost. These are costs already incurred as a result of past decisions, and so are not relevant cash flows.

QueTirwen plc

Answer 1

A   Rights issue price = 4.00 × 0.85 = $3.40.

    I   Theoretical ex rights price = ((5 × 4.00) + 3.40)/6 = $3.90.

    II   Value of rights per existing share = (3.90 – 3.40)/5 = 10c.

B   Value of 1,200 shares after rights issue = 1,200 × 3.90 = $4,680.

Value of 1,000 shares before rights issue = 1,000 × 4.00 = $4,000.

Value of 1,000 shares after rights issue = 1,000 × 3.90 = $3,900.

Cash subscribed for new shares = 200 × 3.40 = $680.

Cash raised from sale of rights = 1,000 × 0.1 = $100.

The investor could do nothing, take up the offered rights, sell the rights into the rights market, or any combination of these actions. The effect of the rights issue on the wealth of the investor depends on which action is taken.

The rights issue has a neutral effect if the rights attached to the 1,000 shares are exercised to purchase an additional 200 shares, since the value of 1,200 shares after the rights issue ($4,680) is equal to the sum of the value of 1,000 shares before the rights issue ($4,000) and the cash subscribed for new shares ($680). Part of the investor's wealth has changed from cash into shares, but no wealth has been gained or lost. The theoretical ex rights per share therefore acts as a benchmark following the rights issue against which other ex rights share prices can be compared.

The rights issue also has a neutral effect on the wealth of the investor if the rights attached to existing shares are sold. The value of 1,000 shares after the rights issue ($3,900) plus the cash received from the sale of rights ($100) is equal to the value of 1,000 shares before the rights issue ($4,000). In this case, part of the investor's wealth has changed from share into cash.

If the investor neither subscribes for the new shares offered nor sells the rights attached to the shares already held, a loss of wealth of $100 will occur, due to the difference between the value of 1,000 shares before the rights issue ($4,000) and the value of 1,000 shares after the rights issue ($3,900).

The theoretical ex rights price is simply a weighted average of the cum rights price and the rights issue price, ignoring any use made of the funds raised. The actual ex rights price will depend on the use made of the funds raised by the rights issue, as well as the expectations of investors and the stock market.

C   Current share price = $4.00.

Earnings per share = 100 × (4.00/15.24) = 26.25c.

Number of ordinary shares = 2m/0.5 = 4m shares.

Earnings of Tirwen = 4m × 0.2625 = $1.05m.

Funds raised from rights issue

= 800,000 × $4.00 × 0.85 = $2,720,000.

Funds raised less issue costs = 2,720,000 – 220,000 = $2,500,000.

Loan note interest saved = 2,500,000 × 0.12 = $300,000.

Profit before tax of Tirwen = 1,050,000/(1 – 0.3) = $1,500,000.

Current loan note interest paid = 4,500,000 × 0.12 = $540,000.

Current overdraft interest = 1,250,000 × 0.07 = $87,500.

Total interest = 540,000 + 87,500 = $627,500.

Current profit before interest and tax

= 1,500,000 + 627,500 = $2,127,500.

Revised total interest = 627,500 – 300,000 = $327,500.

Revised profit after tax

= (2,127,500 – 327,500) × 0.7 = $1,260,000.

(Or revised profit after tax

= 1,050,000 + (300,000 × 0.7) = $1,260,000).

New shares issued = 4m/5 = 800,000.

Shares in issue = 4,000,000 + 800,000 = 4,800,000.

Revised earnings per share

= 100 × (1,260,000/4,800,000) = 26.25c.

D   As the price/earnings ratio is constant, the share price expected after redeeming part of the loan notes will remain unchanged at $4.00 per share (26.25 × 15.24). Since this is greater than the theoretical ex rights share price of $3.90, using the funds raised by the rights issue to redeem part of the loan notes results in a capital gain of 10p per share. The proposal to use the rights issue funds to redeem part of the loan notes therefore results in an increase in shareholder wealth.

E   A rights issue will be an attractive source of finance to Tirwen Inc as it will reduce the gearing of the company. The current debt/equity ratio using book values is:

Debt/equity ratio = 100 × 4,500/3,500 = 129%.

Including the overdraft, debt/equity ratio

= 100 × 5,750/3,500 = 164%.

Both values are above the sector average of 100% and issuing new debt will not be attractive in this situation. A substantial reduction in gearing will occur, however, if the rights issue is used to redeem $2.5m of loan notes:

Debt/equity ratio = 100 × 2,000/6,000 = 33%.

Including the overdraft, debt/equity ratio

= 100 × 3,250/6,000 = 54%.

If the rights issue is not used to redeem the loan notes issue, the decrease in gearing is less dramatic:

Debt/equity ratio = 100 × 4,500/6,000 = 75%.

Including the overdraft, debt/equity ratio

= 100 × 5,750/6,000 = 96%.

In both cases, the debt/equity ratio falls to less than the sector average, signalling a decrease in financial risk. The debt/equity ratio would fall further if increased retained profits were included in the calculation, but the absence of information on Tirwen's dividend policy makes retained profits uncertain.

If the rights issue is used to redeem $2.5m of loan notes, there will be an improvement in interest cover from 3.4 times (2,127,500/627,500), which is below the sector average of 6 times, to 6.5 times (2,127,500/327,500), which is marginally better than the sector average. Interest cover might also increase if the funds raised are invested in profitable projects.

A rights issue will also be attractive to Tirwen Inc since it will make it more likely that the company can raise further debt finance in the future, possibly at a lower interest rate due to its lower financial risk.

It should be noted that a decrease in gearing is likely to increase the average cost of the finance used by Tirwen Inc, since a greater proportion of relatively more expensive equity finance will be used compared to relatively cheaper debt. This will increase the discount rate used by the company and decrease the net present value of any expected future cash flows.

Predator Co

Answer 1

The approaches to use for valuation are:

(1) Net asset valuation.

(2) DVM.

(3) PE ratio valuation.

(1) **Net asset valuation**

Target is being purchased as a going concern, so realisable values are irrelevant.

	$'000
Net assets per accounts $(1,892 – 768)	1,124
adjustment to freehold property $(800 – 460)	340
adjustment to inventory	(50)
Valuation	**1,414**

Say $1.4m

(2) **DVM**

The average rate of growth in Target's dividends over the last 4 years is 7.4% on a compound basis.

85 (1+g)4 = 113.1 hence g = 7.4%

The estimated value of Target using the DVM is therefore:

Valuation $\dfrac{\$113,100 \times 1.074}{0.15 - 0.074}$ = $1,598,282

Say $1.6m

(3) **PE ratio valuation**

A suitable PE ratio for Target will be based on the PE ratio of Predator as both companies are in the same industry.

$$\text{PE of Predator} \quad \frac{70 \times \$4.30}{\$20.04\text{m}} \quad \text{or} \quad \frac{430}{28.63} \quad = \textbf{15.02}$$

The adjustments: – Downwards by 20% or 0.20, i.e. multiply by 0.80.

(1) Target is a private company and its shares may be less liquid.

(2) Target is a private company and it may have a less detailed compliance environment and therefore may be more risky.

A suitable PE ratio is therefore 15.02 × 0.80 = 12.02

(multiplying by 0.80 results in the 20% reduction).

Target's PAT + Adjustment for the savings in the director's remuneration after tax:

$183,000 + ($40,000 × 67%) = $209,800

The estimated value is therefore $209,800 × 12.02 = $2,521,796

Say $2.5m

Advice to the board

On the basis of its tangible assets the value of Target is $1.4 million, which excludes any value for intangibles.

The dividend valuation gives a value of around $1.6 million.

The earnings based valuation indicates a value of around $2.5 million, which is based on the assumption, that not only will the current earnings be maintained, but that they will increase by the savings in the director's remuneration.

On the basis of these valuations an offer of around $2 million would appear to be most suitable, however a review of all potential financial gains from the merger is recommended. The directors should, however, be prepared to increase the offer to maximum price.

Tagna

Answer 1

A   Market efficiency is commonly discussed in terms of pricing efficiency.

A stock market is described as efficient when share prices fully and fairly reflect relevant information.

Weak form efficiency occurs when share prices fully and fairly reflect all past information, such as share price movements in preceding periods. If a stock market is weak-form efficient, investors cannot make abnormal gains by studying and acting upon past information.

Semi-strong form efficiency occurs when share prices fully and fairly reflect not only past information, but all publicly available information as well, such as the information provided by the published financial statements of companies or by reports in the financial press. If a stock market is semi-strong-form efficient, investors cannot make abnormal gains by studying and acting upon publicly available information.

Strong form efficiency occurs when share prices fully and fairly reflect not only all past and publicly available information, but all relevant private information as well, such as confidential minutes of board meetings. If a stock market is strong-form efficient, investors cannot make abnormal gains by acting upon any information, whether publicly available or not. There is no empirical evidence supporting the proposition that stock markets are strong form efficient and so the bank is incorrect in suggesting that in six months the stock market will be strong-form efficient. However, there is a great deal of evidence suggesting that stock markets are semi-strong-form efficient and so Tagna's share are unlikely to be under-priced.

B   A substantial interest rate increase may have several consequences for Tagna in the areas indicated.

   I   As a manufacturer and supplier of luxury goods, it is likely that Tagna will experience a sharp decrease in sales as a result of the increase in interest rates. One reason for this is that sales of luxury goods will be more sensitive to changes in disposable income than sales of basic necessities, and disposable income is likely to fall as a result of the interest rate increase. Another reason is the likely effect of the interest rate increase on consumer demand. If the increase in demand has been supported, even in part, by the increase in consumer credit, the substantial interest rate increase will have a negative effect on demand as the cost of consumer credit increases. It is also likely that many chain store customers will buy Tagna's goods by using credit.

   II   Tagna may experience an increase in operating costs as a result of the substantial interest rate increase, although this is likely to be a smaller effect and one that occurs more slowly than a decrease in sales. As the higher cost of borrowing moves through the various supply chains in the economy, producer prices may increase and the cost of materials and other inputs Tagna may rise by more than the current rate of inflation. Labour costs may also increase sharply if the recent sharp rise in inflation leads to high inflationary expectations being built into wage demands. Acting against this will be the deflationary effect on consumer demand of the interest rate increase. If the Central Bank has made an accurate assessment of the economic situation when determining the interest rate increase, both the growth in consumer demand and the rate of inflation may fall to more acceptable levels, leading to a lower increase in operating costs.

   III   The earnings (profit after tax) of Tagna are likely to fall as a result of the interest rate increase. In addition to the decrease in sales and the possible increase in operating costs discussed above, Tagna will experience an increase in interest costs arising from its overdraft. The combination of these effects is likely to result in a sharp fall in earnings. The level of reported profits has been low in recent years and so Tagna may be faced with insufficient profits to maintain its dividend, or even a reported loss.

C   The objectives of public sector organisations are often difficult to define. Even though the cost of resources used can be measured, the benefits gained from the consumption of those resources can be difficult, if not impossible, to quantify. Because of this difficulty, public sector organisations often have financial targets imposed on them, such as a target rate of return on capital employed. Furthermore, they will tend to focus on maximising the return on resources consumed by producing the best possible combination of services for the lowest possible cost. This is the meaning of 'value for money', often referred to as the pursuit of economy, efficiency and effectiveness.

Economy refers to seeking the lowest level of input costs for a given level of output. Efficiency refers to seeking the highest level of output for a given level of input resources. Effectiveness refers to the extent to which output produced meets the specified objectives, for example in terms of provision of a required range of services.

In contrast, private sector organisations have to compete for funds in the capital markets and must offer an adequate return to investors. The objective of maximisation of shareholder wealth equates to the view that the primary financial objective of companies is to reward their owners. If this objective is not followed, the directors may be replaced or a company may find it difficult to obtain funds in the market, since investors will prefer companies that increase their wealth. However, shareholder wealth cannot be maximised if companies do not seek both economy and efficiency in their business operations.

Exchange rate systems

Answer 1

Key answer tips

This question is standard bookwork. It is vital that you discuss the implications of each system to multinationals.

Managed floating exchange rate

A managed floating exchange rate will be mainly influenced by the market supply and demand for a currency, but is also subject to intervention by the relevant government. The government will buy or sell the currency in order to influence the exchange rate, often to keep it within a desired range against the dollar or other key currency. The government will not normally reveal how or when it will intervene in the foreign exchange market, and floating exchange rates such as this are difficult to forecast as they directly respond to economic events, relevant new information and to government intervention. This could lead to volatility in foreign exchange rates, which might be a deterrent to foreign trade.

In theory, managed exchange rates should gradually adjust to changing economic relationships between nations. For example, as a country moves into a balance of trade deficit, this would normally lead to a fall in the value of the country's currency, which in turn will make the country's exports more attractive, and will reduce the trade deficit. Floating exchange rates should prevent persistent deficits, and result in fewer large speculative international movements of funds. From a multinational company's perspective the difficulty in forecasting such rates makes accurate cash budgeting for international activities more onerous, increases currency risk, and in many cases makes some form of currency hedging essential.

Fixed exchange rate linked to a basket of currencies

An economy that fixes its exchange rate against the dollar or other major currency will inevitably be affected by the state of the economy and the policies of the country to which it has linked. For example, if inflation or the money supply increases in the USA, similar effects may be experienced in countries which have their currencies tied to the dollar.

An exchange rate linked to a basket of currencies is less susceptible to economic influences from a single country, although if the basket is weighted by international trade, a dominant trade partner might still have a major influence. In theory, fixed exchange rates offer greater stability, and future rates should be easier to forecast, which reduces risk and aids international pricing and cash budgeting. However, fixed exchange rates do not remain fixed forever; devaluation or revaluation may occur if inflation, interest rates and other economic variables diverge between the relevant countries. The direction of a possible change in rates is quite easy to predict, but not the exact timing of devaluation or revaluation, or the magnitude of any change in currency values. Fixed rates are also more susceptible to currency speculation.

Fixed exchange rates backed by a currency board system

This type of exchange rate regime shares many characteristics of other fixed exchange rate systems, but the currency board means that any domestic currency issues are backed by an equal amount of some 'hard' currency, such as the dollar. In theory the domestic currency could be converted at any time into the hard currency at a fixed exchange rate. This backing by a 'hard' currency is aimed at achieving greater economic stability, and less exchange rate volatility. A currency board system might result in a fall in the domestic money supply, high interest rates, and thus high 'local' financing costs for multinational companies. For some countries, such as Hong Kong, a currency board has proved successful. For others, such as Argentina, it has failed. A multinational company will normally experience lower inflation and more stable economic conditions when a currency board exists.

Index

Index

KAPLAN PUBLISHING

Index

Index

KAPLAN PUBLISHING

Index

U

V

W

Y

Index